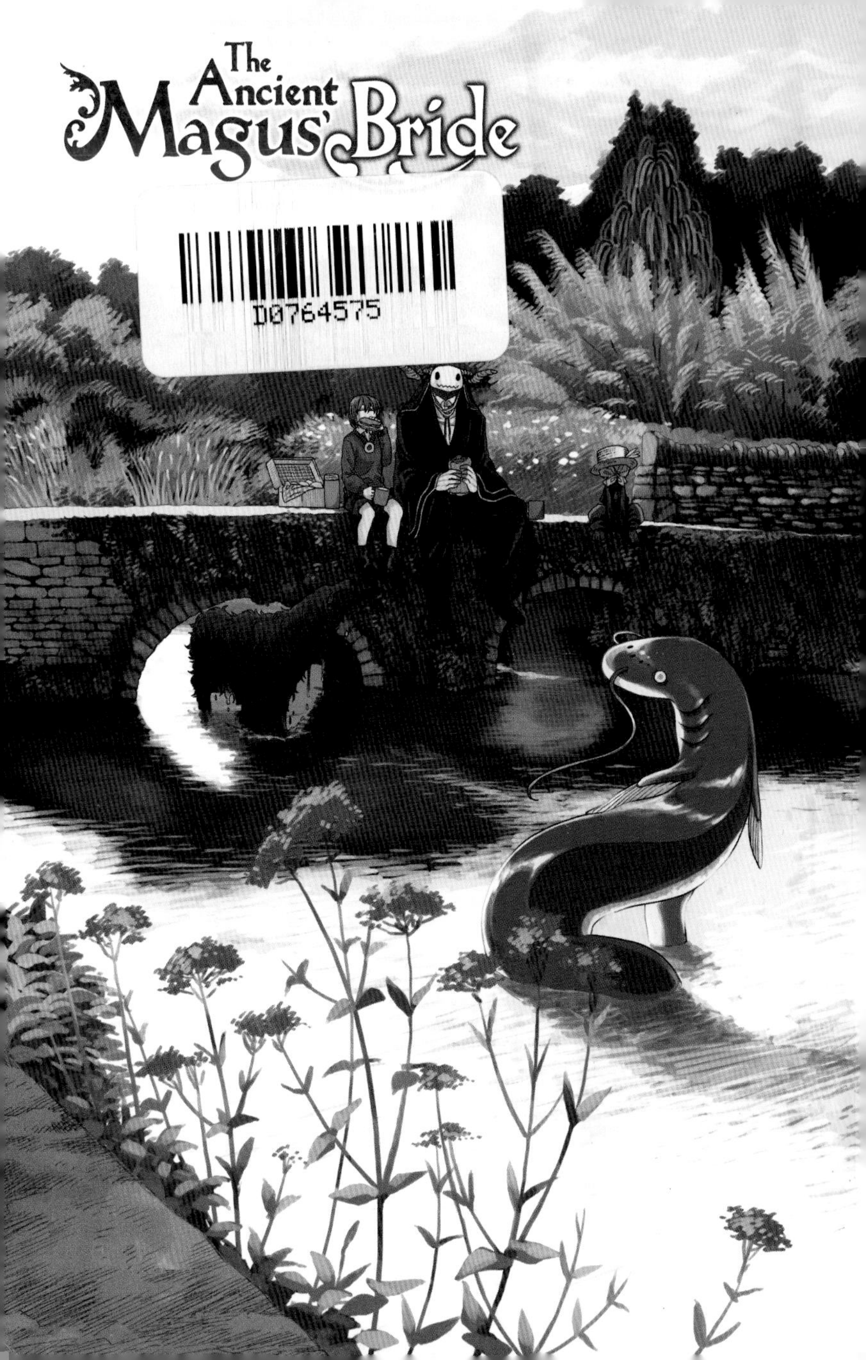
The Ancient Magus' Bride

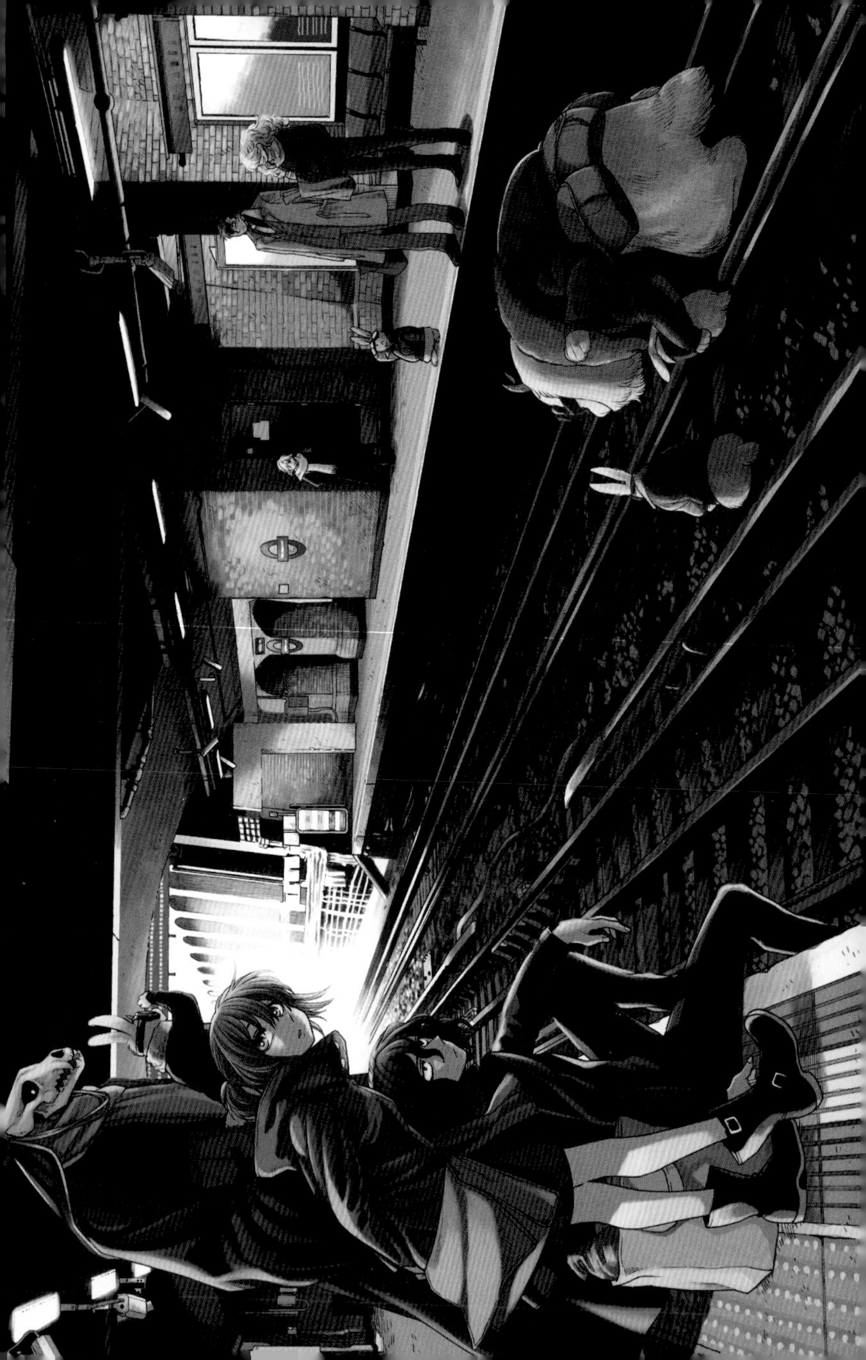

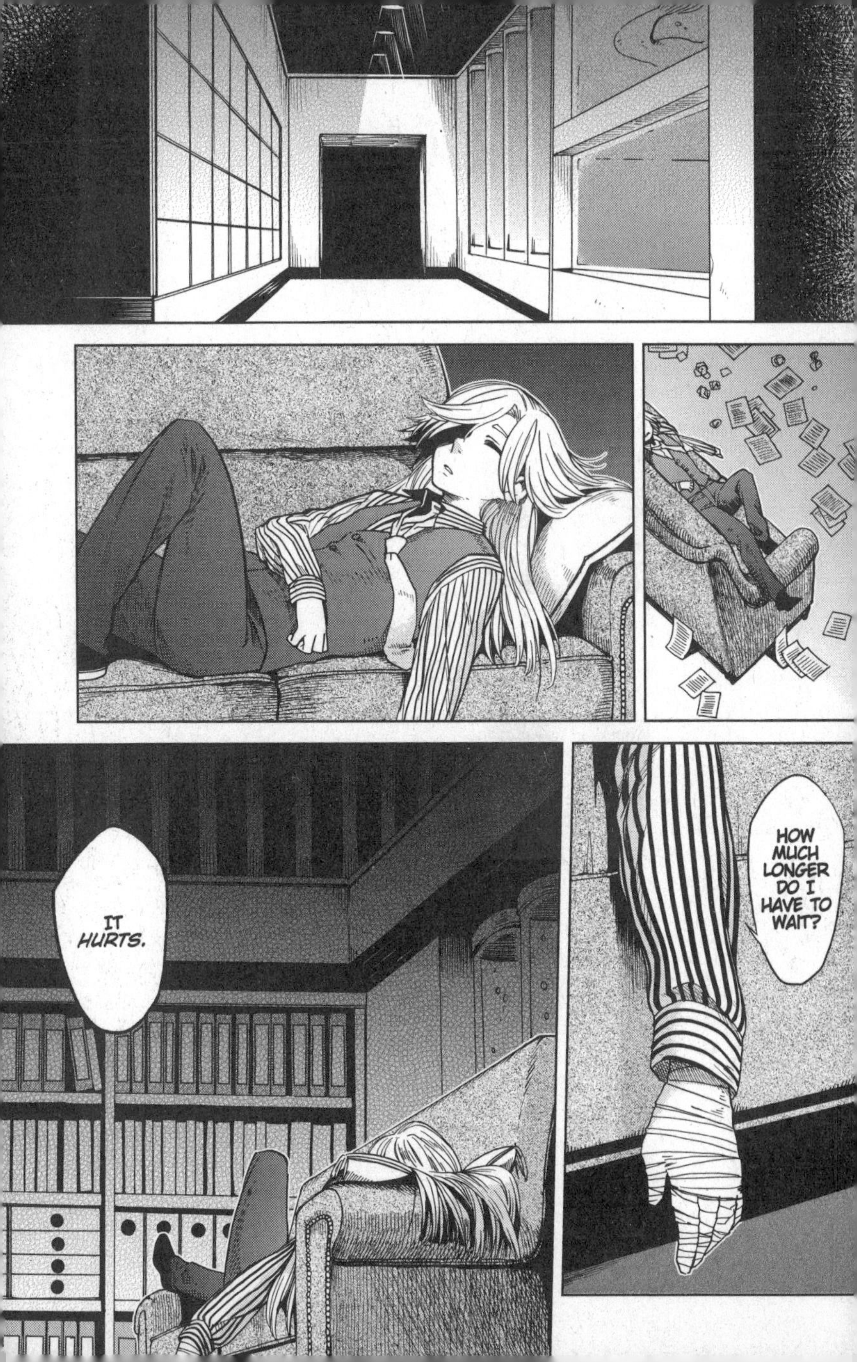
HOW MUCH LONGER DO I HAVE TO WAIT?
IT *HURTS.*

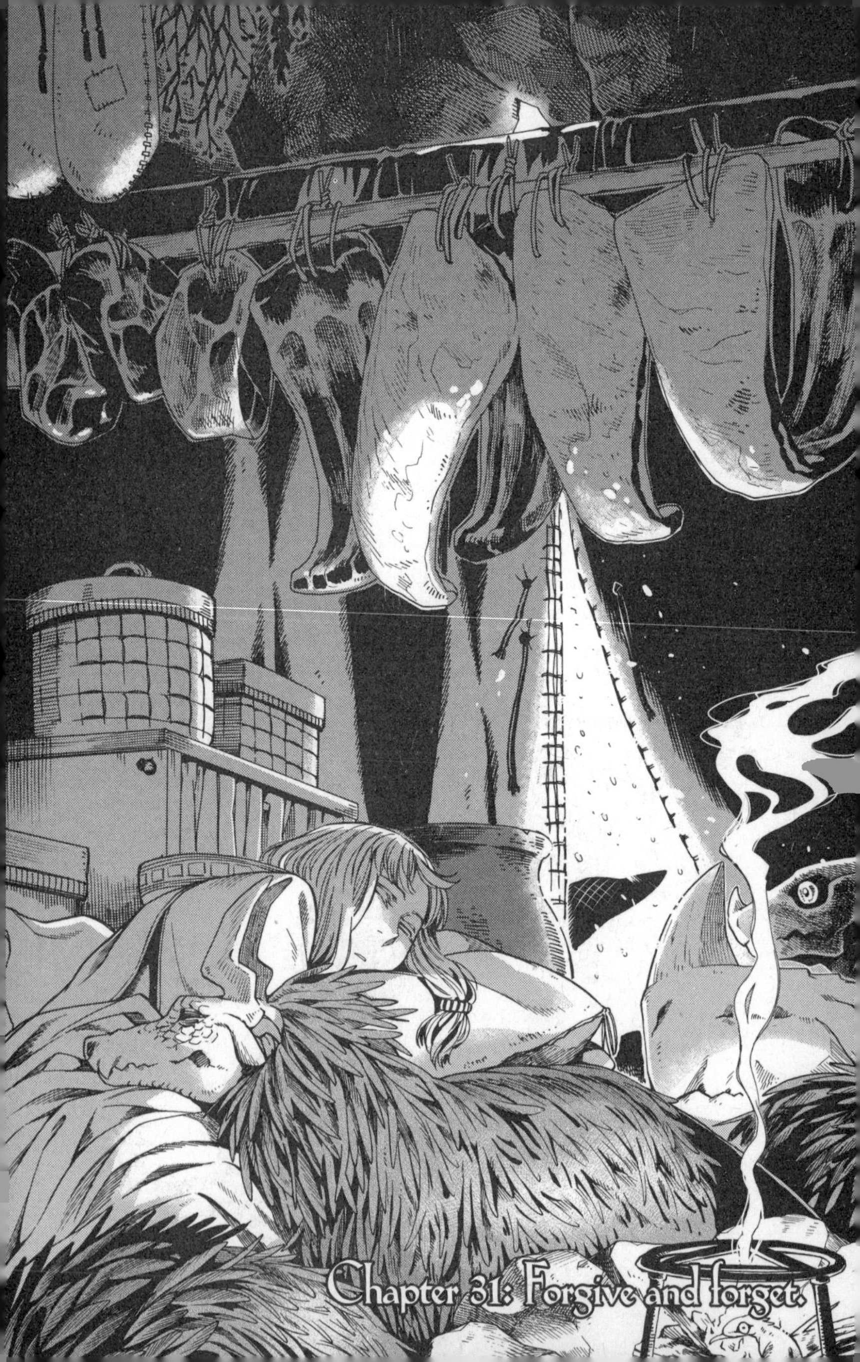
Chapter 31: Forgive and forget.

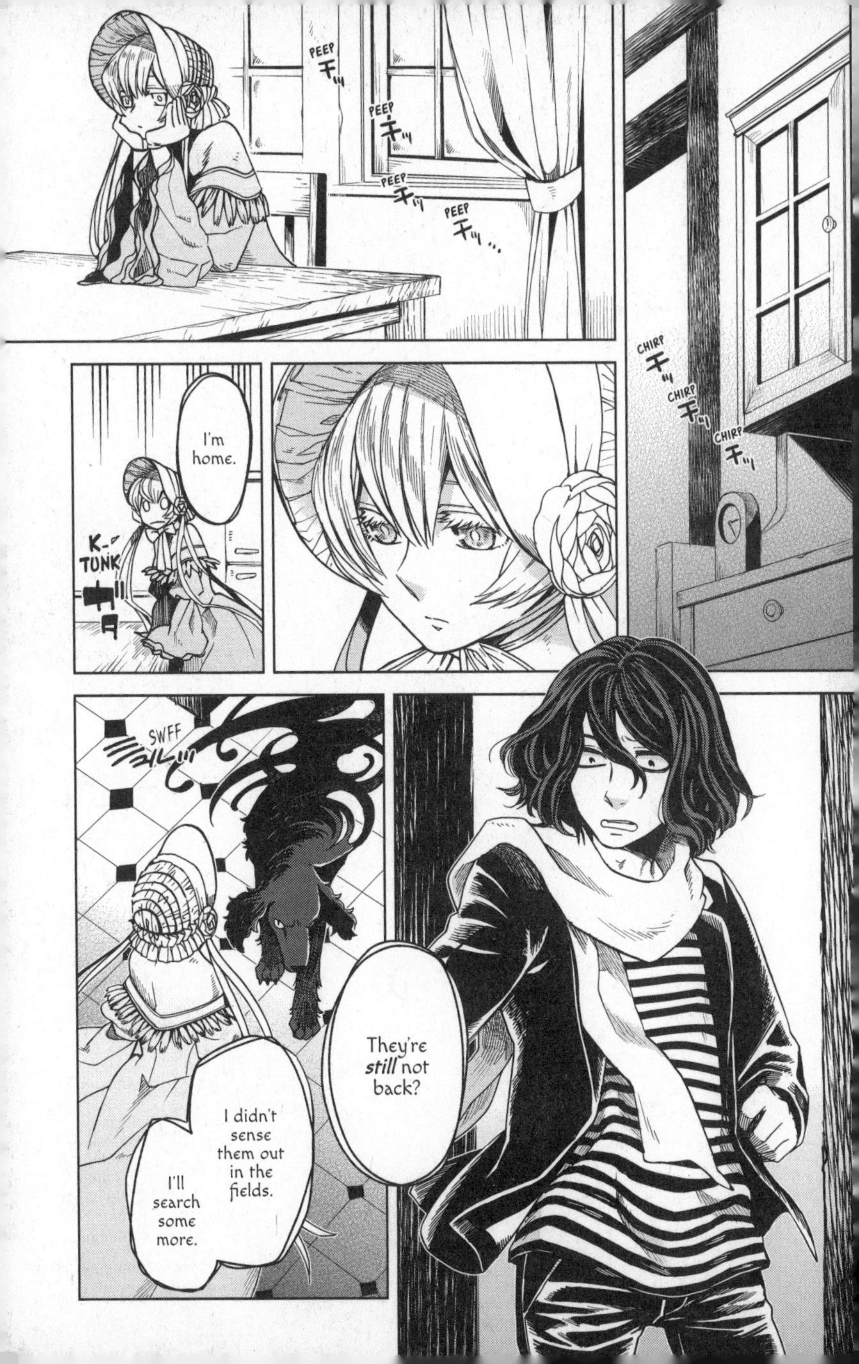
CHIRP
CHIRP
CHIRP
PEEP
PEEP
PEEP
PEEP
I'm home.
K-TUNK
They're ***still*** not back?
SWFF
I didn't sense them out in the fields.
I'll search some more.

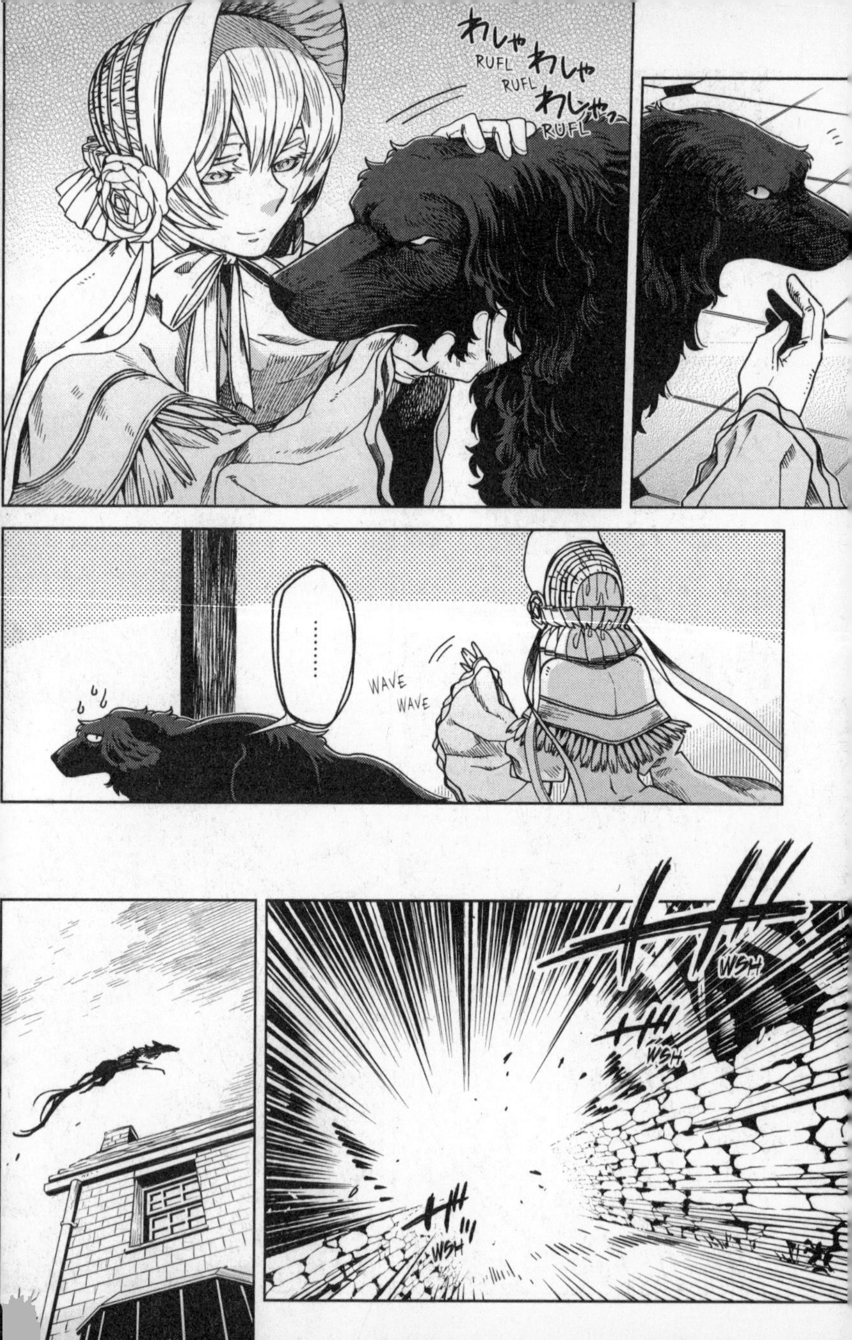
わしゃ RUFL
わしゃ RUFL
わしゃっ RUFL
......
WAVE WAVE
WSH
WSH
WSH

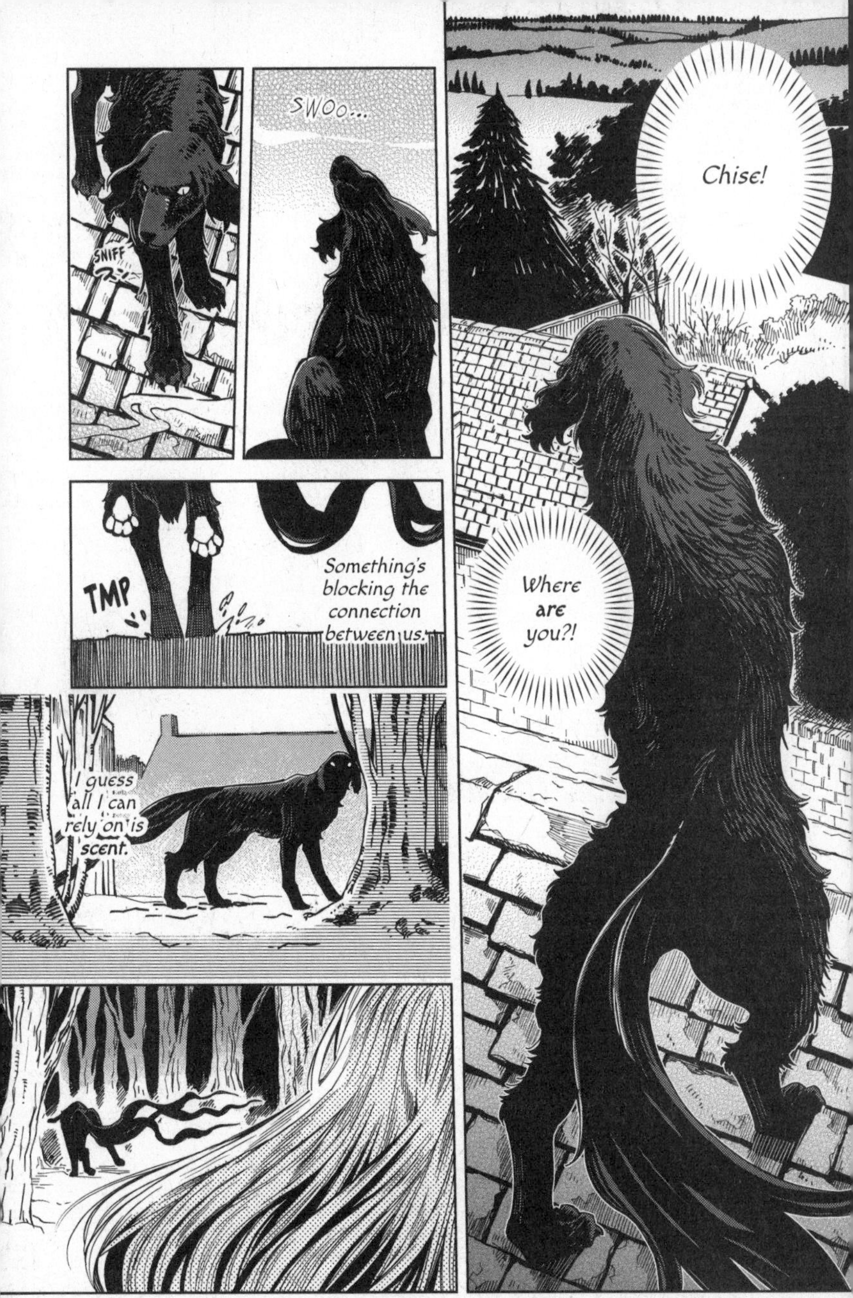
Chise!
Where are you?!
SWOO...
SNIFF
Something's blocking the connection between us.
TMP
I guess all I can rely on is scent.

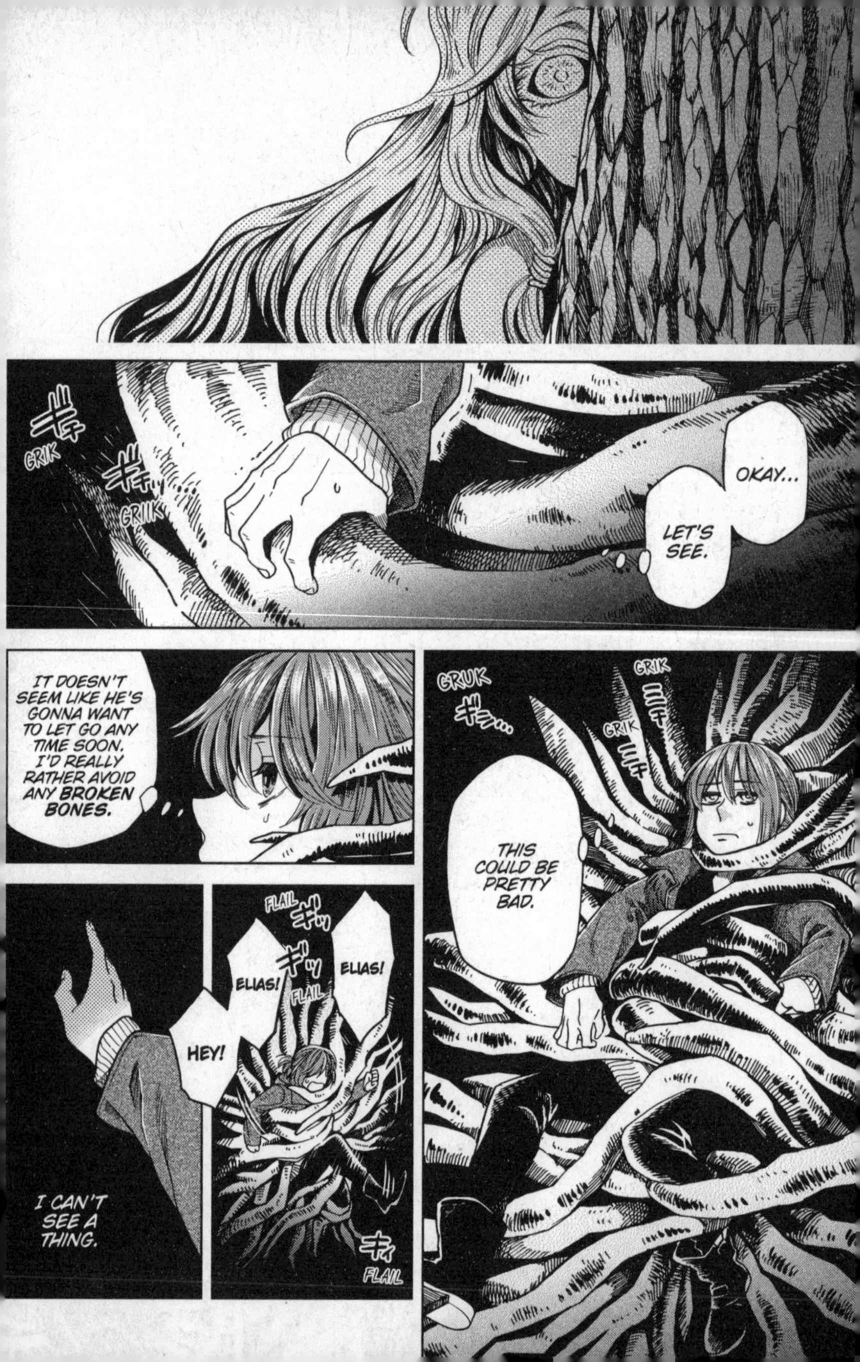
OKAY...
LET'S SEE.
GRIK
GRIIK
GRUK
GRIK
GRIK
THIS COULD BE PRETTY BAD.
IT DOESN'T SEEM LIKE HE'S GONNA WANT TO LET GO ANY TIME SOON. I'D REALLY RATHER AVOID ANY BROKEN BONES.
FLAIL
ELIAS!
ELIAS!
FLAIL
HEY!
FLAIL
I CAN'T SEE A THING.

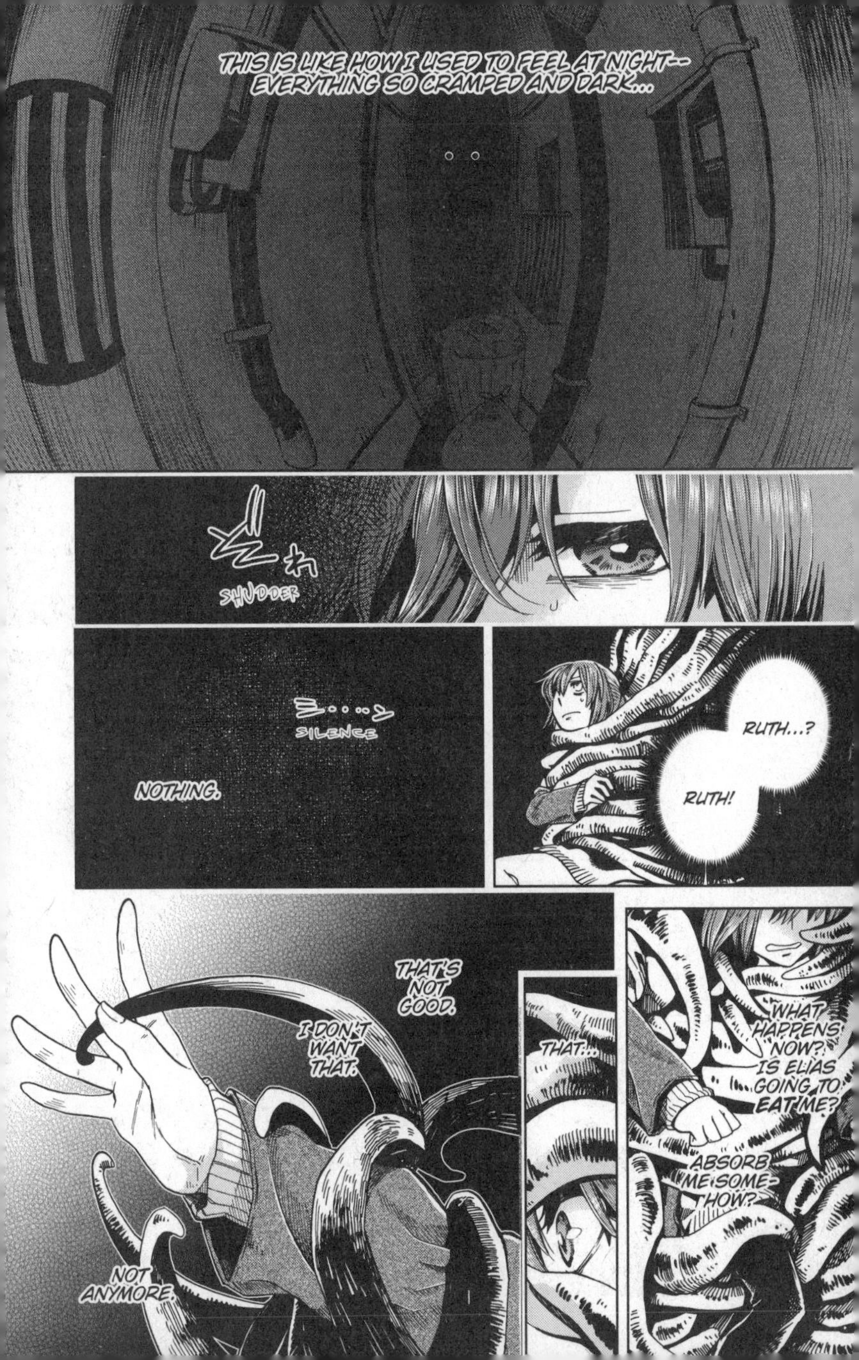
THIS IS LIKE HOW I USED TO FEEL AT NIGHT--
EVERYTHING SO CRAMPED AND DARK...
SHUDDER
RUTH...?
RUTH!
SILENCE
NOTHING.
WHAT HAPPENS NOW? IS ELIAS GOING TO EAT ME?
ABSORB ME SOME-HOW?
THAT...
THAT'S NOT GOOD.
I DON'T WANT THAT.
NOT ANYMORE.

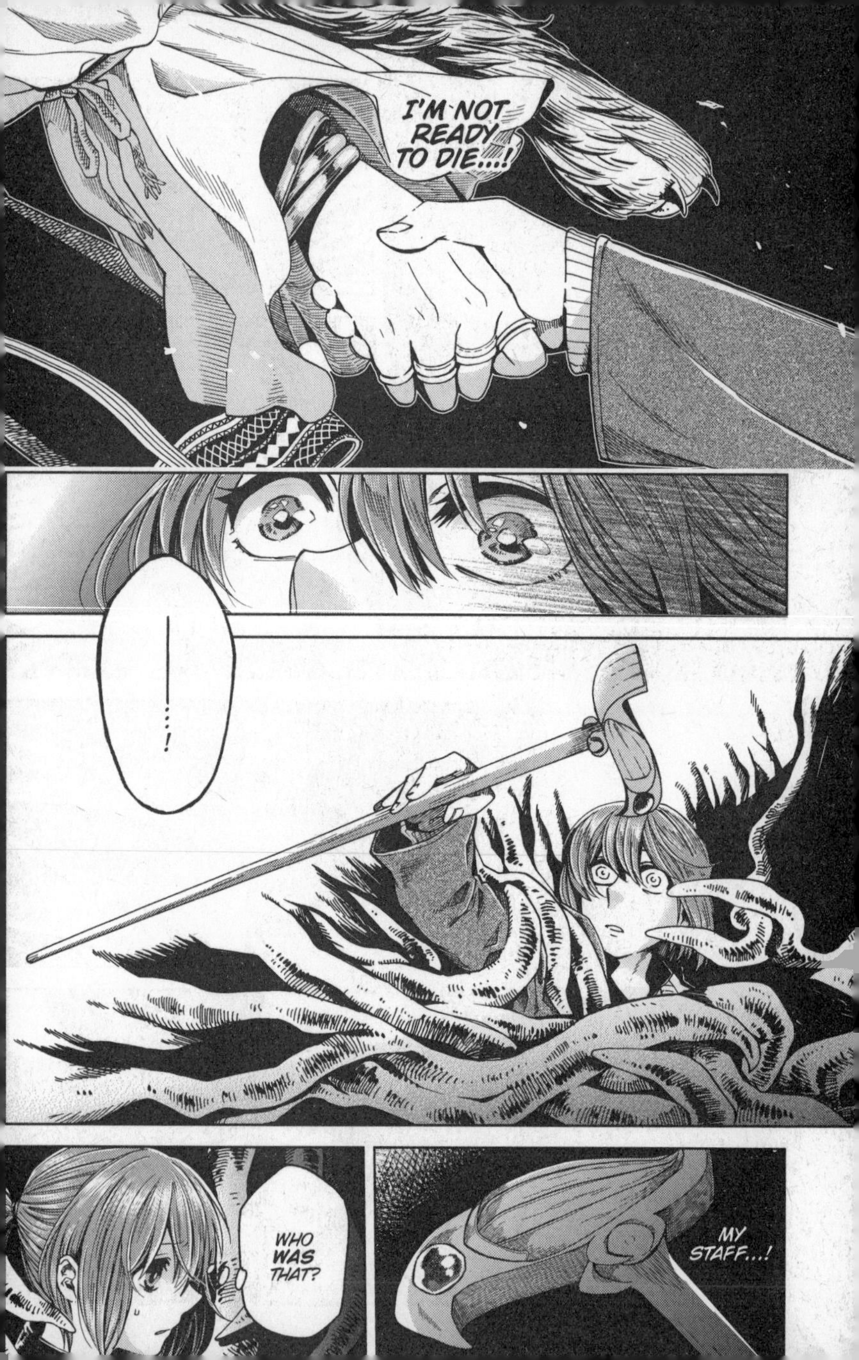
I'M NOT READY TO DIE...!
......!
MY STAFF...!
WHO WAS THAT?

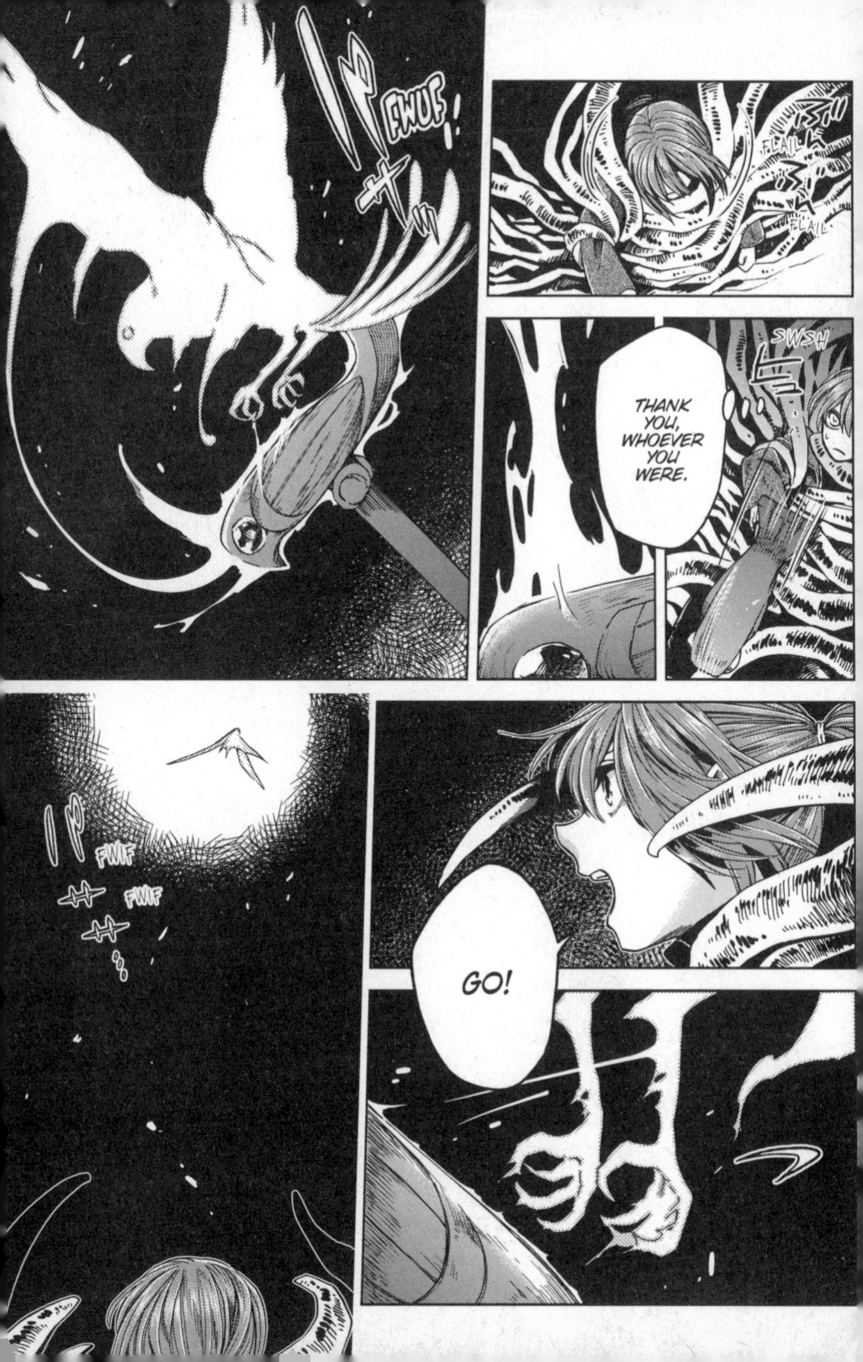
FLAIL
FLAIL
SWSH
THANK YOU, WHOEVER YOU WERE.
FWUF
GO!
FWIF
FWIF

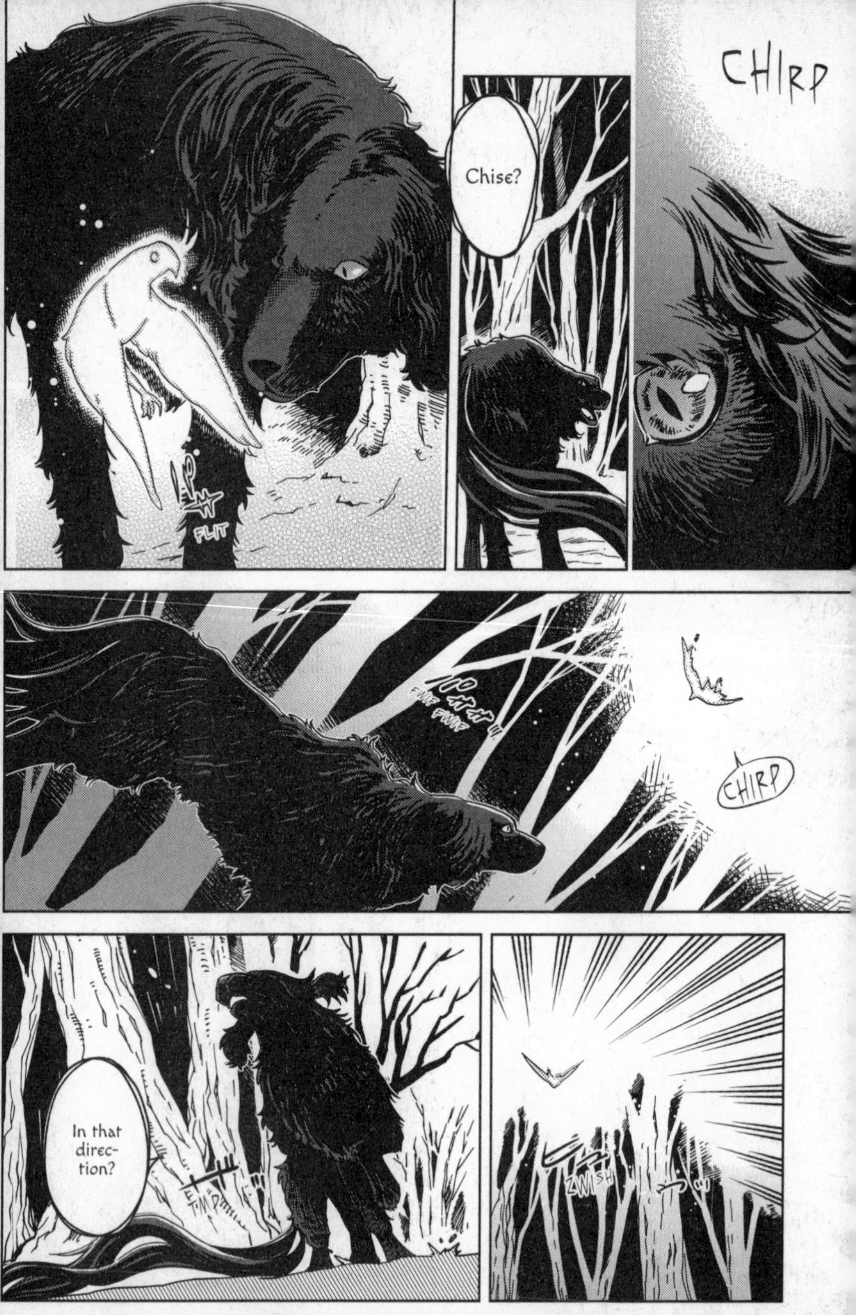
CHIRP
Chise?
FLIT
FWIP FWIP
CHIRP
ZWISH
In that direc-tion?

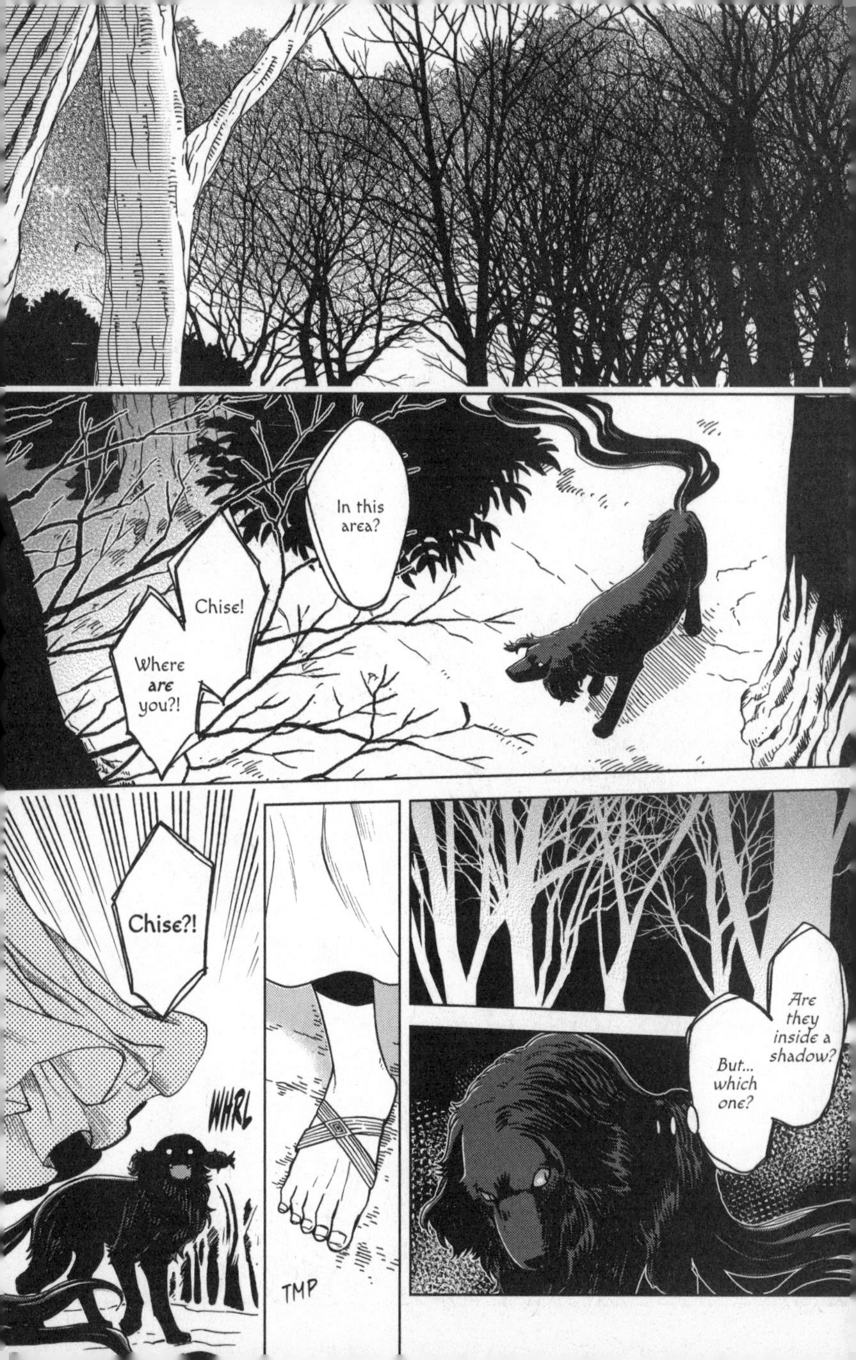
In this area?
Chise!
Where are you?!
Are they inside a shadow?
But... which one?
TMP
Chise?!
WHRL

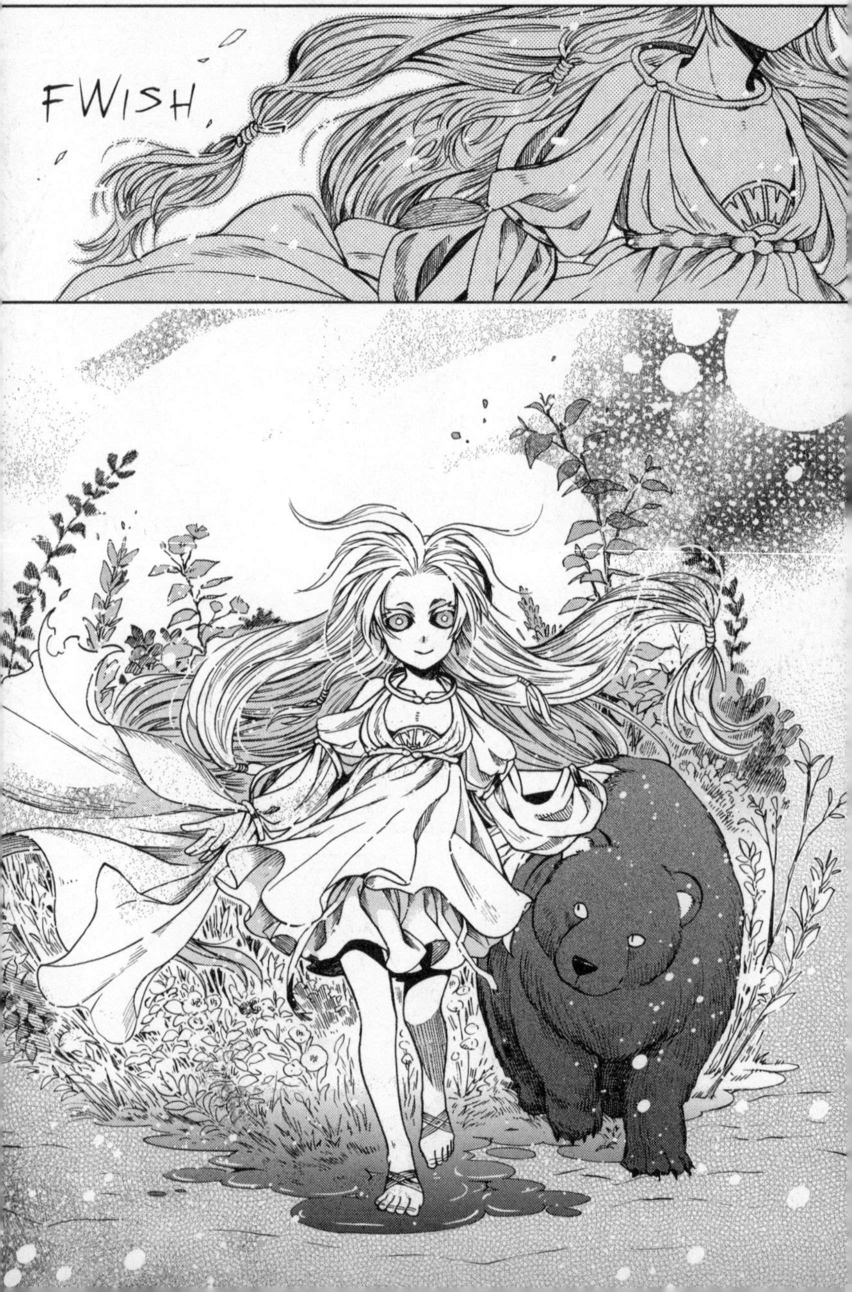
FWISH

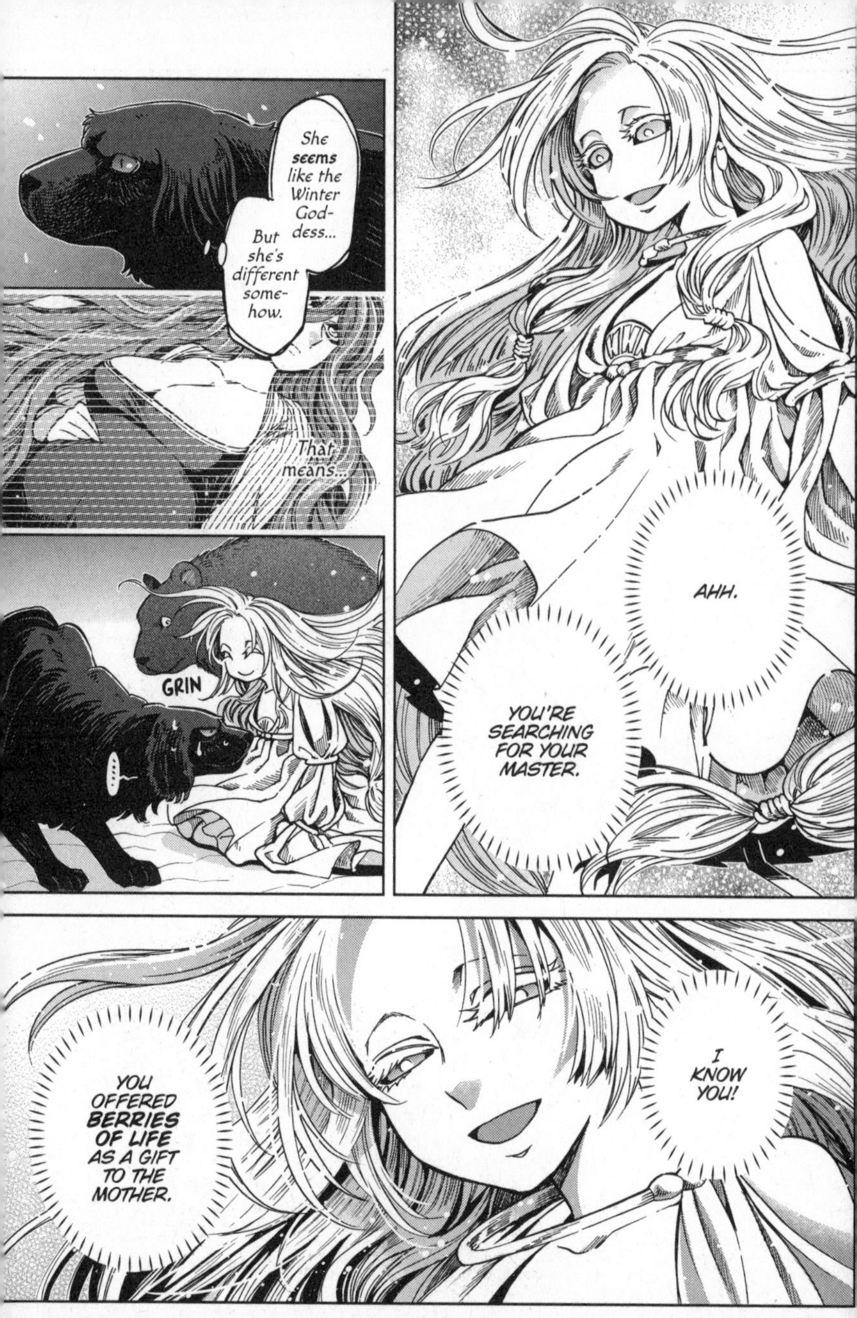
AHH.
YOU'RE SEARCHING FOR YOUR MASTER.
She **seems** like the Winter God-dess...
But she's different some-how.
That means...
GRIN
....
I KNOW YOU!
YOU OFFERED **BERRIES OF LIFE** AS A GIFT TO THE MOTHER.

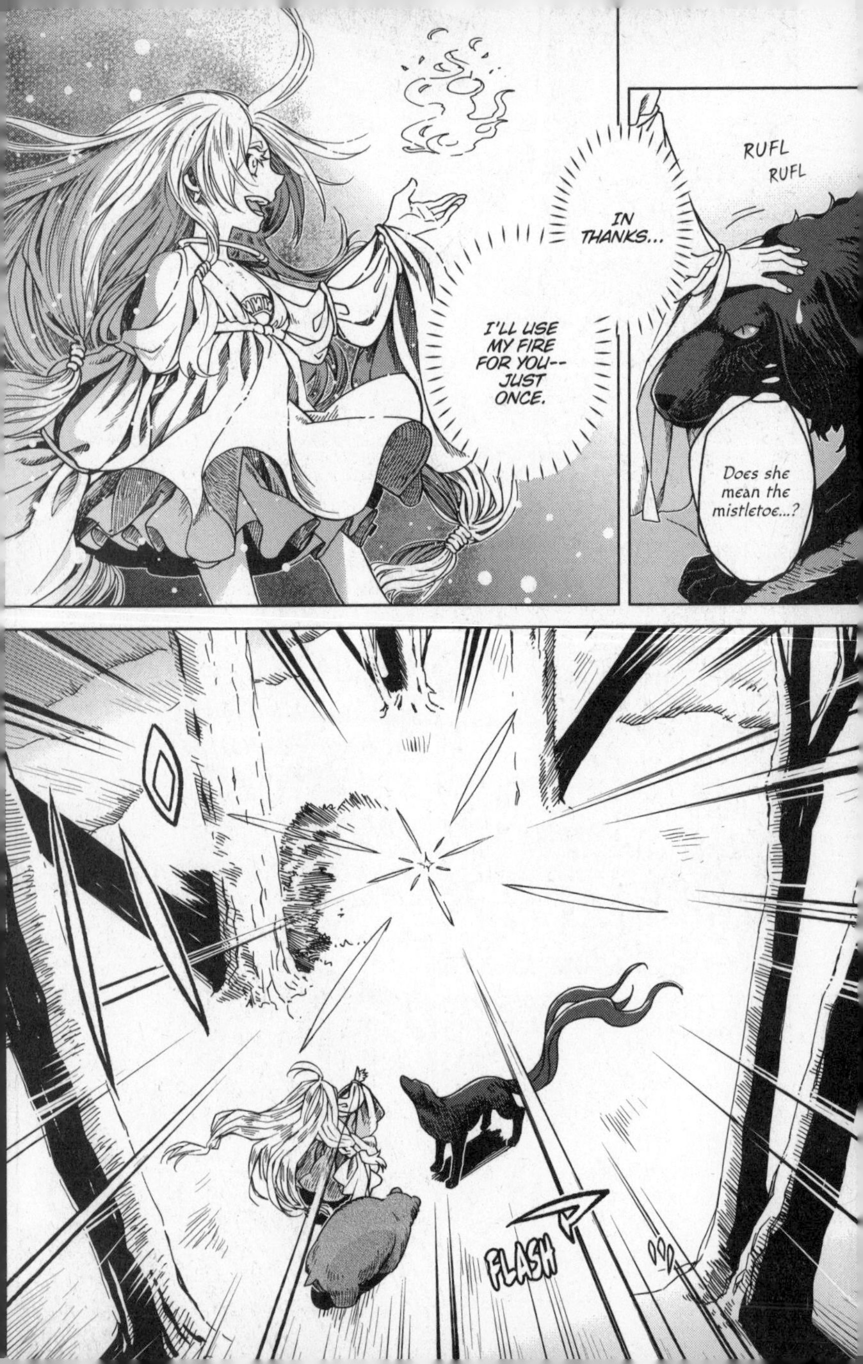
RUFL
RUFL
IN THANKS...
I'LL USE MY FIRE FOR YOU--JUST ONCE.
Does she mean the mistletoe...?
FLASH

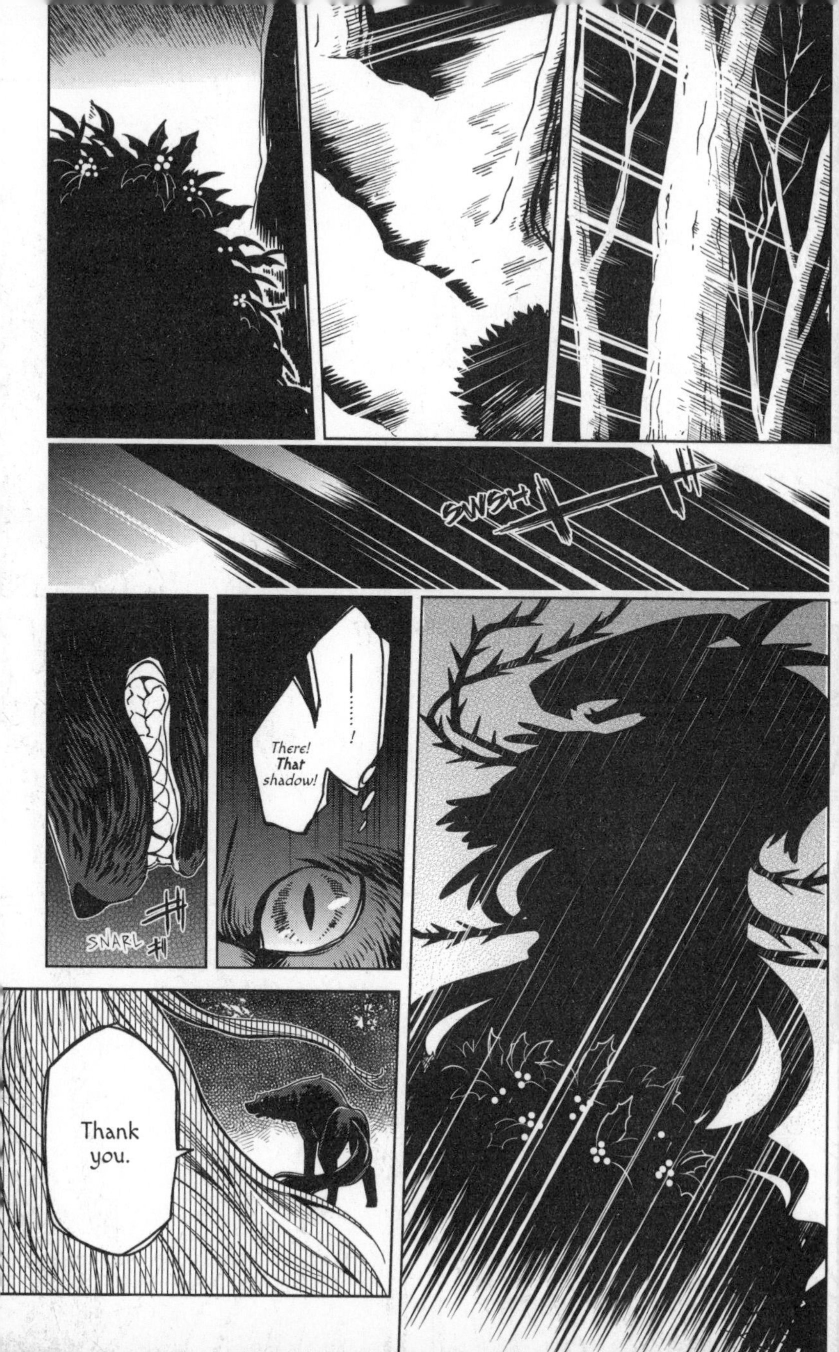
SWISH
......!
There! That shadow!
SNARL
Thank you.

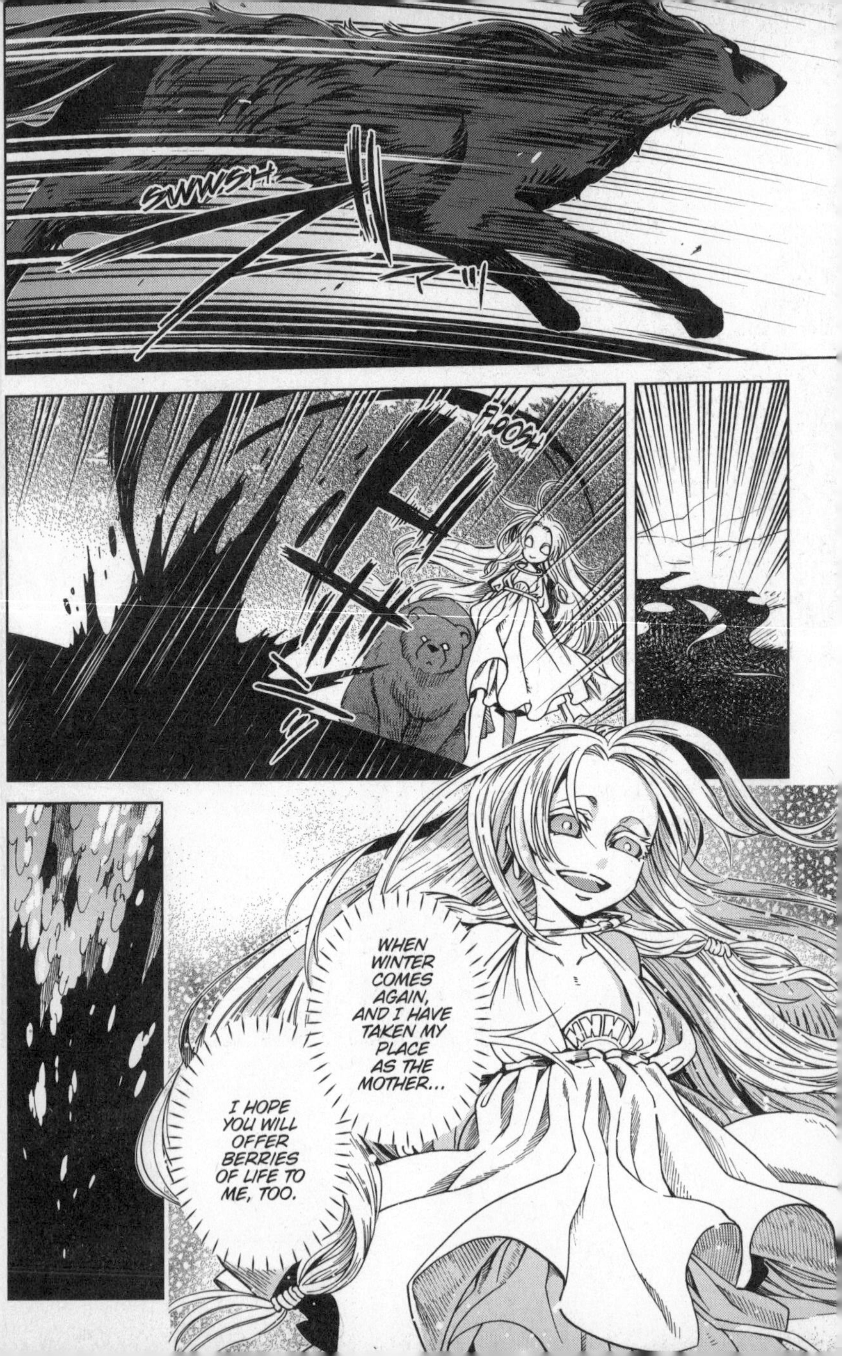
SWUSH
FLOOSH
WHEN WINTER COMES AGAIN, AND I HAVE TAKEN MY PLACE AS THE MOTHER...
I HOPE YOU WILL OFFER BERRIES OF LIFE TO ME, TOO.

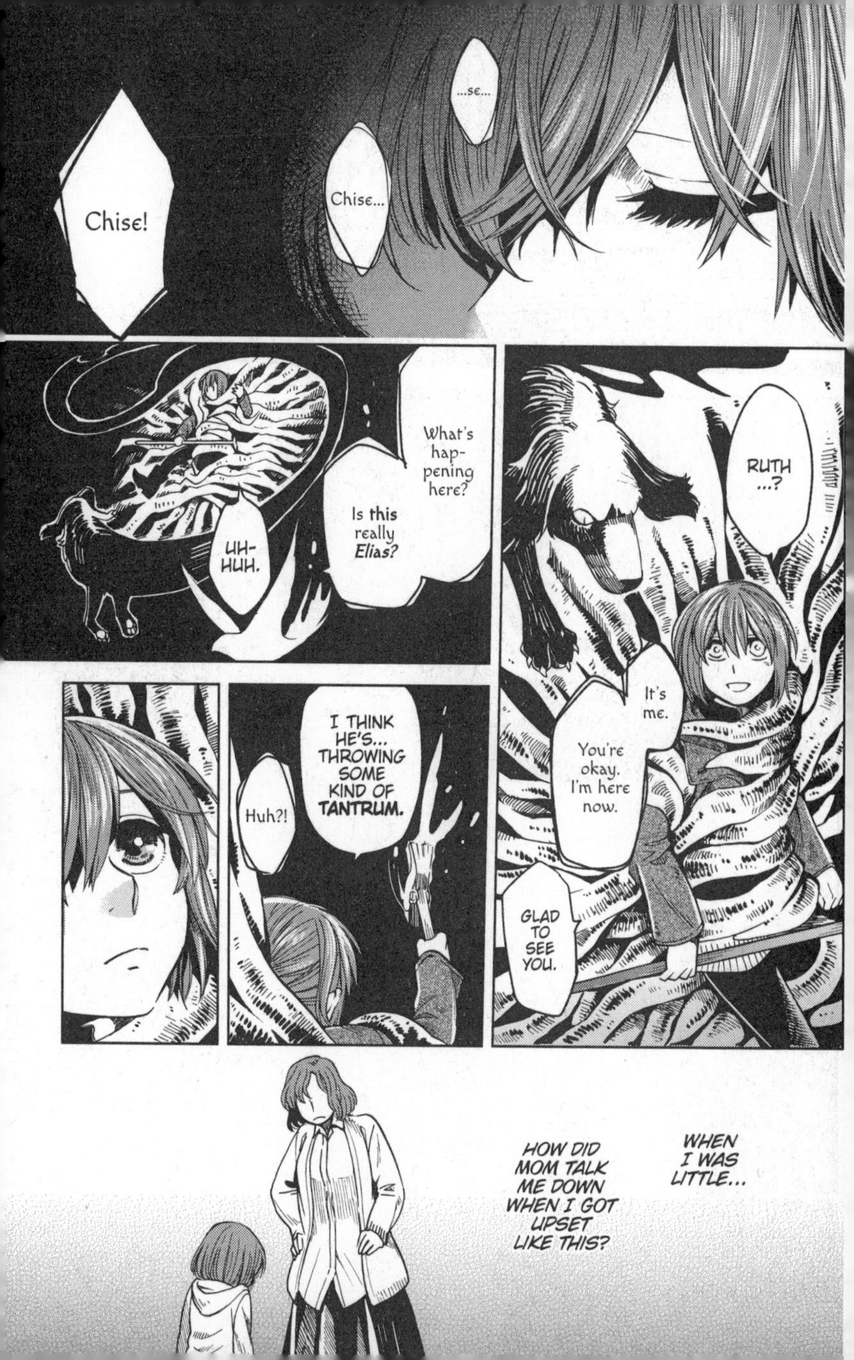
...se...
Chise...
Chise!
RUTH ...?
What's hap-pening here?
Is this really *Elias?*
UH-HUH.
It's me.
You're okay. I'm here now.
GLAD TO SEE YOU.
I THINK HE'S... THROWING SOME KIND OF **TANTRUM.**
Huh?!
WHEN I WAS LITTLE...
HOW DID MOM TALK ME DOWN WHEN I GOT UPSET LIKE THIS?

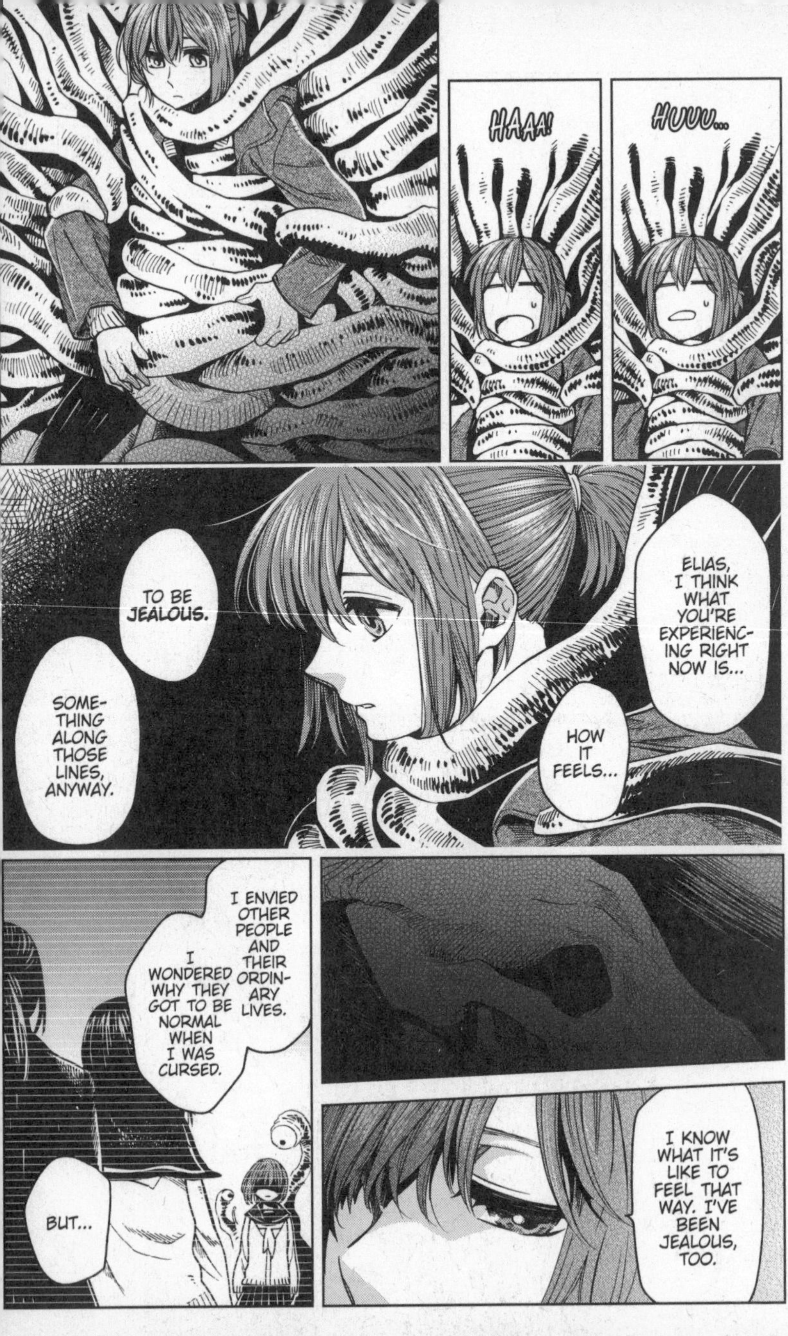
HUUU...
HAAA!
ELIAS, I THINK WHAT YOU'RE EXPERIENCING RIGHT NOW IS...
HOW IT FEELS...
TO BE JEALOUS.
SOMETHING ALONG THOSE LINES, ANYWAY.
I KNOW WHAT IT'S LIKE TO FEEL THAT WAY. I'VE BEEN JEALOUS, TOO.
I ENVIED OTHER PEOPLE AND THEIR ORDINARY LIVES.
I WONDERED WHY THEY GOT TO BE NORMAL WHEN I WAS CURSED.
BUT...

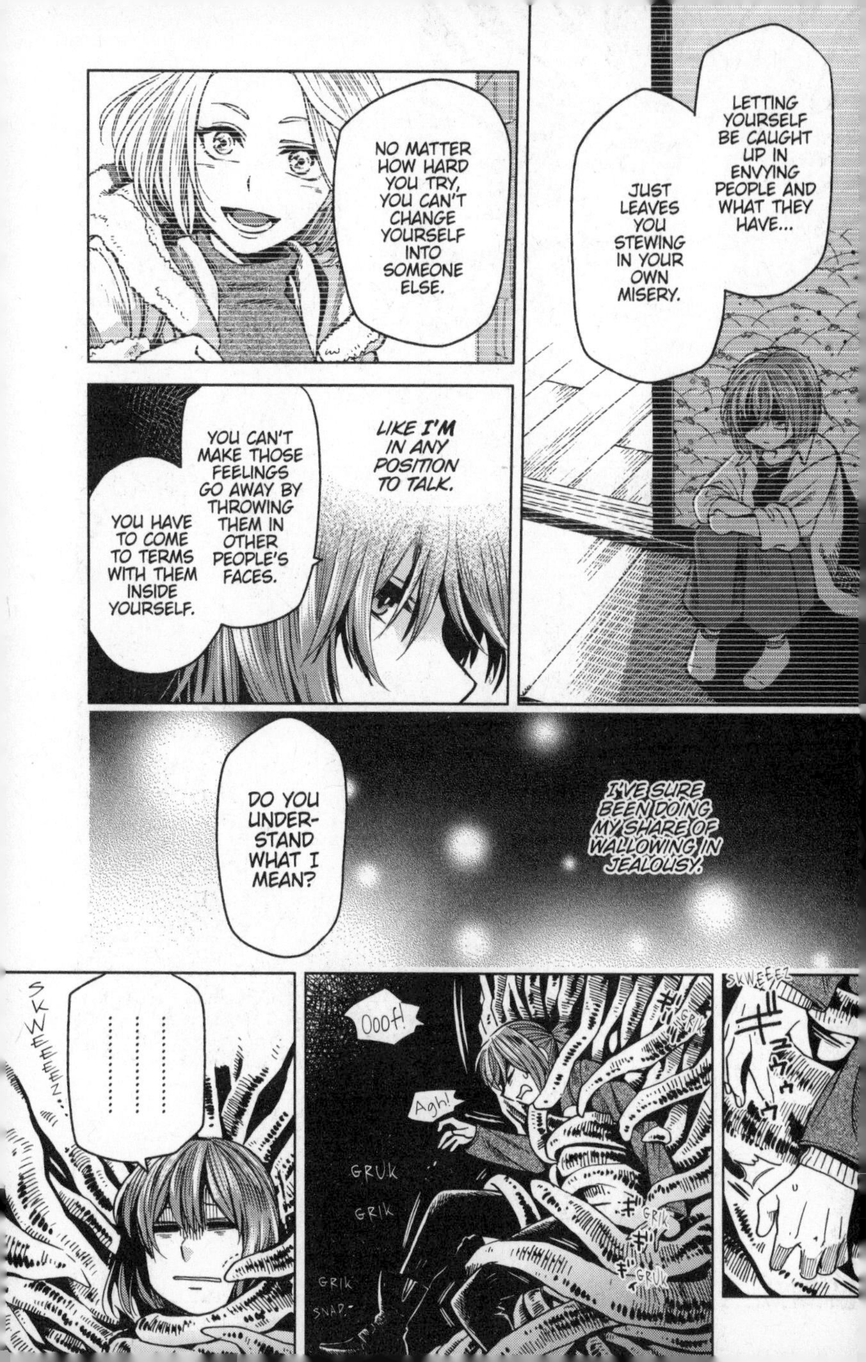

LETTING YOURSELF BE CAUGHT UP IN ENVYING PEOPLE AND WHAT THEY HAVE...
JUST LEAVES YOU STEWING IN YOUR OWN MISERY.
NO MATTER HOW HARD YOU TRY, YOU CAN'T CHANGE YOURSELF INTO SOMEONE ELSE.
LIKE I'M IN ANY POSITION TO TALK.
YOU CAN'T MAKE THOSE FEELINGS GO AWAY BY THROWING THEM IN OTHER PEOPLE'S FACES.
YOU HAVE TO COME TO TERMS WITH THEM INSIDE YOURSELF.
I'VE SURE BEEN DOING MY SHARE OF WALLOWING IN JEALOUSY.
DO YOU UNDERSTAND WHAT I MEAN?
SKWEEEZ
Ooof!
GRIK
Agh!
GRUK
GRIK
GRIK
GRUK
GRIK
SNAP
SKWEEEZ...
......

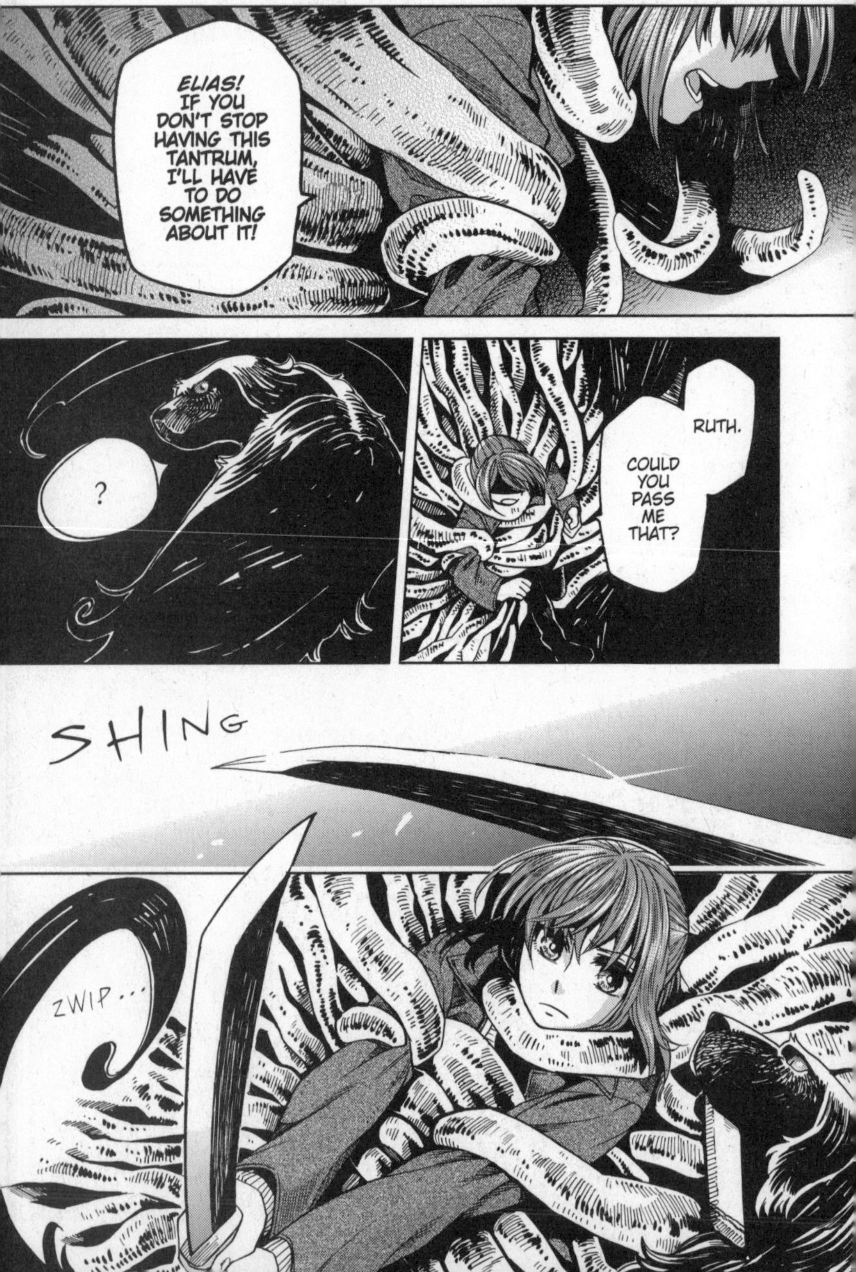
ELIAS! IF YOU DON'T STOP HAVING THIS TANTRUM, I'LL HAVE TO DO SOMETHING ABOUT IT!
RUTH.
COULD YOU PASS ME THAT?
?
SHING
ZWIP...

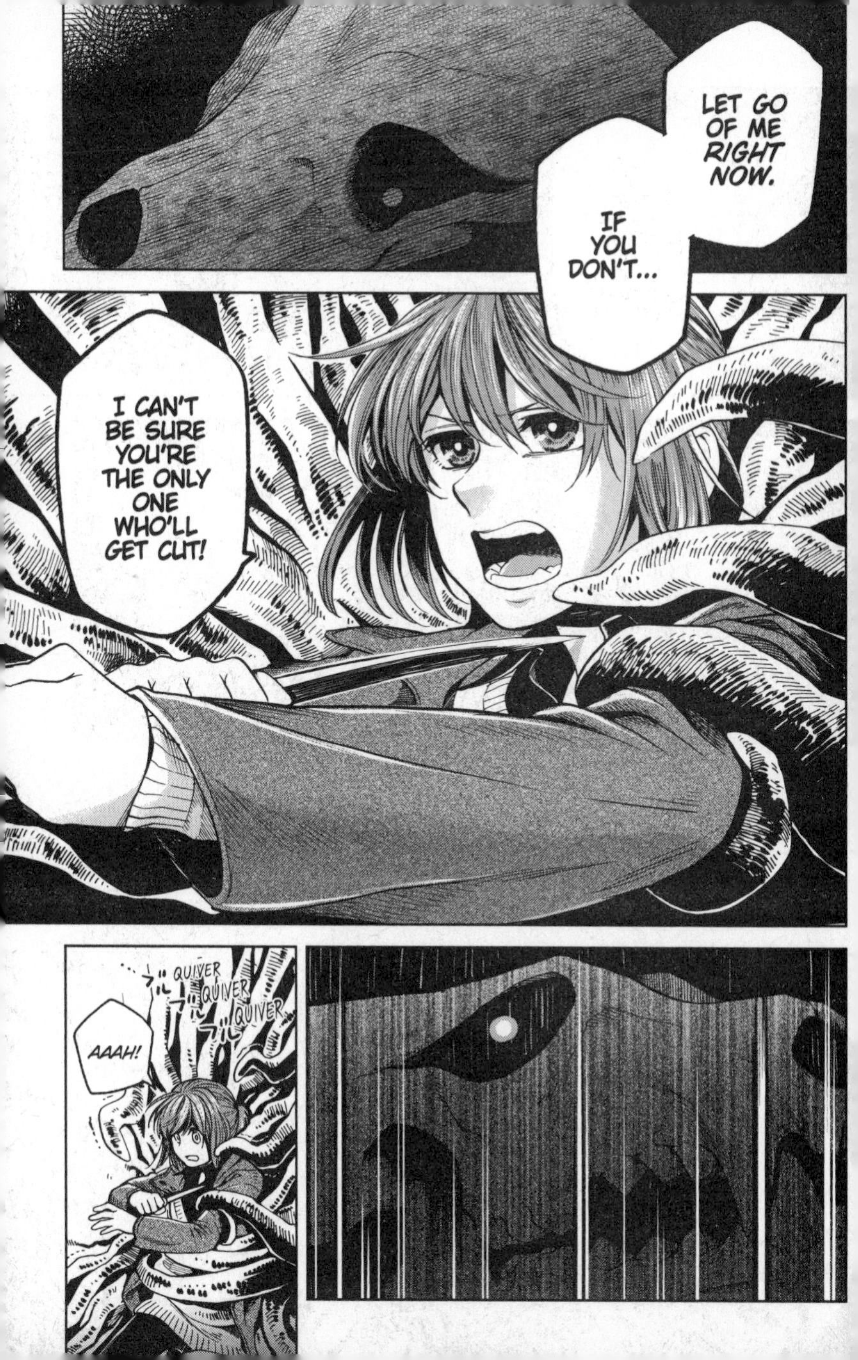
LET GO OF ME RIGHT NOW.
IF YOU DON'T...
I CAN'T BE SURE YOU'RE THE ONLY ONE WHO'LL GET CUT!
QUIVER
QUIVER
QUIVER
AAAH!

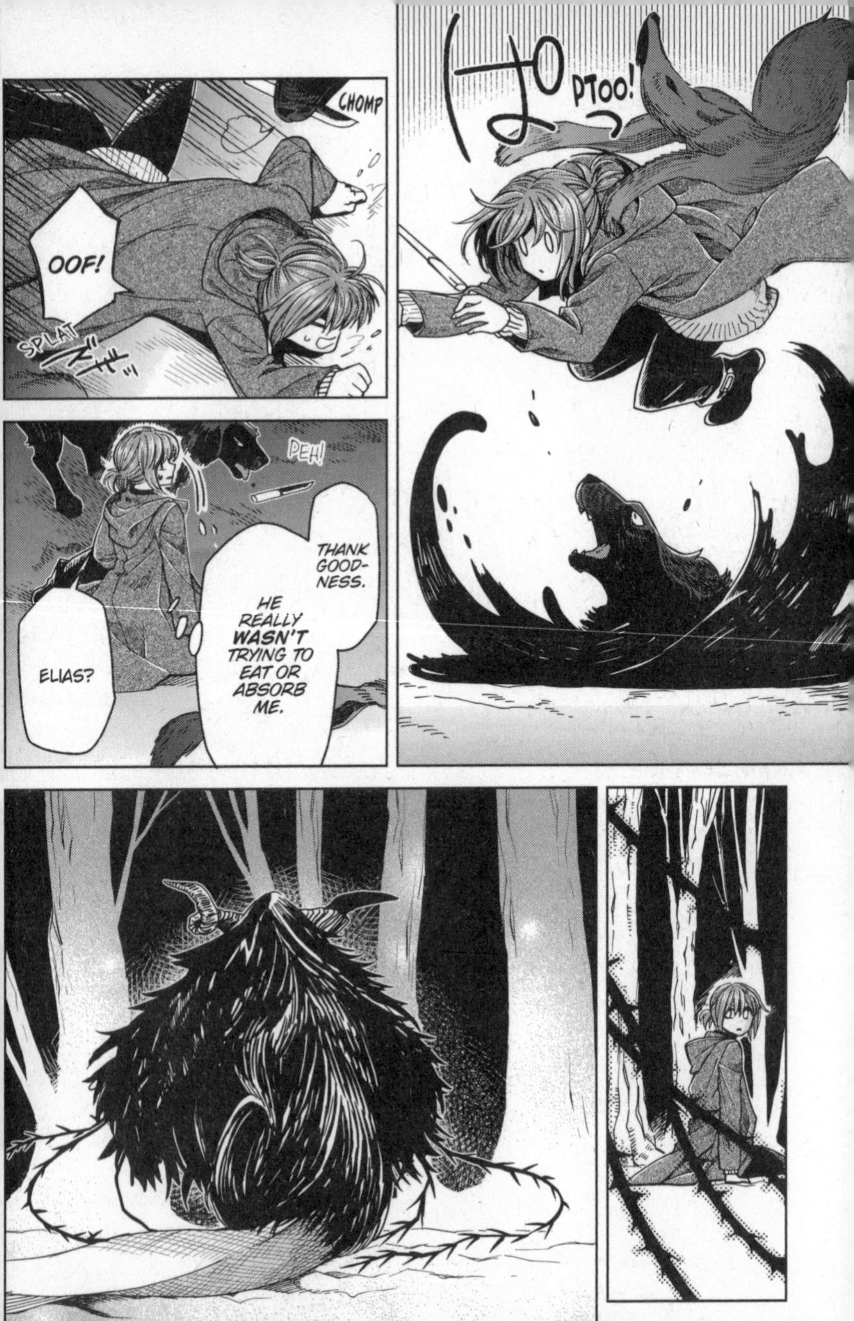
PTOO!
CHOMP
OOF!
SPLAT
PEH!
THANK GOODNESS.
HE REALLY WASN'T TRYING TO EAT OR ABSORB ME.
ELIAS?

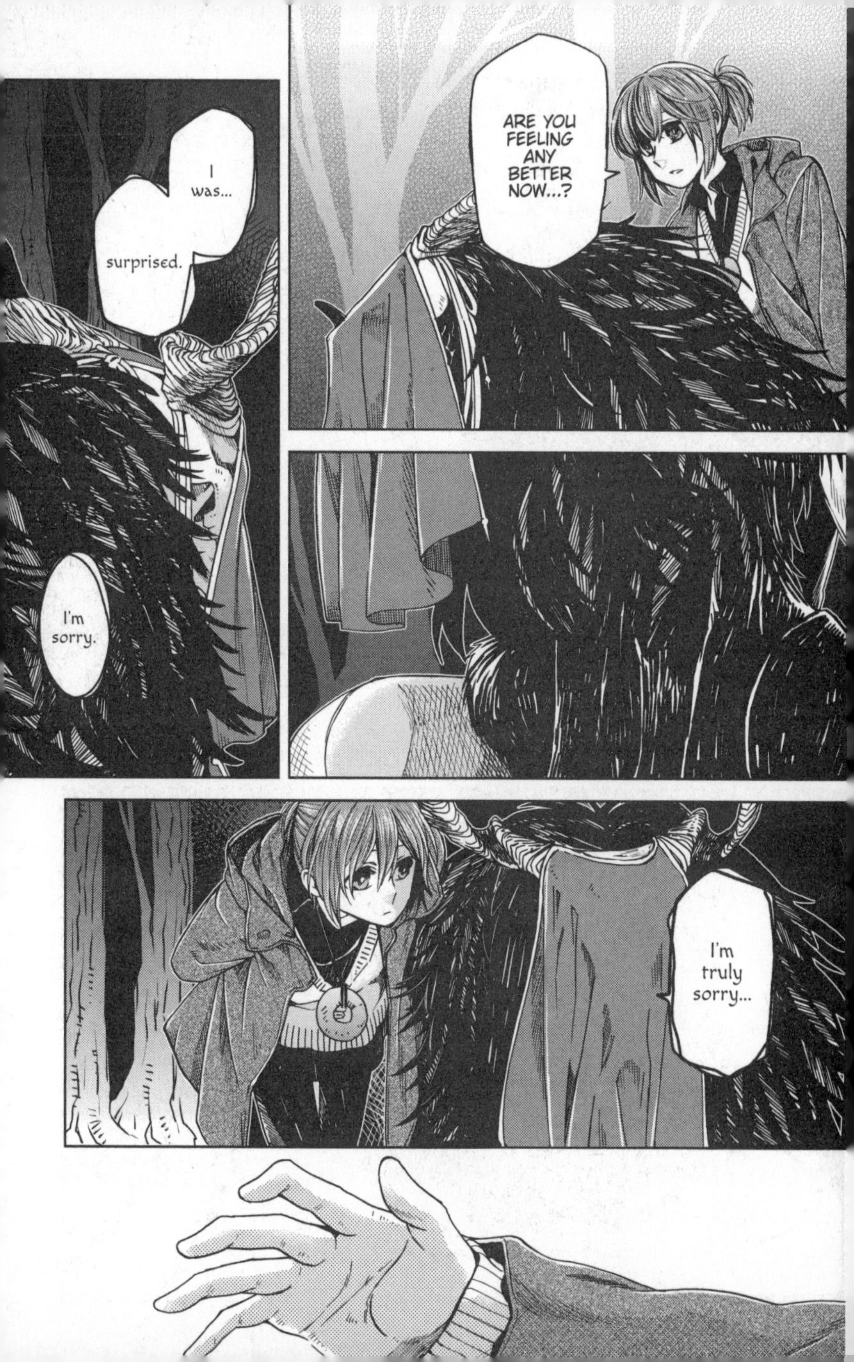
ARE YOU FEELING ANY BETTER NOW...?
I was... surprised.
I'm sorry.
I'm truly sorry...

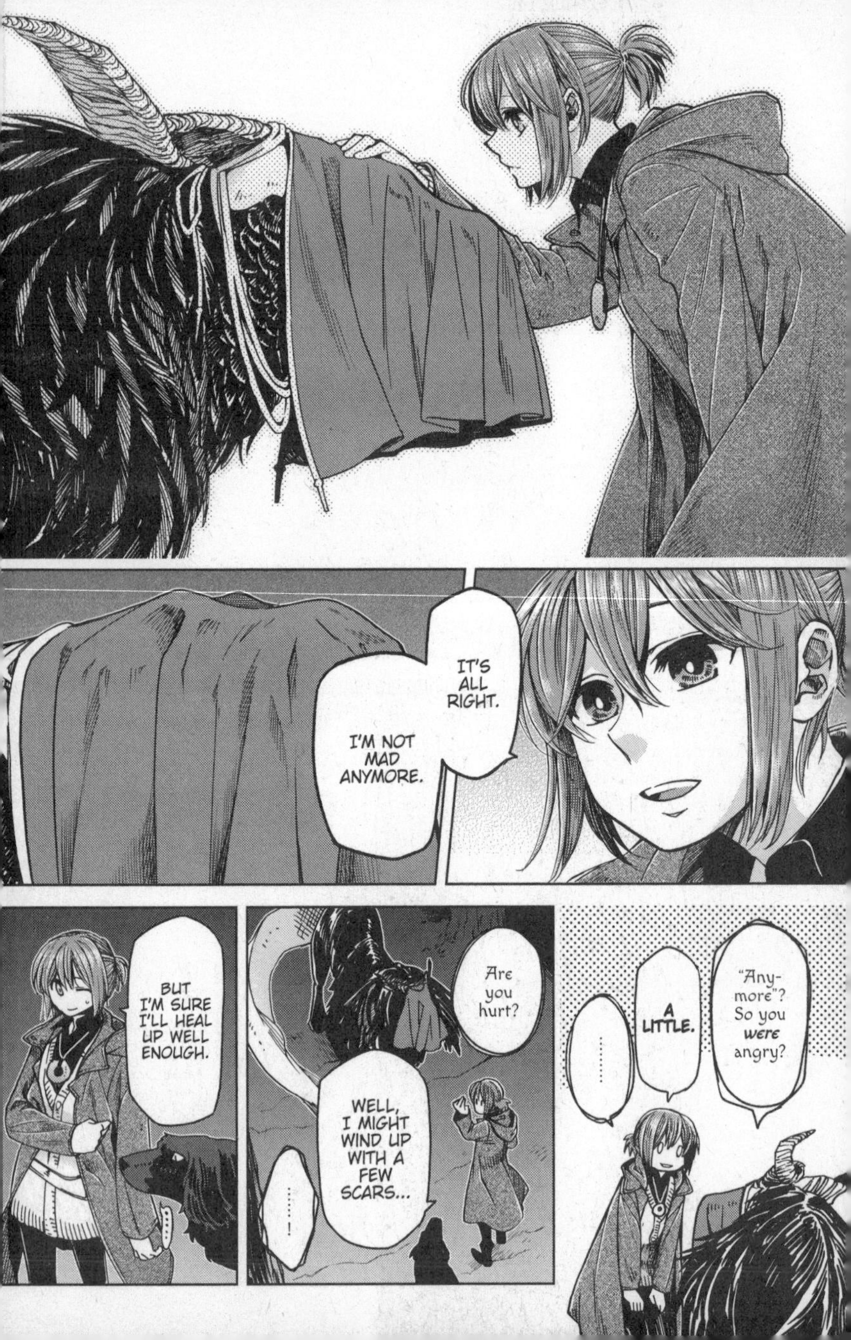
IT'S ALL RIGHT.
I'M NOT MAD ANYMORE.
"Any-more"? So you *were* angry?
A LITTLE.
......
Are you hurt?
WELL, I MIGHT WIND UP WITH A FEW SCARS...
......!
BUT I'M SURE I'LL HEAL UP WELL ENOUGH.

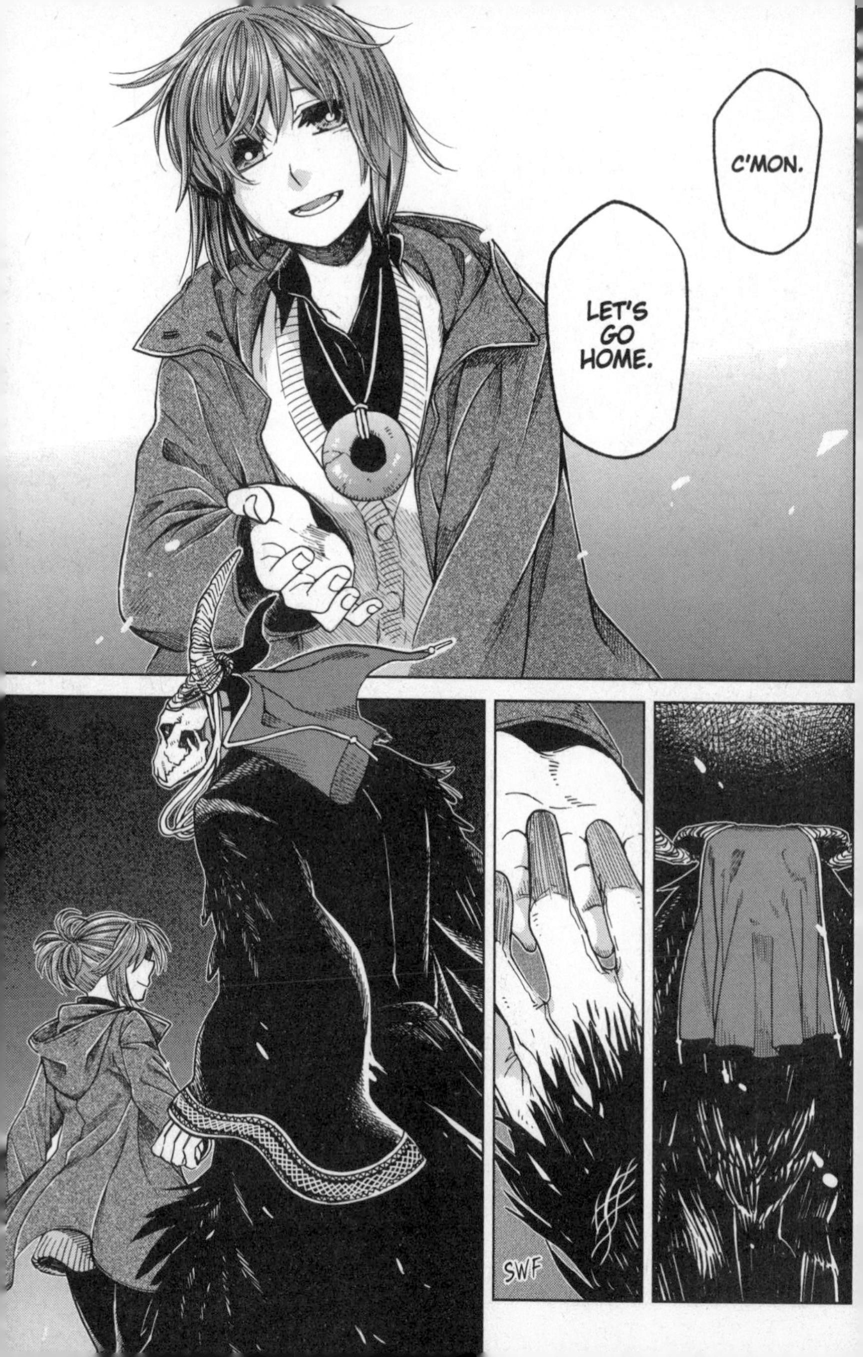
C'MON.
LET'S GO HOME.
SWF

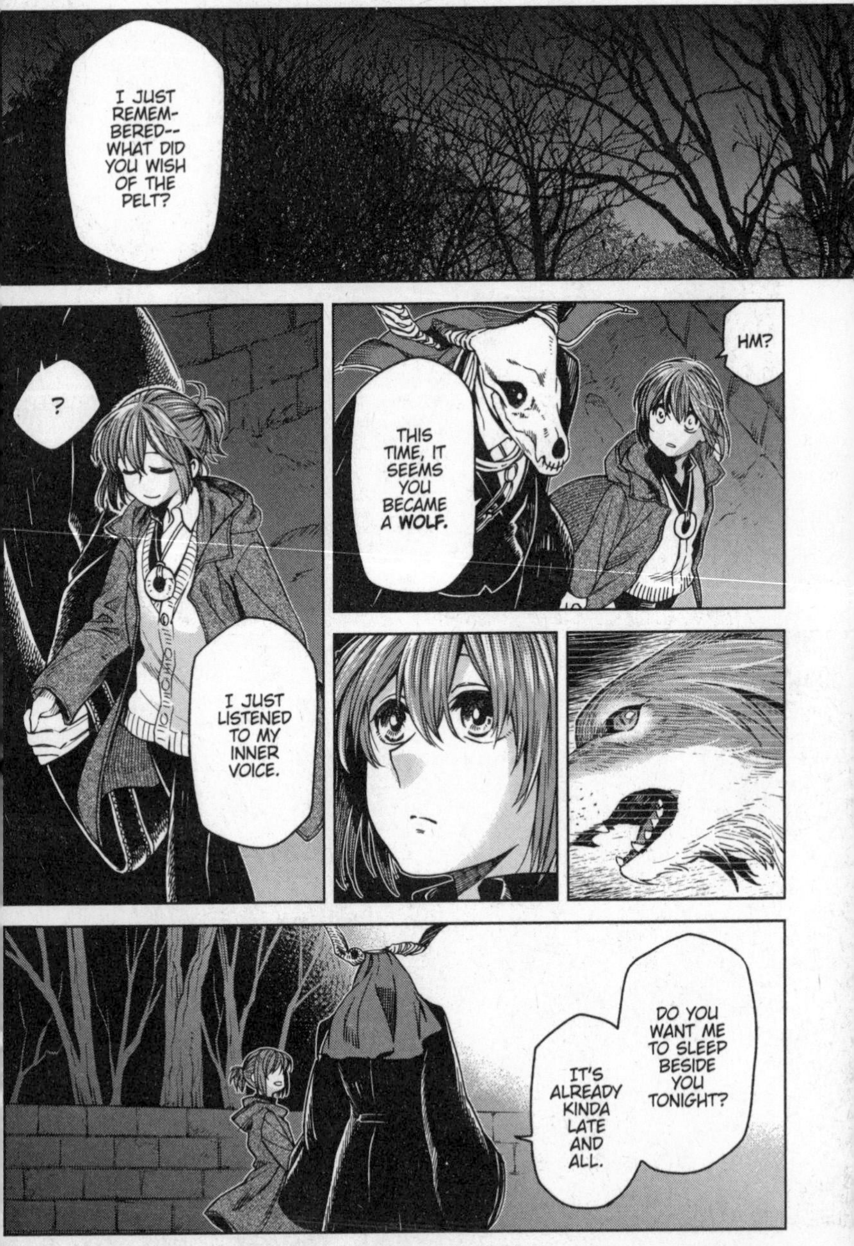
I JUST REMEMBERED-- WHAT DID YOU WISH OF THE PELT?
HM?
THIS TIME, IT SEEMS YOU BECAME A **WOLF.**
?
I JUST LISTENED TO MY INNER VOICE.
DO YOU WANT ME TO SLEEP BESIDE YOU TONIGHT?
IT'S ALREADY KINDA LATE AND ALL.

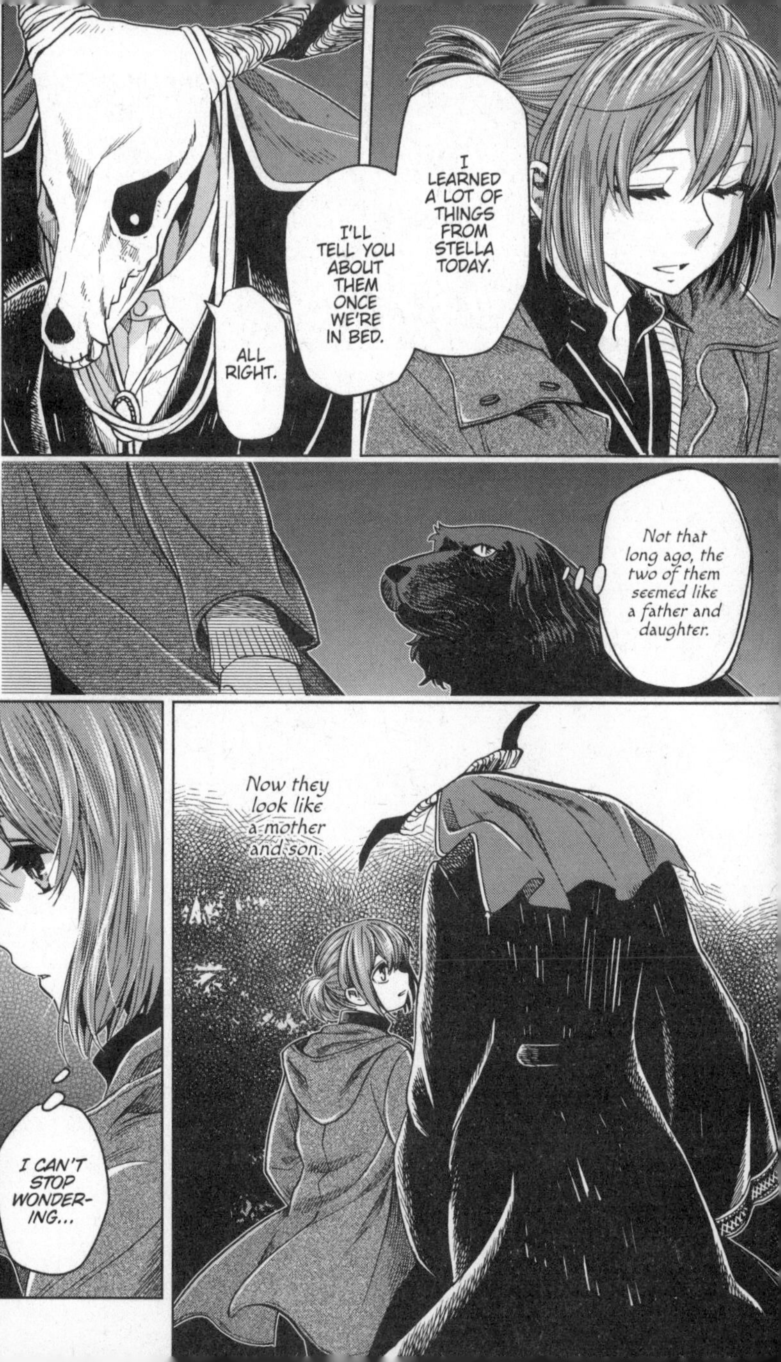
I LEARNED A LOT OF THINGS FROM STELLA TODAY.
I'LL TELL YOU ABOUT THEM ONCE WE'RE IN BED.
ALL RIGHT.
Not that long ago, the two of them seemed like a father and daughter.
Now they look like a mother and son.
I CAN'T STOP WONDERING...

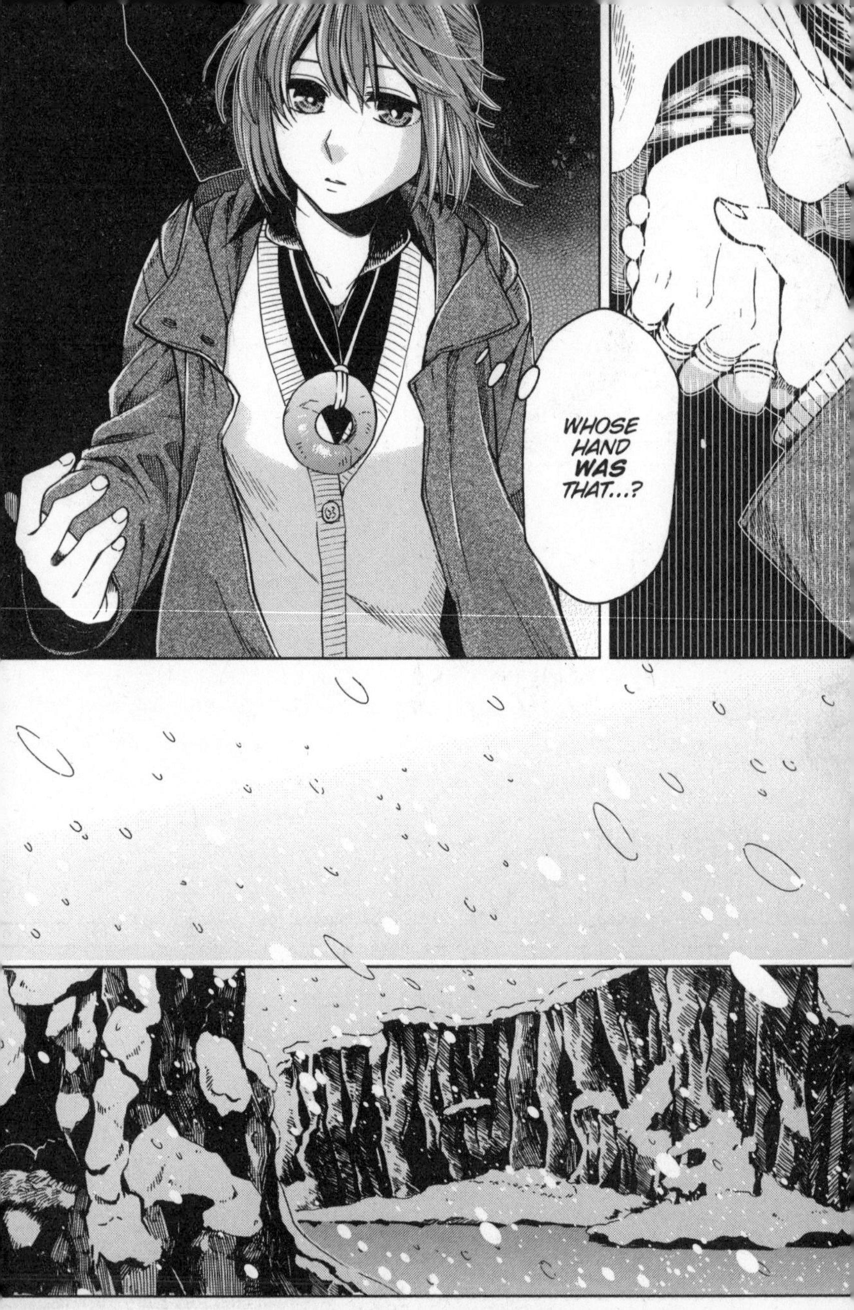
WHOSE HAND WAS THAT...?

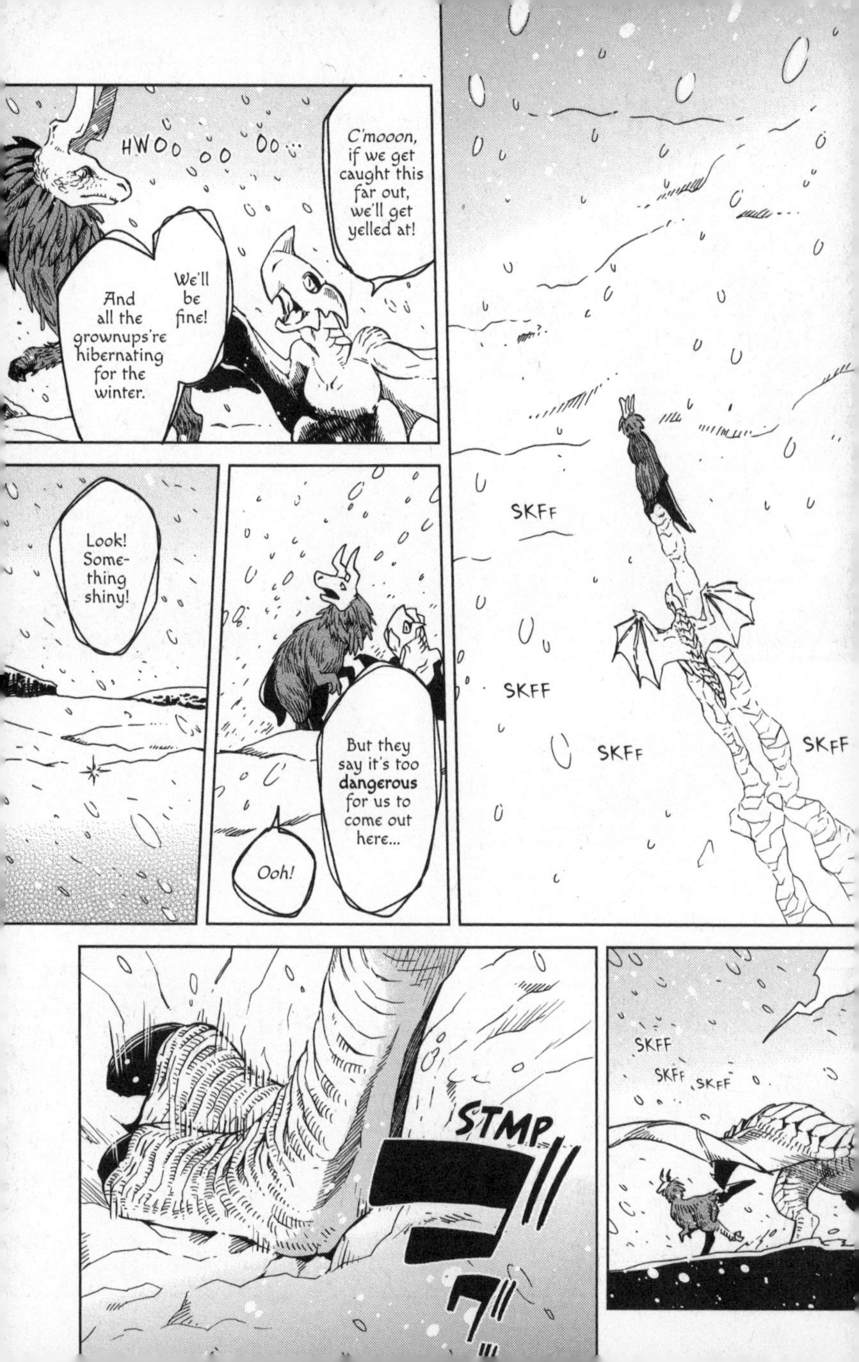
SKFF
SKFF
SKFF
SKFF
C'mooon, if we get caught this far out, we'll get yelled at!
HWOOOOOO...
We'll be fine!
And all the grownups're hibernating for the winter.
But they say it's too **dangerous** for us to come out here...
Ooh!
Look! Something shiny!
SKFF
SKFF
SKFF
STMP

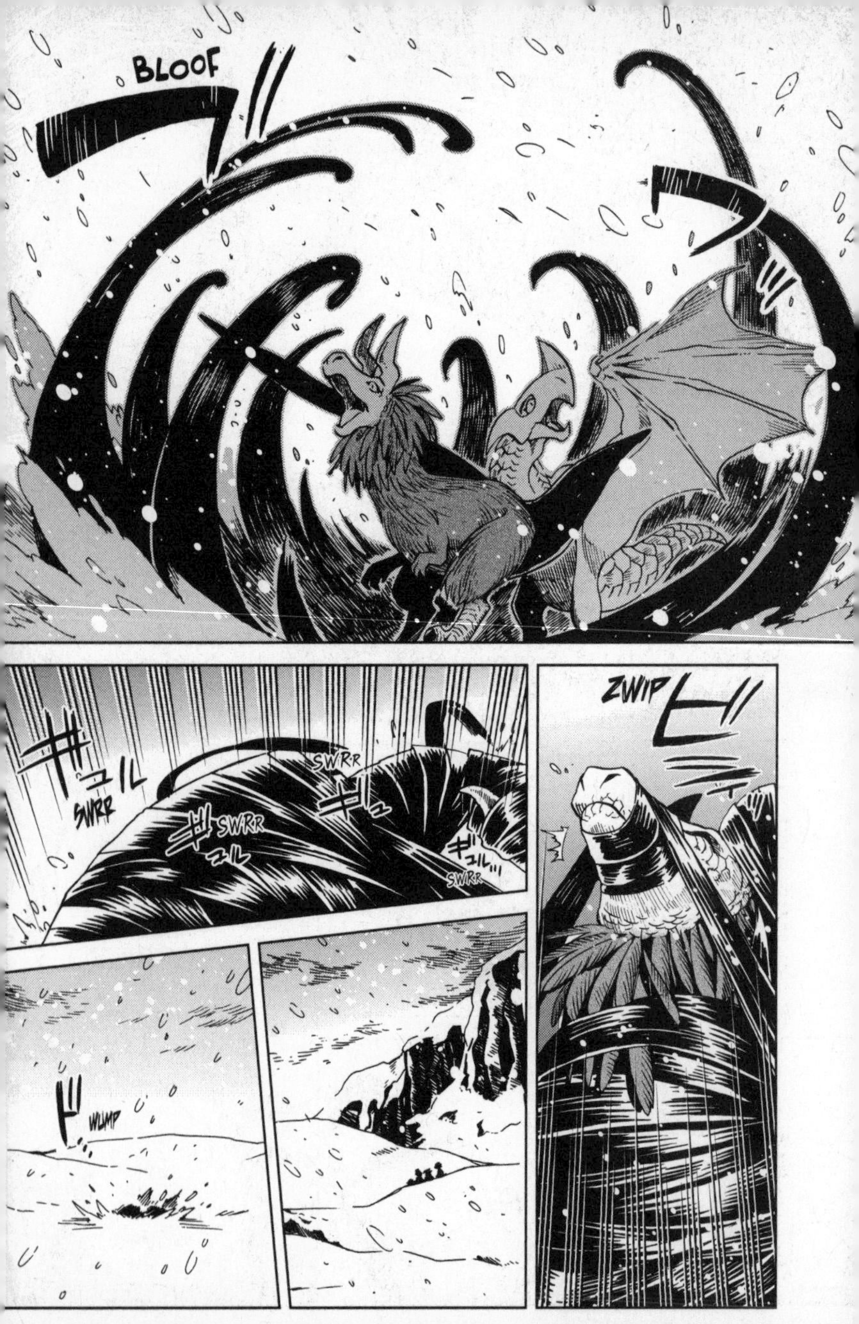
BLOOF
ZWIP
SWRR
SWRR
SWRR
SWRR
WUMP

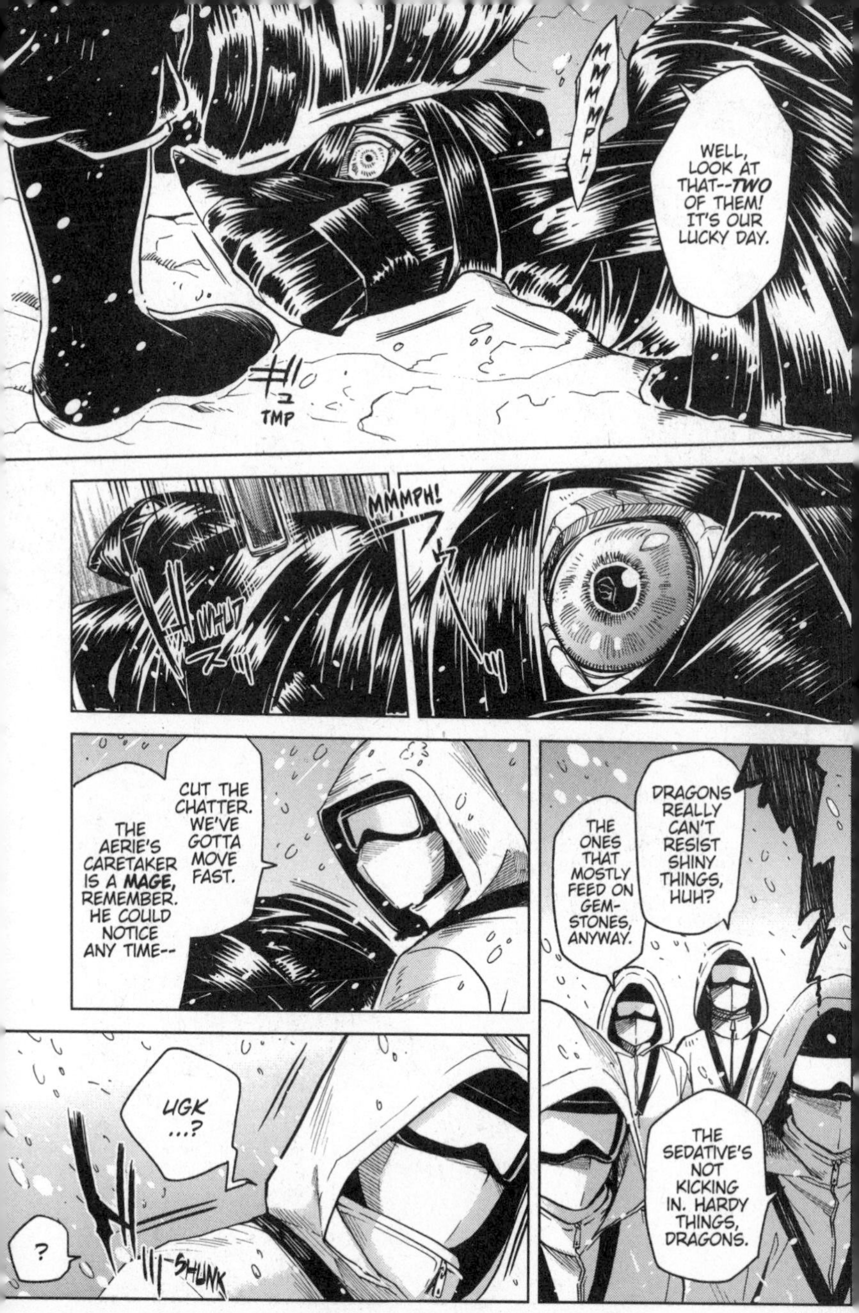
WELL, LOOK AT THAT--TWO OF THEM! IT'S OUR LUCKY DAY.
MMMMMPH!
TMP
MMMPH!
WHUD
DRAGONS REALLY CAN'T RESIST SHINY THINGS, HUH?
THE ONES THAT MOSTLY FEED ON GEM-STONES, ANYWAY.
THE SEDATIVE'S NOT KICKING IN. HARDY THINGS, DRAGONS.
CUT THE CHATTER. WE'VE GOTTA MOVE FAST.
THE AERIE'S CARETAKER IS A MAGE, REMEMBER. HE COULD NOTICE ANY TIME--
UGK ...?
?
SHUNK

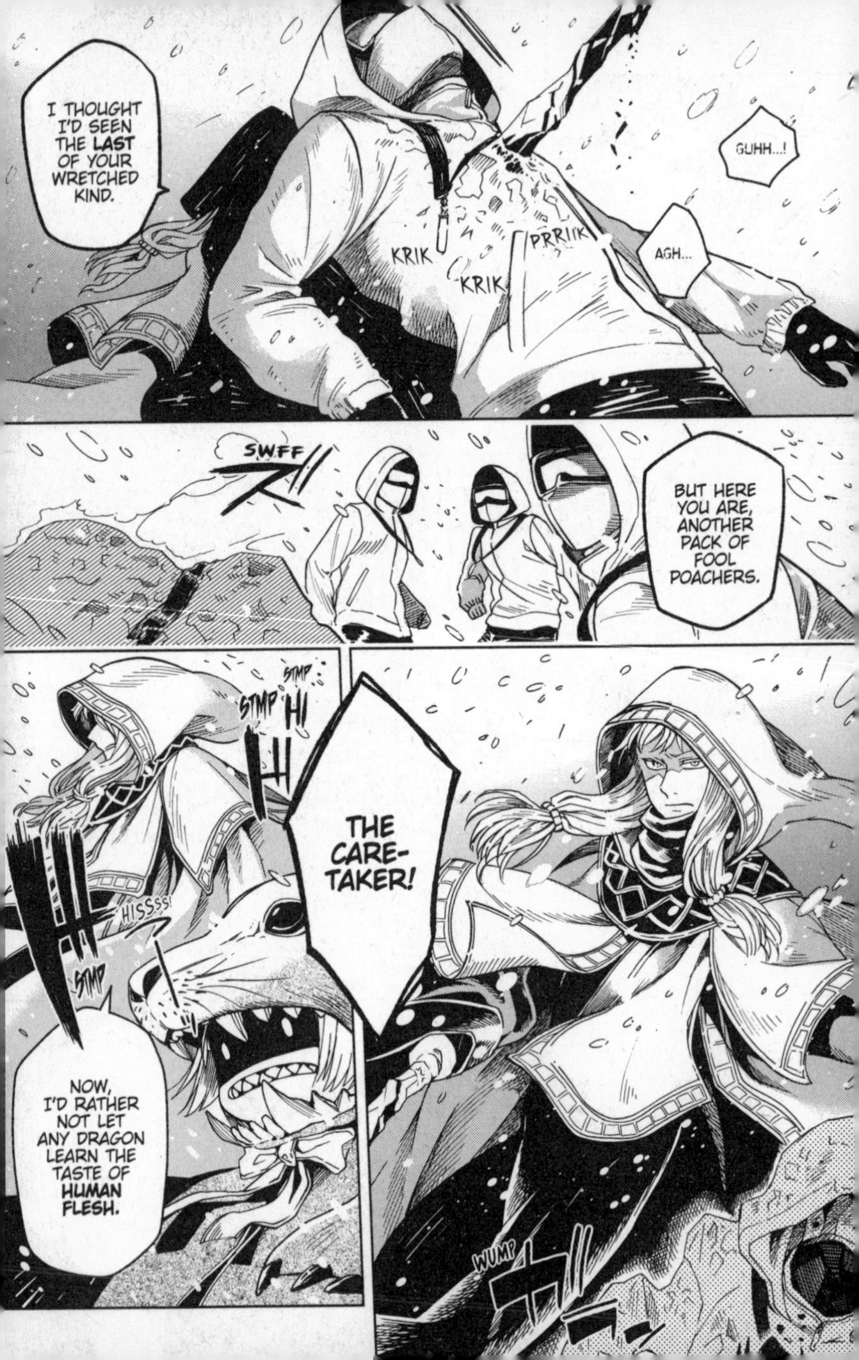
GUHH...!
AGH...
PRRIIK
KRIK
KRIK
I THOUGHT I'D SEEN THE **LAST** OF YOUR WRETCHED KIND.
BUT HERE YOU ARE, ANOTHER PACK OF FOOL POACHERS.
SWFF
THE CARE-TAKER!
WUMP
STMP
STMP
HISSSS!
STMP
NOW, I'D RATHER NOT LET ANY DRAGON LEARN THE TASTE OF **HUMAN FLESH.**

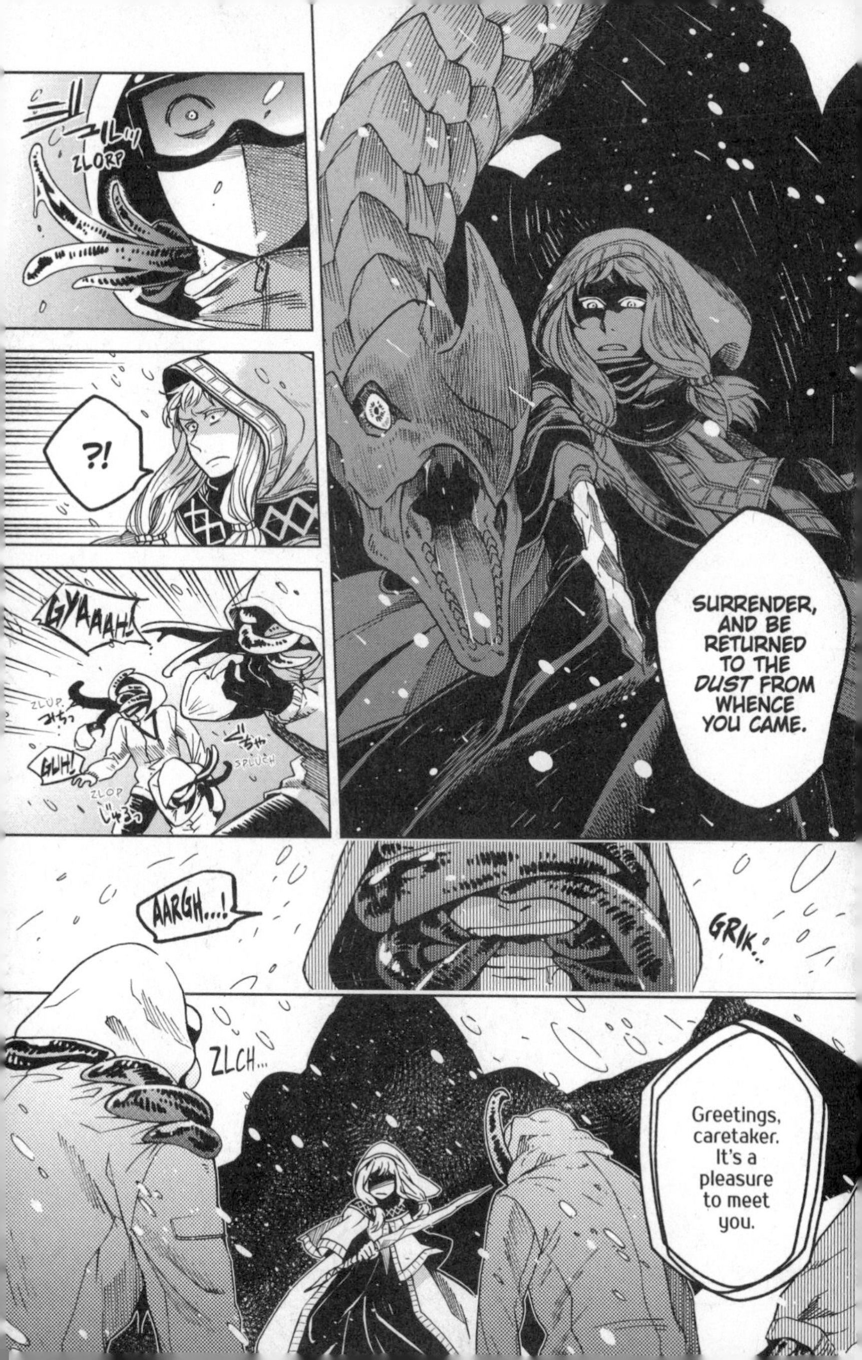
SURRENDER, AND BE RETURNED TO THE DUST FROM WHENCE YOU CAME.
ZLORP
?!
GYAAAH!
ZLUP
みちっ
GUH!
ぐちゃ
SPLUCH
ZLOP
じゅるっ
GRIK...
AARGH...!
ZLCH...
Greetings, caretaker. It's a pleasure to meet you.

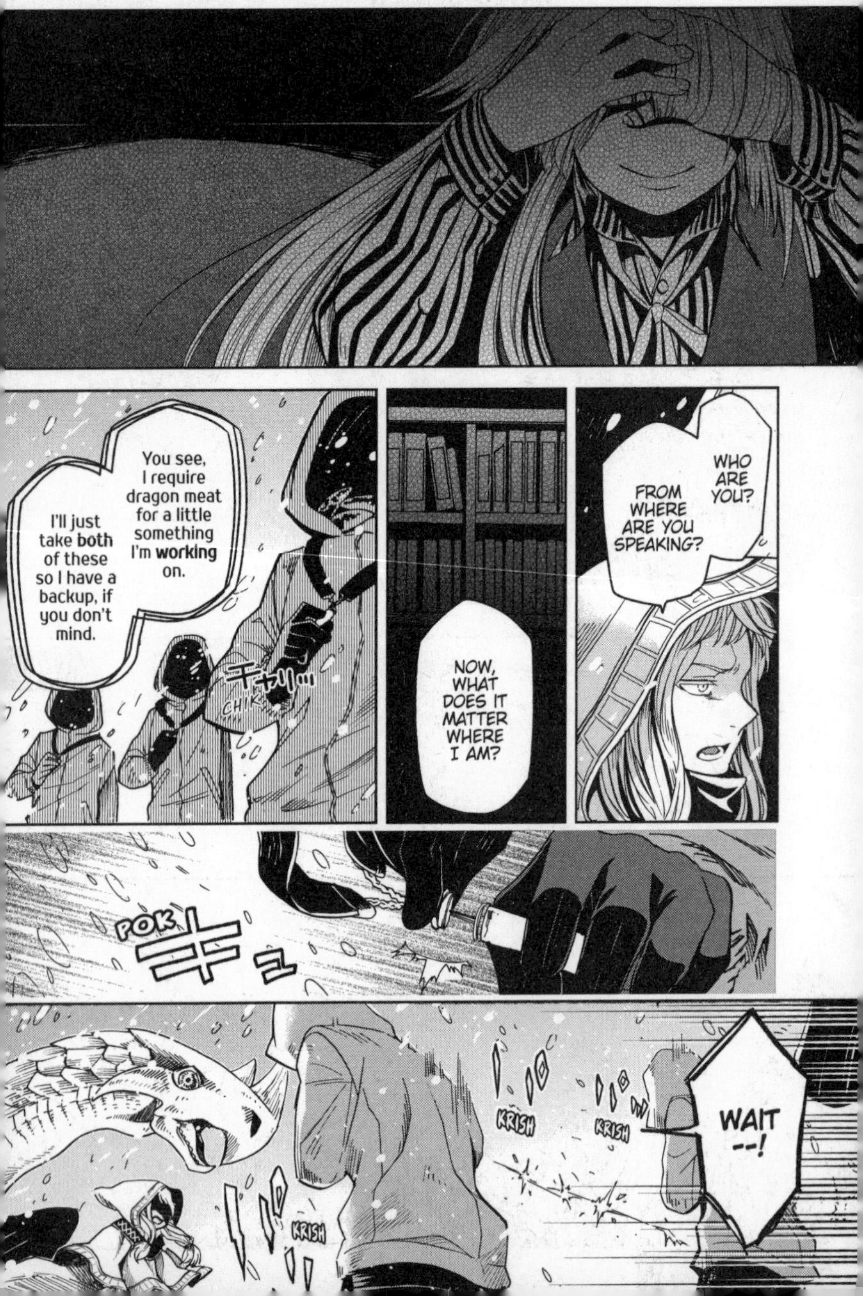
WHO ARE YOU?
FROM WHERE ARE YOU SPEAKING?
NOW, WHAT DOES IT MATTER WHERE I AM?
You see, I require dragon meat for a little something I'm working on.
I'll just take both of these so I have a backup, if you don't mind.
CHIK
POK
WAIT--!
KRISH
KRISH
KRISH

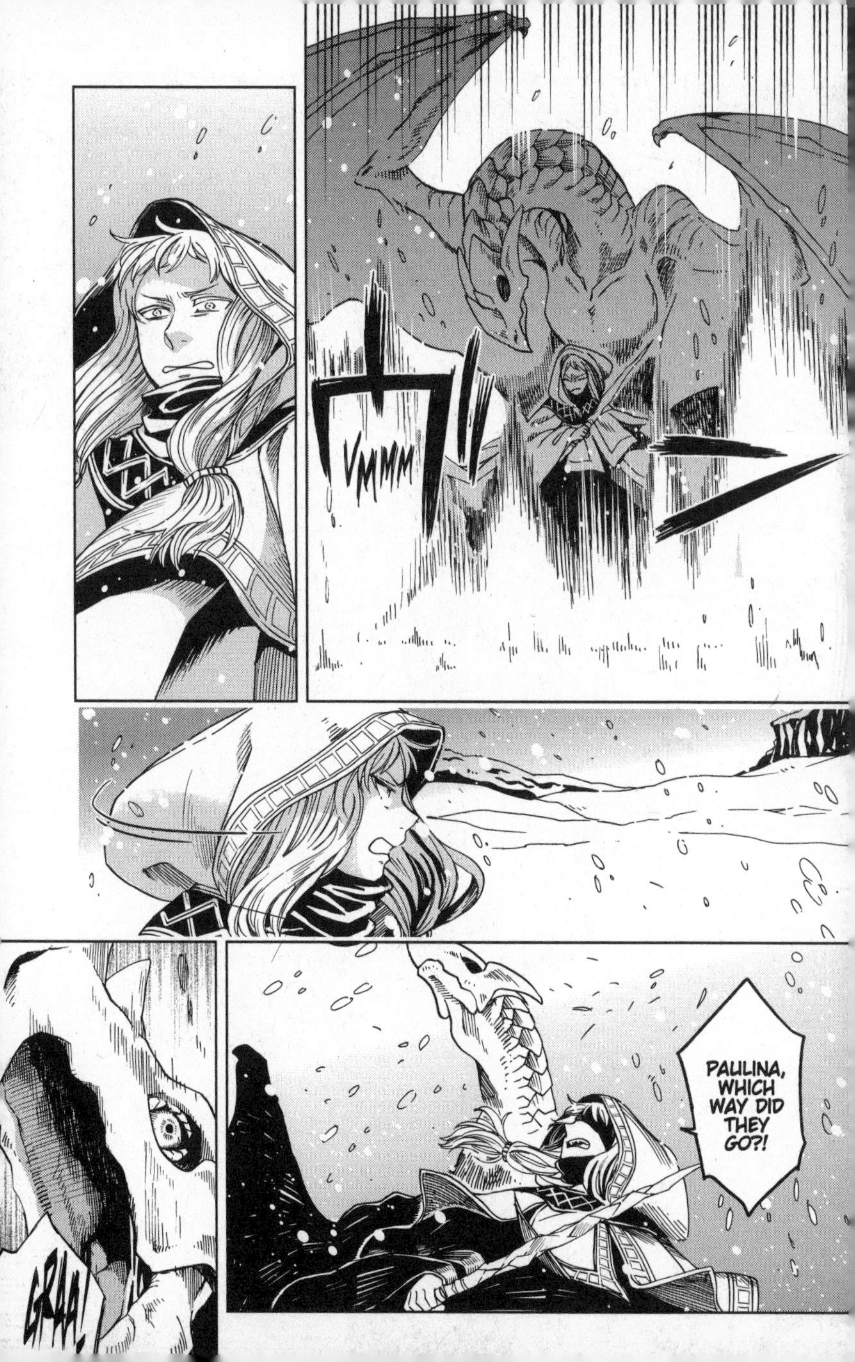
VMMM
PAULINA, WHICH WAY DID THEY GO?!
GRAA!

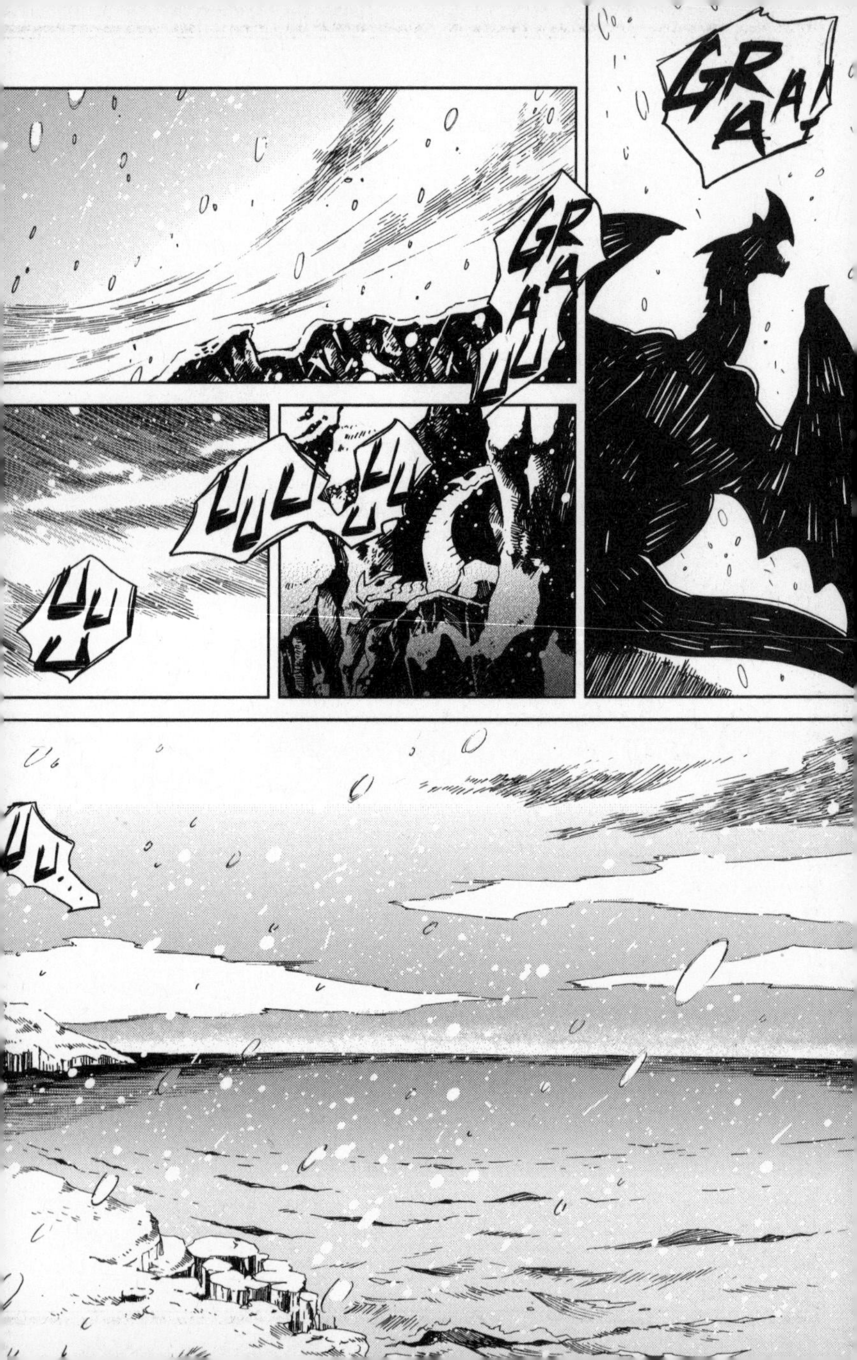
GRAA!
GRAAUU
UUUUUU
UUU
UU

The Ancient Magus' Bride

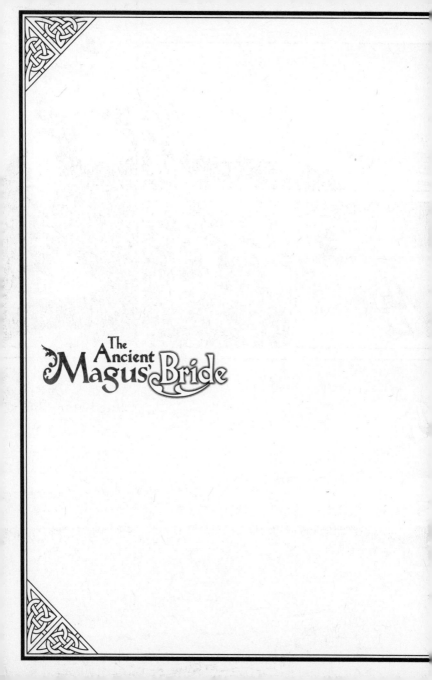

The Ancient Magus' Bride

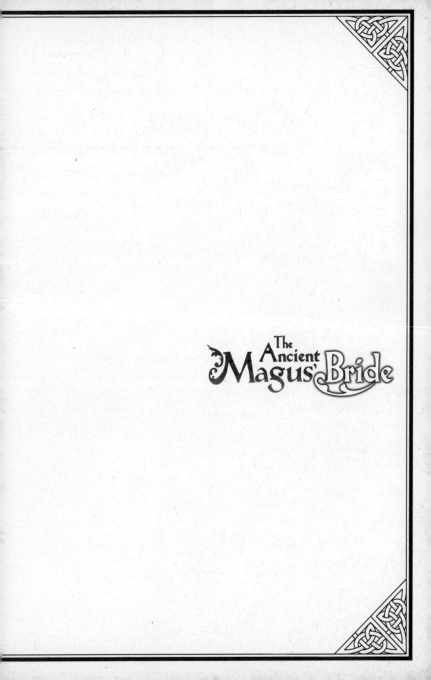

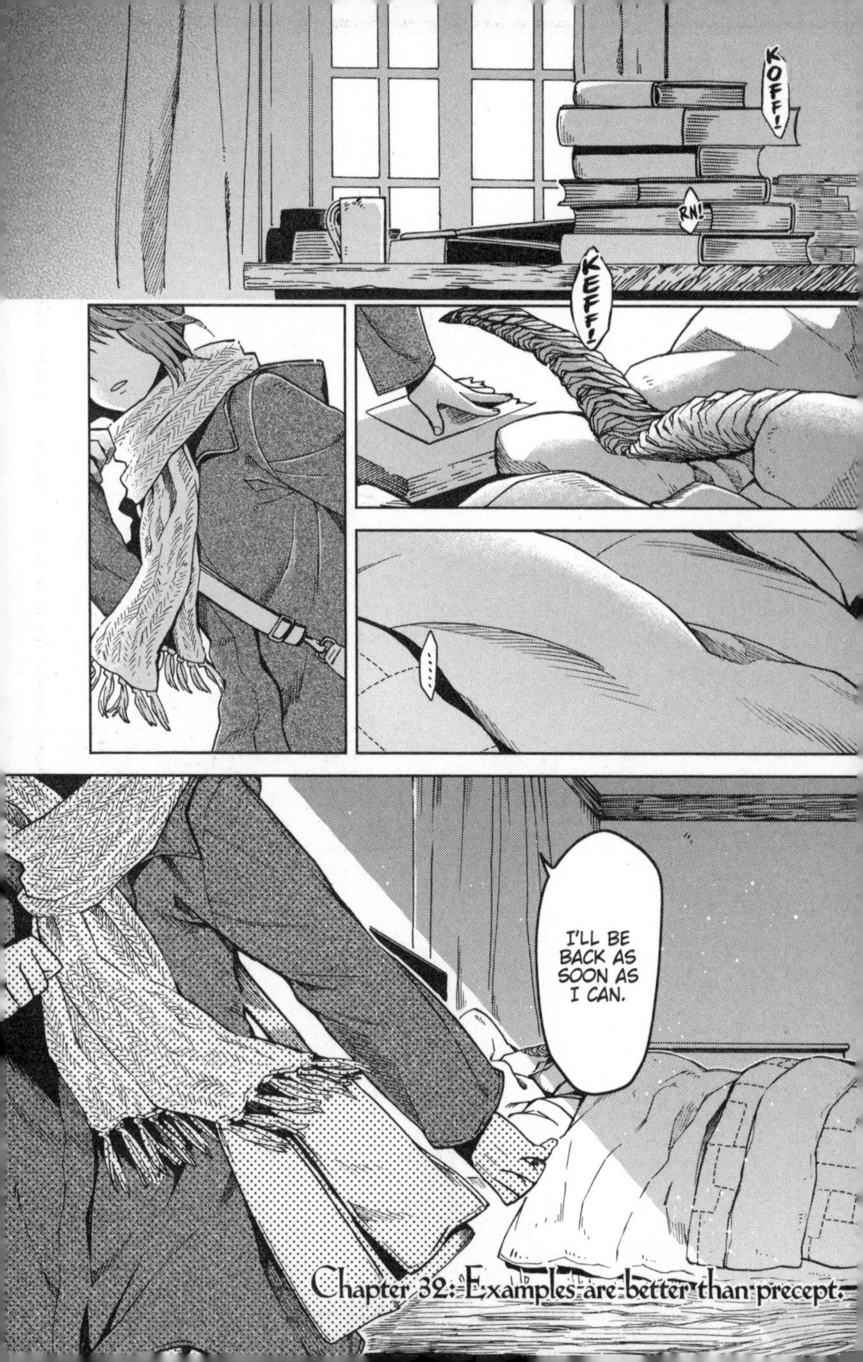
KOFF!
RN!
KEFF!
....
I'LL BE BACK AS SOON AS I CAN.
Chapter 32: Examples are better than precept.

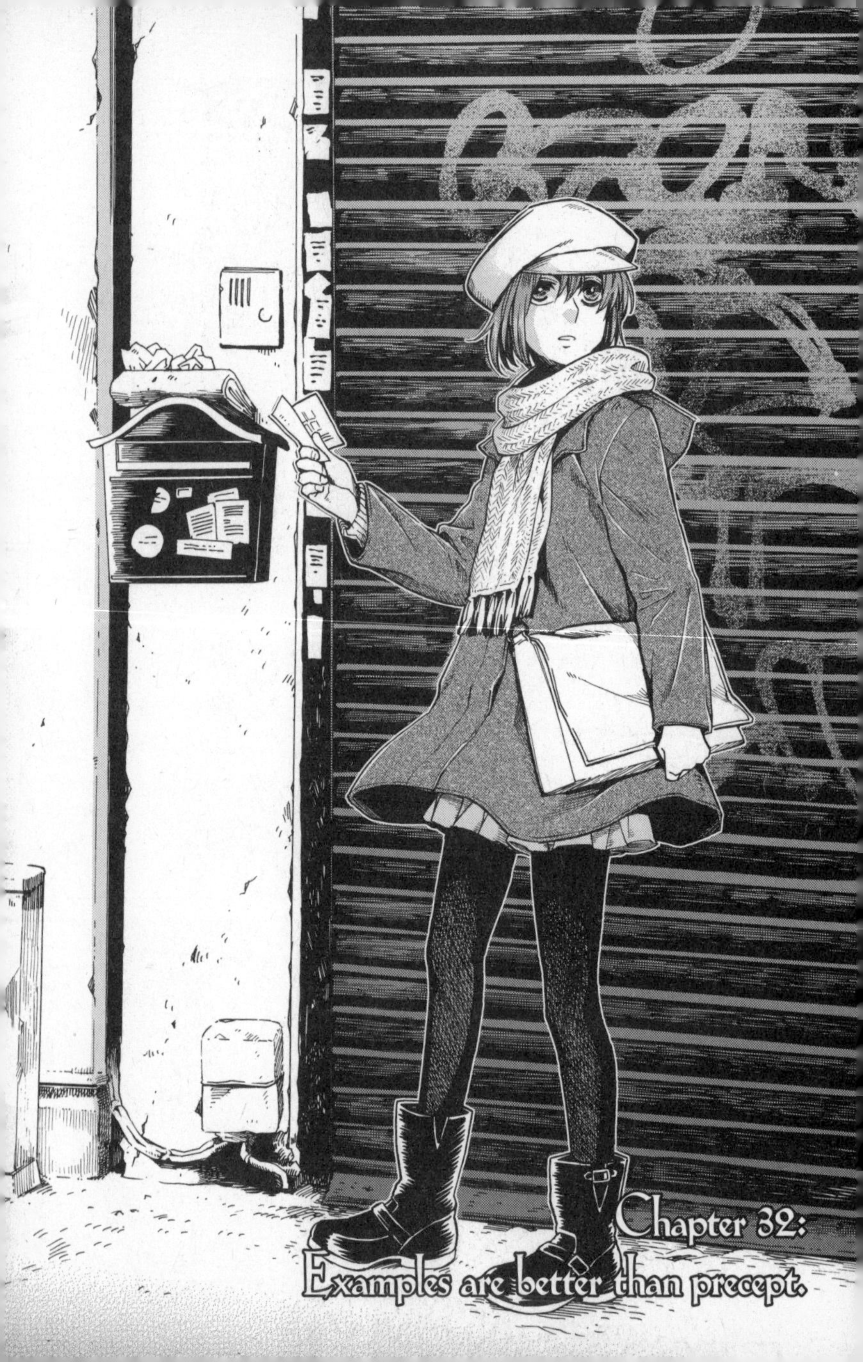
Chapter 32:
Examples are better than precept.

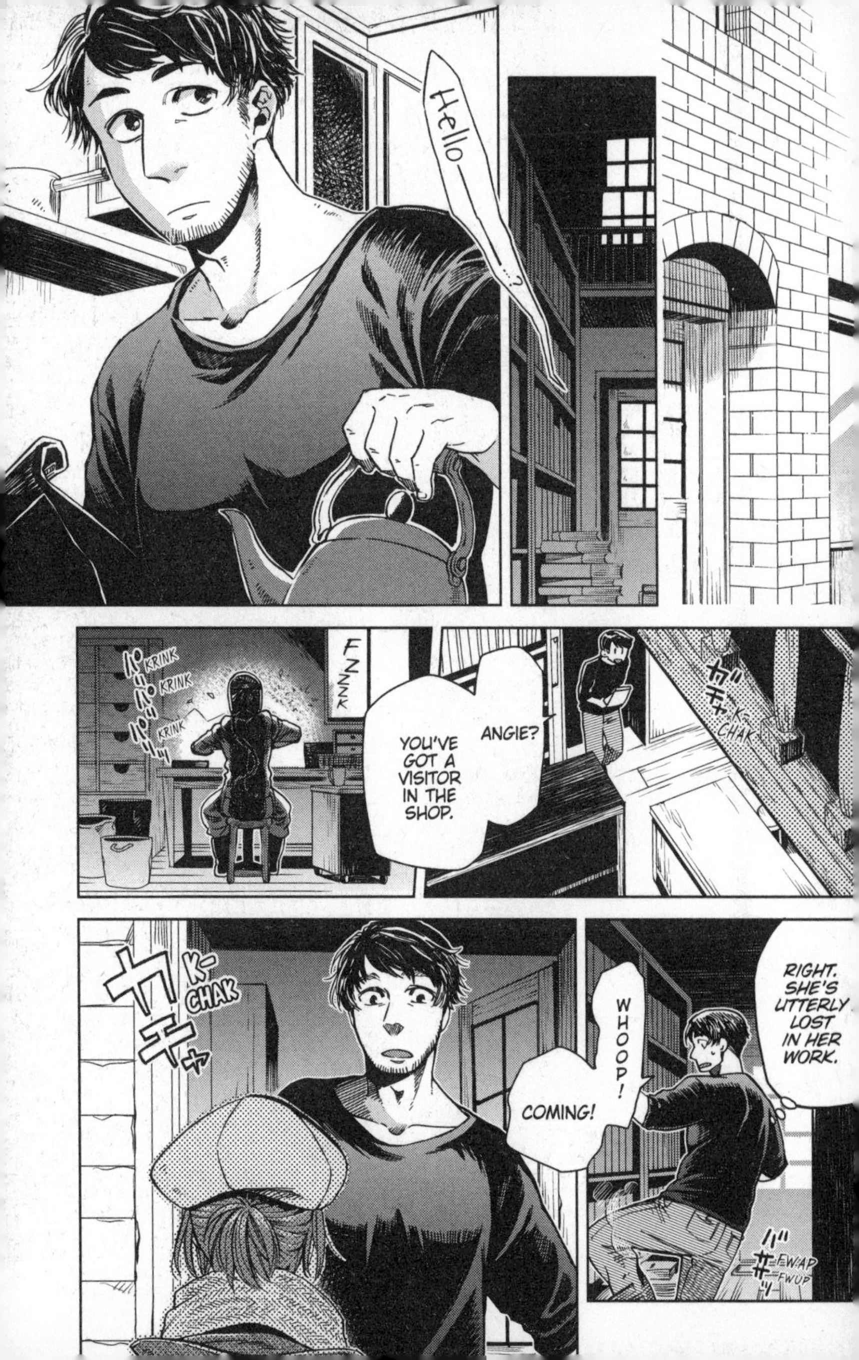
Hello ...?
K-CHAK
ANGIE?
YOU'VE GOT A VISITOR IN THE SHOP.
FZZZK
KRINK
KRINK
KRINK
RIGHT. SHE'S UTTERLY LOST IN HER WORK.
WHOOP!
COMING!
FWAP
FWUP
K-CHAK

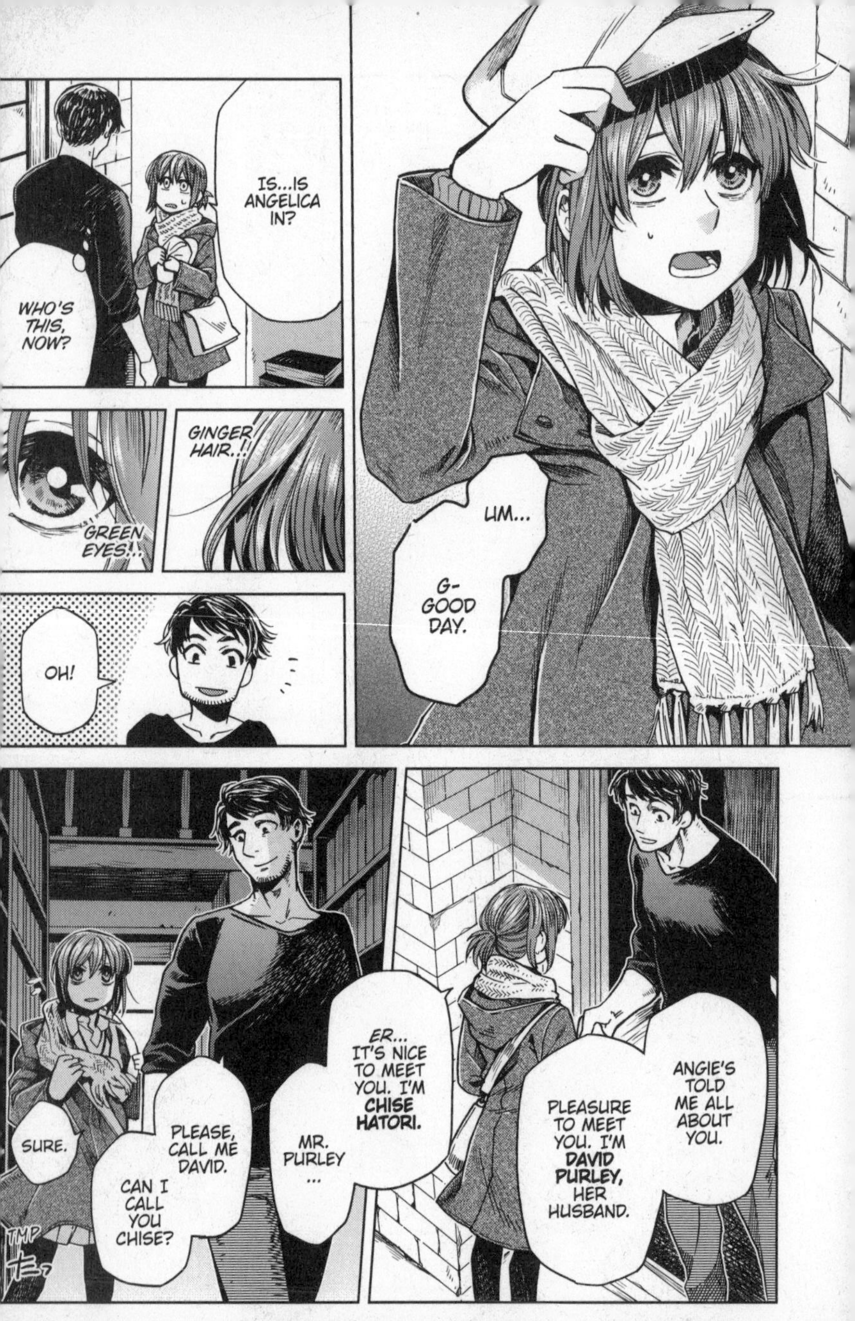
UM...
G-GOOD DAY.
IS...IS ANGELICA IN?
WHO'S THIS, NOW?
GINGER HAIR...!
GREEN EYES...!
OH!
ANGIE'S TOLD ME ALL ABOUT YOU.
PLEASURE TO MEET YOU. I'M **DAVID PURLEY,** HER HUSBAND.
ER... IT'S NICE TO MEET YOU. I'M **CHISE HATORI.**
MR. PURLEY...
PLEASE, CALL ME DAVID.
CAN I CALL YOU CHISE?
SURE.
TMP

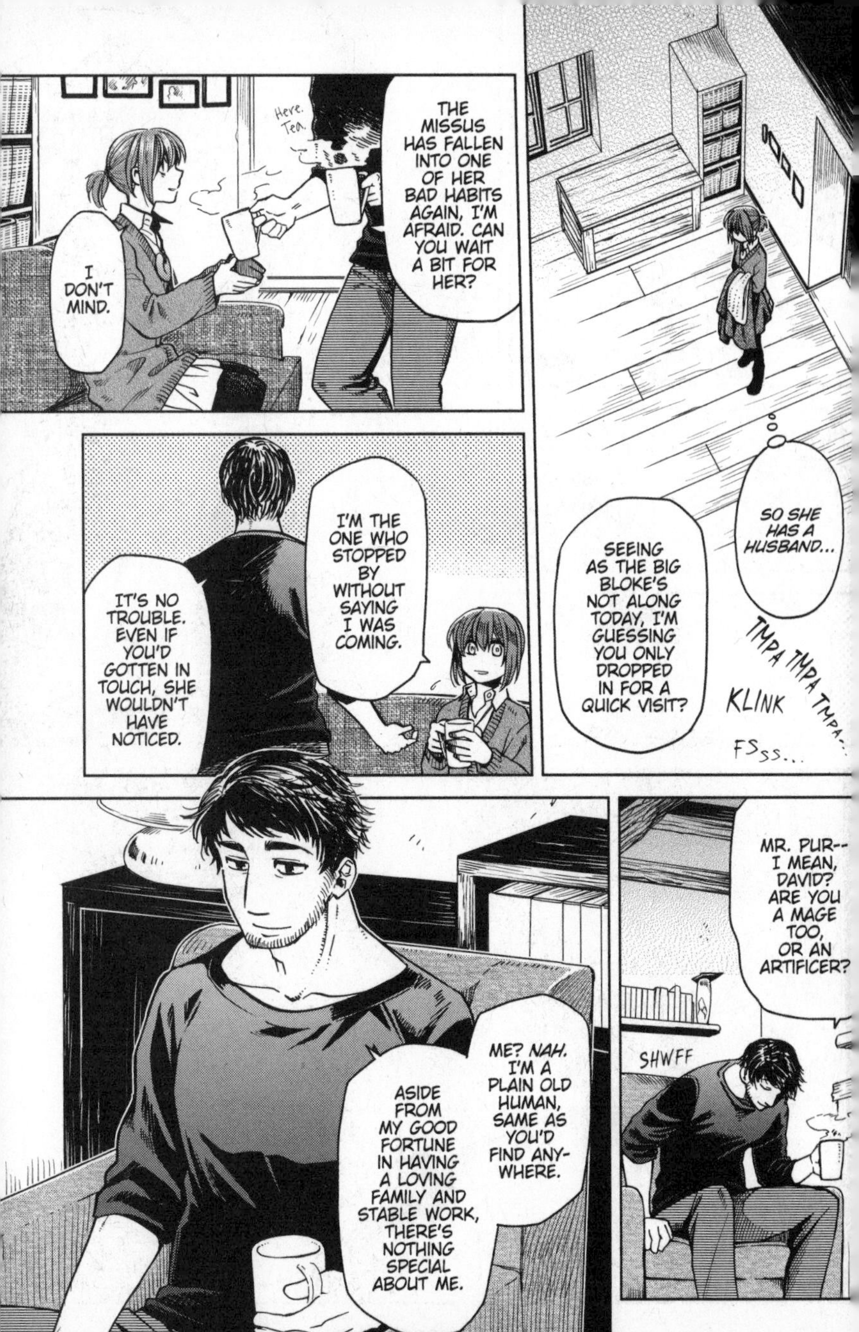

SO SHE HAS A HUSBAND...
TMPA TMPA TMPA...
SEEING AS THE BIG BLOKE'S NOT ALONG TODAY, I'M GUESSING YOU ONLY DROPPED IN FOR A QUICK VISIT?
KLINK
FSss...
THE MISSUS HAS FALLEN INTO ONE OF HER BAD HABITS AGAIN, I'M AFRAID. CAN YOU WAIT A BIT FOR HER?
Here. Tea.
I DON'T MIND.
I'M THE ONE WHO STOPPED BY WITHOUT SAYING I WAS COMING.
IT'S NO TROUBLE. EVEN IF YOU'D GOTTEN IN TOUCH, SHE WOULDN'T HAVE NOTICED.
MR. PUR-- I MEAN, DAVID? ARE YOU A MAGE TOO, OR AN ARTIFICER?
SHWFF
ME? *NAH.* I'M A PLAIN OLD HUMAN, SAME AS YOU'D FIND ANYWHERE.
ASIDE FROM MY GOOD FORTUNE IN HAVING A LOVING FAMILY AND STABLE WORK, THERE'S NOTHING SPECIAL ABOUT ME.

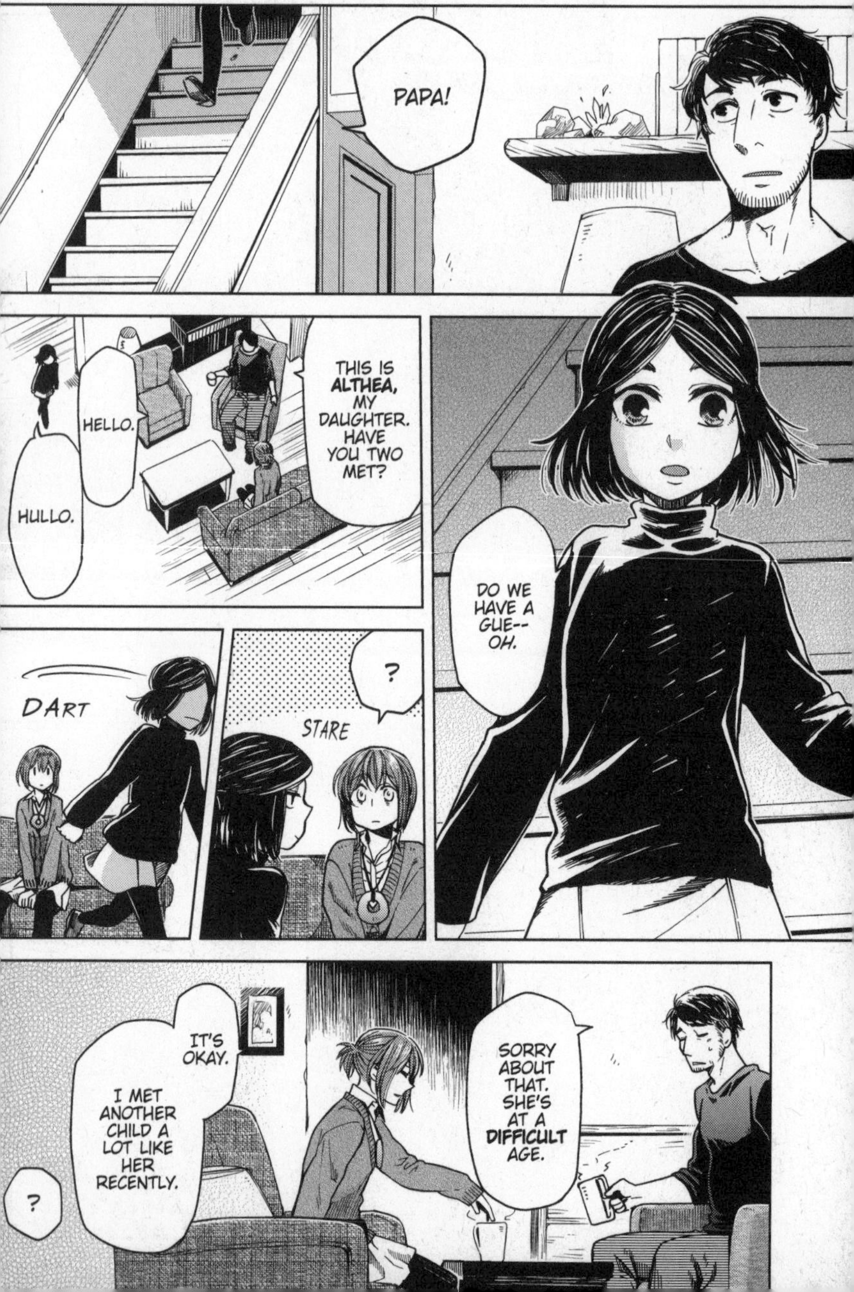
PAPA!
DO WE HAVE A GUE-- OH.
THIS IS **ALTHEA**, MY DAUGHTER. HAVE YOU TWO MET?
HELLO.
HULLO.
?
STARE
DART
SORRY ABOUT THAT. SHE'S AT A **DIFFICULT** AGE.
IT'S OKAY.
I MET ANOTHER CHILD A LOT LIKE HER RECENTLY.
?

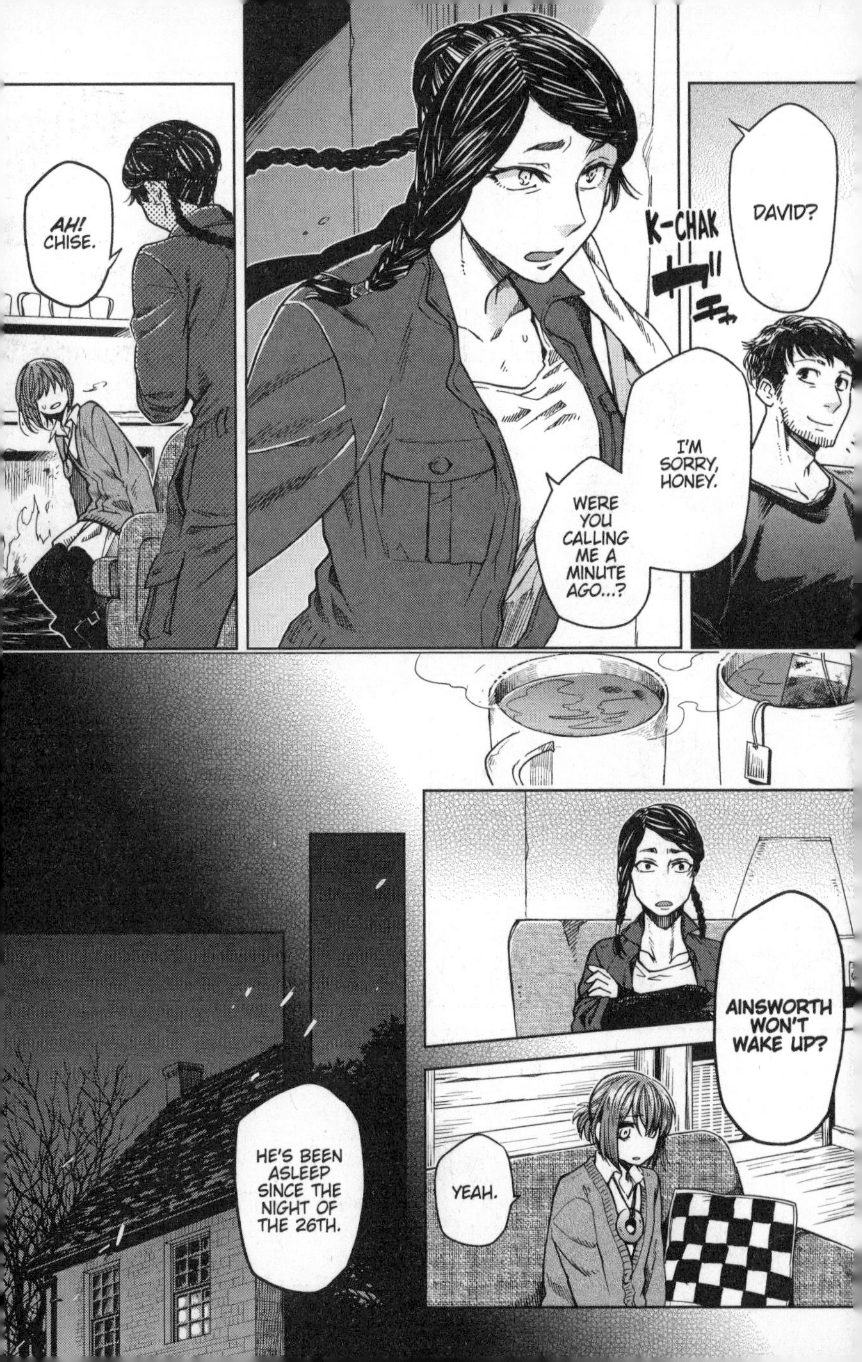
DAVID?
K-CHAK
I'M SORRY, HONEY.
WERE YOU CALLING ME A MINUTE AGO...?
AH! CHISE.
AINSWORTH WON'T WAKE UP?
YEAH.
HE'S BEEN ASLEEP SINCE THE NIGHT OF THE 26TH.

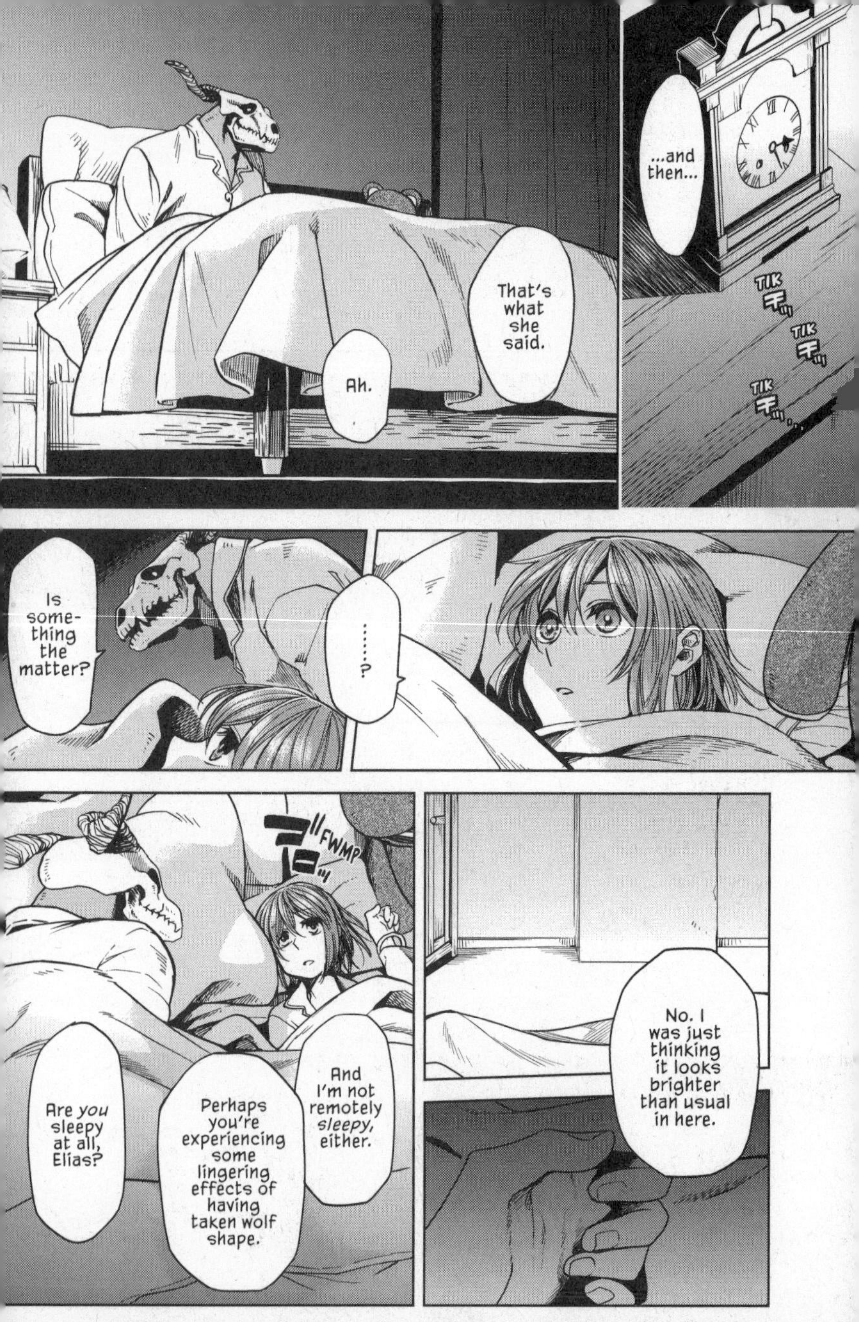
...and then...
TIK
TIK
TIK
That's what she said.
Ah.
......?
Is some-thing the matter?
No. I was just thinking it looks brighter than usual in here.
FWMP
And I'm not remotely *sleepy*, either.
Perhaps you're experiencing some lingering effects of having taken wolf shape.
Are *you* sleepy at all, Elias?

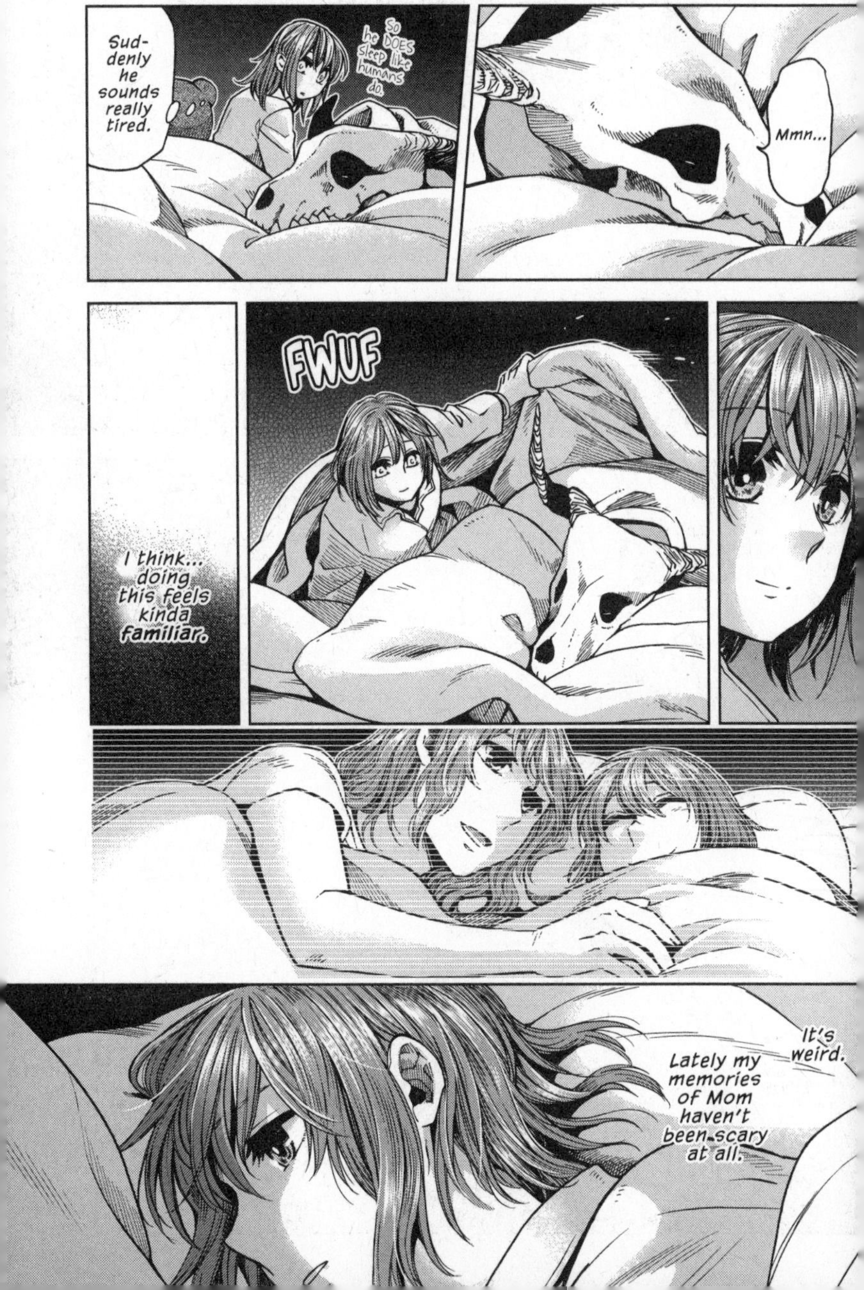
Mmn...
So he DOES sleep like humans do.
Sud-denly he sounds really tired.
FWUF
I think... doing this feels kinda familiar.
It's weird.
Lately my memories of Mom haven't been scary at all.

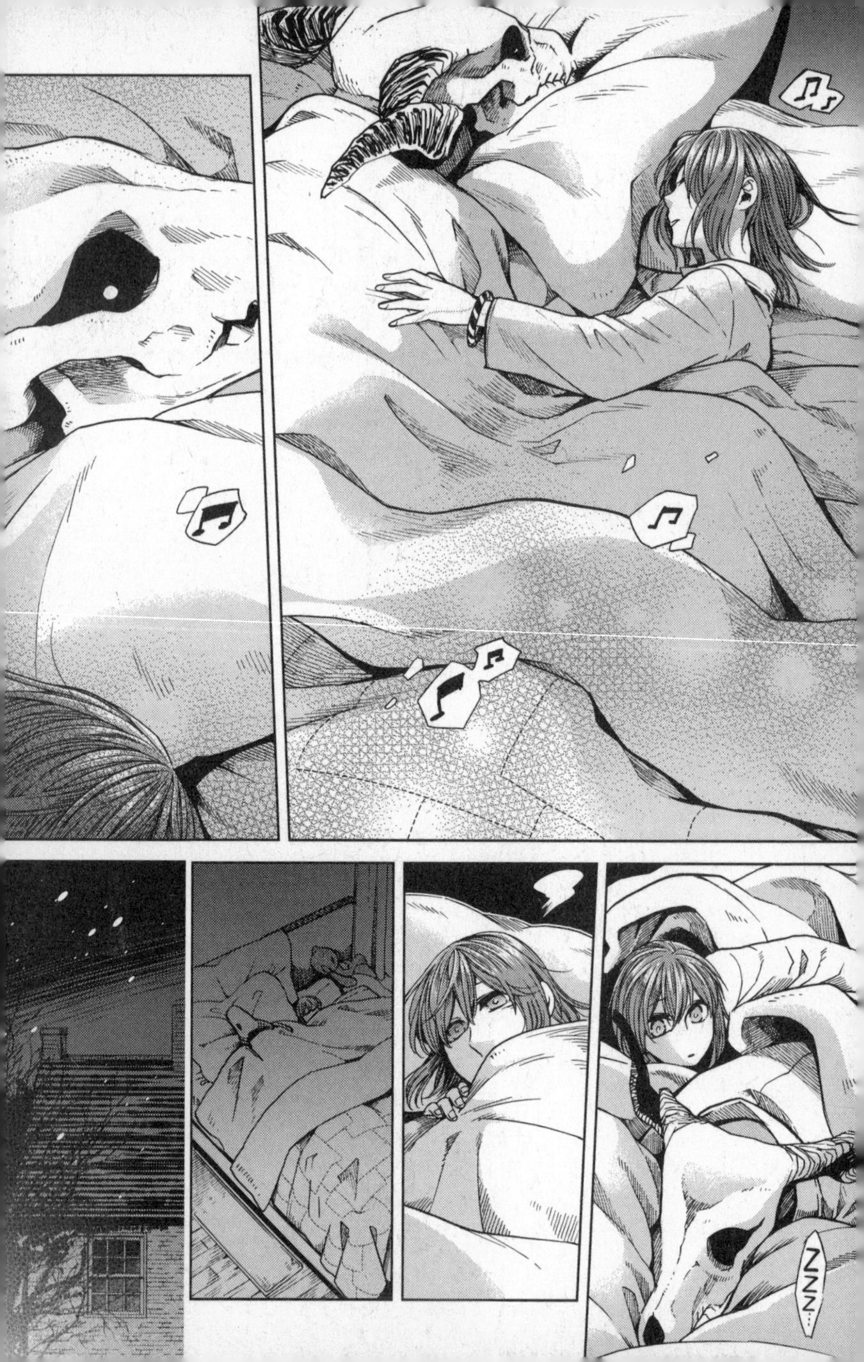
ZZZ...

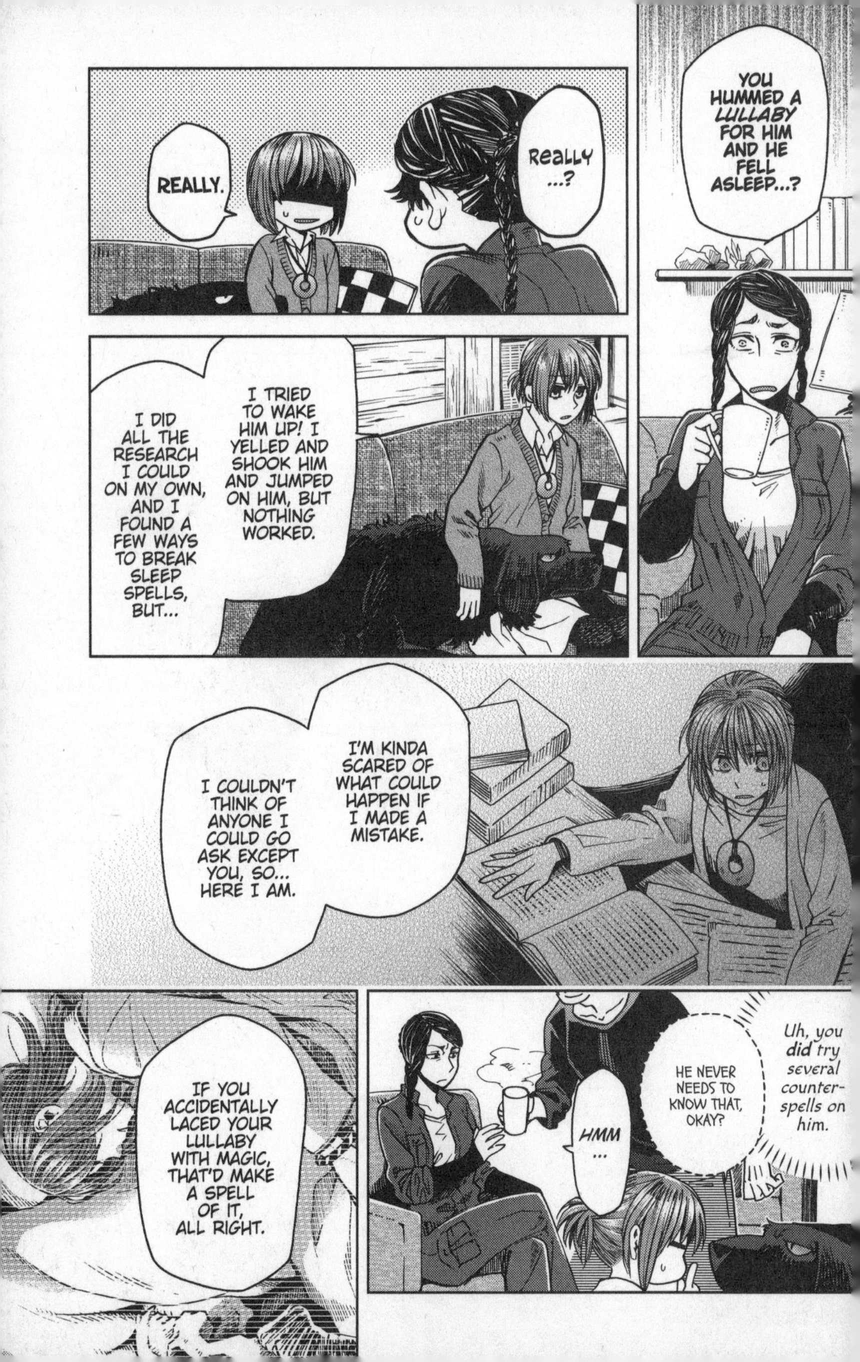
YOU HUMMED A *LULLABY* FOR HIM AND HE FELL ASLEEP...?
Really ...?
REALLY.
I TRIED TO WAKE HIM UP! I YELLED AND SHOOK HIM AND JUMPED ON HIM, BUT NOTHING WORKED.
I DID ALL THE RESEARCH I COULD ON MY OWN, AND I FOUND A FEW WAYS TO BREAK SLEEP SPELLS, BUT...
I'M KINDA SCARED OF WHAT COULD HAPPEN IF I MADE A MISTAKE.
I COULDN'T THINK OF ANYONE I COULD GO ASK EXCEPT YOU, SO... HERE I AM.
Uh, you **did** try several counter-spells on him.
HE NEVER NEEDS TO KNOW THAT, OKAY?
HMM ...
IF YOU ACCIDENTALLY LACED YOUR LULLABY WITH MAGIC, THAT'D MAKE A SPELL OF IT, ALL RIGHT.

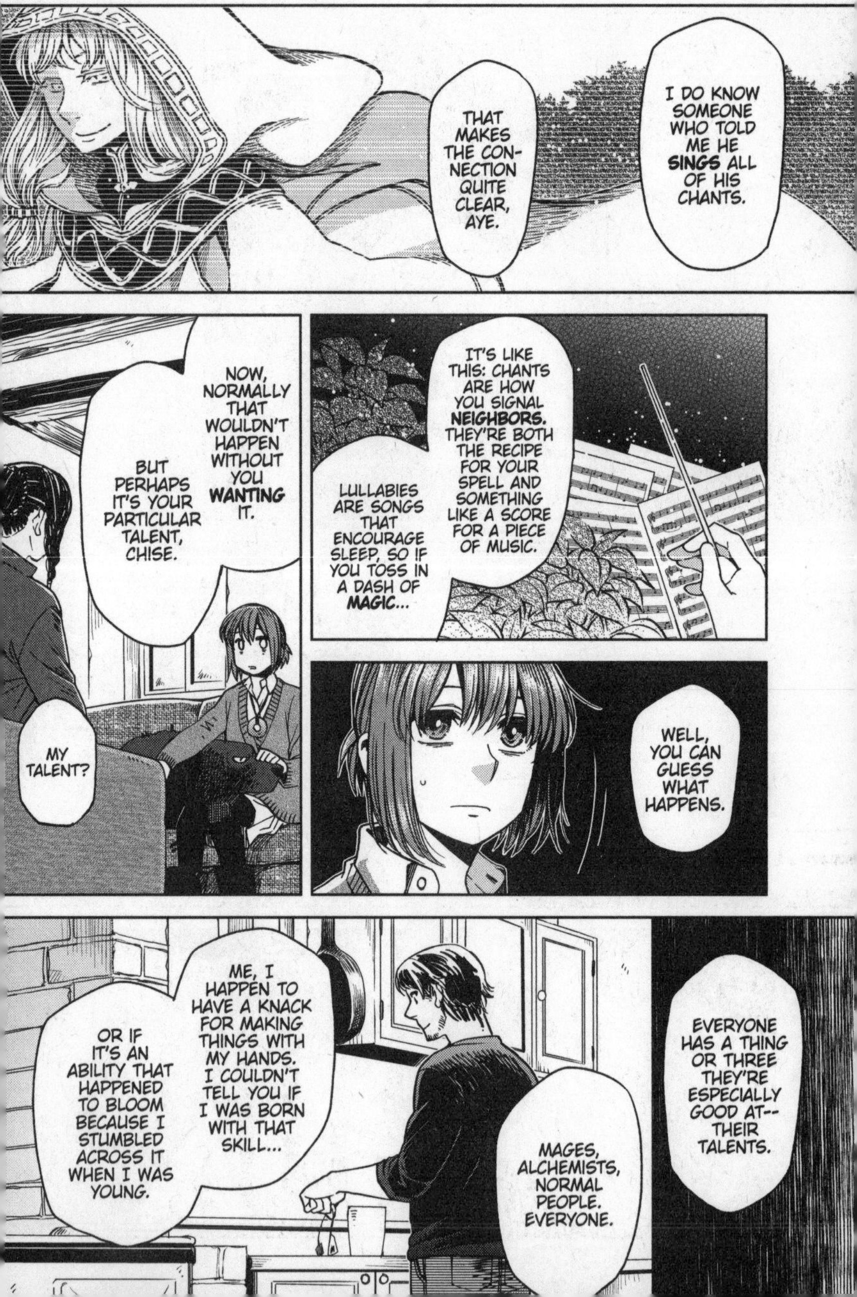
I DO KNOW SOMEONE WHO TOLD ME HE SINGS ALL OF HIS CHANTS.
THAT MAKES THE CON-NECTION QUITE CLEAR, AYE.
IT'S LIKE THIS: CHANTS ARE HOW YOU SIGNAL NEIGHBORS. THEY'RE BOTH THE RECIPE FOR YOUR SPELL AND SOMETHING LIKE A SCORE FOR A PIECE OF MUSIC.
LULLABIES ARE SONGS THAT ENCOURAGE SLEEP, SO IF YOU TOSS IN A DASH OF MAGIC...
WELL, YOU CAN GUESS WHAT HAPPENS.
NOW, NORMALLY THAT WOULDN'T HAPPEN WITHOUT YOU WANTING IT.
BUT PERHAPS IT'S YOUR PARTICULAR TALENT, CHISE.
MY TALENT?
EVERYONE HAS A THING OR THREE THEY'RE ESPECIALLY GOOD AT-- THEIR TALENTS.
MAGES, ALCHEMISTS, NORMAL PEOPLE. EVERYONE.
ME, I HAPPEN TO HAVE A KNACK FOR MAKING THINGS WITH MY HANDS. I COULDN'T TELL YOU IF I WAS BORN WITH THAT SKILL...
OR IF IT'S AN ABILITY THAT HAPPENED TO BLOOM BECAUSE I STUMBLED ACROSS IT WHEN I WAS YOUNG.

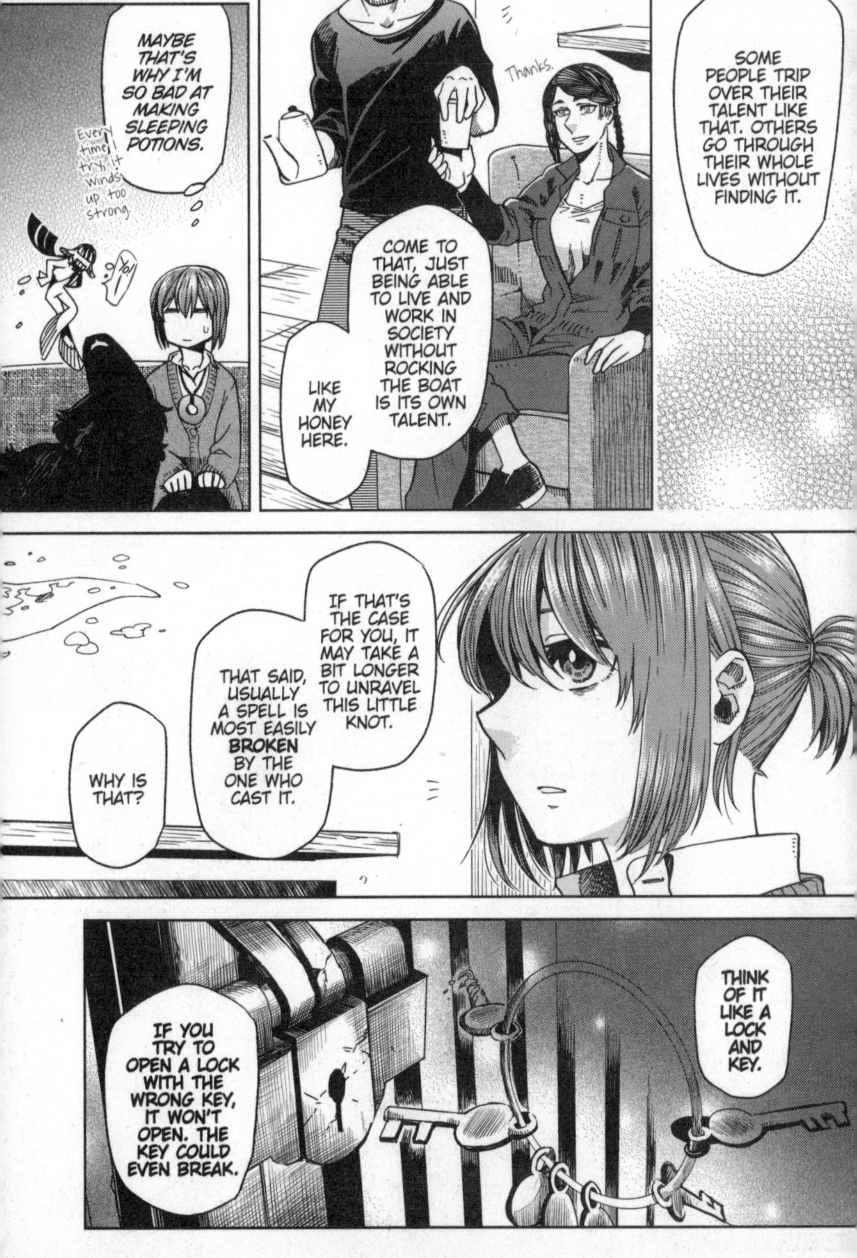
SOME PEOPLE TRIP OVER THEIR TALENT LIKE THAT. OTHERS GO THROUGH THEIR WHOLE LIVES WITHOUT FINDING IT.
Thanks.
COME TO THAT, JUST BEING ABLE TO LIVE AND WORK IN SOCIETY WITHOUT ROCKING THE BOAT IS ITS OWN TALENT.
LIKE MY HONEY HERE.
MAYBE THAT'S WHY I'M SO BAD AT MAKING SLEEPING POTIONS.
Every time I try, it winds up too strong.
YO!
IF THAT'S THE CASE FOR YOU, IT MAY TAKE A BIT LONGER TO UNRAVEL THIS LITTLE KNOT.
THAT SAID, USUALLY A SPELL IS MOST EASILY **BROKEN** BY THE ONE WHO CAST IT.
WHY IS THAT?
THINK OF IT LIKE A LOCK AND KEY.
IF YOU TRY TO OPEN A LOCK WITH THE WRONG KEY, IT WON'T OPEN. THE KEY COULD EVEN BREAK.

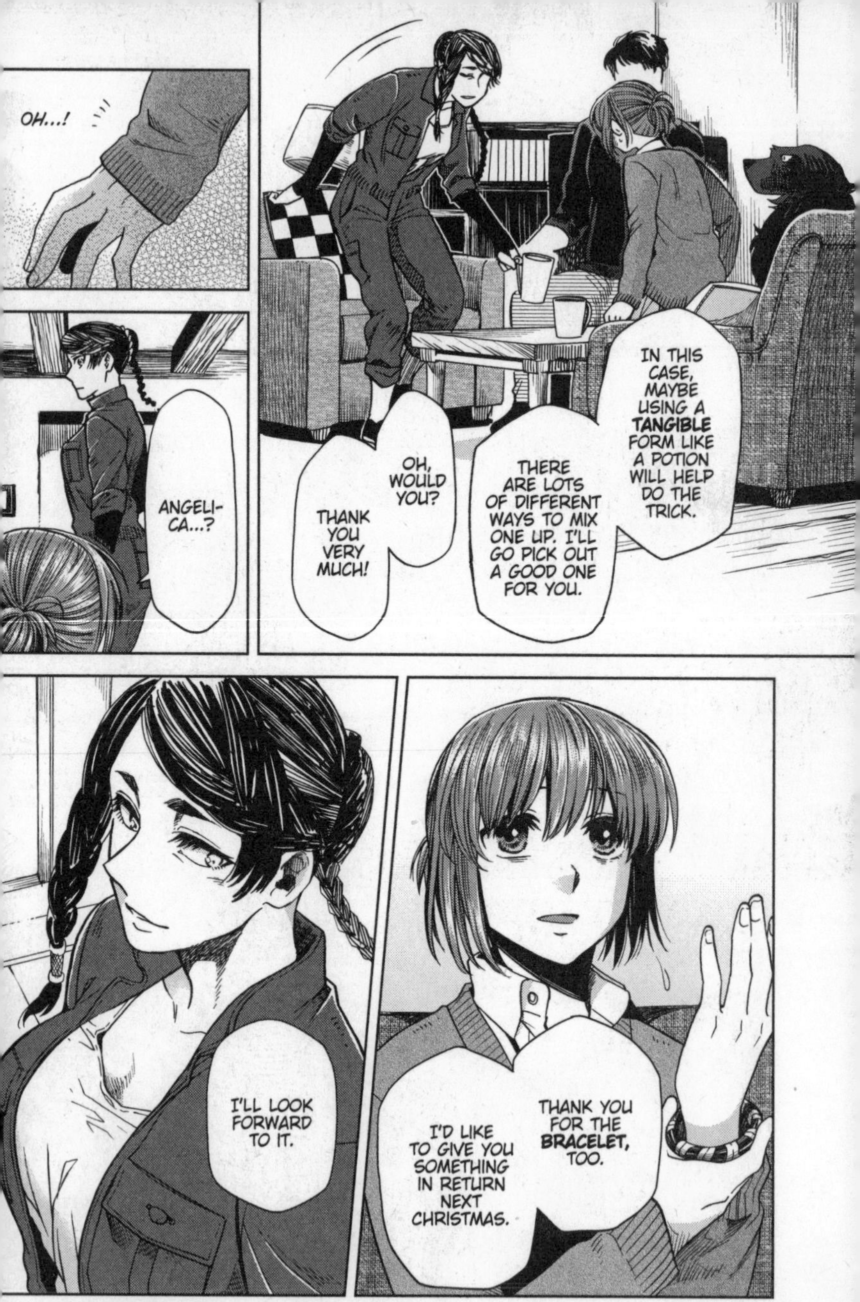
IN THIS CASE, MAYBE USING A **TANGIBLE** FORM LIKE A POTION WILL HELP DO THE TRICK.
THERE ARE LOTS OF DIFFERENT WAYS TO MIX ONE UP. I'LL GO PICK OUT A GOOD ONE FOR YOU.
OH, WOULD YOU?
THANK YOU VERY MUCH!
OH...!
ANGELI-CA...?
THANK YOU FOR THE **BRACELET,** TOO.
I'D LIKE TO GIVE YOU SOMETHING IN RETURN NEXT CHRISTMAS.
I'LL LOOK FORWARD TO IT.

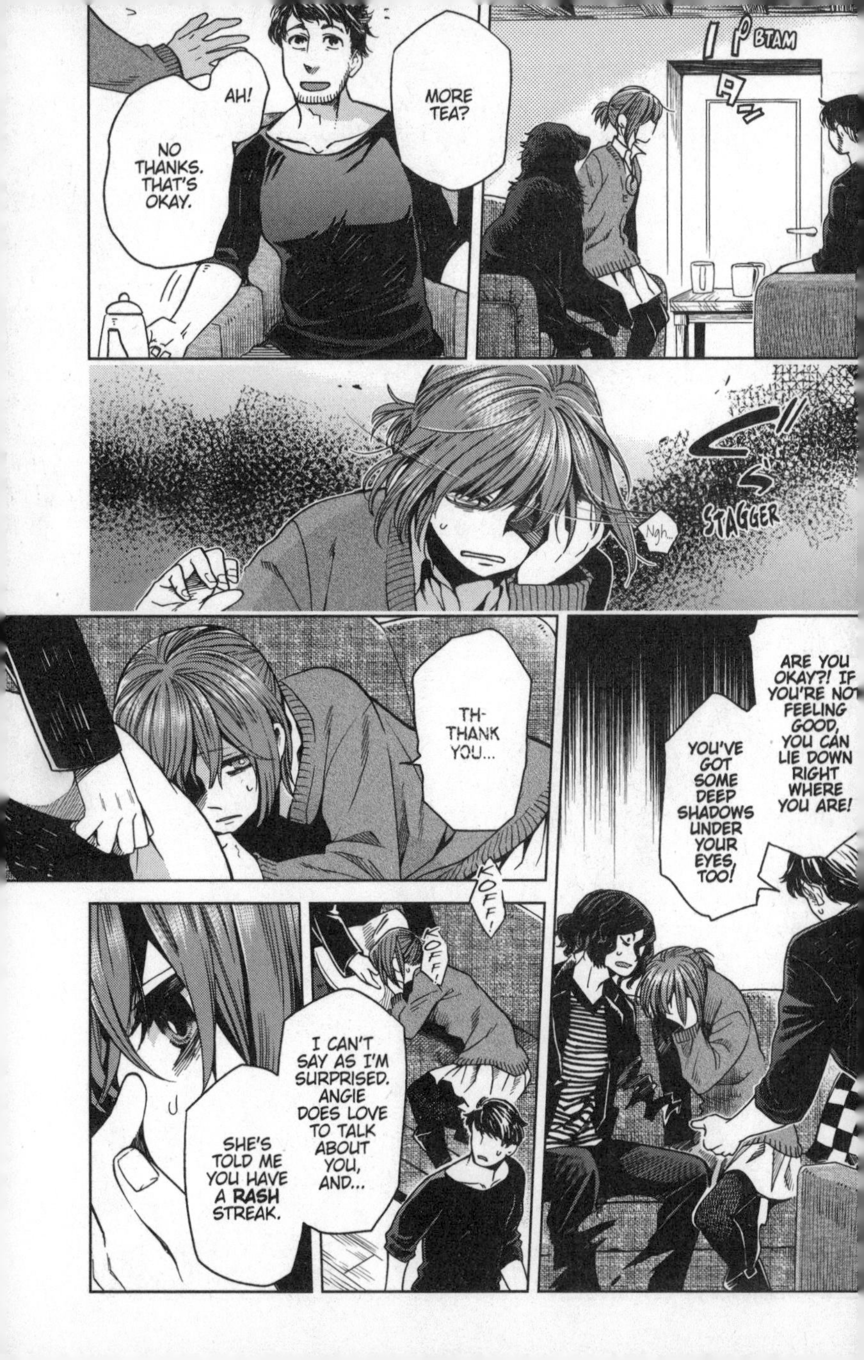
BTAM
MORE TEA?
AH!
NO THANKS. THAT'S OKAY.
Ngh...
STAGGER
ARE YOU OKAY?! IF YOU'RE NOT FEELING GOOD, YOU CAN LIE DOWN RIGHT WHERE YOU ARE!
YOU'VE GOT SOME DEEP SHADOWS UNDER YOUR EYES, TOO!
TH-THANK YOU...
KOFF!
KOFF!
I CAN'T SAY AS I'M SURPRISED. ANGIE DOES LOVE TO TALK ABOUT YOU, AND...
SHE'S TOLD ME YOU HAVE A **RASH** STREAK.

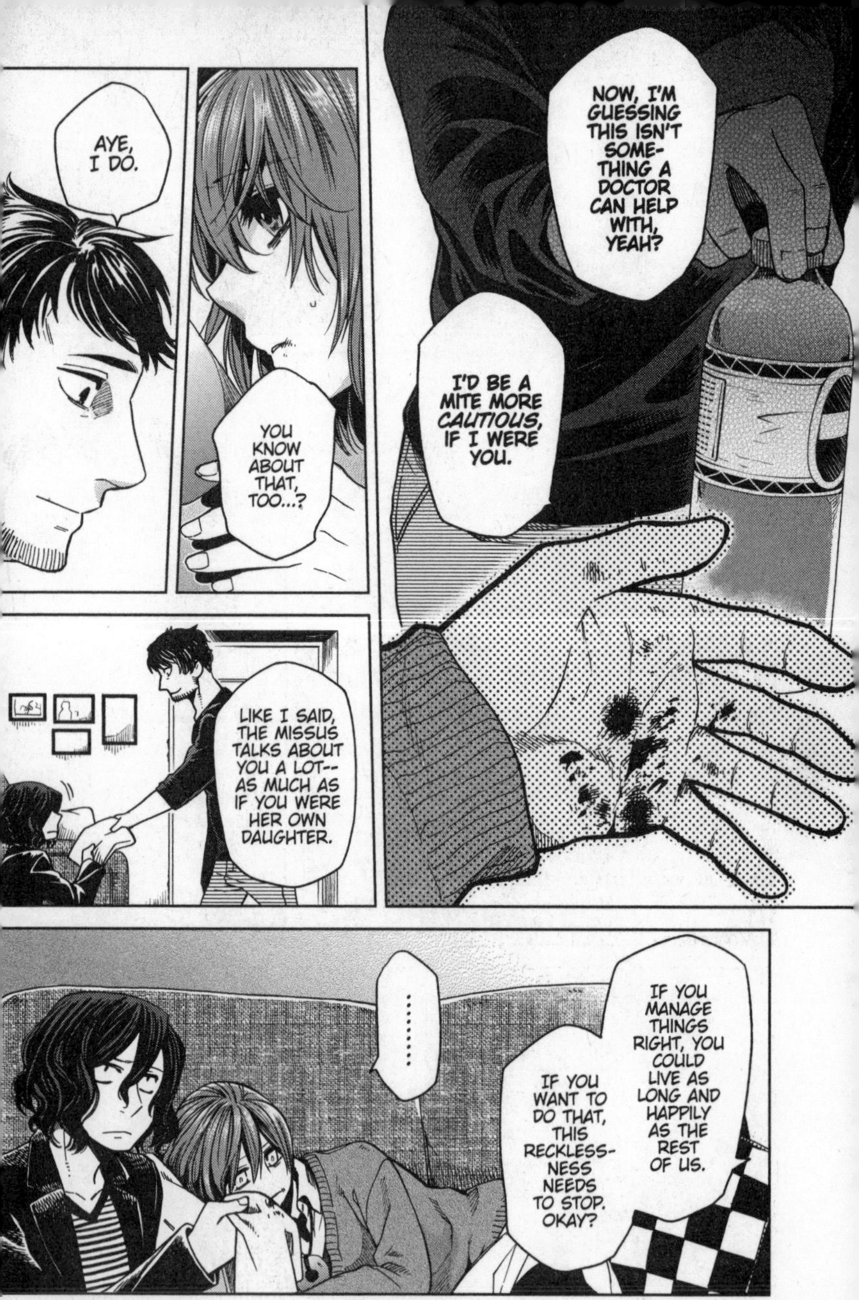
NOW, I'M GUESSING THIS ISN'T SOME-THING A DOCTOR CAN HELP WITH, YEAH?
I'D BE A MITE MORE CAUTIOUS, IF I WERE YOU.
YOU KNOW ABOUT THAT, TOO...?
AYE, I DO.
LIKE I SAID, THE MISSUS TALKS ABOUT YOU A LOT--AS MUCH AS IF YOU WERE HER OWN DAUGHTER.
IF YOU MANAGE THINGS RIGHT, YOU COULD LIVE AS LONG AND HAPPILY AS THE REST OF US.
IF YOU WANT TO DO THAT, THIS RECKLESS-NESS NEEDS TO STOP. OKAY?
....

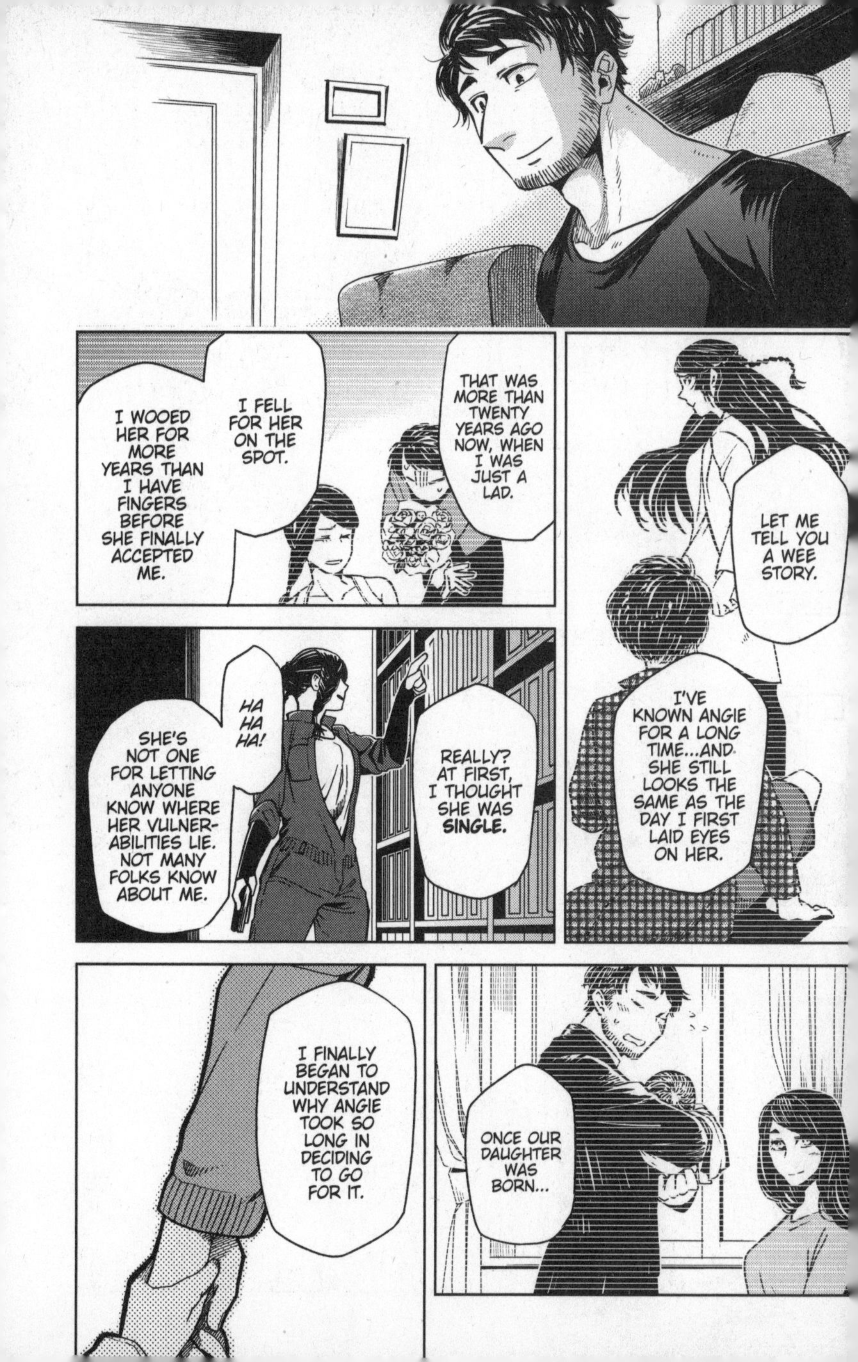
LET ME TELL YOU A WEE STORY.
I'VE KNOWN ANGIE FOR A LONG TIME...AND SHE STILL LOOKS THE SAME AS THE DAY I FIRST LAID EYES ON HER.
THAT WAS MORE THAN TWENTY YEARS AGO NOW, WHEN I WAS JUST A LAD.
I FELL FOR HER ON THE SPOT.
I WOOED HER FOR MORE YEARS THAN I HAVE FINGERS BEFORE SHE FINALLY ACCEPTED ME.
REALLY? AT FIRST, I THOUGHT SHE WAS **SINGLE.**
HA HA HA!
SHE'S NOT ONE FOR LETTING ANYONE KNOW WHERE HER VULNER-ABILITIES LIE. NOT MANY FOLKS KNOW ABOUT ME.
ONCE OUR DAUGHTER WAS BORN...
I FINALLY BEGAN TO UNDERSTAND WHY ANGIE TOOK SO LONG IN DECIDING TO GO FOR IT.

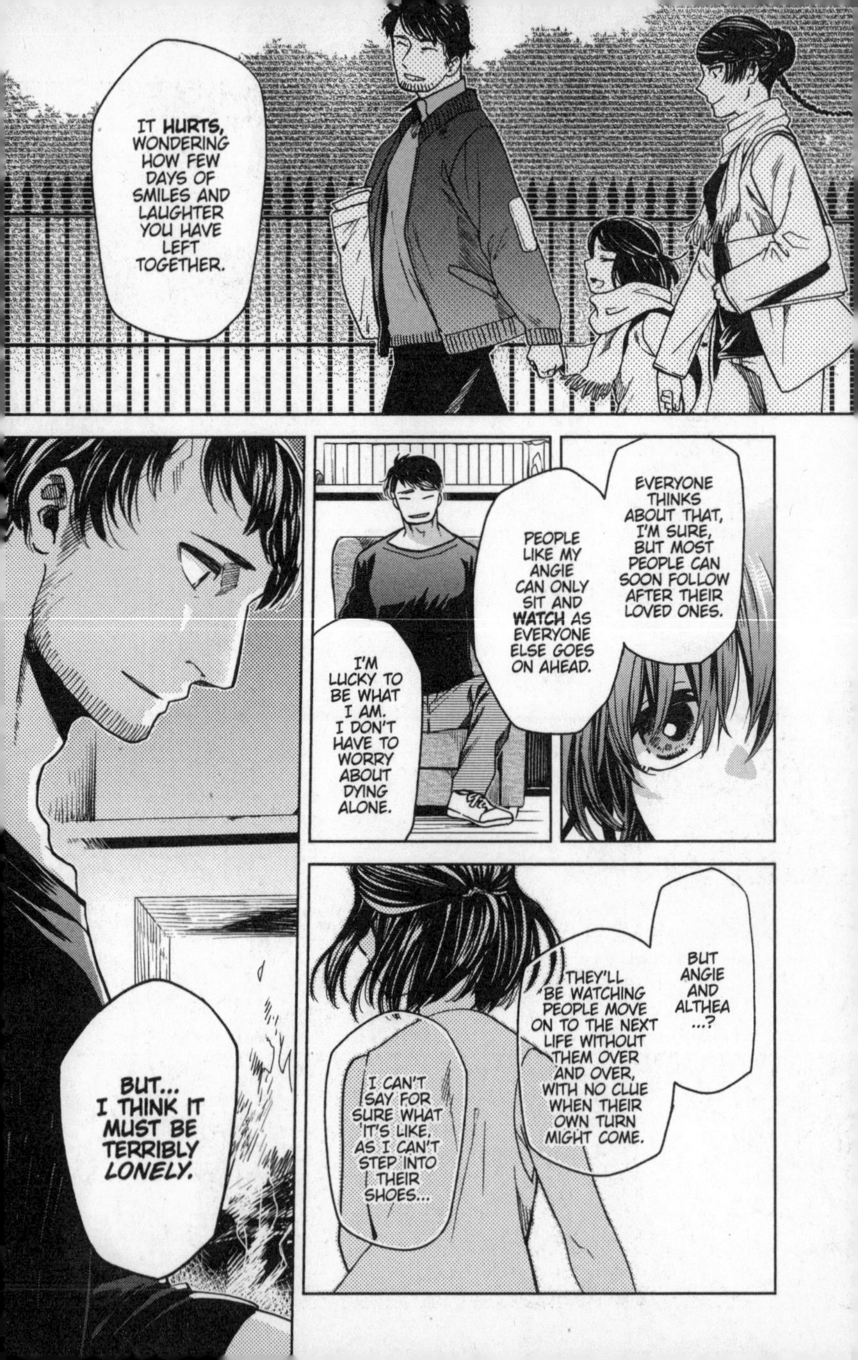
IT HURTS, WONDERING HOW FEW DAYS OF SMILES AND LAUGHTER YOU HAVE LEFT TOGETHER.
EVERYONE THINKS ABOUT THAT, I'M SURE, BUT MOST PEOPLE CAN SOON FOLLOW AFTER THEIR LOVED ONES.
PEOPLE LIKE MY ANGIE CAN ONLY SIT AND WATCH AS EVERYONE ELSE GOES ON AHEAD.
I'M LUCKY TO BE WHAT I AM. I DON'T HAVE TO WORRY ABOUT DYING ALONE.
BUT ANGIE AND ALTHEA ...?
THEY'LL BE WATCHING PEOPLE MOVE ON TO THE NEXT LIFE WITHOUT THEM OVER AND OVER, WITH NO CLUE WHEN THEIR OWN TURN MIGHT COME.
I CAN'T SAY FOR SURE WHAT IT'S LIKE, AS I CAN'T STEP INTO THEIR SHOES...
BUT... I THINK IT MUST BE TERRIBLY LONELY.

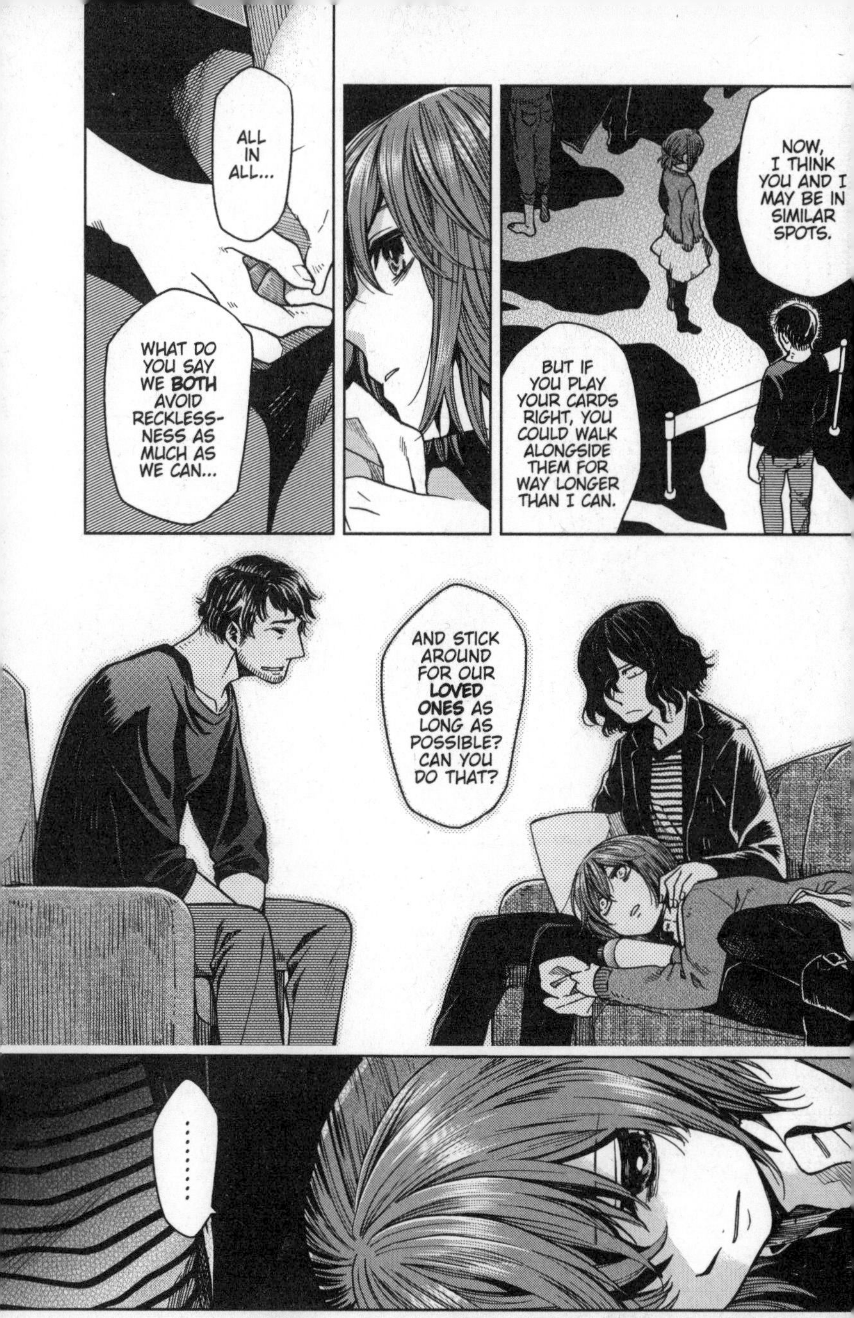
NOW, I THINK YOU AND I MAY BE IN SIMILAR SPOTS.
BUT IF YOU PLAY YOUR CARDS RIGHT, YOU COULD WALK ALONGSIDE THEM FOR WAY LONGER THAN I CAN.
ALL IN ALL...
WHAT DO YOU SAY WE **BOTH** AVOID RECKLESS-NESS AS MUCH AS WE CAN...
AND STICK AROUND FOR OUR **LOVED ONES** AS LONG AS POSSIBLE? CAN YOU DO THAT?
....

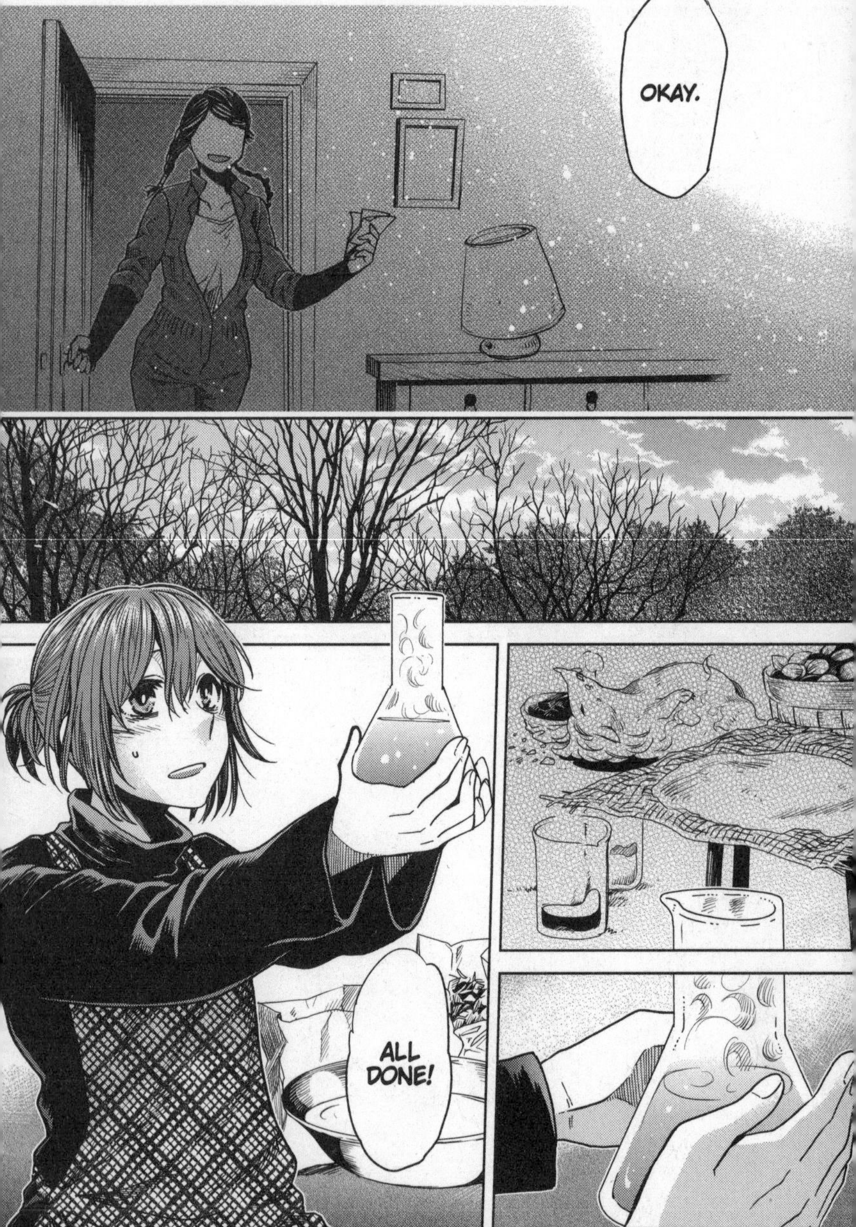
OKAY.
ALL DONE!

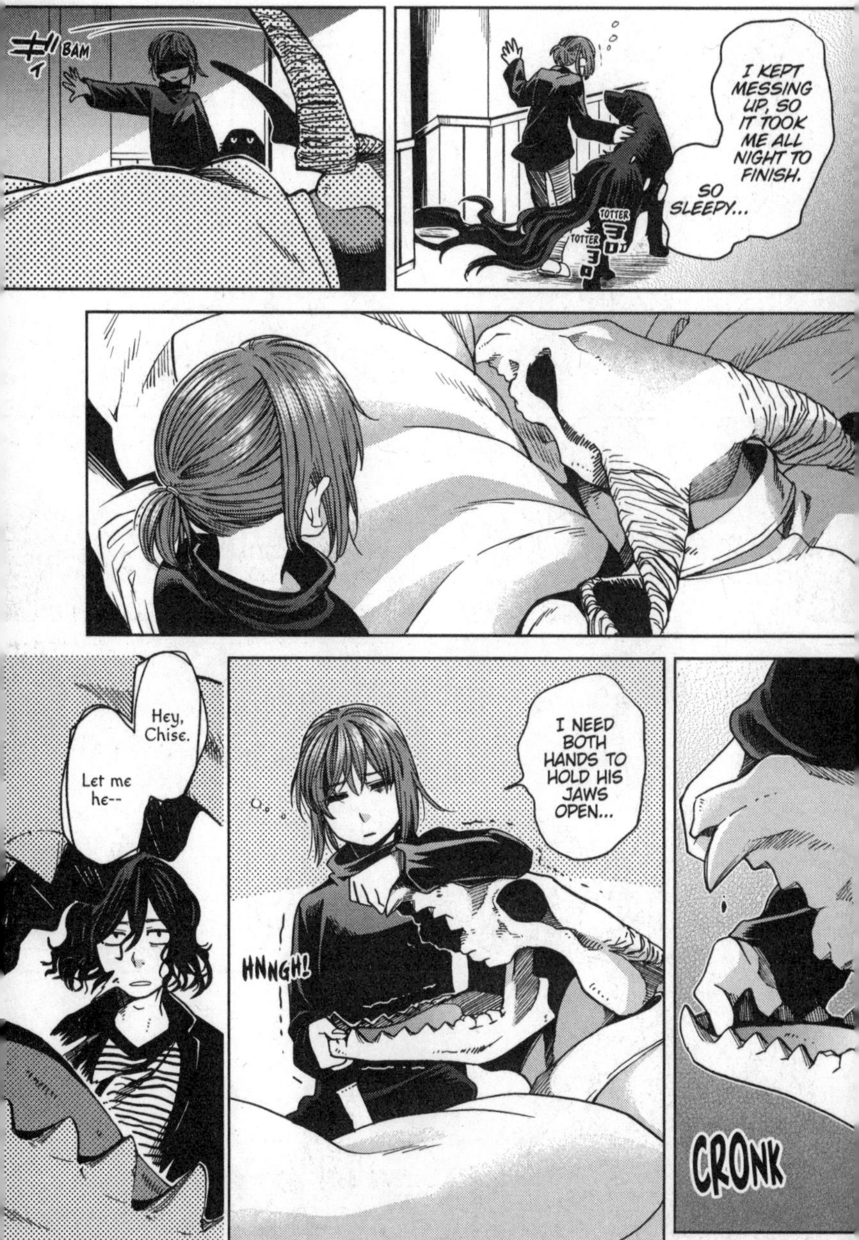
I KEPT MESSING UP, SO IT TOOK ME ALL NIGHT TO FINISH.
SO SLEEPY...
TOTTER
TOTTER
BAM
CRONK
I NEED BOTH HANDS TO HOLD HIS JAWS OPEN...
HNNGH!
Hey, Chise.
Let me he--

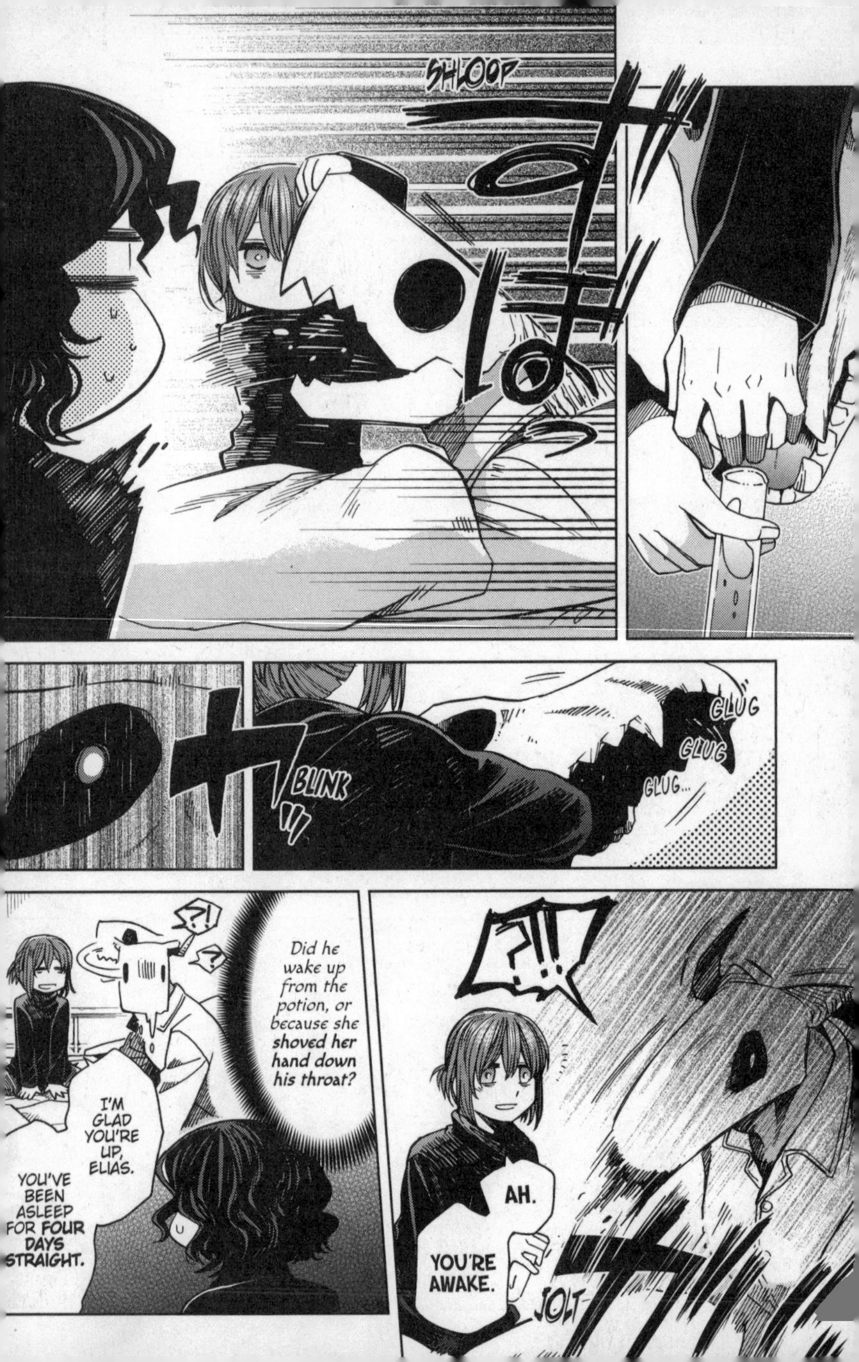

SHLOOP
BLINK
GLUG
GLUG
GLUG...
JOLT
?!!
AH.
YOU'RE AWAKE.
?!
?!
Did he wake up from the potion, or because she shoved her hand down his throat?
I'M GLAD YOU'RE UP, ELIAS.
YOU'VE BEEN ASLEEP FOR FOUR DAYS STRAIGHT.

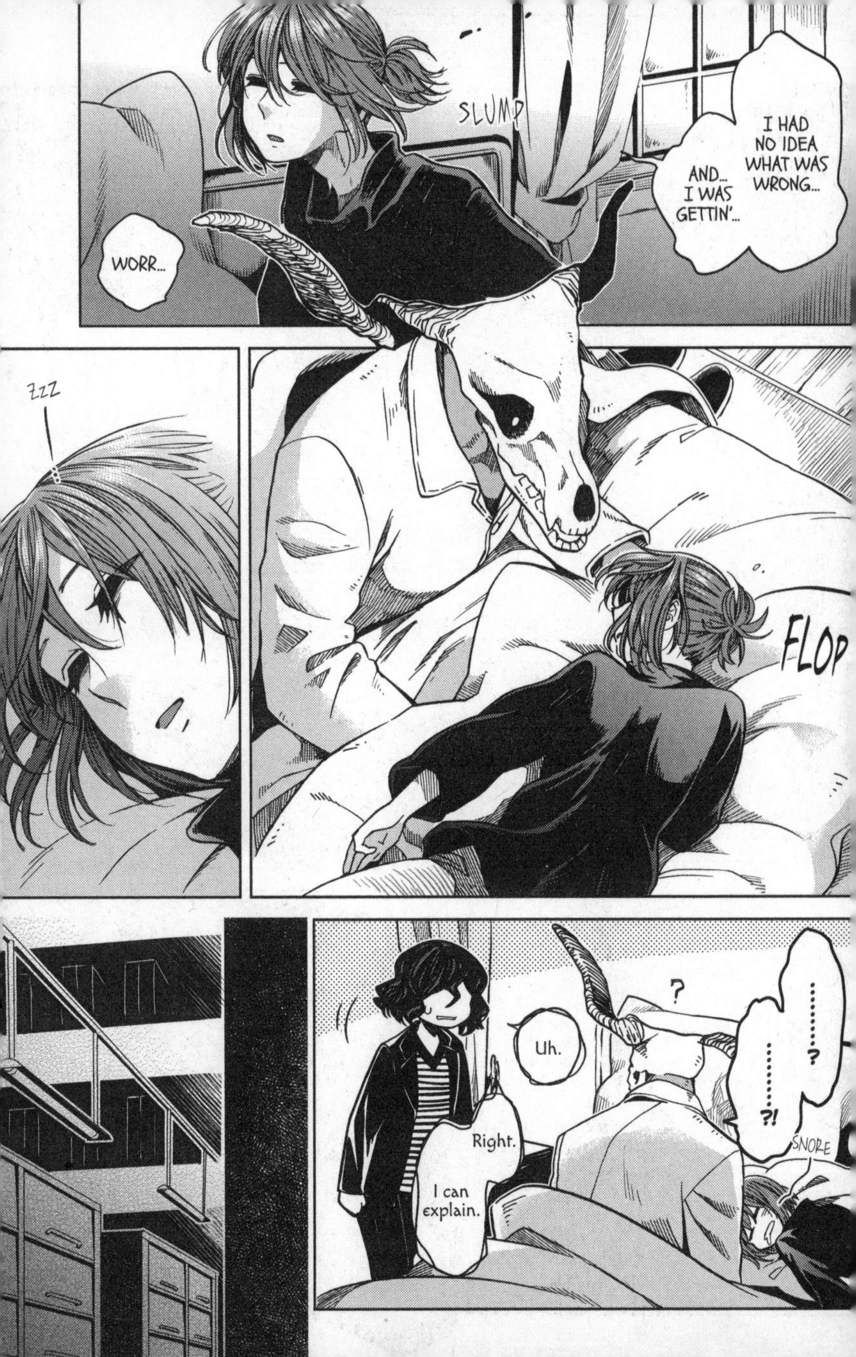
I HAD NO IDEA WHAT WAS WRONG...
AND... I WAS GETTIN'...
SLUMP
WORR...
FLOP
ZZZ
........?
........?!
?
SNORE
Uh.
Right.
I can explain.

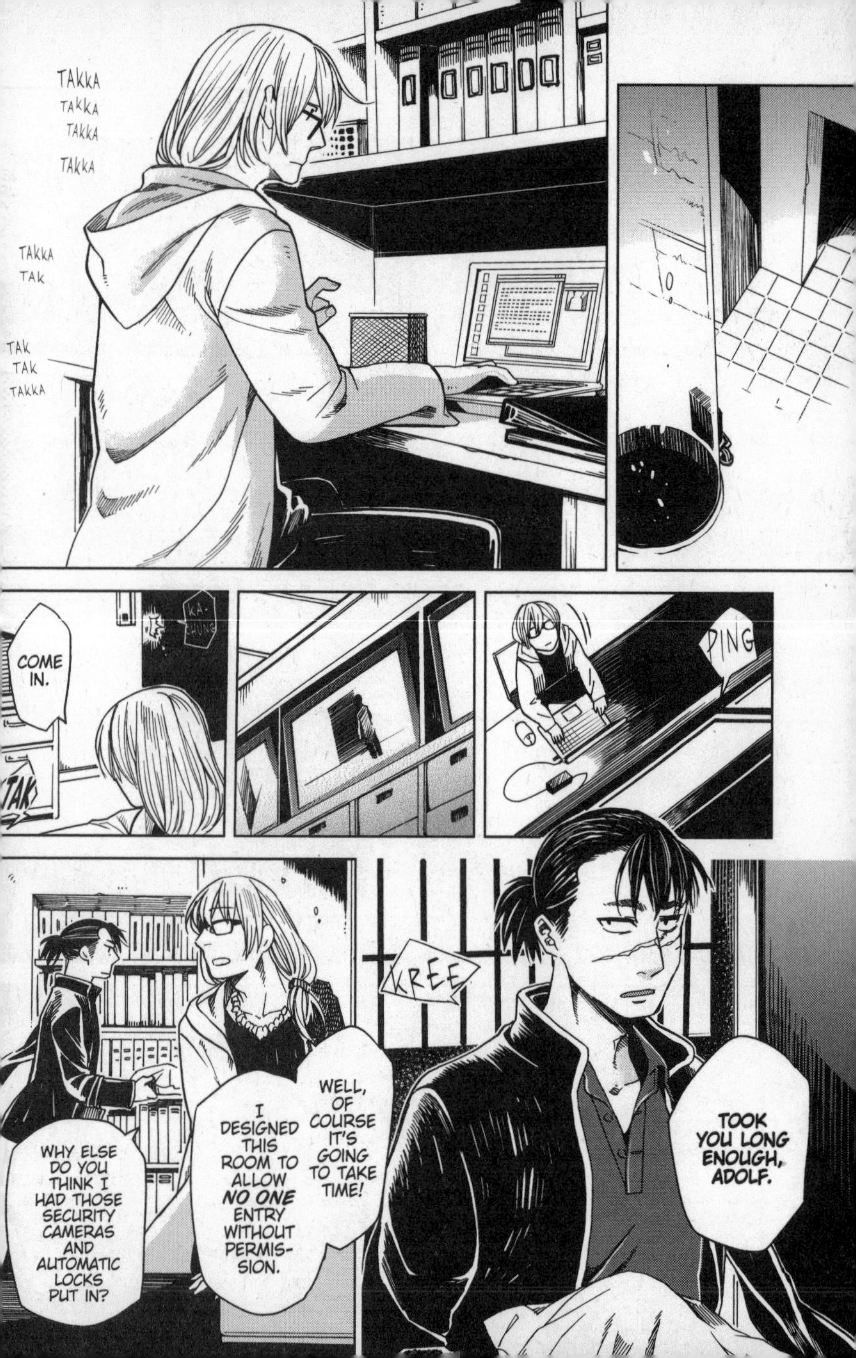
TAKKA
TAKKA
TAKKA
TAKKA
TAKKA
TAK
TAK
TAK
TAKKA
PING
KA-CHUNG
COME IN.
TAK
KREE
TOOK YOU LONG ENOUGH, ADOLF.
WELL, OF COURSE IT'S GOING TO TAKE TIME!
I DESIGNED THIS ROOM TO ALLOW ***NO ONE*** ENTRY WITHOUT PERMIS- SION.
WHY ELSE DO YOU THINK I HAD THOSE SECURITY CAMERAS AND AUTOMATIC LOCKS PUT IN?

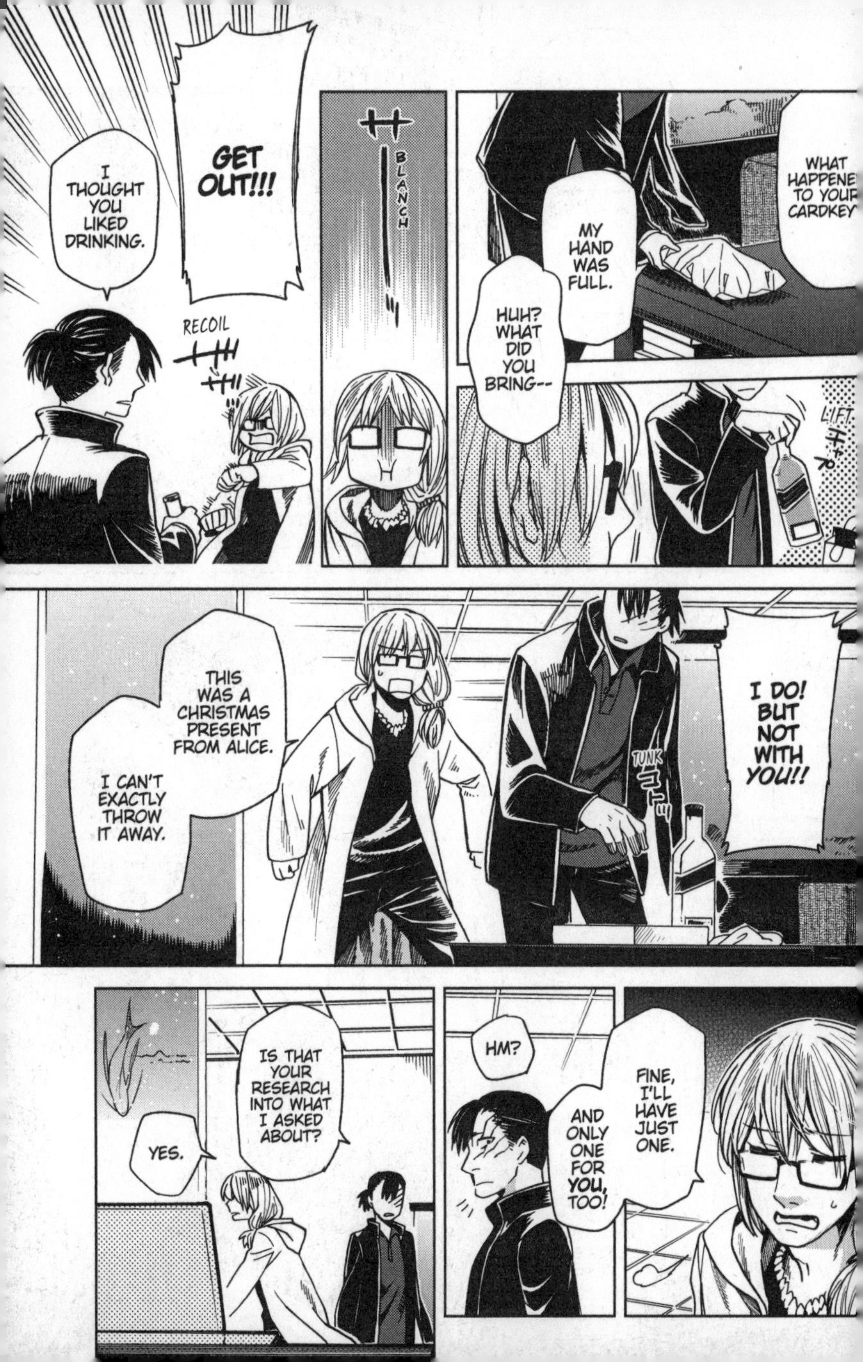
WHAT HAPPENE TO YOUR CARDKEY
MY HAND WAS FULL.
HUH? WHAT DID YOU BRING--
LIFT
BLANCH
GET OUT!!!
I THOUGHT YOU LIKED DRINKING.
RECOIL
I DO! BUT NOT WITH YOU!!
TUNK
THIS WAS A CHRISTMAS PRESENT FROM ALICE.
I CAN'T EXACTLY THROW IT AWAY.
FINE, I'LL HAVE JUST ONE.
HM?
AND ONLY ONE FOR YOU, TOO!
IS THAT YOUR RESEARCH INTO WHAT I ASKED ABOUT?
YES.

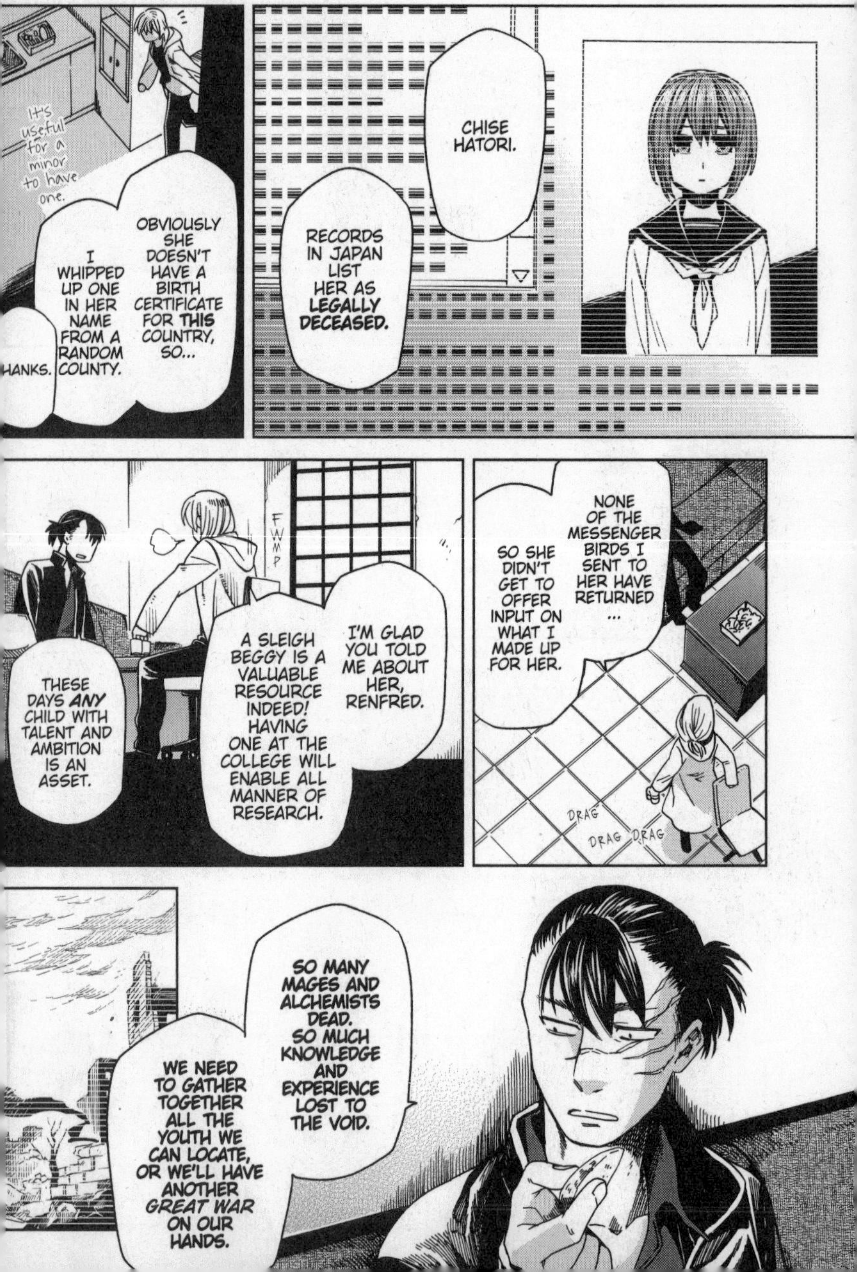
CHISE HATORI.
RECORDS IN JAPAN LIST HER AS LEGALLY DECEASED.
OBVIOUSLY SHE DOESN'T HAVE A BIRTH CERTIFICATE FOR THIS COUNTRY, SO...
I WHIPPED UP ONE IN HER NAME FROM A RANDOM COUNTY.
It's useful for a minor to have one.
HANKS.
NONE OF THE MESSENGER BIRDS I SENT TO HER HAVE RETURNED...
SO SHE DIDN'T GET TO OFFER INPUT ON WHAT I MADE UP FOR HER.
DRAG DRAG DRAG
FWMP
I'M GLAD YOU TOLD ME ABOUT HER, RENFRED.
A SLEIGH BEGGY IS A VALUABLE RESOURCE INDEED! HAVING ONE AT THE COLLEGE WILL ENABLE ALL MANNER OF RESEARCH.
THESE DAYS ANY CHILD WITH TALENT AND AMBITION IS AN ASSET.
SO MANY MAGES AND ALCHEMISTS DEAD. SO MUCH KNOWLEDGE AND EXPERIENCE LOST TO THE VOID.
WE NEED TO GATHER TOGETHER ALL THE YOUTH WE CAN LOCATE, OR WE'LL HAVE ANOTHER GREAT WAR ON OUR HANDS.

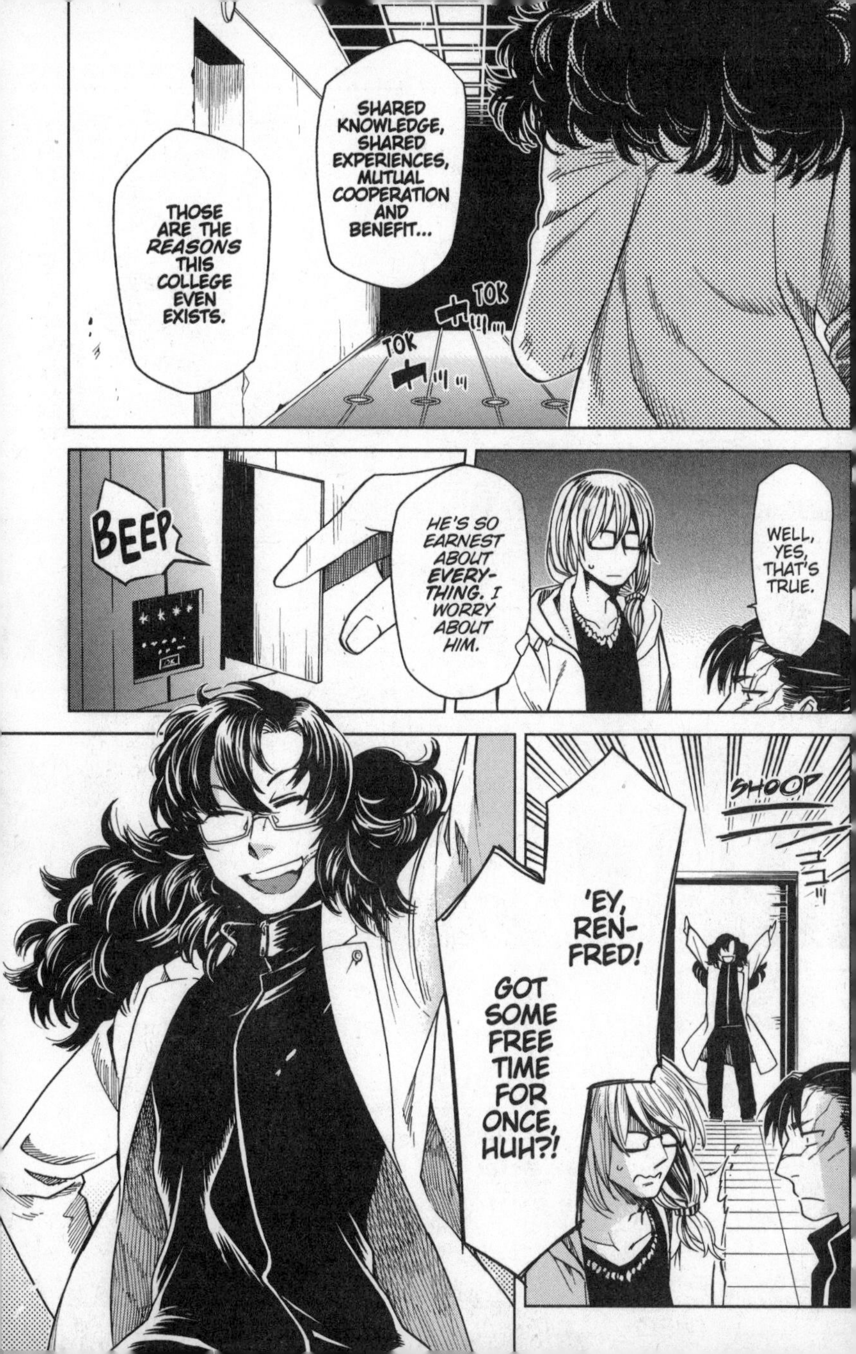
SHARED KNOWLEDGE, SHARED EXPERIENCES, MUTUAL COOPERATION AND BENEFIT...
THOSE ARE THE *REASONS* THIS COLLEGE EVEN EXISTS.
TOK
TOK
WELL, YES, THAT'S TRUE.
HE'S SO EARNEST ABOUT **EVERYTHING**. *I WORRY ABOUT HIM.*
BEEP
SHOOP
'EY, REN-FRED!
GOT SOME FREE TIME FOR ONCE, HUH?!

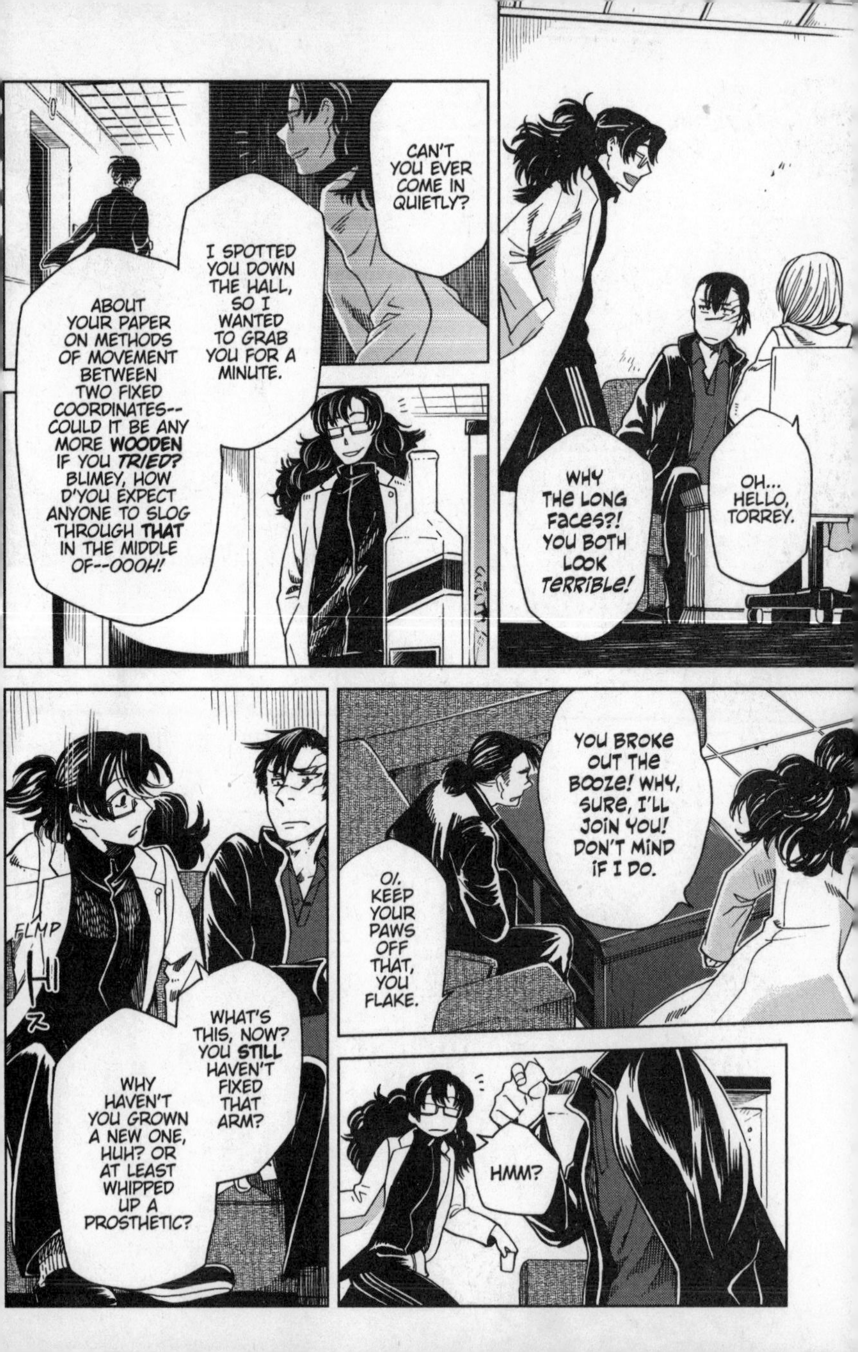

OH... HELLO, TORREY.
WHY THE LONG FACES?! YOU BOTH LOOK TERRIBLE!
CAN'T YOU EVER COME IN QUIETLY?
I SPOTTED YOU DOWN THE HALL, SO I WANTED TO GRAB YOU FOR A MINUTE.
ABOUT YOUR PAPER ON METHODS OF MOVEMENT BETWEEN TWO FIXED COORDINATES--COULD IT BE ANY MORE WOODEN IF YOU TRIED? BLIMEY, HOW D'YOU EXPECT ANYONE TO SLOG THROUGH THAT IN THE MIDDLE OF--OOOH!
YOU BROKE OUT THE BOOZE! WHY, SURE, I'LL JOIN YOU! DON'T MIND IF I DO.
OI. KEEP YOUR PAWS OFF THAT, YOU FLAKE.
HMM?
WHAT'S THIS, NOW? YOU STILL HAVEN'T FIXED THAT ARM?
WHY HAVEN'T YOU GROWN A NEW ONE, HUH? OR AT LEAST WHIPPED UP A PROSTHETIC?
FLMP

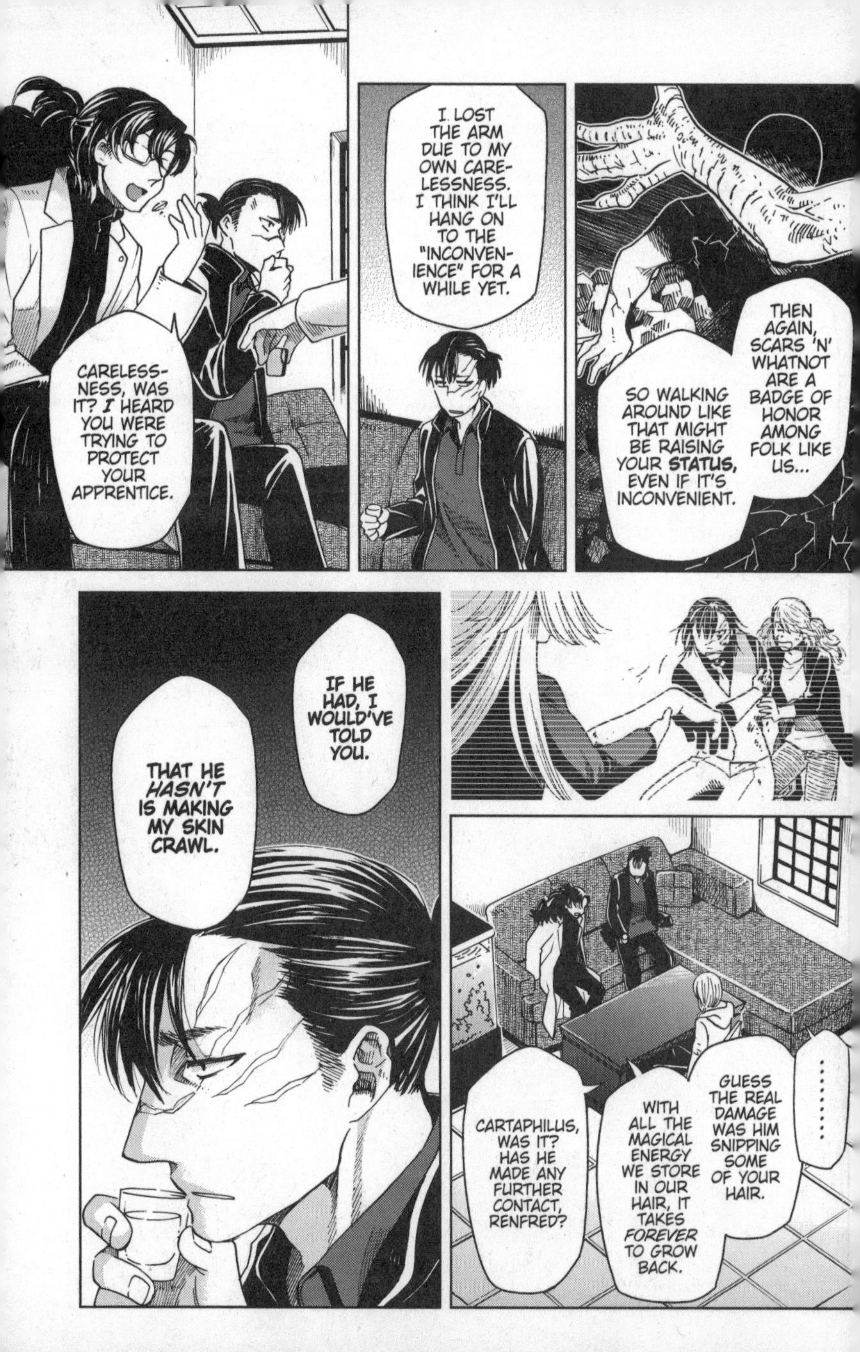
THEN AGAIN, SCARS 'N' WHATNOT ARE A BADGE OF HONOR AMONG FOLK LIKE US...
SO WALKING AROUND LIKE THAT MIGHT BE RAISING YOUR **STATUS**, EVEN IF IT'S INCONVENIENT.
I LOST THE ARM DUE TO MY OWN CARE-LESSNESS. I THINK I'LL HANG ON TO THE "INCONVEN-IENCE" FOR A WHILE YET.
CARELESS-NESS, WAS IT? *I* HEARD YOU WERE TRYING TO PROTECT YOUR APPRENTICE.
......
GUESS THE REAL DAMAGE WAS HIM SNIPPING SOME OF YOUR HAIR.
WITH ALL THE MAGICAL ENERGY WE STORE IN OUR HAIR, IT TAKES *FOREVER* TO GROW BACK.
CARTAPHILUS, WAS IT? HAS HE MADE ANY FURTHER CONTACT, RENFRED?
IF HE HAD, I WOULD'VE TOLD YOU.
THAT HE *HASN'T* IS MAKING MY SKIN CRAWL.

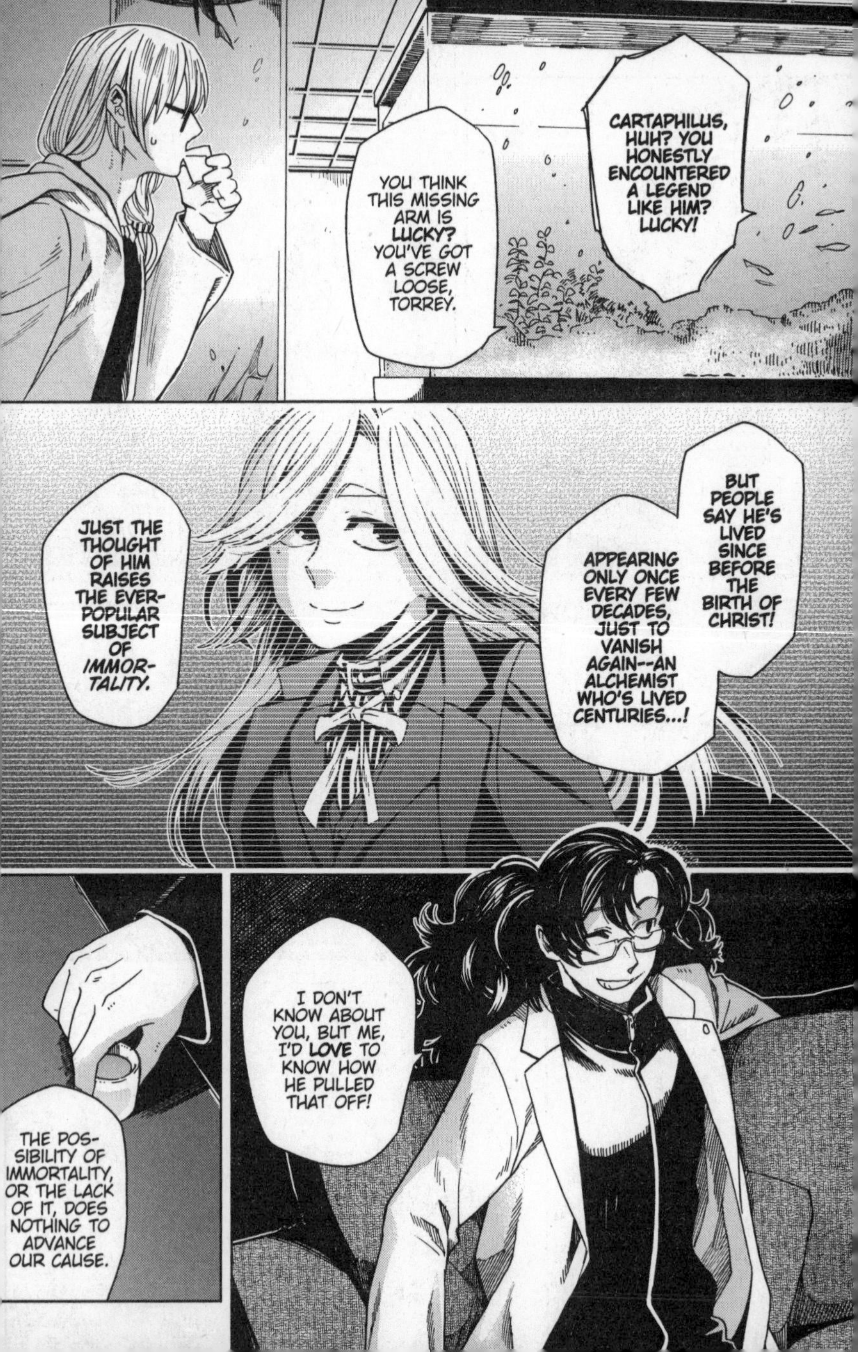
CARTAPHILUS, HUH? YOU HONESTLY ENCOUNTERED A LEGEND LIKE HIM? LUCKY!
YOU THINK THIS MISSING ARM IS LUCKY? YOU'VE GOT A SCREW LOOSE, TORREY.
BUT PEOPLE SAY HE'S LIVED SINCE BEFORE THE BIRTH OF CHRIST!
APPEARING ONLY ONCE EVERY FEW DECADES, JUST TO VANISH AGAIN--AN ALCHEMIST WHO'S LIVED CENTURIES...!
JUST THE THOUGHT OF HIM RAISES THE EVER-POPULAR SUBJECT OF IMMORTALITY.
I DON'T KNOW ABOUT YOU, BUT ME, I'D LOVE TO KNOW HOW HE PULLED THAT OFF!
THE POSSIBILITY OF IMMORTALITY, OR THE LACK OF IT, DOES NOTHING TO ADVANCE OUR CAUSE.

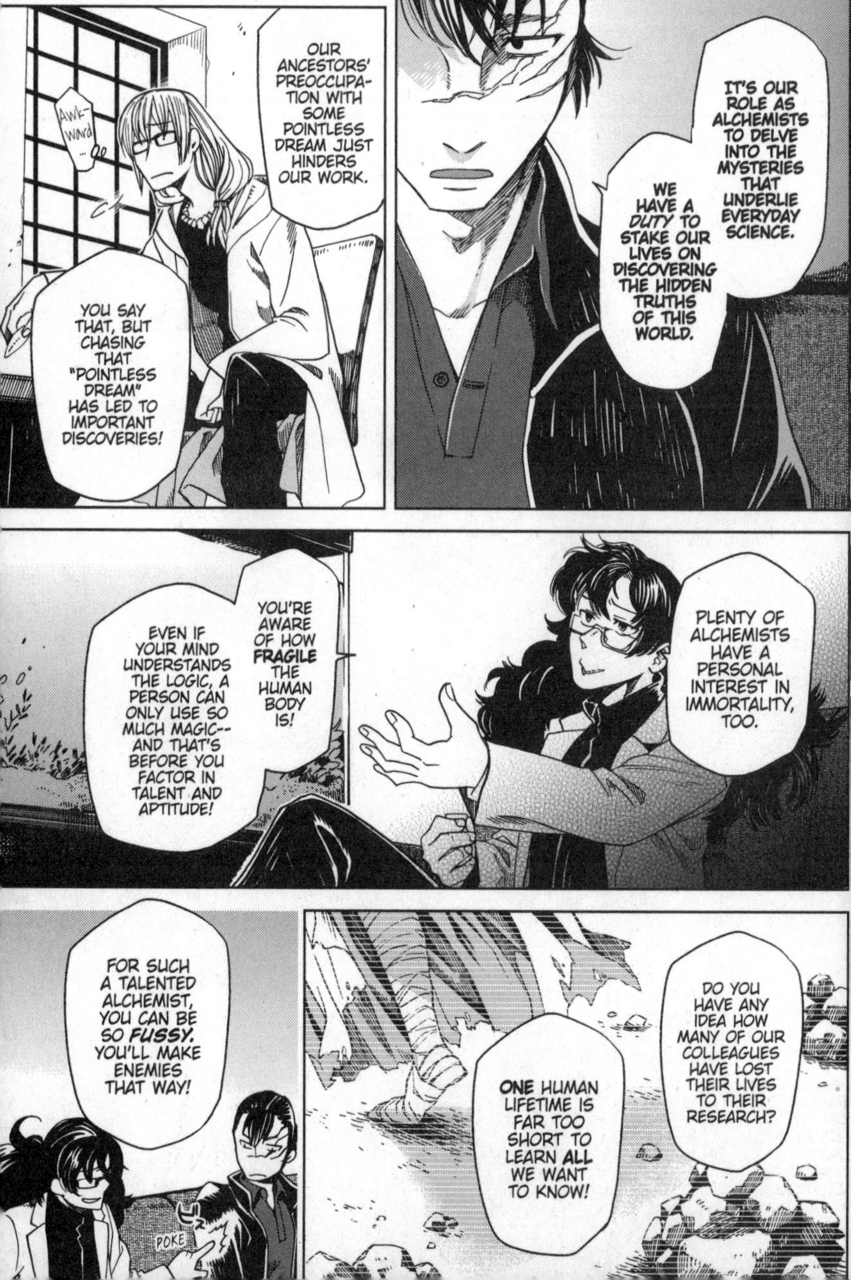
IT'S OUR ROLE AS ALCHEMISTS TO DELVE INTO THE MYSTERIES THAT UNDERLIE EVERYDAY SCIENCE.
WE HAVE A *DUTY* TO STAKE OUR LIVES ON DISCOVERING THE HIDDEN TRUTHS OF THIS WORLD.
OUR ANCESTORS' PREOCCUPATION WITH SOME POINTLESS DREAM JUST HINDERS OUR WORK.
Awk-ward ...
YOU SAY THAT, BUT CHASING THAT "POINTLESS DREAM" HAS LED TO IMPORTANT DISCOVERIES!
PLENTY OF ALCHEMISTS HAVE A PERSONAL INTEREST IN IMMORTALITY, TOO.
YOU'RE AWARE OF HOW **FRAGILE** THE HUMAN BODY IS!
EVEN IF YOUR MIND UNDERSTANDS THE LOGIC, A PERSON CAN ONLY USE SO MUCH MAGIC-- AND THAT'S BEFORE YOU FACTOR IN TALENT AND APTITUDE!
DO YOU HAVE ANY IDEA HOW MANY OF OUR COLLEAGUES HAVE LOST THEIR LIVES TO THEIR RESEARCH?
ONE HUMAN LIFETIME IS FAR TOO SHORT TO LEARN **ALL** WE WANT TO KNOW!
FOR SUCH A TALENTED ALCHEMIST, YOU CAN BE SO ***FUSSY.*** YOU'LL MAKE ENEMIES THAT WAY!
POKE

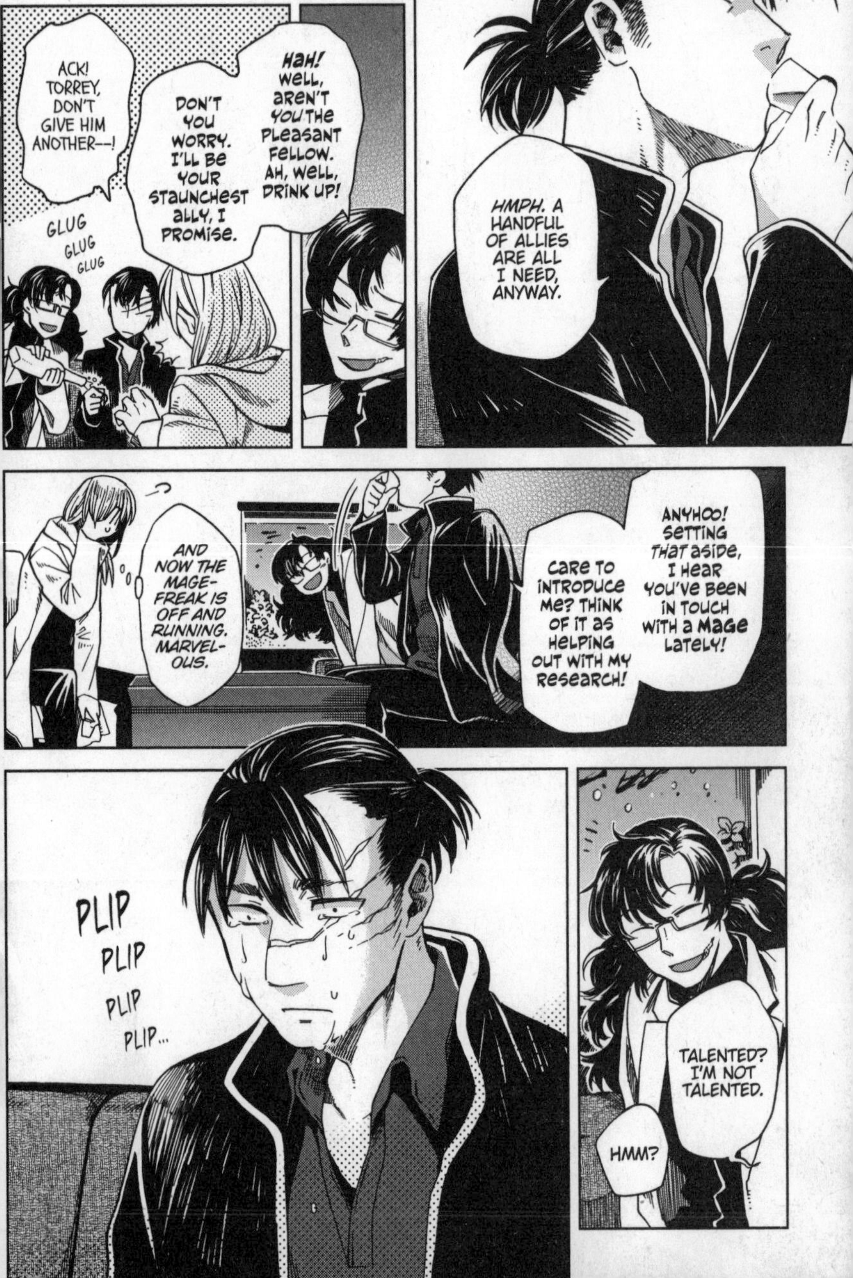
HMPH. A HANDFUL OF ALLIES ARE ALL I NEED, ANYWAY.
HAH! WELL, AREN'T YOU THE PLEASANT FELLOW. AH, WELL, DRINK UP!
DON'T YOU WORRY. I'LL BE YOUR STAUNCHEST ALLY, I PROMISE.
ACK! TORREY, DON'T GIVE HIM ANOTHER--!
GLUG GLUG GLUG
ANYHOO! SETTING THAT ASIDE, I HEAR YOU'VE BEEN IN TOUCH WITH A MAGE LATELY!
CARE TO INTRODUCE ME? THINK OF IT AS HELPING OUT WITH MY RESEARCH!
AND NOW THE MAGE-FREAK IS OFF AND RUNNING. MARVELOUS.
TALENTED? I'M NOT TALENTED.
HMM?
PLIP PLIP PLIP PLIP...

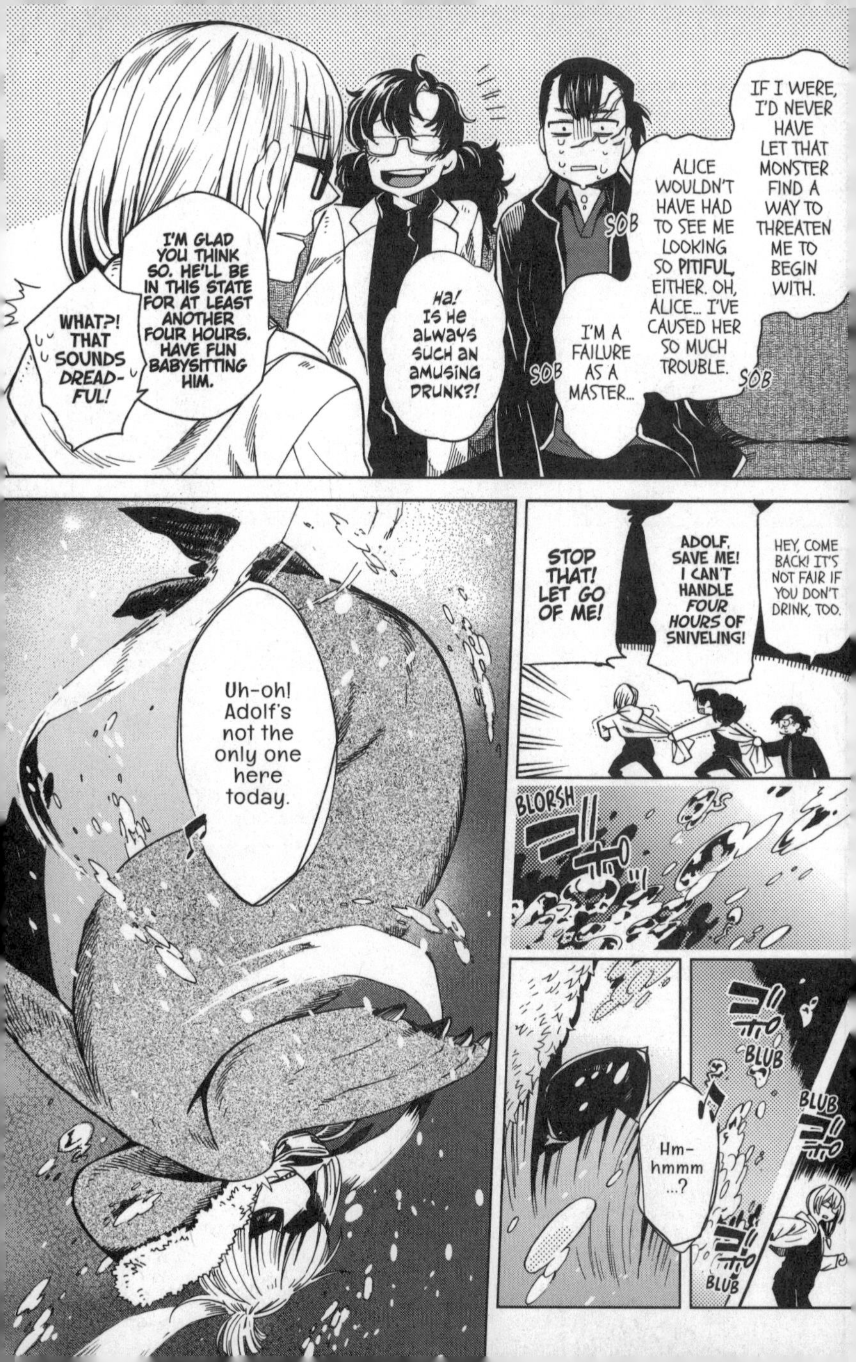
IF I WERE, I'D NEVER HAVE LET THAT MONSTER FIND A WAY TO THREATEN ME TO BEGIN WITH.
SOB
ALICE WOULDN'T HAVE HAD TO SEE ME LOOKING SO PITIFUL, EITHER. OH, ALICE... I'VE CAUSED HER SO MUCH TROUBLE.
SOB
SOB
I'M A FAILURE AS A MASTER...
Ha! Is he always such an amusing drunk?!
I'M GLAD YOU THINK SO. HE'LL BE IN THIS STATE FOR AT LEAST ANOTHER FOUR HOURS. HAVE FUN BABYSITTING HIM.
WHAT?! THAT SOUNDS DREADFUL!
HEY, COME BACK! IT'S NOT FAIR IF YOU DON'T DRINK, TOO.
ADOLF, SAVE ME! I CAN'T HANDLE FOUR HOURS OF SNIVELING!
STOP THAT! LET GO OF ME!
BLORSH
BLUB
BLUB
Hm-hmmm...?
BLUB
Uh-oh! Adolf's not the only one here today.

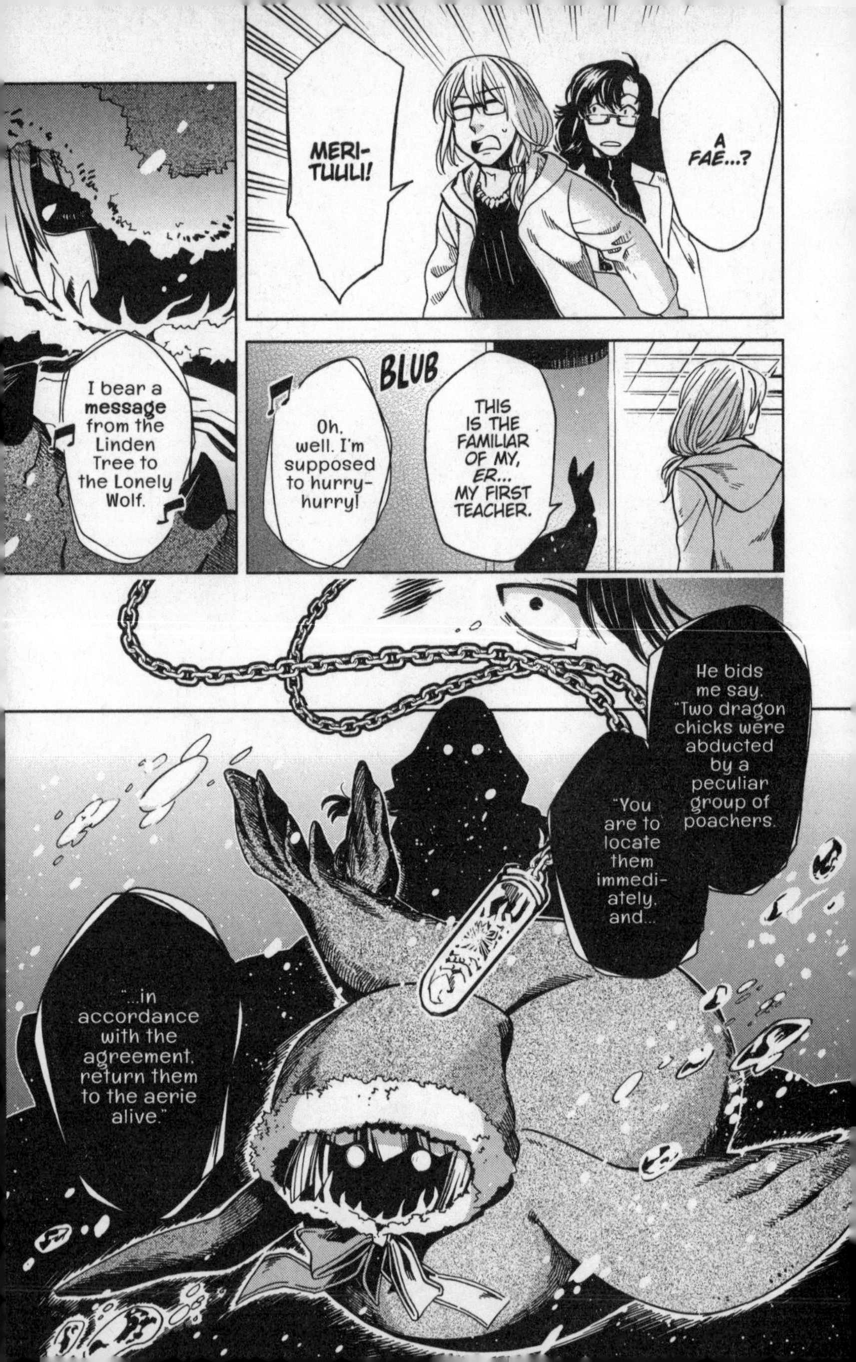
A FAE...?
MERI-TUULI!
THIS IS THE FAMILIAR OF MY, *ER*... MY FIRST TEACHER.
BLUB
Oh, well. I'm supposed to hurry-hurry!
I bear a **message** from the Linden Tree to the Lonely Wolf.
He bids me say, "Two dragon chicks were abducted by a peculiar group of poachers.
"You are to locate them immediately, and...
"...in accordance with the agreement, return them to the aerie alive."

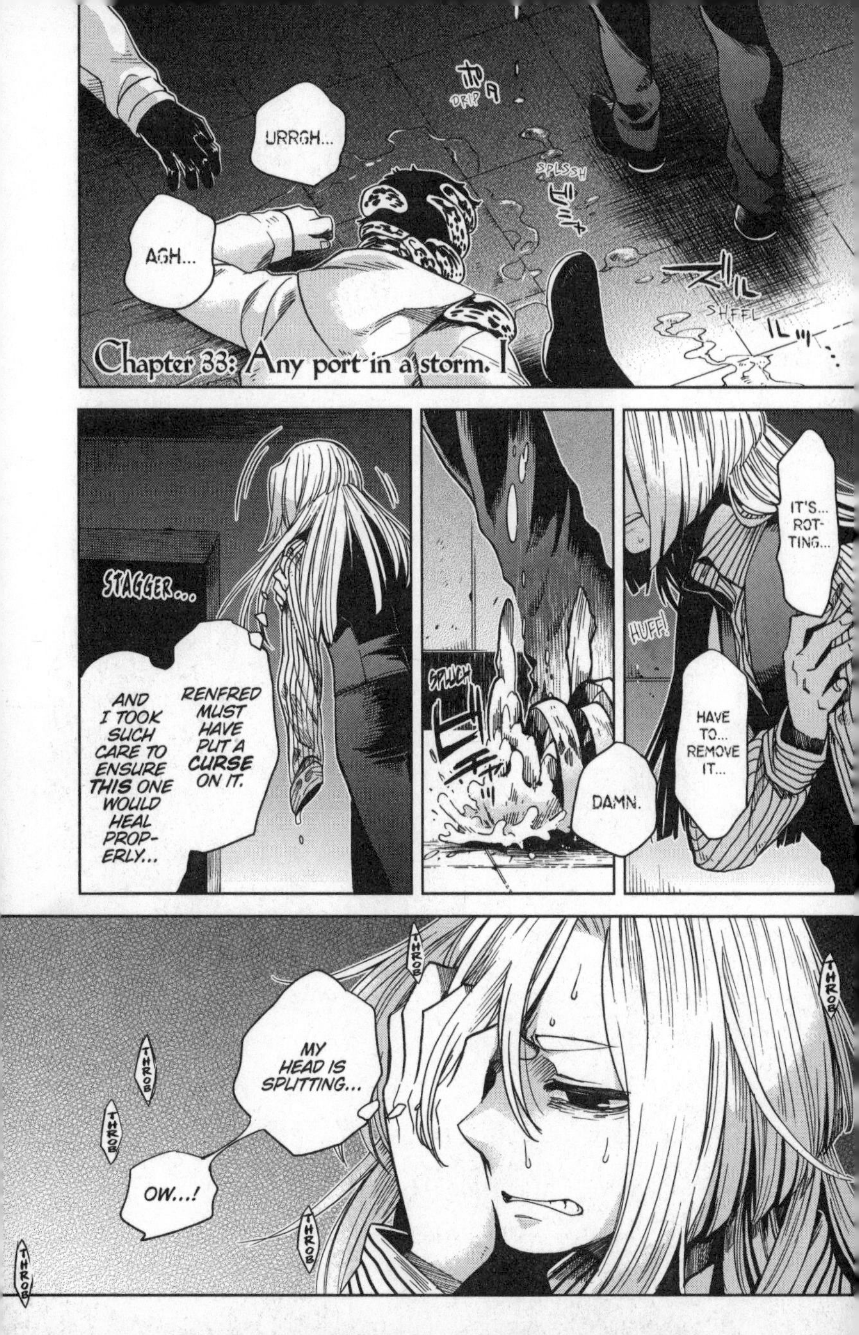
SHFFL
DRIP
URRGH...
AGH...
Chapter 33: Any port in a storm. I
IT'S... ROT-TING...
HUFF!
HAVE TO... REMOVE IT...
SPLUCH
DAMN.
STAGGER...
RENFRED MUST HAVE PUT A CURSE ON IT.
AND I TOOK SUCH CARE TO ENSURE THIS ONE WOULD HEAL PROPERLY...
THROB
THROB
MY HEAD IS SPLITTING...
THROB
THROB
OW...!
THROB
THROB

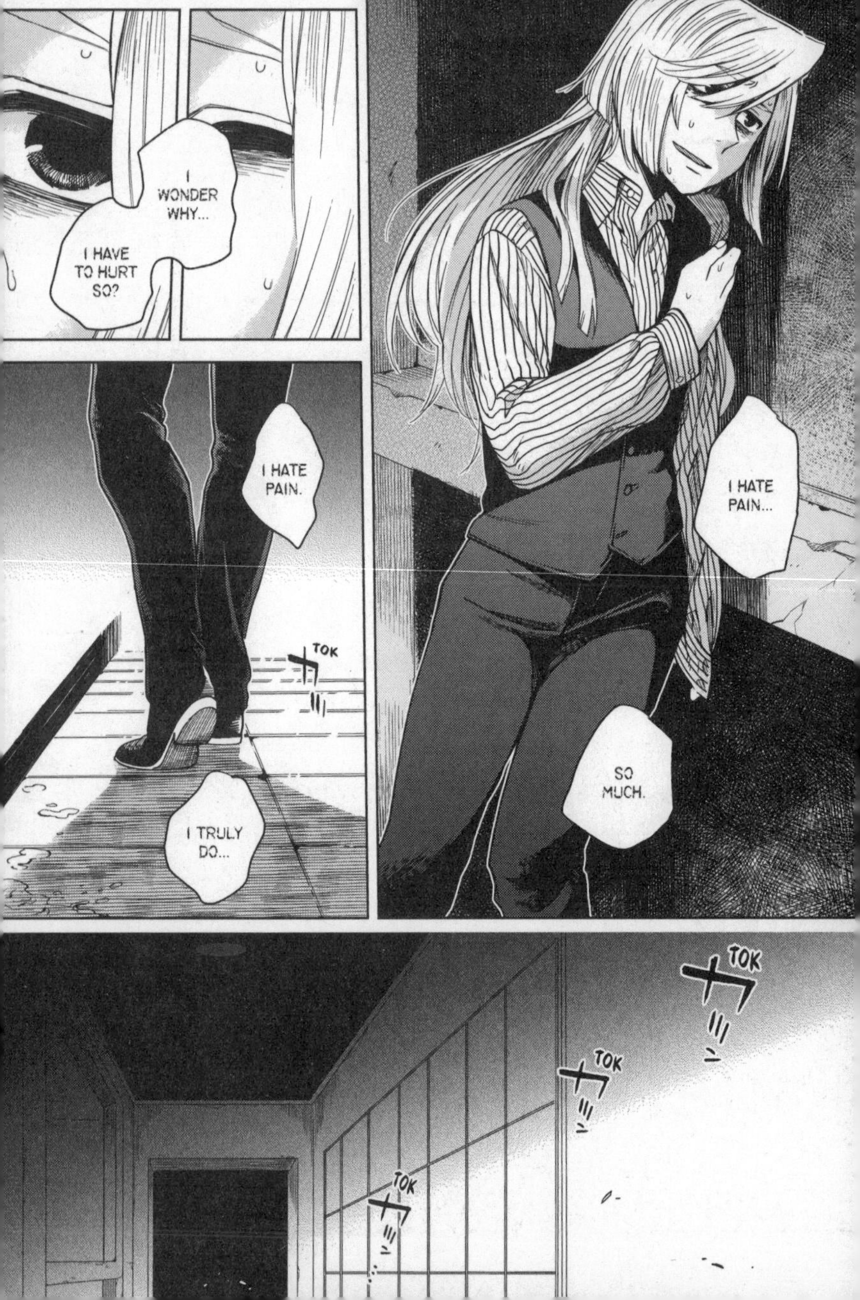
I HATE PAIN...
SO MUCH.
I WONDER WHY...
I HAVE TO HURT SO?
I HATE PAIN.
TOK
I TRULY DO...
TOK
TOK
TOK

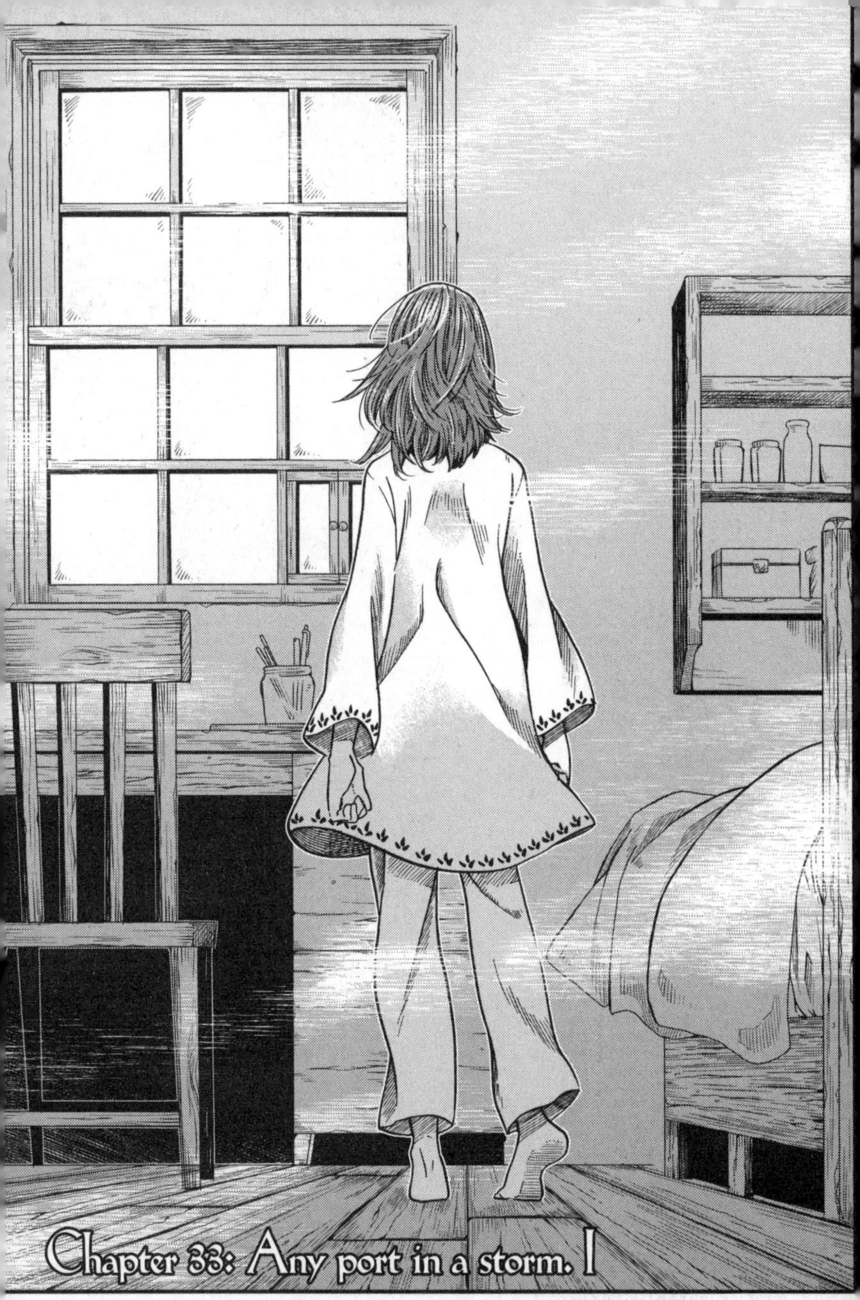
Chapter 33: Any port in a storm. I

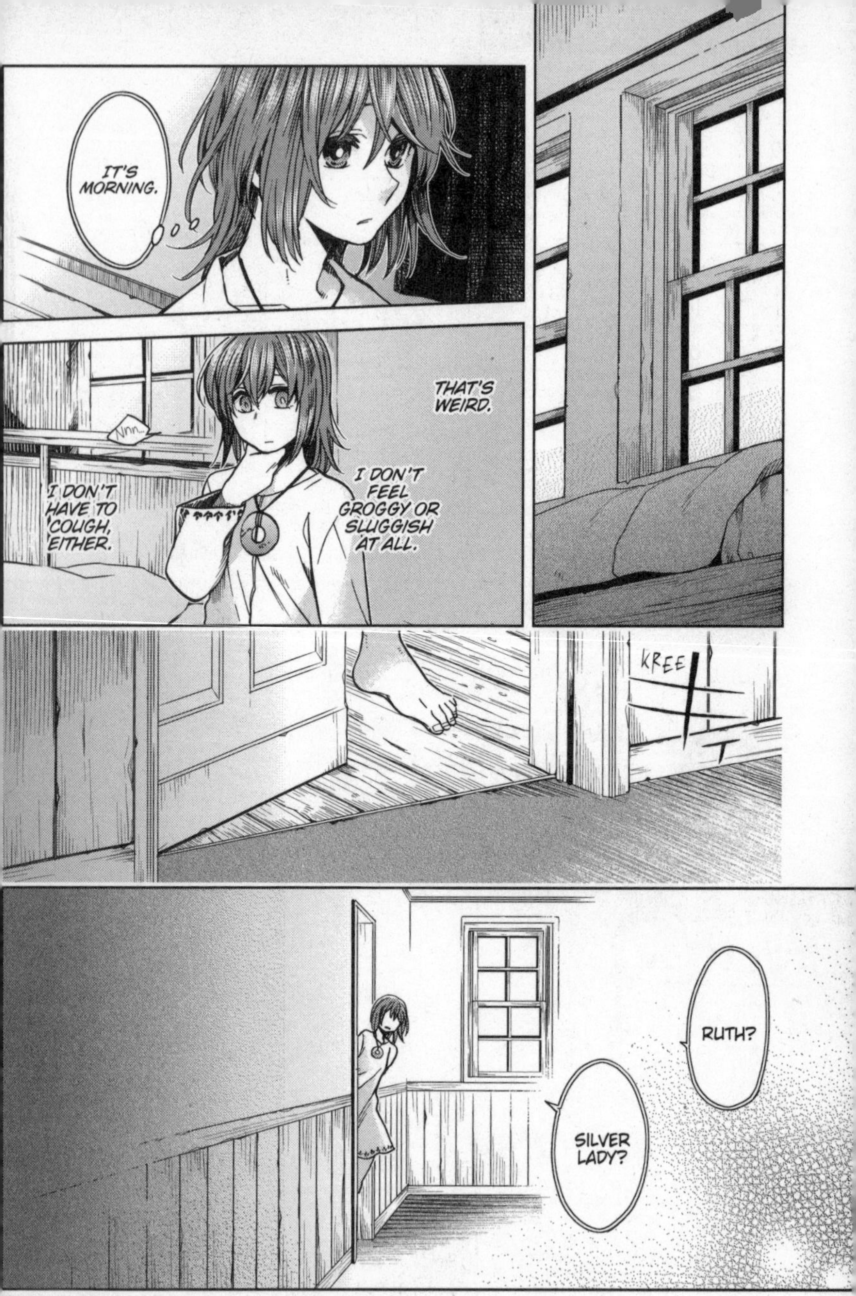
IT'S MORNING.
THAT'S WEIRD.
Nnn...
I DON'T FEEL GROGGY OR SLUGGISH AT ALL.
I DON'T HAVE TO COUGH, EITHER.
KREE
RUTH?
SILVER LADY?

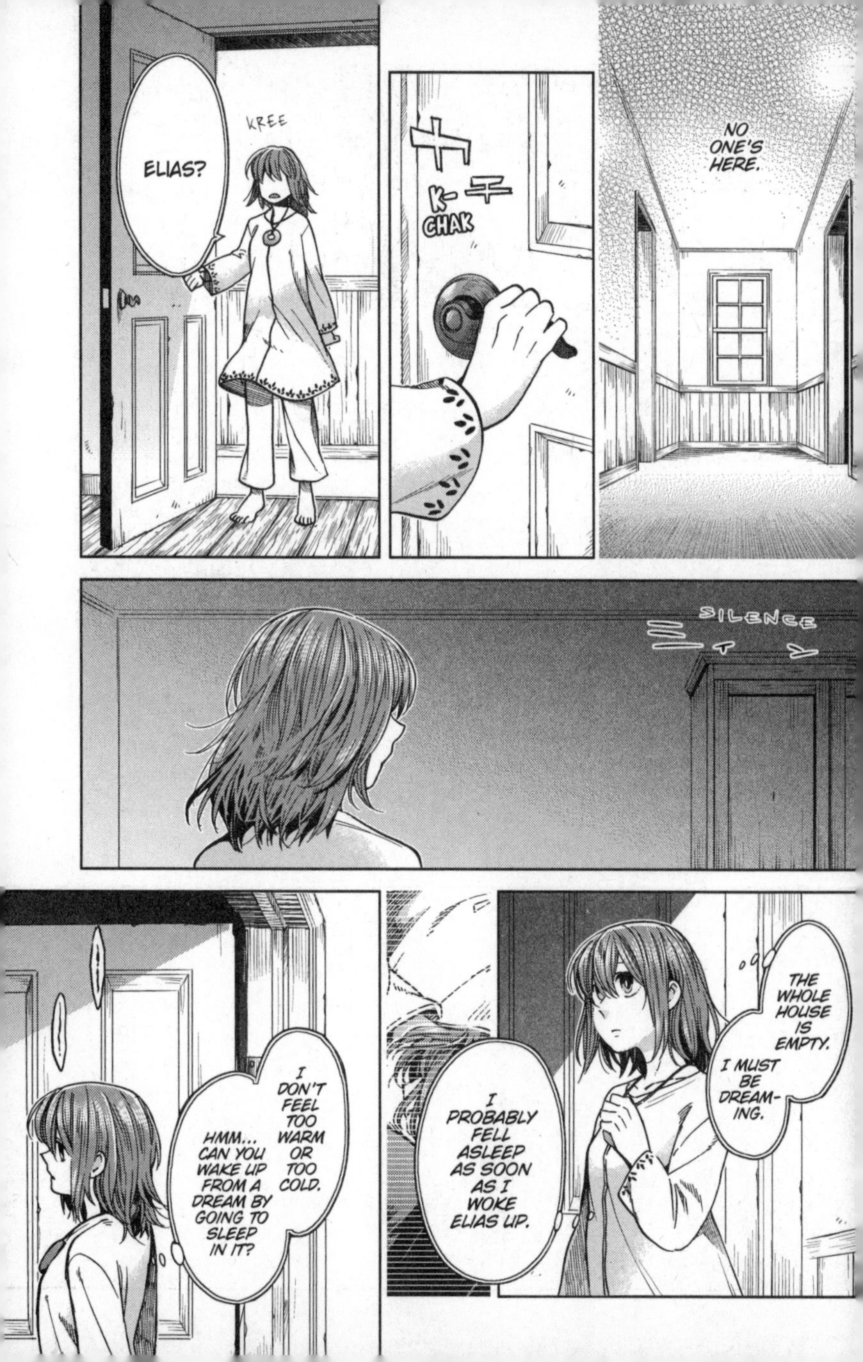
NO ONE'S HERE.
K-CHAK
KREE
ELIAS?
SILENCE
THE WHOLE HOUSE IS EMPTY.
I MUST BE DREAMING.
I PROBABLY FELL ASLEEP AS SOON AS I WOKE ELIAS UP.
I DON'T FEEL TOO WARM OR TOO COLD.
HMM... CAN YOU WAKE UP FROM A DREAM BY GOING TO SLEEP IN IT?

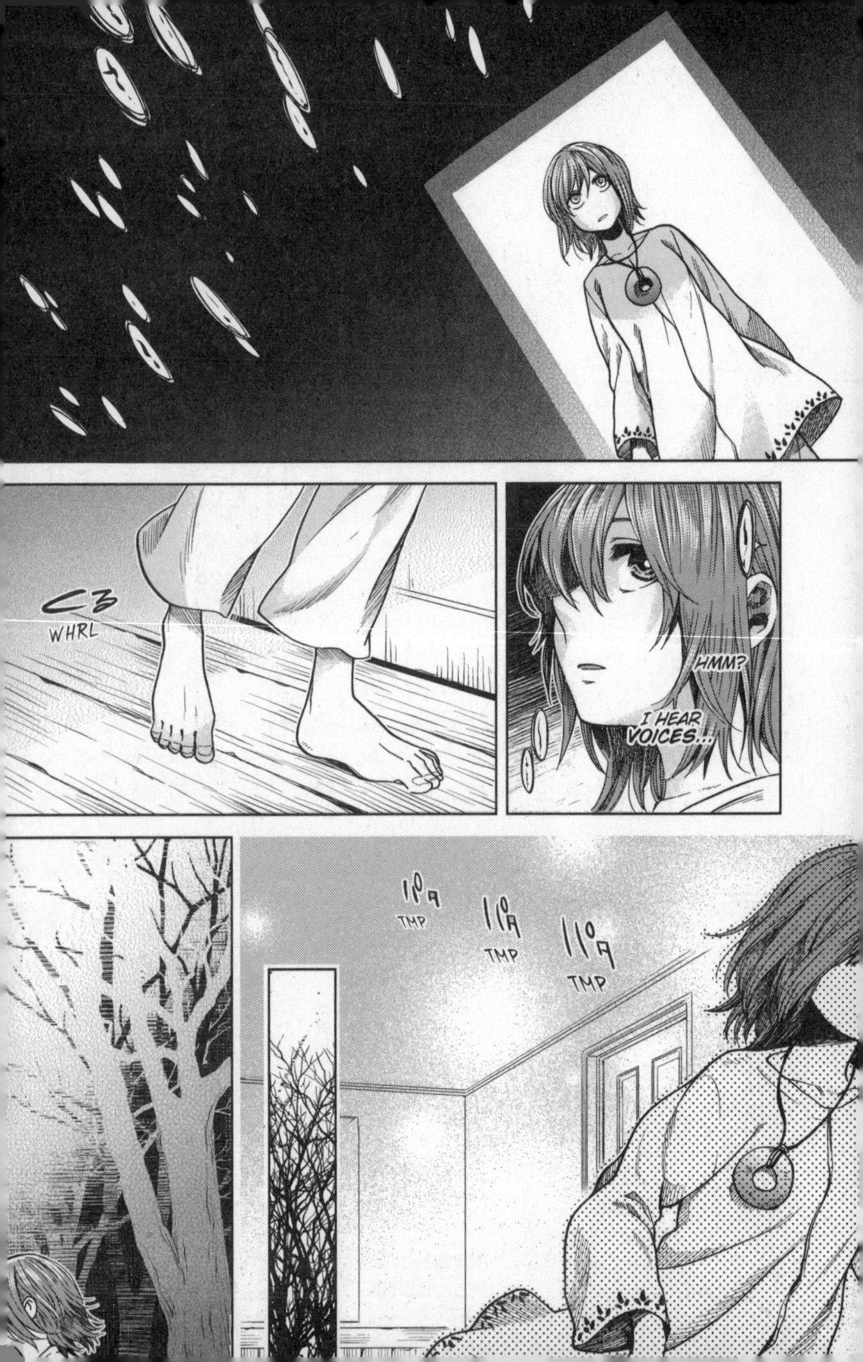
HMM?
I HEAR VOICES...
WHRL
TMP
TMP
TMP

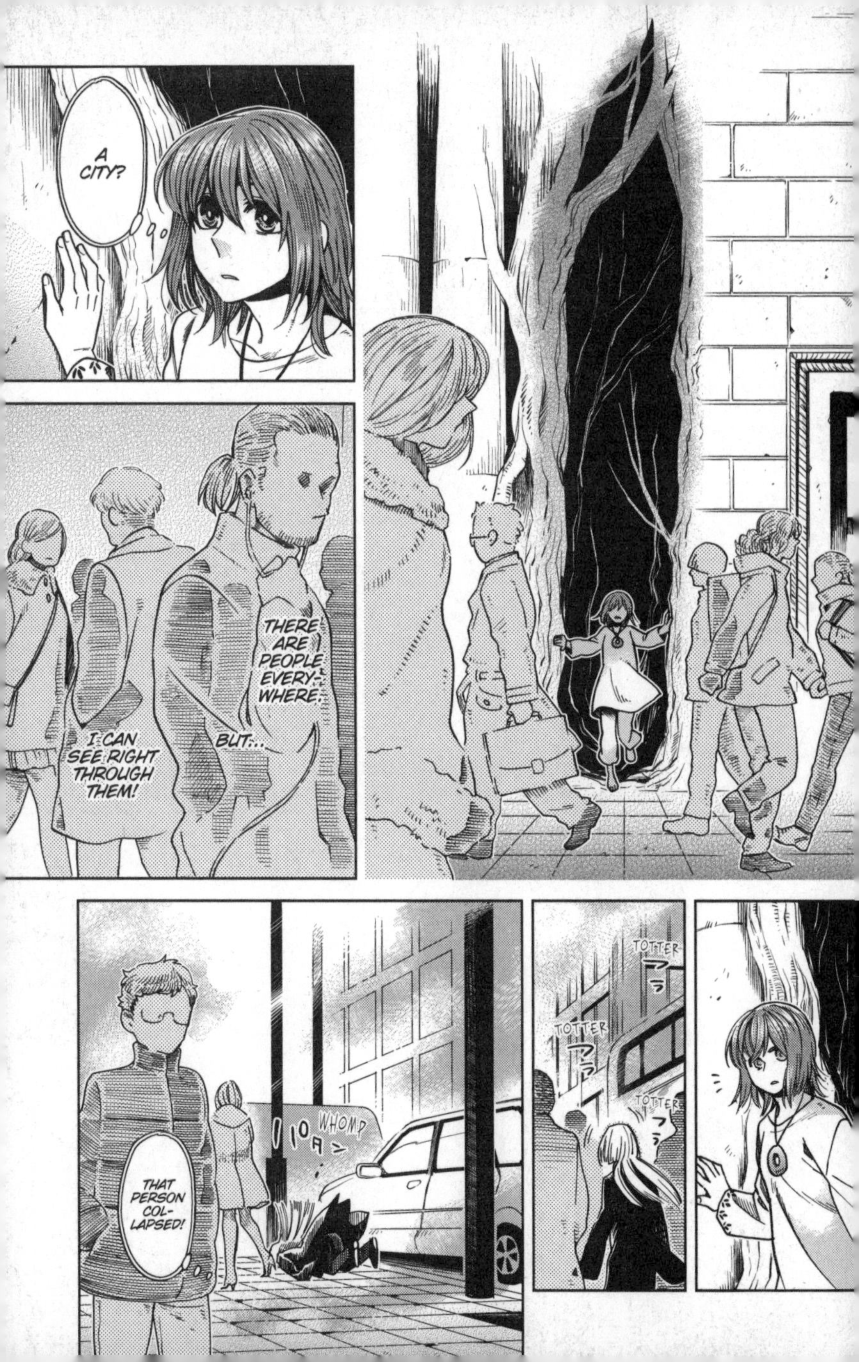
A CITY?
THERE ARE PEOPLE EVERY-WHERE.
BUT...
I CAN SEE RIGHT THROUGH THEM!
TOTTER
TOTTER
TOTTER
WHOMP
THAT PERSON COL-LAPSED!

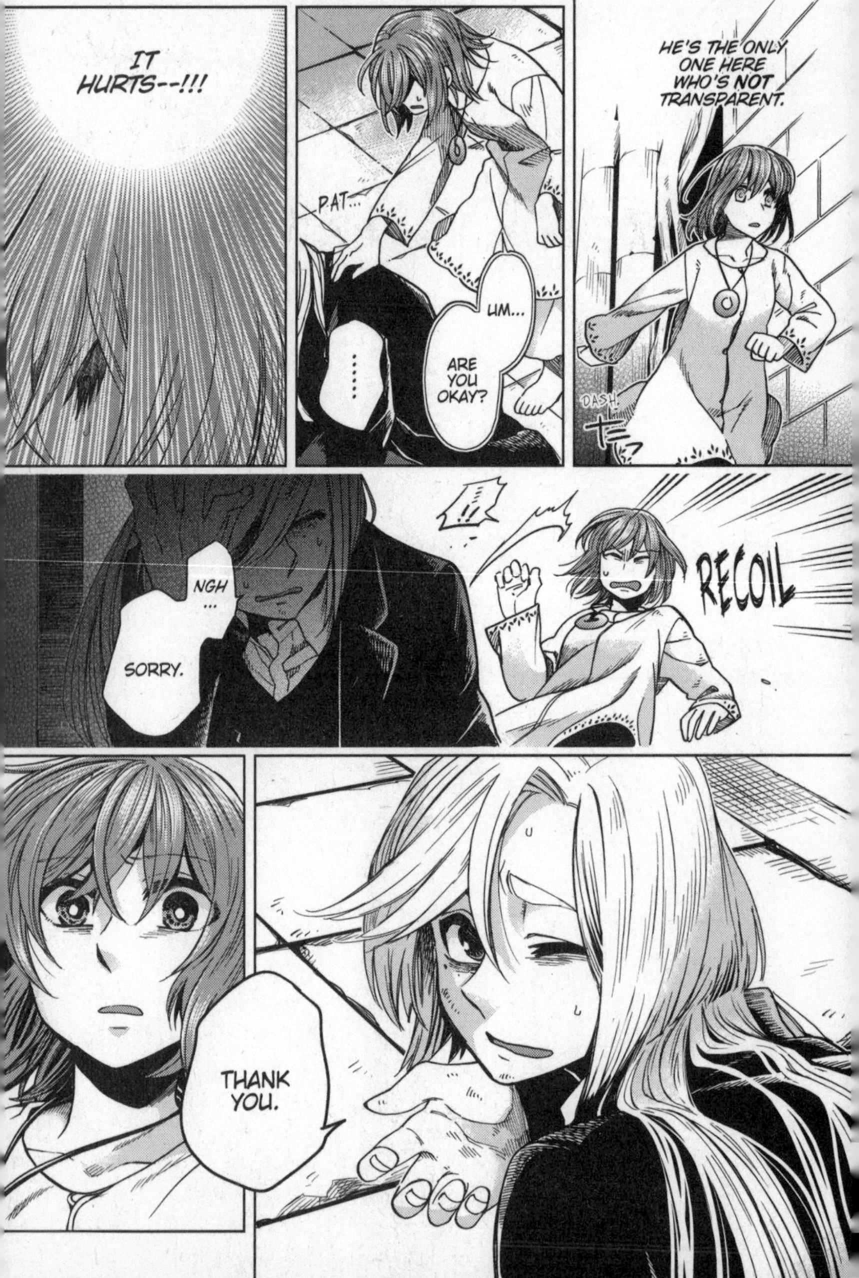
HE'S THE ONLY ONE HERE WHO'S NOT TRANSPARENT.
DASH!
PAT...
UM...
ARE YOU OKAY?
......
IT HURTS--!!!
!!
RECOIL
NGH ...
SORRY.
THANK YOU.

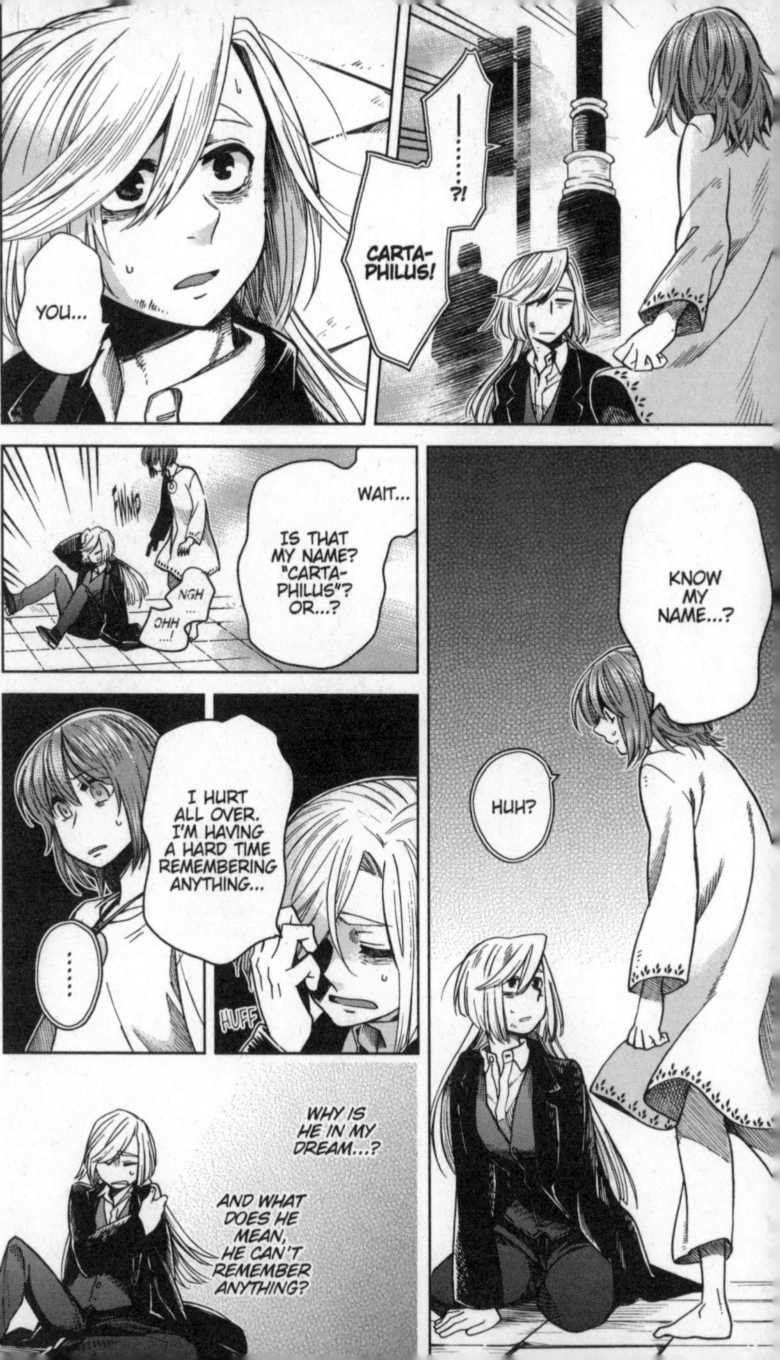
......?!
CARTA-PHILUS!
YOU...
KNOW MY NAME...?
HUH?
WAIT...
IS THAT MY NAME? "CARTA-PHILUS"? OR...?
FWMP
NGH... OHH...!
I HURT ALL OVER. I'M HAVING A HARD TIME REMEMBERING ANYTHING...
HUFF
......
WHY IS HE IN MY DREAM...?
AND WHAT DOES HE MEAN, HE CAN'T REMEMBER ANYTHING?

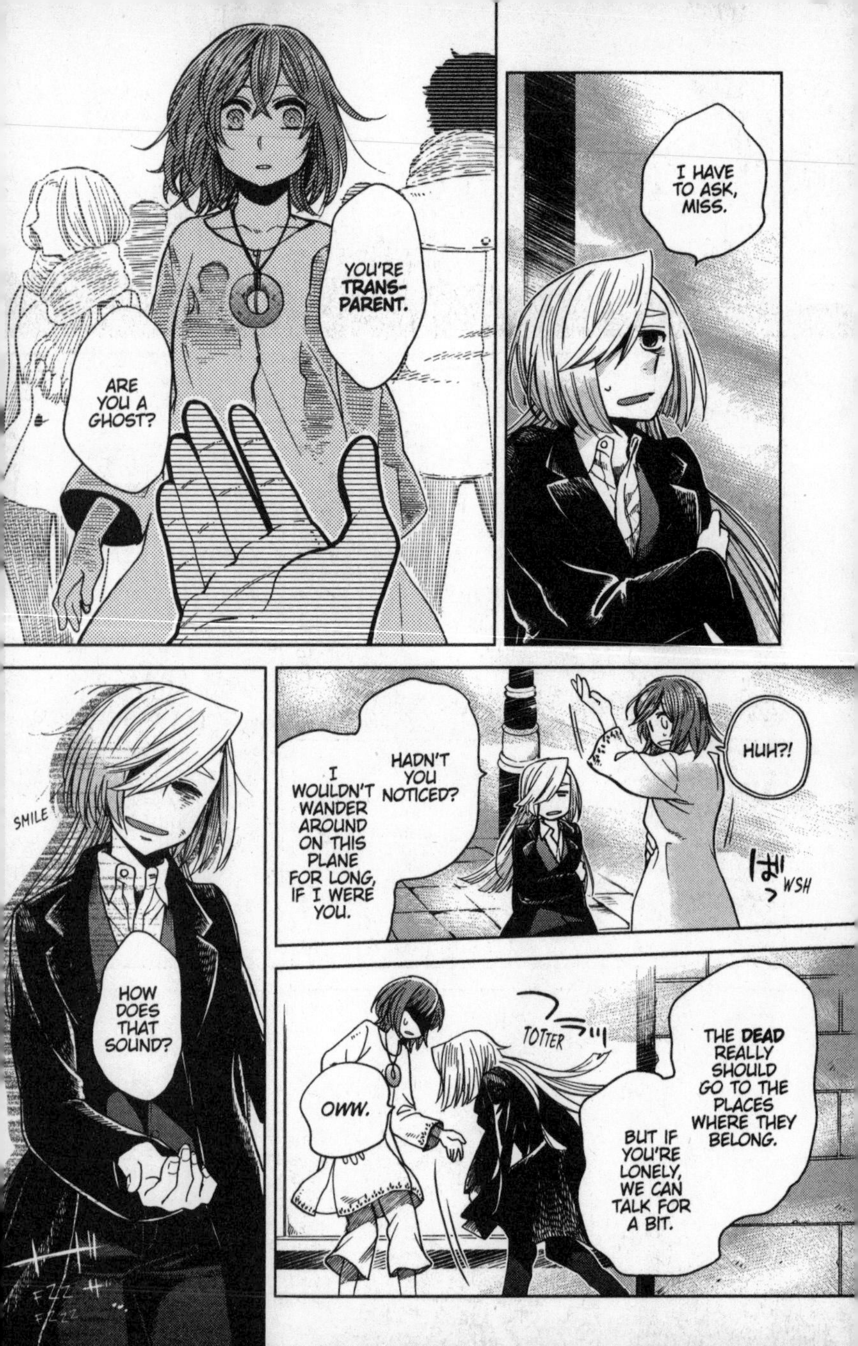
I HAVE TO ASK, MISS.
YOU'RE TRANS-PARENT.
ARE YOU A GHOST?
HUH?!
ぱっ
WSH
HADN'T YOU NOTICED?
I WOULDN'T WANDER AROUND ON THIS PLANE FOR LONG, IF I WERE YOU.
THE **DEAD** REALLY SHOULD GO TO THE PLACES WHERE THEY BELONG.
BUT IF YOU'RE LONELY, WE CAN TALK FOR A BIT.
TOTTER
OWW.
SMILE
HOW DOES THAT SOUND?
FZZ FZZ

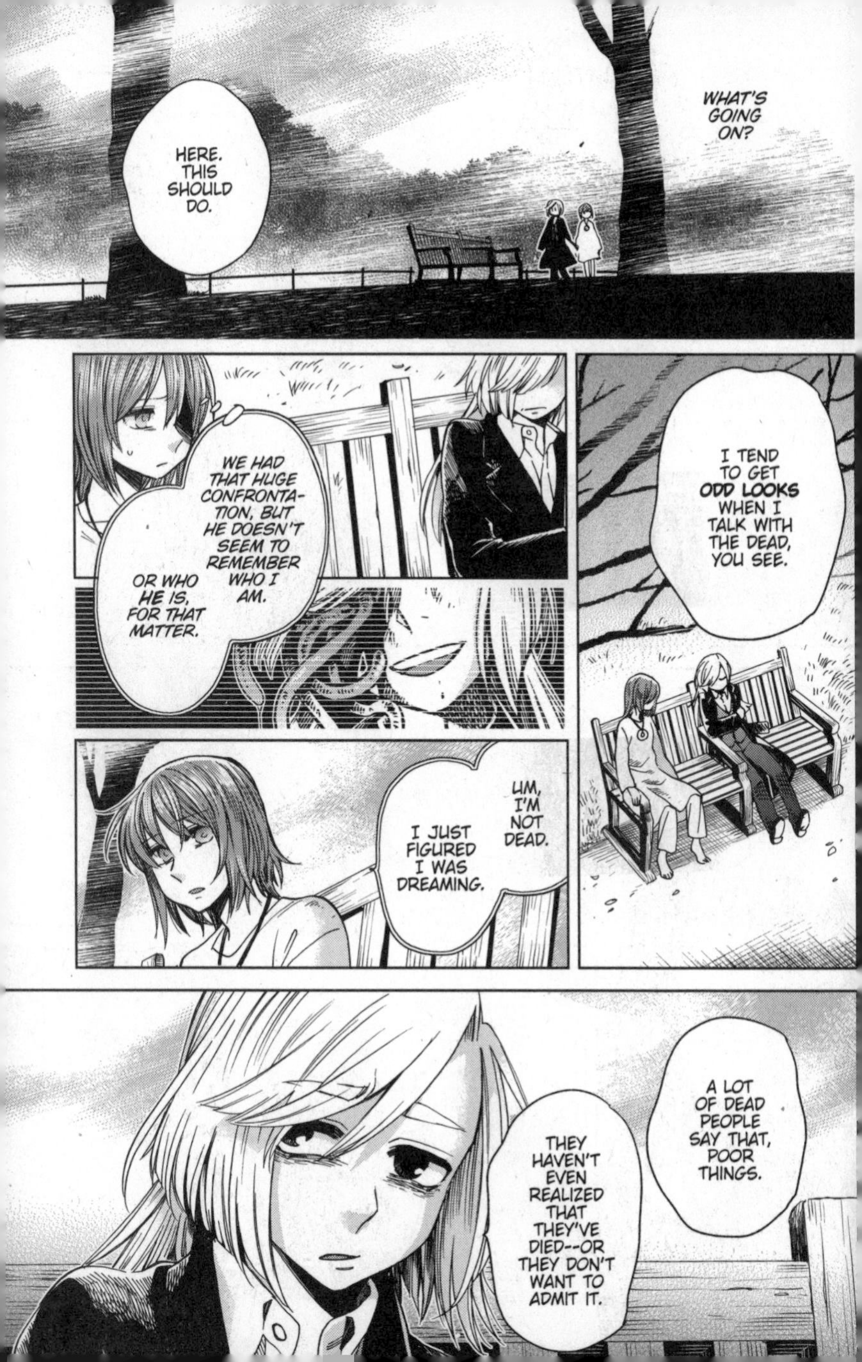
WHAT'S GOING ON?
HERE. THIS SHOULD DO.
I TEND TO GET **ODD LOOKS** WHEN I TALK WITH THE DEAD, YOU SEE.
WE HAD THAT HUGE CONFRONTATION, BUT HE DOESN'T SEEM TO REMEMBER WHO I AM.
OR WHO **HE** IS, FOR THAT MATTER.
UM, I'M NOT DEAD.
I JUST FIGURED I WAS DREAMING.
A LOT OF DEAD PEOPLE SAY THAT, POOR THINGS.
THEY HAVEN'T EVEN REALIZED THAT THEY'VE DIED--OR THEY DON'T WANT TO ADMIT IT.

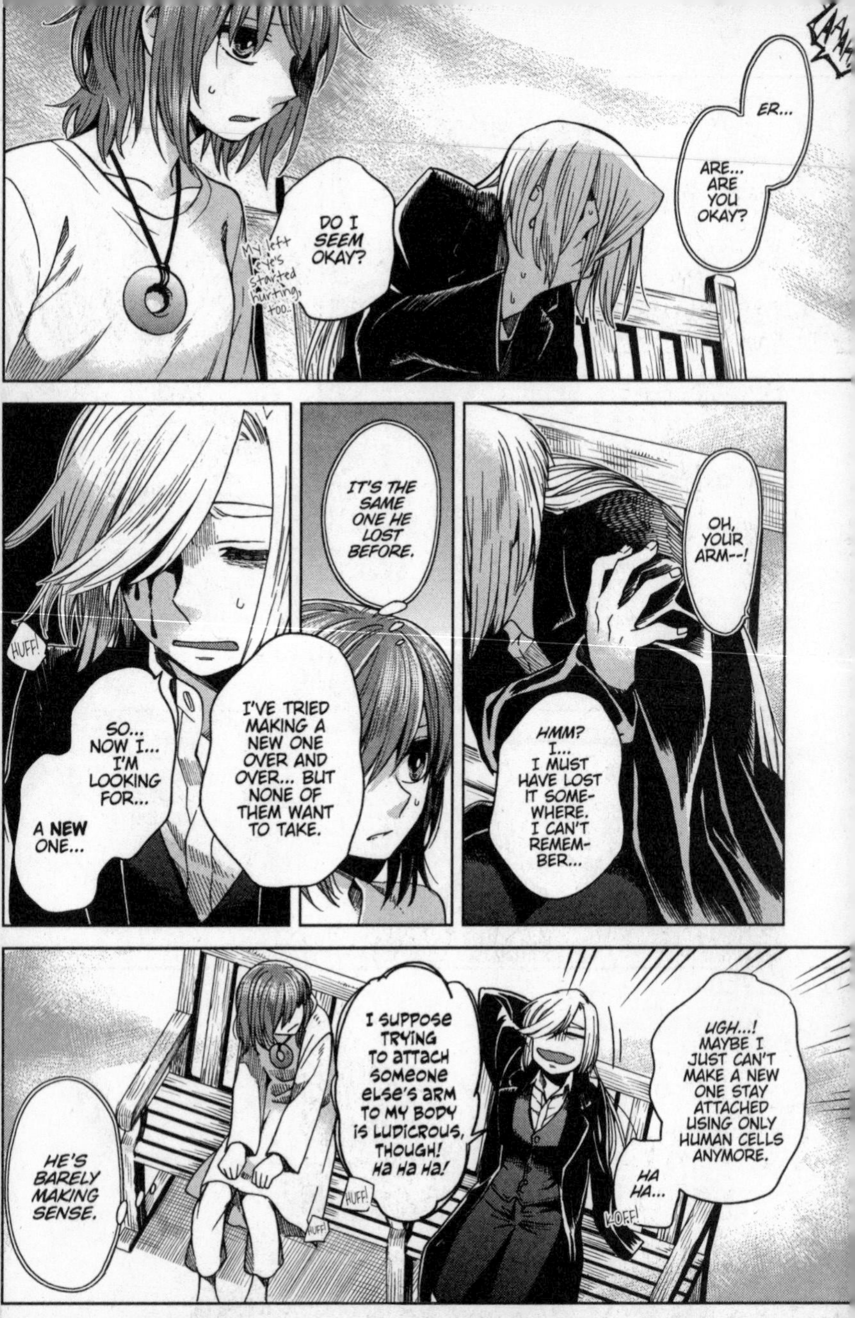
AAAK!
ER...
ARE... ARE YOU OKAY?
DO I SEEM OKAY?
My left eye's started hurting, too...
OH, YOUR ARM--!
HMM? I... I MUST HAVE LOST IT SOMEWHERE. I CAN'T REMEMBER...
IT'S THE SAME ONE HE LOST BEFORE.
I'VE TRIED MAKING A NEW ONE OVER AND OVER... BUT NONE OF THEM WANT TO TAKE.
HUFF!
SO... NOW I... I'M LOOKING FOR... A NEW ONE...
UGH...! MAYBE I JUST CAN'T MAKE A NEW ONE STAY ATTACHED USING ONLY HUMAN CELLS ANYMORE.
HA HA...
KOFF!
I SUPPOSE TRYING TO ATTACH SOMEONE ELSE'S ARM TO MY BODY IS LUDICROUS, THOUGH! HA HA HA!
HUFF!
HUFF!
HE'S BARELY MAKING SENSE.

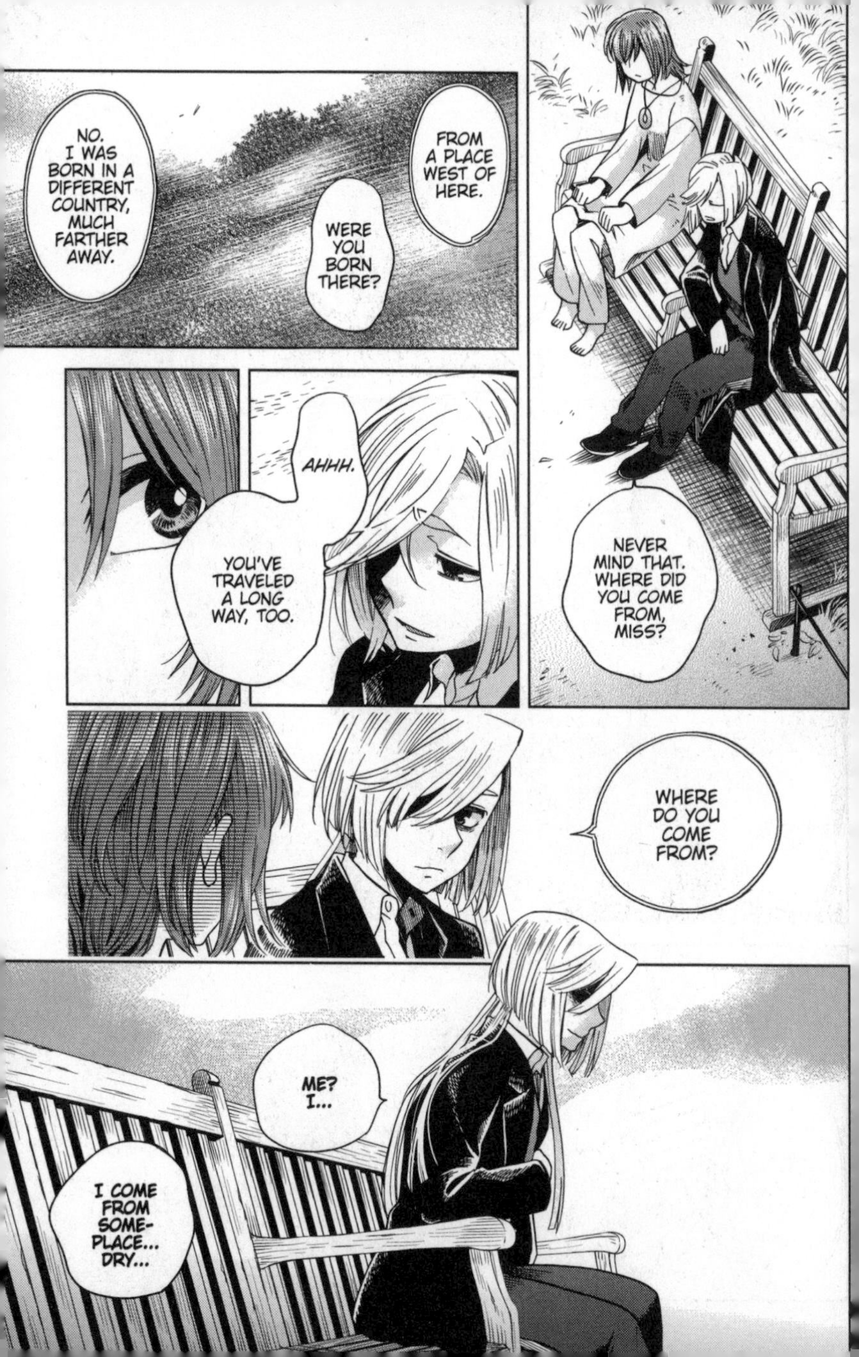
NEVER MIND THAT. WHERE DID YOU COME FROM, MISS?
FROM A PLACE WEST OF HERE.
WERE YOU BORN THERE?
NO. I WAS BORN IN A DIFFERENT COUNTRY, MUCH FARTHER AWAY.
AHHH.
YOU'VE TRAVELED A LONG WAY, TOO.
WHERE DO YOU COME FROM?
ME? I...
I COME FROM SOME-PLACE... DRY...

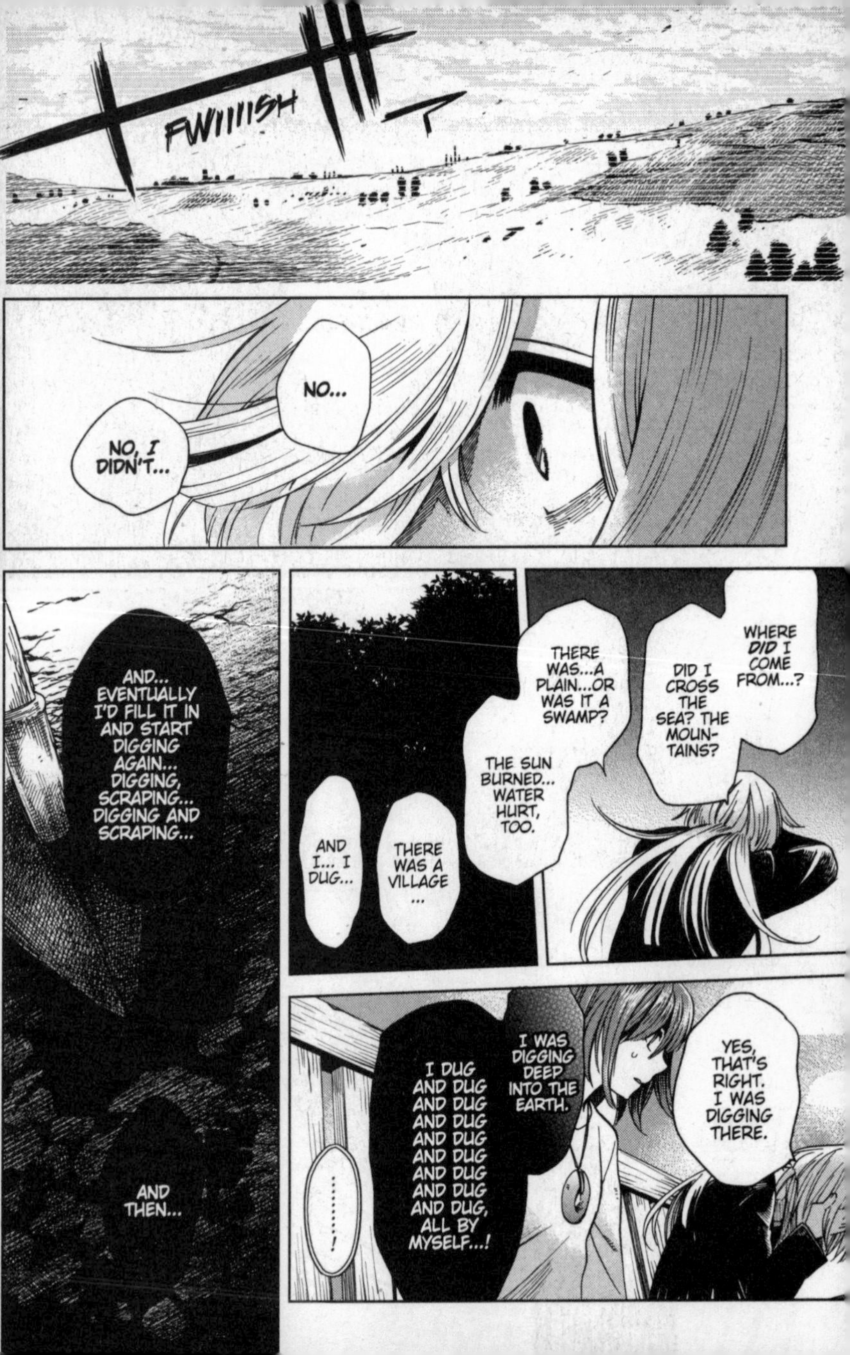
FWIIIISH
NO...
NO, I DIDN'T...
WHERE *DID* I COME FROM...?
DID I CROSS THE SEA? THE MOUNTAINS?
THERE WAS...A PLAIN...OR WAS IT A SWAMP?
THE SUN BURNED... WATER HURT, TOO.
THERE WAS A VILLAGE...
AND I... I DUG...
YES, THAT'S RIGHT. I WAS DIGGING THERE.
I WAS DIGGING DEEP INTO THE EARTH.
I DUG AND DUG AND DUG AND DUG AND DUG AND DUG AND DUG AND DUG AND DUG, ALL BY MYSELF...!
........!
AND... EVENTUALLY I'D FILL IT IN AND START DIGGING AGAIN... DIGGING, SCRAPING... DIGGING AND SCRAPING...
AND THEN...

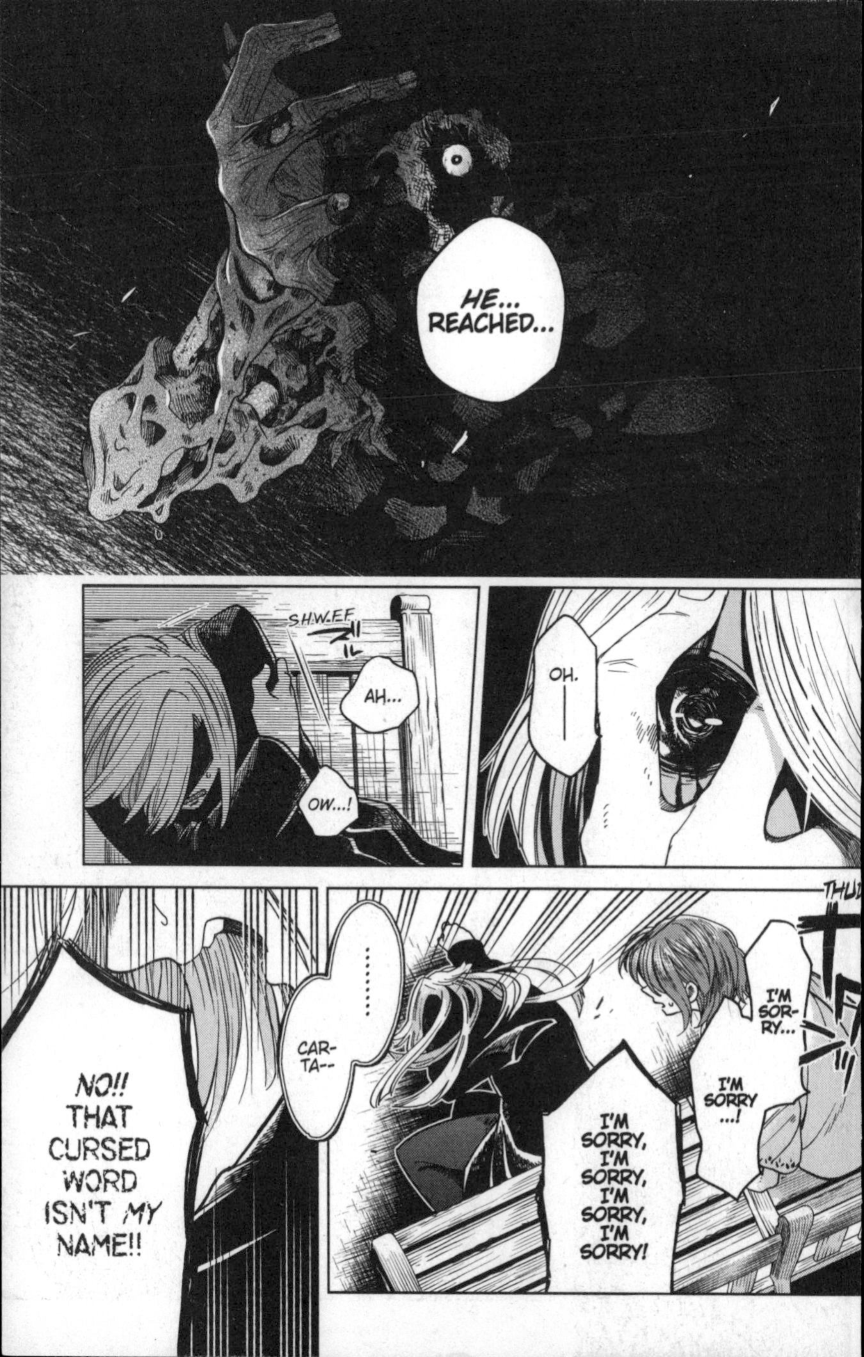
HE... REACHED...
OH.
SHWFF
AH...
OW...!
I'M SORRY...
I'M SORRY ...!
I'M SORRY, I'M SORRY, I'M SORRY, I'M SORRY!
......
CAR-TA--
NO!! THAT CURSED WORD ISN'T MY NAME!!

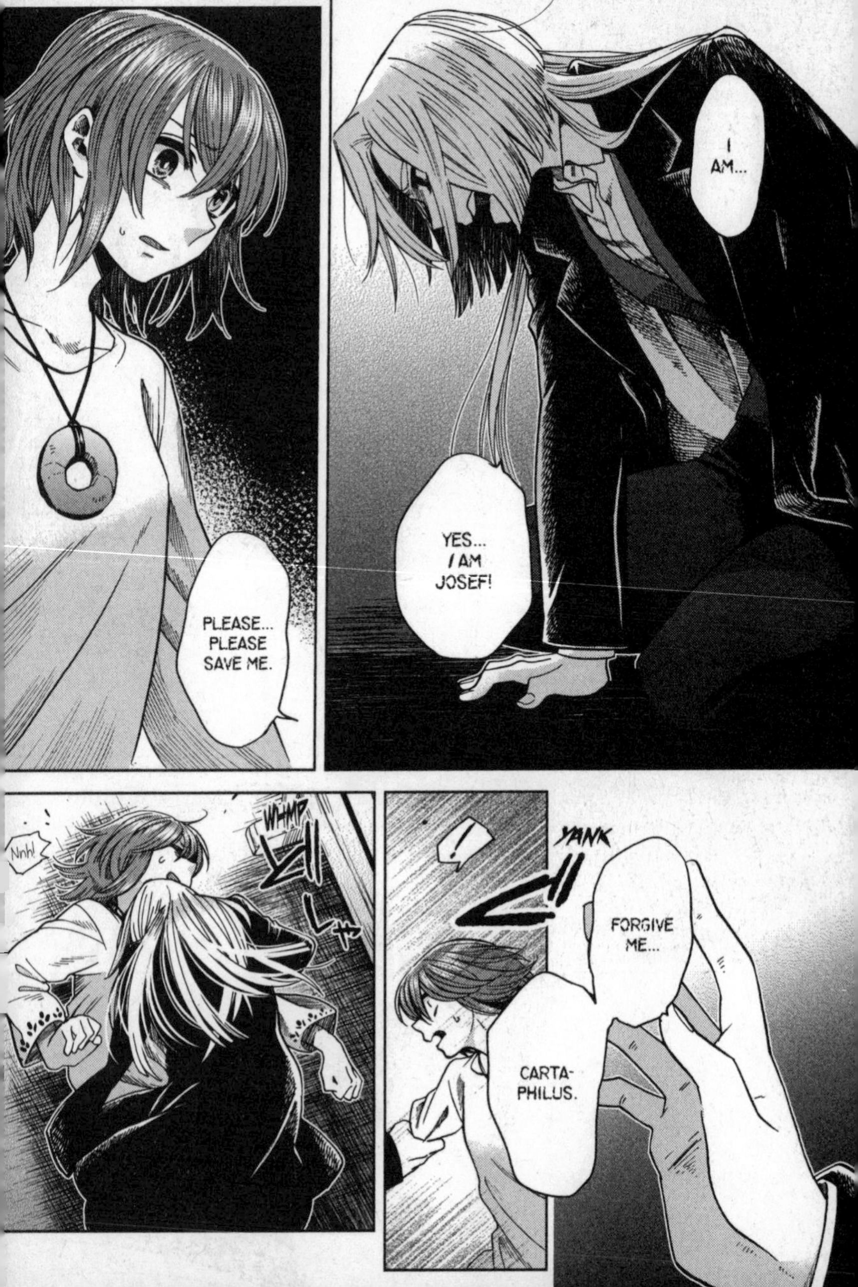
I AM...
YES... I AM JOSEF!
PLEASE... PLEASE SAVE ME.
!
YANK
FORGIVE ME...
CARTA-PHILUS.
Nnh!
!
WHMP

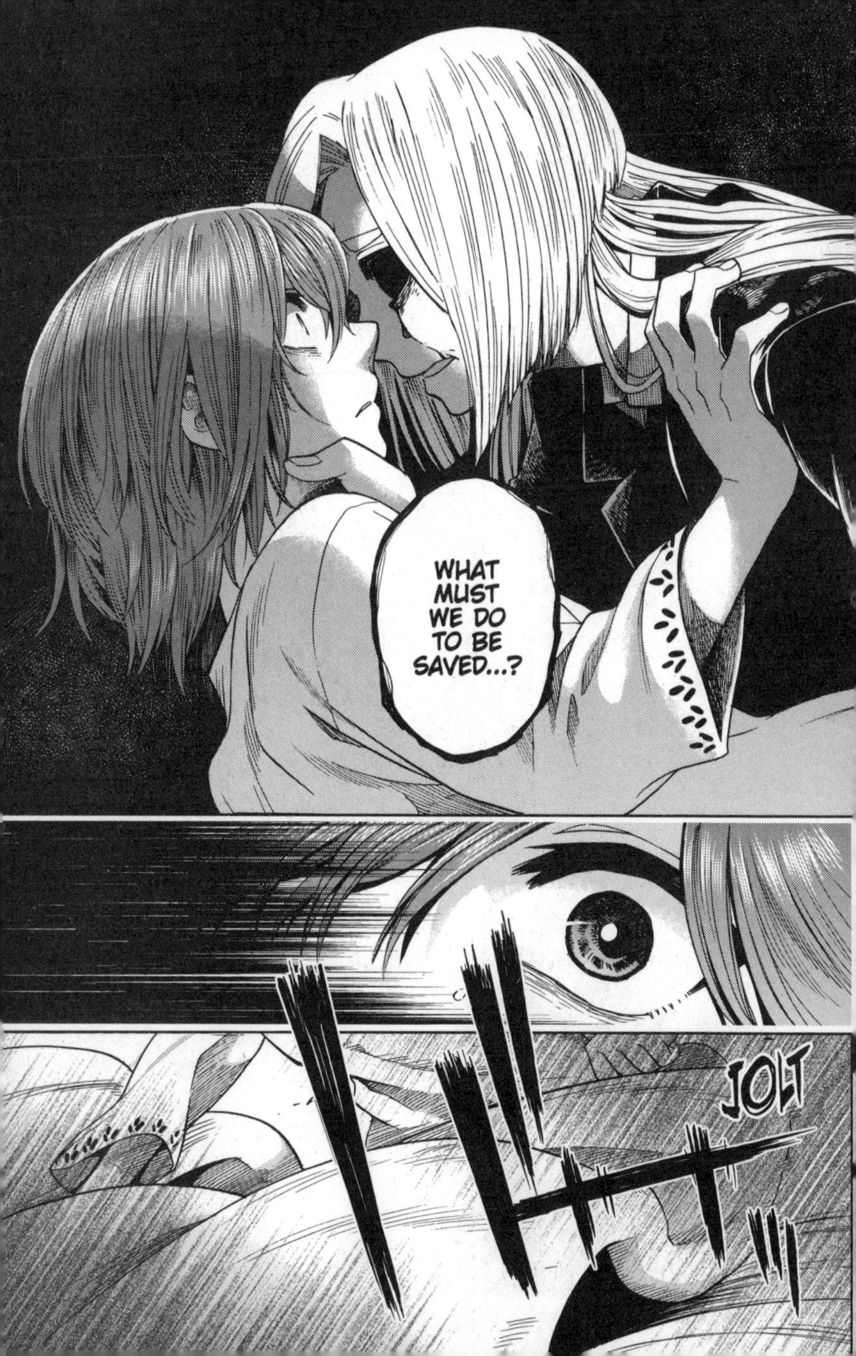
WHAT MUST WE DO TO BE SAVED...?
JOLT

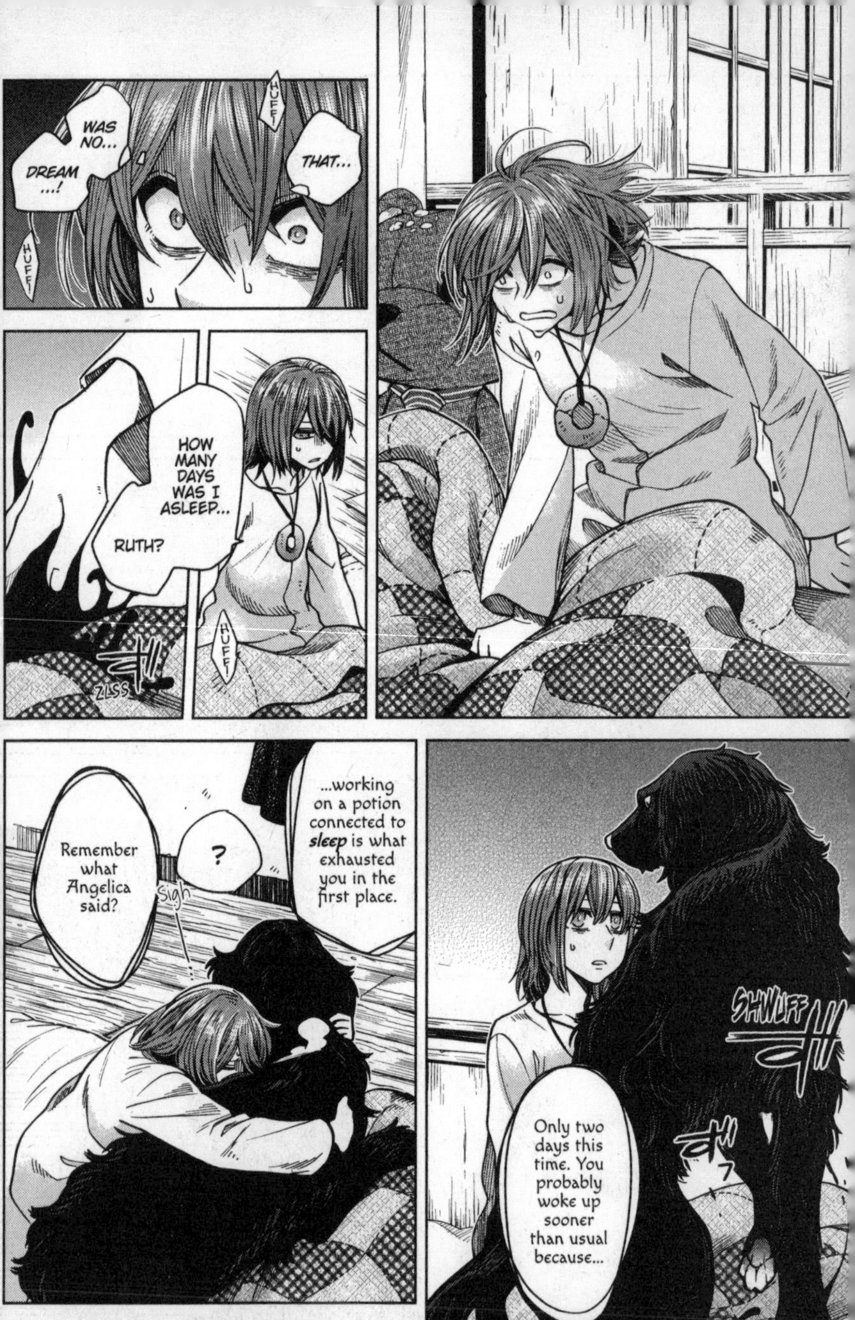
HUFF!
THAT...
WAS NO...
DREAM ...!
HUFF!
HUFF!
HOW MANY DAYS WAS I ASLEEP...
RUTH?
ZLSS
SHWUFF
Only two days this time. You probably woke up sooner than usual because...
...working on a potion connected to **sleep** is what exhausted you in the first place.
?
Remember what Angelica said?
Sigh

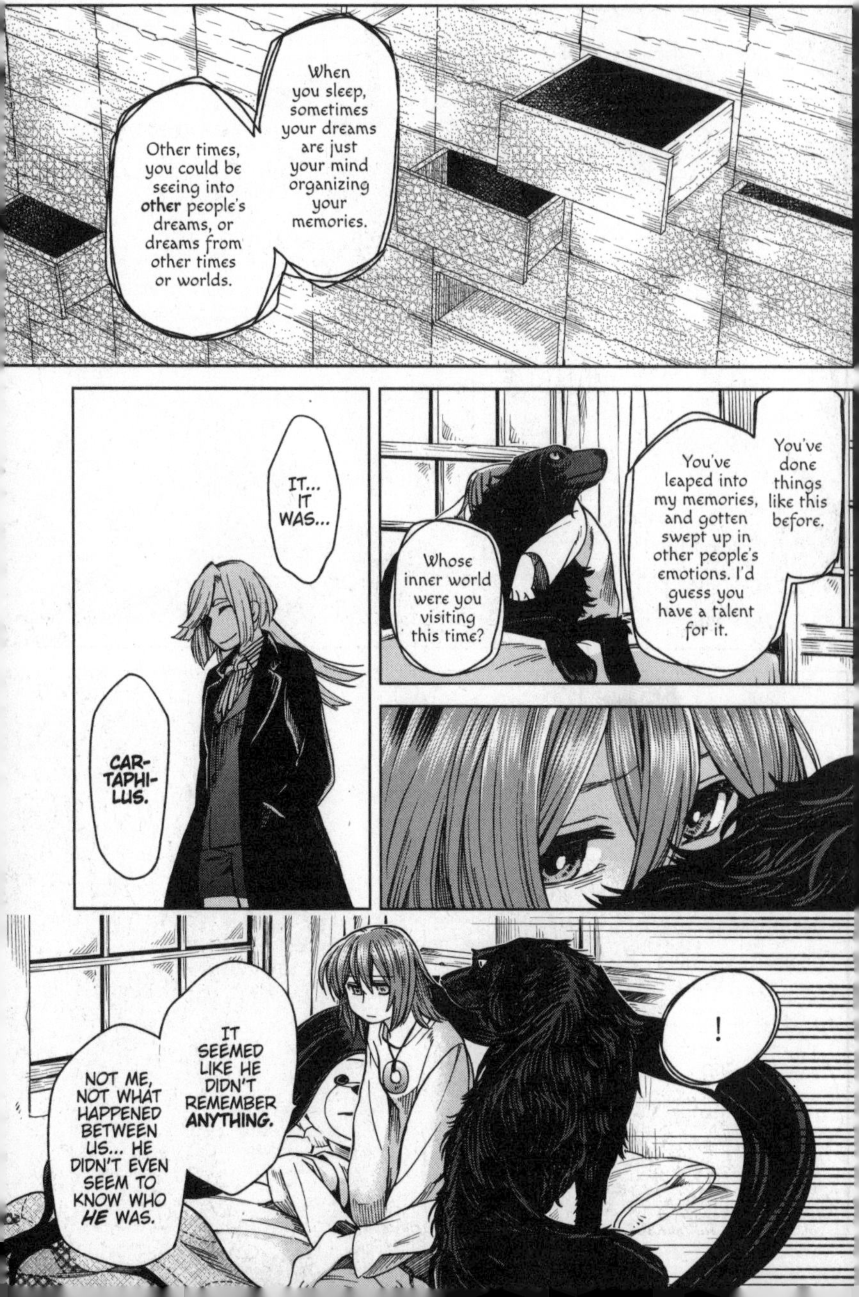
When you sleep, sometimes your dreams are just your mind organizing your memories.
Other times, you could be seeing into **other** people's dreams, or dreams from other times or worlds.
You've done things like this before.
You've leaped into my memories, and gotten swept up in other people's emotions. I'd guess you have a talent for it.
Whose inner world were you visiting this time?
IT... IT WAS...
CAR-TAPHI-LUS.
!
IT SEEMED LIKE HE DIDN'T REMEMBER **ANYTHING.**
NOT ME, NOT WHAT HAPPENED BETWEEN US... HE DIDN'T EVEN SEEM TO KNOW WHO ***HE*** WAS.

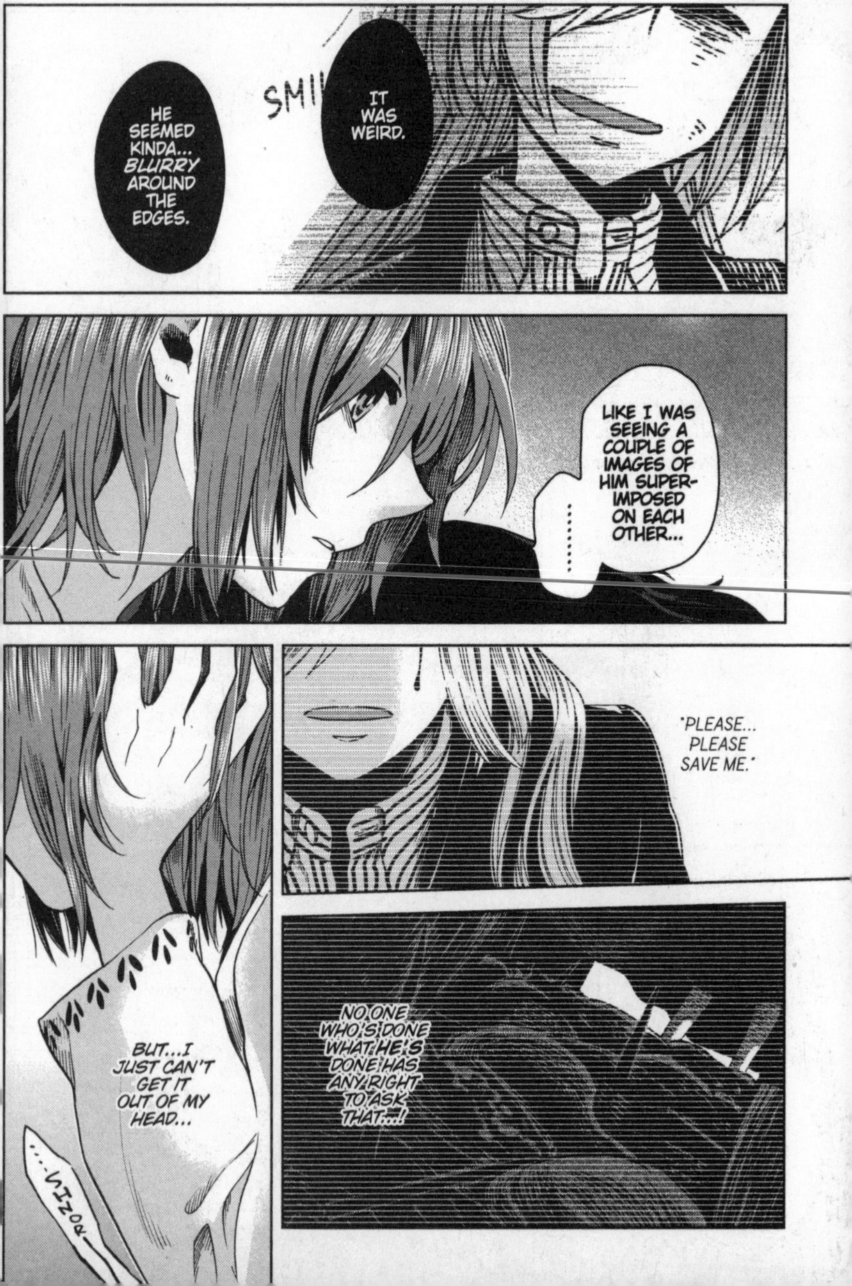
IT WAS WEIRD.
SMI
HE SEEMED KINDA... BLURRY AROUND THE EDGES.
LIKE I WAS SEEING A COUPLE OF IMAGES OF HIM SUPER-IMPOSED ON EACH OTHER...
......
"PLEASE... PLEASE SAVE ME."
NO ONE WHO'S DONE WHAT HE'S DONE HAS ANY RIGHT TO ASK THAT...!
BUT...I JUST CAN'T GET IT OUT OF MY HEAD...
...VIZOR

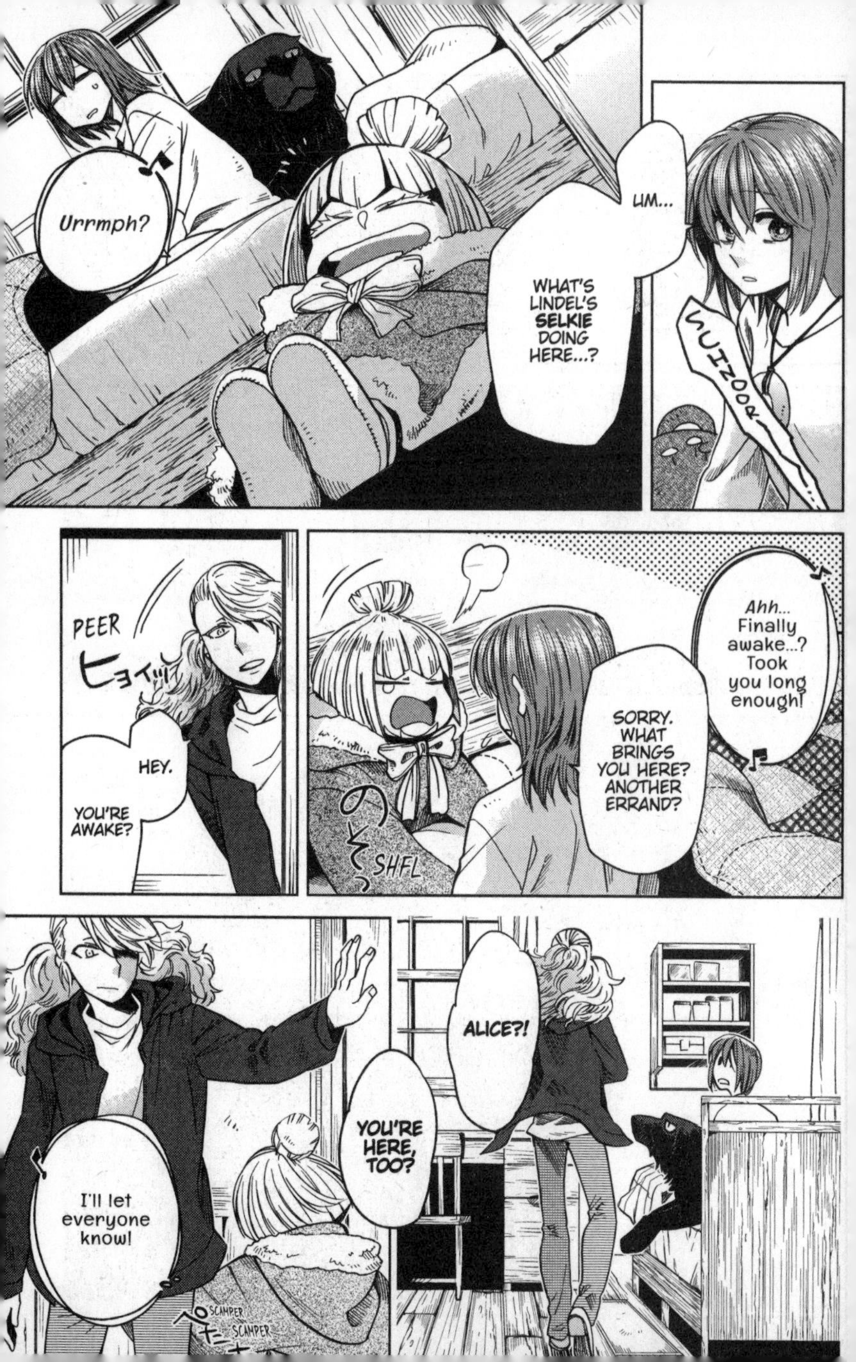
UM...
WHAT'S LINDEL'S SELKIE DOING HERE...?
Urrmph?
Ahh... Finally awake...? Took you long enough!
SORRY. WHAT BRINGS YOU HERE? ANOTHER ERRAND?
のそっ
SHFL
PEER
ヒョイッ
HEY.
YOU'RE AWAKE?
ALICE?!
YOU'RE HERE, TOO?
I'll let everyone know!
SCAMPER
SCAMPER

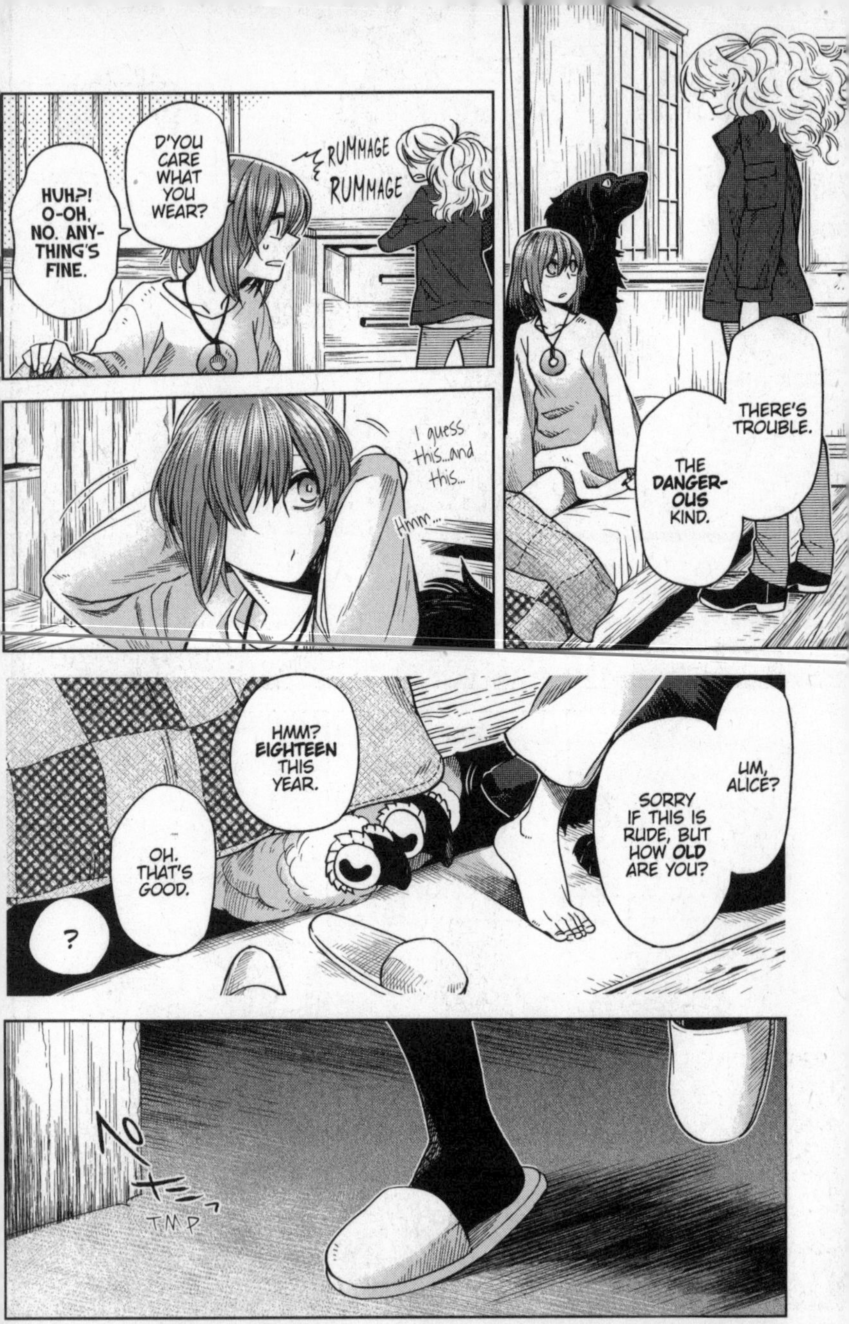
THERE'S TROUBLE.
THE DANGER-OUS KIND.
RUMMAGE RUMMAGE
D'YOU CARE WHAT YOU WEAR?
HUH?! O-OH. NO. ANY-THING'S FINE.
I guess this...and this...
Hmm...
UM, ALICE?
SORRY IF THIS IS RUDE, BUT HOW OLD ARE YOU?
HMM? EIGHTEEN THIS YEAR.
OH. THAT'S GOOD.
?
TMP

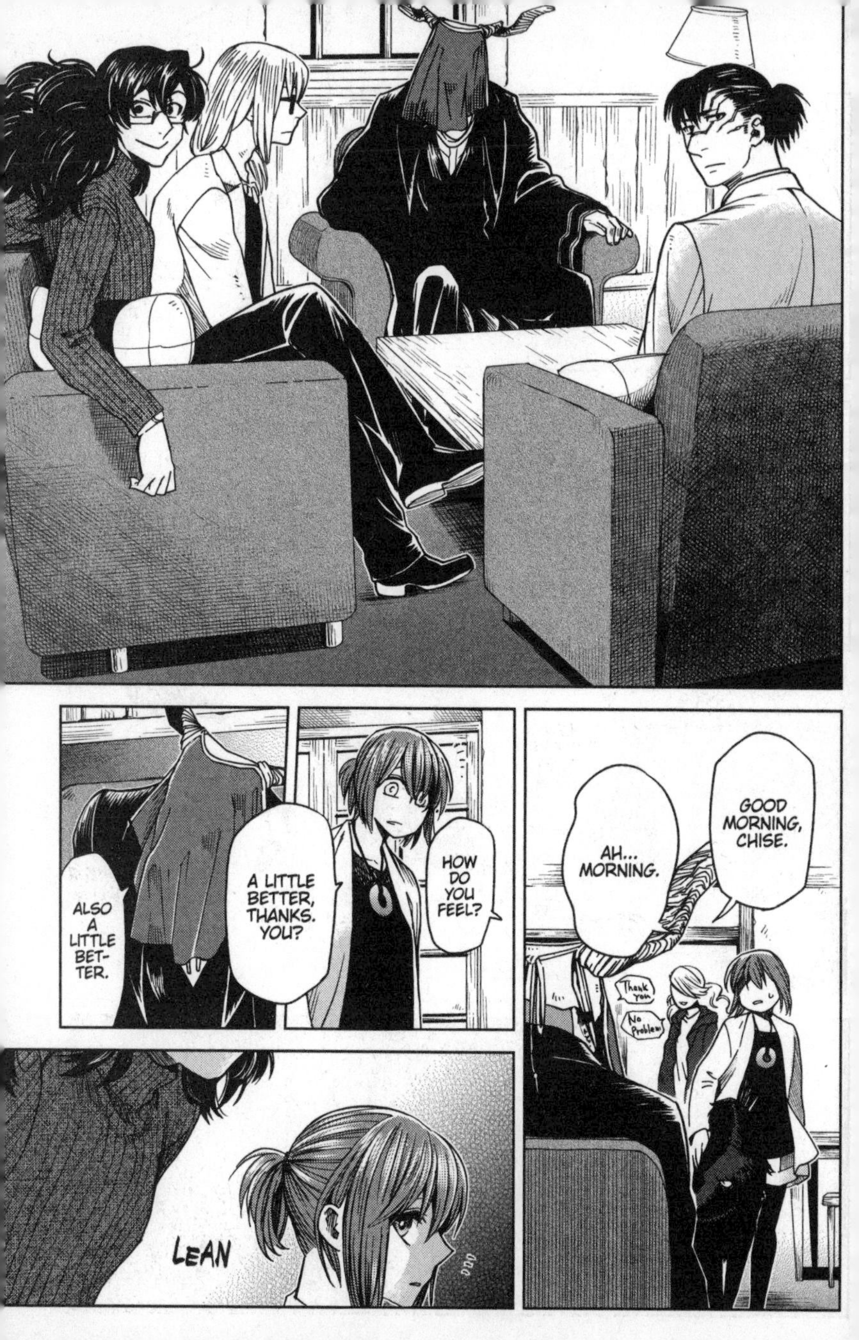
GOOD MORNING, CHISE.
AH... MORNING.
Thank you
No Problem
HOW DO YOU FEEL?
A LITTLE BETTER, THANKS. YOU?
ALSO A LITTLE BET-TER.
LEAN

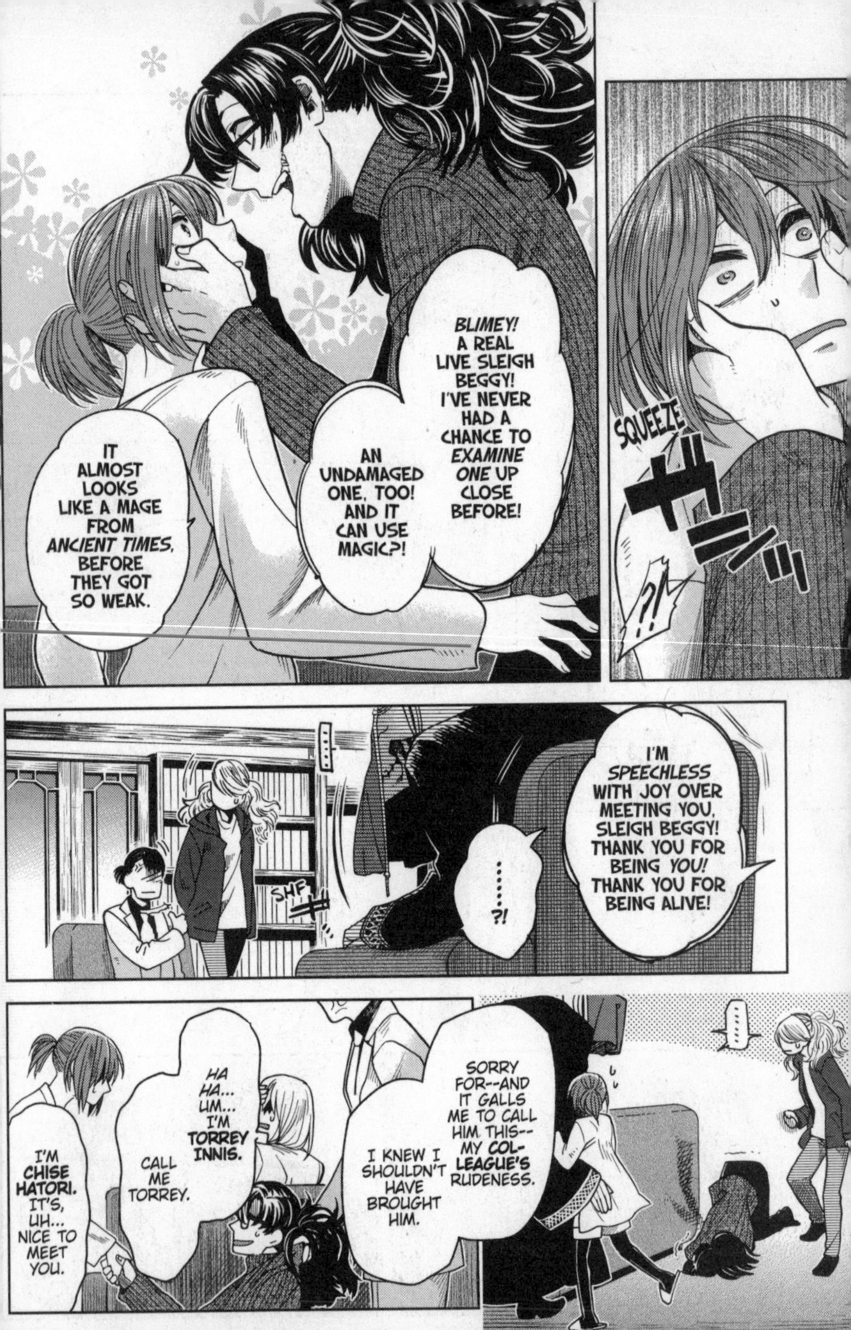
SQUEEZE
?!
BLIMEY! A REAL LIVE SLEIGH BEGGY! I'VE NEVER HAD A CHANCE TO *EXAMINE ONE* UP CLOSE BEFORE!
AN UNDAMAGED ONE, TOO! AND IT CAN USE MAGIC?!
IT ALMOST LOOKS LIKE A MAGE FROM *ANCIENT TIMES*, BEFORE THEY GOT SO WEAK.
I'M *SPEECHLESS* WITH JOY OVER MEETING YOU, SLEIGH BEGGY! THANK YOU FOR BEING *YOU!* THANK YOU FOR BEING ALIVE!
......?!
......
SHF
......
SORRY FOR--AND IT GALLS ME TO CALL HIM THIS--MY **COL-LEAGUE'S** RUDENESS.
I KNEW I SHOULDN'T HAVE BROUGHT HIM.
HA HA... UM... I'M **TORREY INNIS.**
CALL ME TORREY.
I'M **CHISE HATORI.** IT'S, UH... NICE TO MEET YOU.

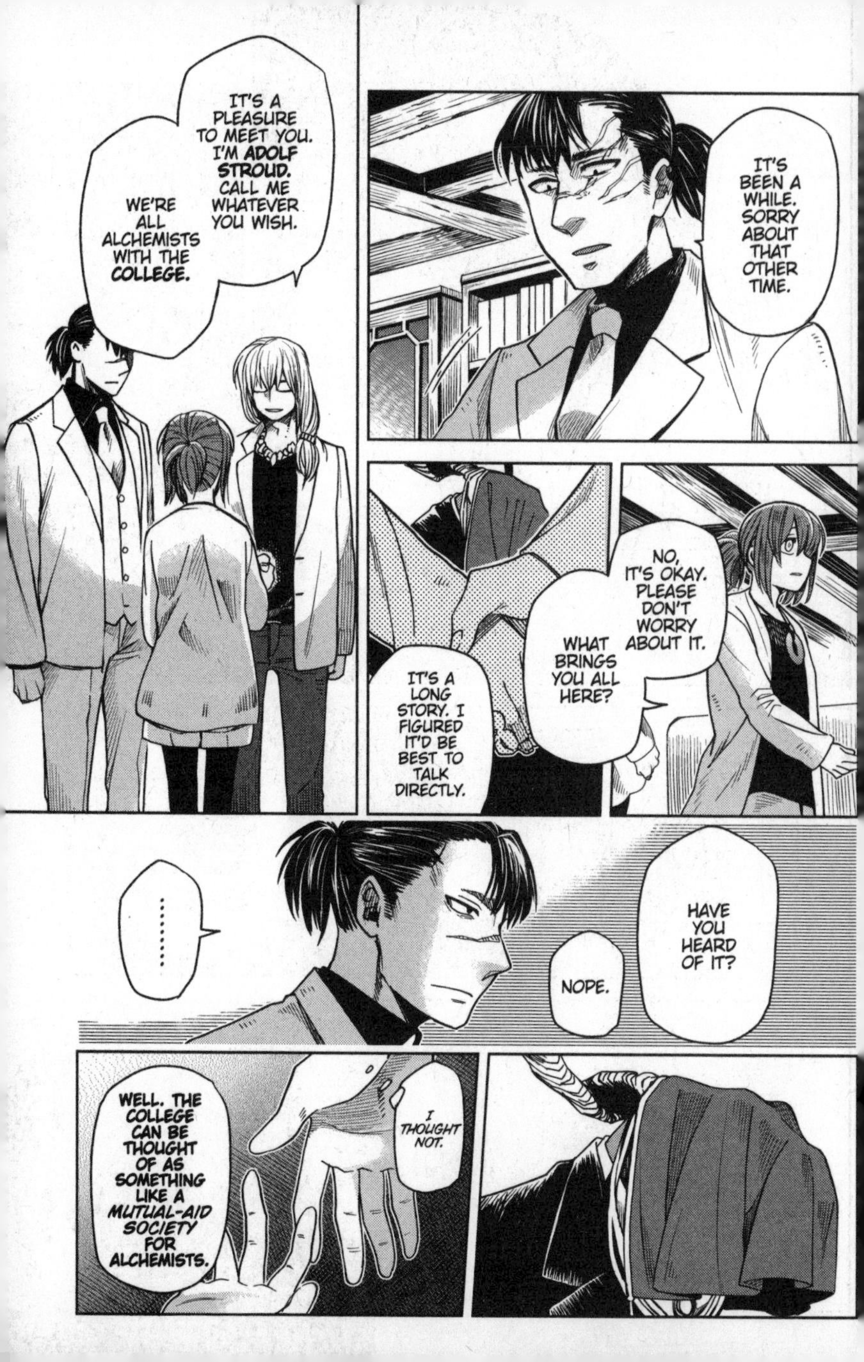
IT'S BEEN A WHILE. SORRY ABOUT THAT OTHER TIME.
NO, IT'S OKAY. PLEASE DON'T WORRY ABOUT IT.
WHAT BRINGS YOU ALL HERE?
IT'S A LONG STORY. I FIGURED IT'D BE BEST TO TALK DIRECTLY.
IT'S A PLEASURE TO MEET YOU. I'M **ADOLF STROUD.** CALL ME WHATEVER YOU WISH.
WE'RE ALL ALCHEMISTS WITH THE **COLLEGE.**
HAVE YOU HEARD OF IT?
NOPE.
....
I THOUGHT NOT.
WELL. THE COLLEGE CAN BE THOUGHT OF AS SOMETHING LIKE A *MUTUAL-AID SOCIETY* FOR ALCHEMISTS.

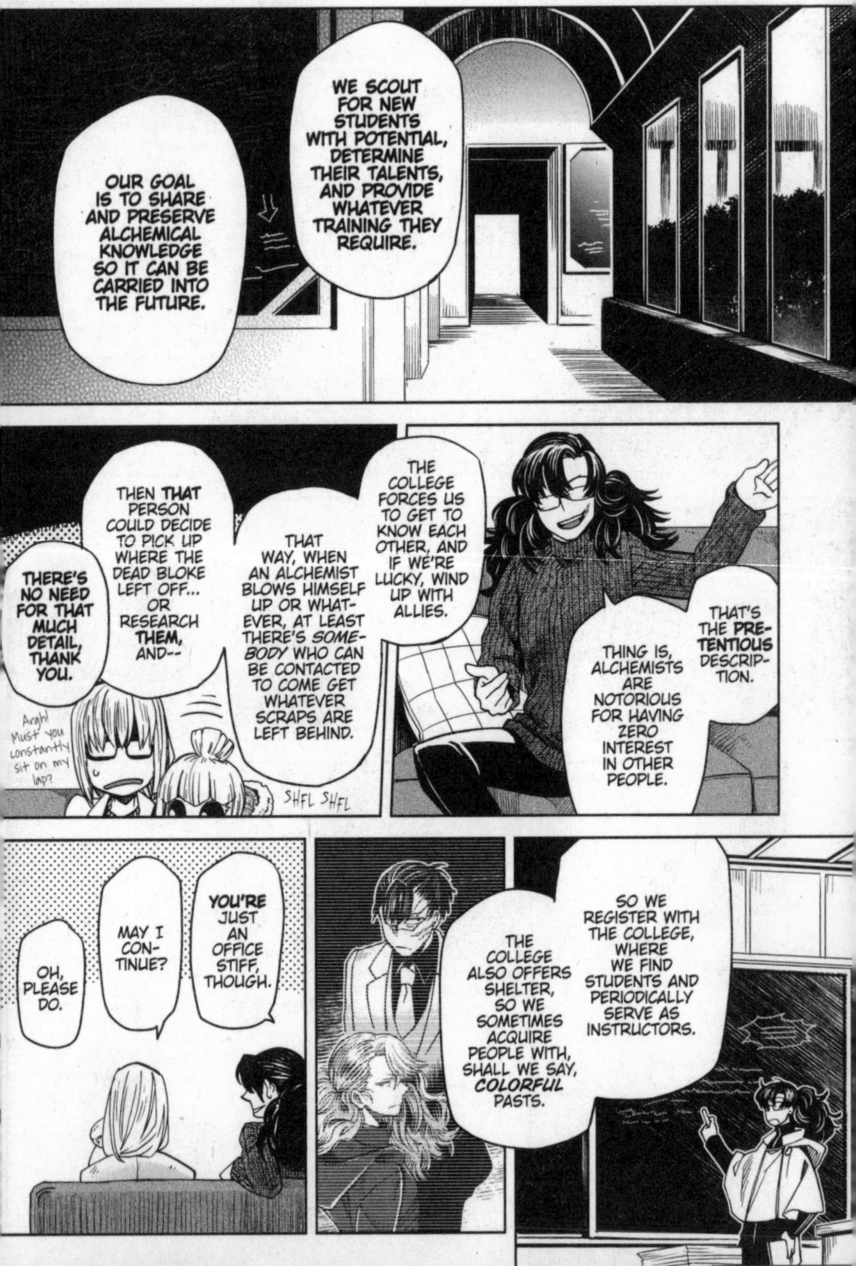
WE SCOUT FOR NEW STUDENTS WITH POTENTIAL, DETERMINE THEIR TALENTS, AND PROVIDE WHATEVER TRAINING THEY REQUIRE.
OUR GOAL IS TO SHARE AND PRESERVE ALCHEMICAL KNOWLEDGE SO IT CAN BE CARRIED INTO THE FUTURE.
THAT'S THE **PRETENTIOUS** DESCRIPTION.
THING IS, ALCHEMISTS ARE NOTORIOUS FOR HAVING ZERO INTEREST IN OTHER PEOPLE.
THE COLLEGE FORCES US TO GET TO KNOW EACH OTHER, AND IF WE'RE LUCKY, WIND UP WITH ALLIES.
THAT WAY, WHEN AN ALCHEMIST BLOWS HIMSELF UP OR WHAT-EVER, AT LEAST THERE'S *SOME-BODY* WHO CAN BE CONTACTED TO COME GET WHATEVER SCRAPS ARE LEFT BEHIND.
THEN **THAT** PERSON COULD DECIDE TO PICK UP WHERE THE DEAD BLOKE LEFT OFF... OR RESEARCH **THEM**, AND--
THERE'S NO NEED FOR THAT MUCH DETAIL, THANK YOU.
Argh! Must you constantly sit on my lap?
SHFL SHFL
SO WE REGISTER WITH THE COLLEGE, WHERE WE FIND STUDENTS AND PERIODICALLY SERVE AS INSTRUCTORS.
THE COLLEGE ALSO OFFERS SHELTER, SO WE SOMETIMES ACQUIRE PEOPLE WITH, SHALL WE SAY, ***COLORFUL*** PASTS.
YOU'RE JUST AN OFFICE STIFF, THOUGH.
MAY I CON-TINUE?
OH, PLEASE DO.

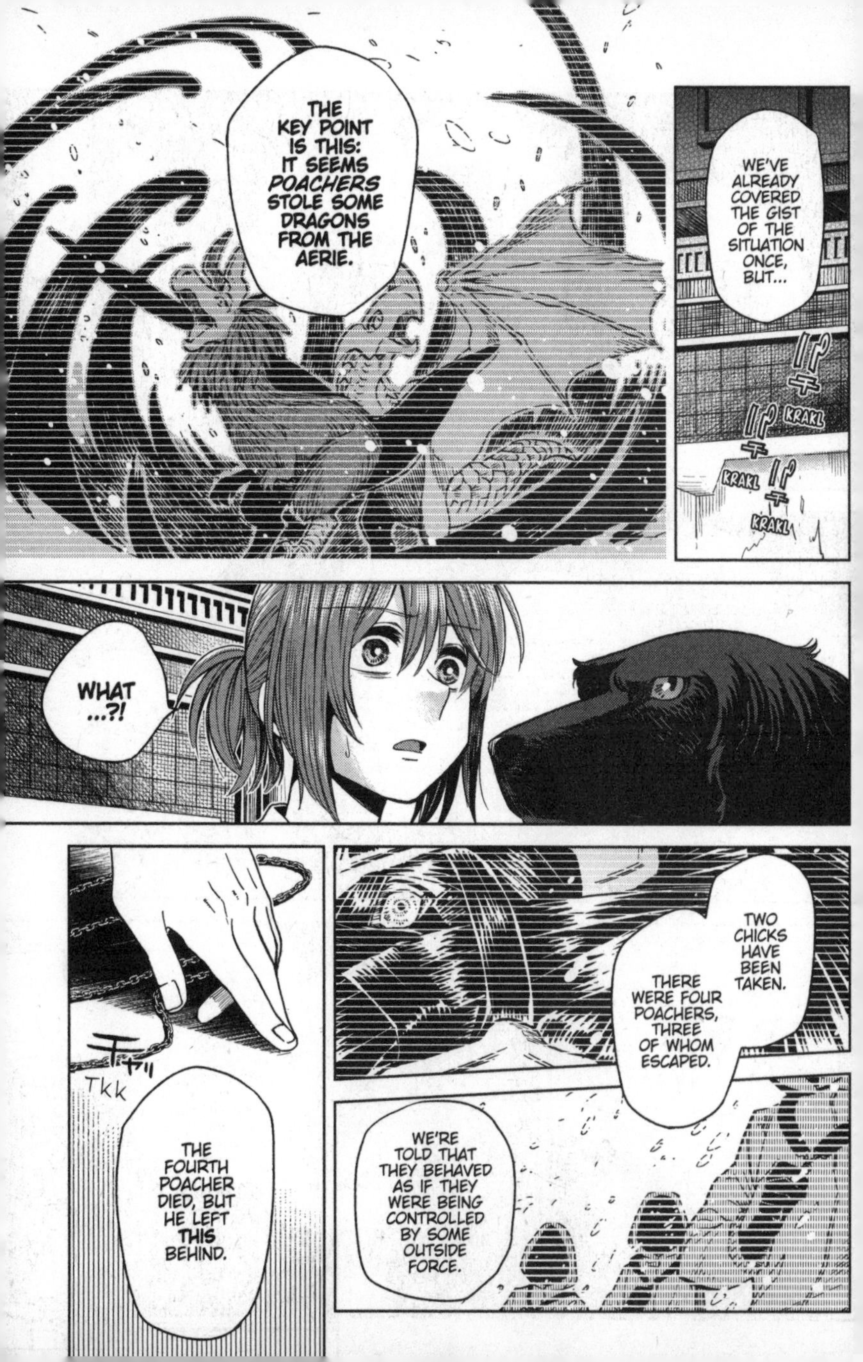
WE'VE ALREADY COVERED THE GIST OF THE SITUATION ONCE, BUT...
KRAKL
KRAKL
KRAKL
THE KEY POINT IS THIS: IT SEEMS *POACHERS* STOLE SOME DRAGONS FROM THE AERIE.
WHAT ...?!
TWO CHICKS HAVE BEEN TAKEN.
THERE WERE FOUR POACHERS, THREE OF WHOM ESCAPED.
WE'RE TOLD THAT THEY BEHAVED AS IF THEY WERE BEING CONTROLLED BY SOME OUTSIDE FORCE.
Tkk
THE FOURTH POACHER DIED, BUT HE LEFT **THIS** BEHIND.

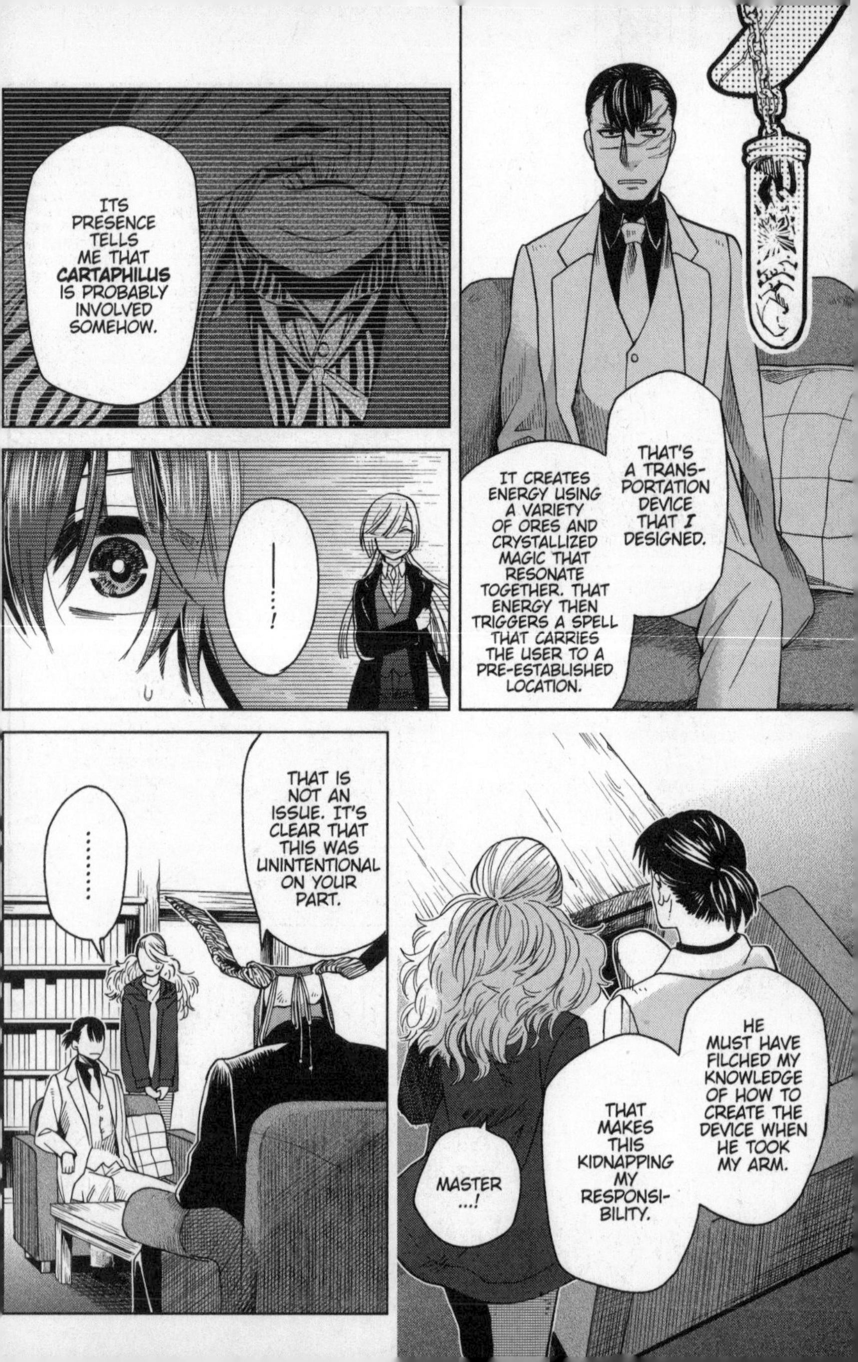
THAT'S A TRANS-PORTATION DEVICE THAT I DESIGNED.
IT CREATES ENERGY USING A VARIETY OF ORES AND CRYSTALLIZED MAGIC THAT RESONATE TOGETHER. THAT ENERGY THEN TRIGGERS A SPELL THAT CARRIES THE USER TO A PRE-ESTABLISHED LOCATION.
ITS PRESENCE TELLS ME THAT **CARTAPHILUS** IS PROBABLY INVOLVED SOMEHOW.
......!
HE MUST HAVE FILCHED MY KNOWLEDGE OF HOW TO CREATE THE DEVICE WHEN HE TOOK MY ARM.
THAT MAKES THIS KIDNAPPING MY RESPONSI-BILITY.
MASTER ...!
THAT IS NOT AN ISSUE. IT'S CLEAR THAT THIS WAS UNINTENTIONAL ON YOUR PART.
......

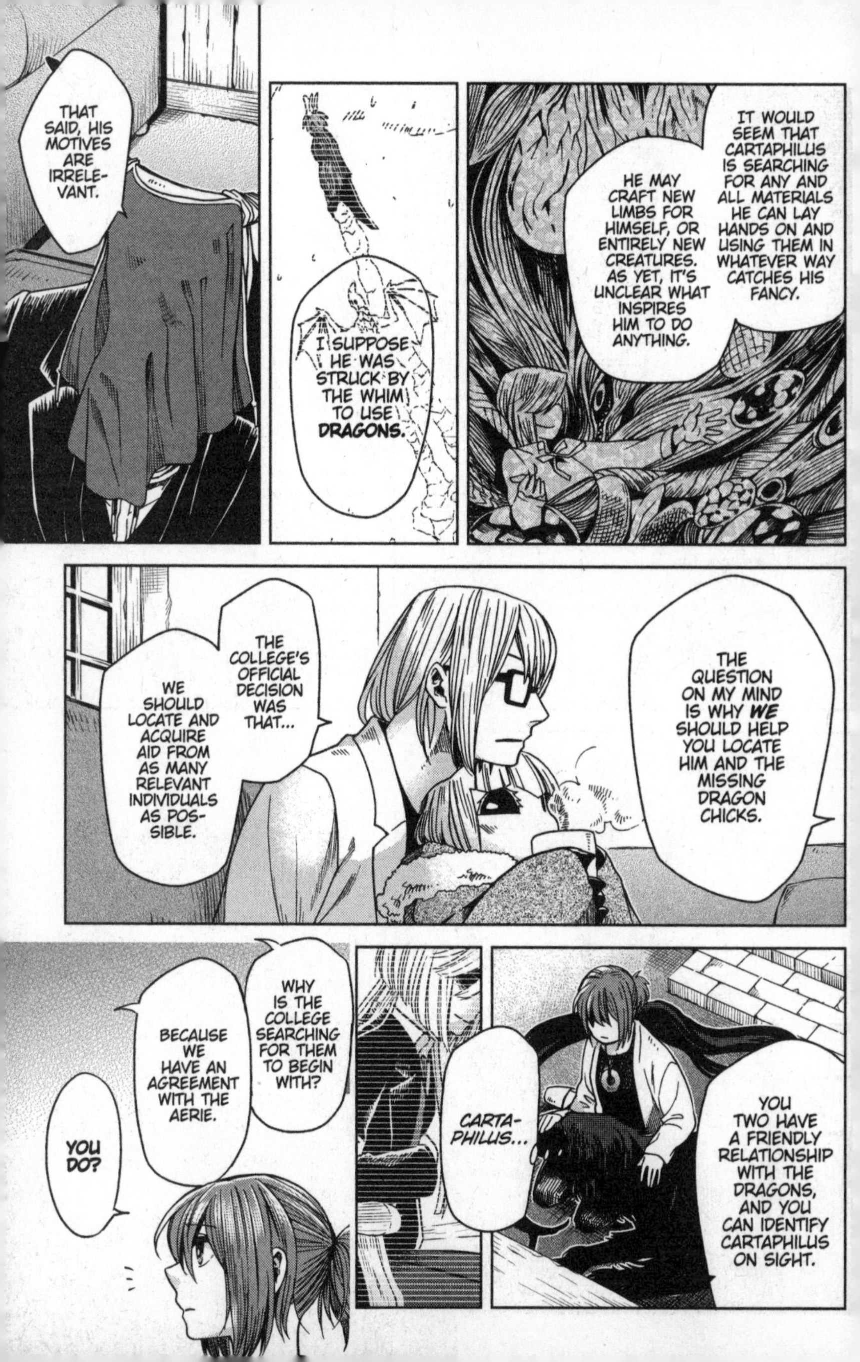
IT WOULD SEEM THAT CARTAPHILUS IS SEARCHING FOR ANY AND ALL MATERIALS HE CAN LAY HANDS ON AND USING THEM IN WHATEVER WAY CATCHES HIS FANCY.
HE MAY CRAFT NEW LIMBS FOR HIMSELF, OR ENTIRELY NEW CREATURES. AS YET, IT'S UNCLEAR WHAT INSPIRES HIM TO DO ANYTHING.
I SUPPOSE HE WAS STRUCK BY THE WHIM TO USE **DRAGONS.**
THAT SAID, HIS MOTIVES ARE IRRELE-VANT.
THE QUESTION ON MY MIND IS WHY ***WE*** SHOULD HELP YOU LOCATE HIM AND THE MISSING DRAGON CHICKS.
THE COLLEGE'S OFFICIAL DECISION WAS THAT...
WE SHOULD LOCATE AND ACQUIRE AID FROM AS MANY RELEVANT INDIVIDUALS AS POS-SIBLE.
YOU TWO HAVE A FRIENDLY RELATIONSHIP WITH THE DRAGONS, AND YOU CAN IDENTIFY CARTAPHILUS ON SIGHT.
CARTA-PHILUS...
WHY IS THE COLLEGE SEARCHING FOR THEM TO BEGIN WITH?
BECAUSE WE HAVE AN AGREEMENT WITH THE AERIE.
YOU DO?

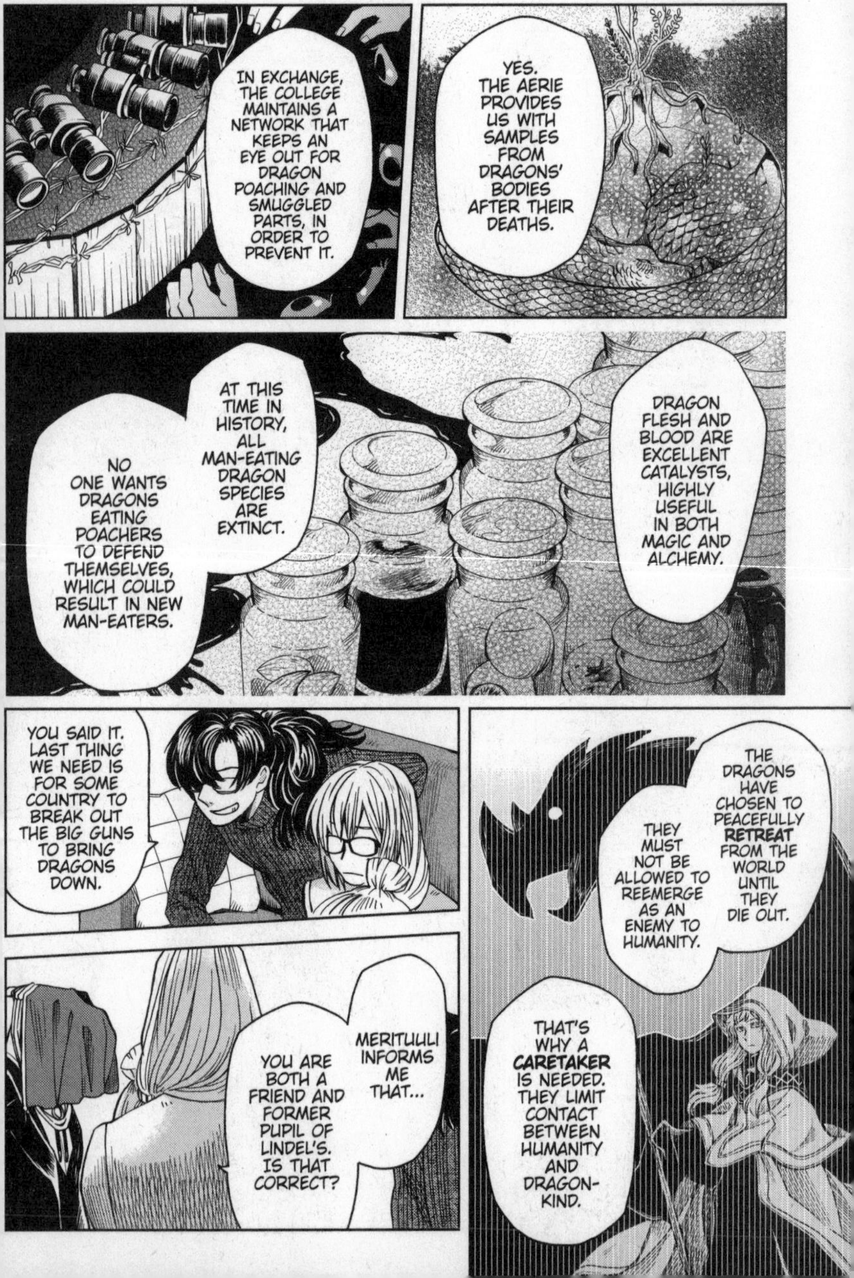
YES. THE AERIE PROVIDES US WITH SAMPLES FROM DRAGONS' BODIES AFTER THEIR DEATHS.
IN EXCHANGE, THE COLLEGE MAINTAINS A NETWORK THAT KEEPS AN EYE OUT FOR DRAGON POACHING AND SMUGGLED PARTS, IN ORDER TO PREVENT IT.
DRAGON FLESH AND BLOOD ARE EXCELLENT CATALYSTS, HIGHLY USEFUL IN BOTH MAGIC AND ALCHEMY.
AT THIS TIME IN HISTORY, ALL MAN-EATING DRAGON SPECIES ARE EXTINCT.
NO ONE WANTS DRAGONS EATING POACHERS TO DEFEND THEMSELVES, WHICH COULD RESULT IN NEW MAN-EATERS.
THE DRAGONS HAVE CHOSEN TO PEACEFULLY **RETREAT** FROM THE WORLD UNTIL THEY DIE OUT.
THEY MUST NOT BE ALLOWED TO REEMERGE AS AN ENEMY TO HUMANITY.
THAT'S WHY A **CARETAKER** IS NEEDED. THEY LIMIT CONTACT BETWEEN HUMANITY AND DRAGON-KIND.
YOU SAID IT. LAST THING WE NEED IS FOR SOME COUNTRY TO BREAK OUT THE BIG GUNS TO BRING DRAGONS DOWN.
MERITUULI INFORMS ME THAT...
YOU ARE BOTH A FRIEND AND FORMER PUPIL OF LINDEL'S. IS THAT CORRECT?

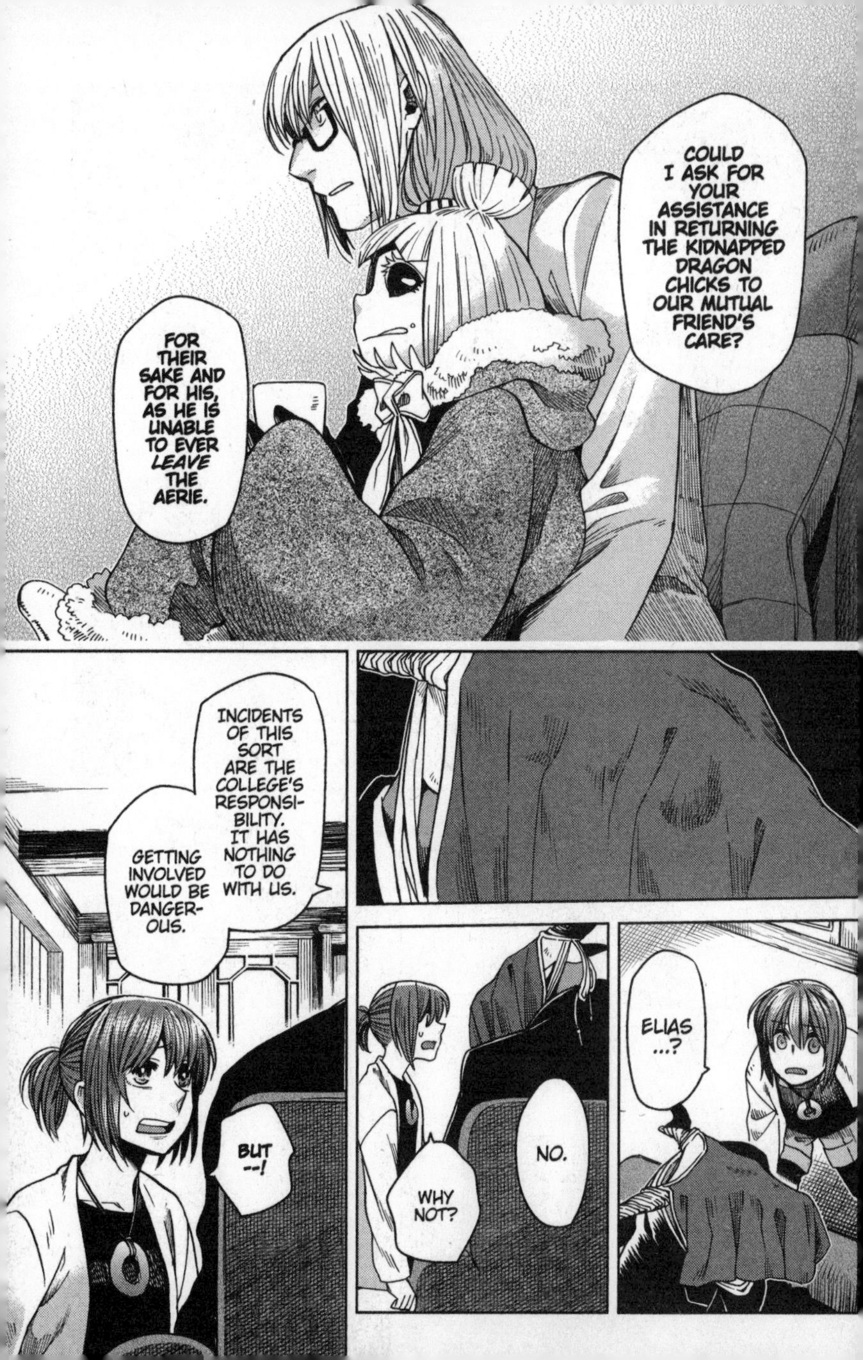
COULD I ASK FOR YOUR ASSISTANCE IN RETURNING THE KIDNAPPED DRAGON CHICKS TO OUR MUTUAL FRIEND'S CARE?
FOR THEIR SAKE AND FOR HIS, AS HE IS UNABLE TO EVER *LEAVE* THE AERIE.
ELIAS ...?
NO.
WHY NOT?
INCIDENTS OF THIS SORT ARE THE COLLEGE'S RESPONSI-BILITY. IT HAS NOTHING TO DO WITH US.
GETTING INVOLVED WOULD BE DANGER-OUS.
BUT --!

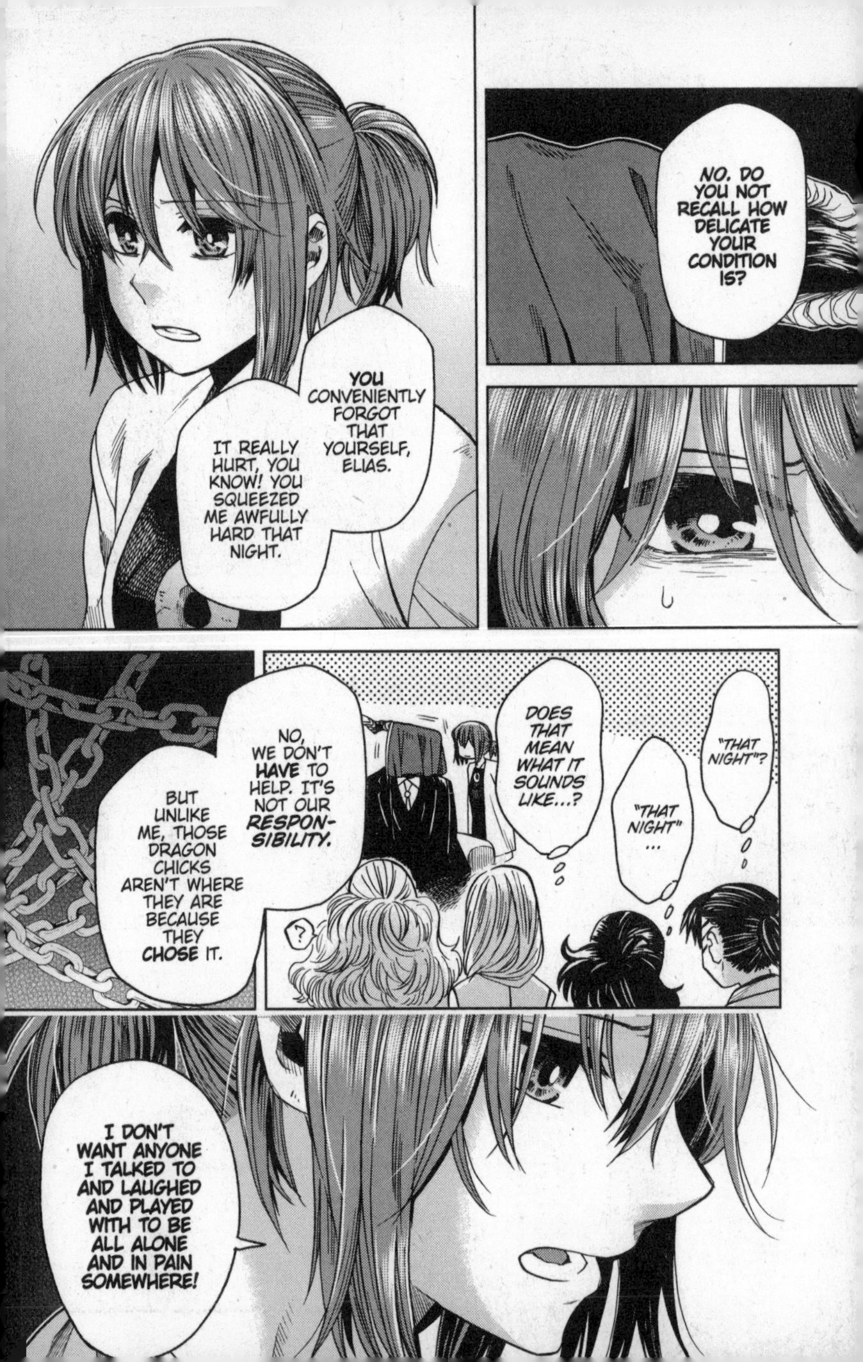
NO. DO YOU NOT RECALL HOW DELICATE YOUR CONDITION IS?
YOU CONVENIENTLY FORGOT THAT YOURSELF, ELIAS.
IT REALLY HURT, YOU KNOW! YOU SQUEEZED ME AWFULLY HARD THAT NIGHT.
"THAT NIGHT"?
"THAT NIGHT" ...
DOES THAT MEAN WHAT IT SOUNDS LIKE...?
NO, WE DON'T HAVE TO HELP. IT'S NOT OUR RESPONSIBILITY.
?
BUT UNLIKE ME, THOSE DRAGON CHICKS AREN'T WHERE THEY ARE BECAUSE THEY CHOSE IT.
I DON'T WANT ANYONE I TALKED TO AND LAUGHED AND PLAYED WITH TO BE ALL ALONE AND IN PAIN SOMEWHERE!

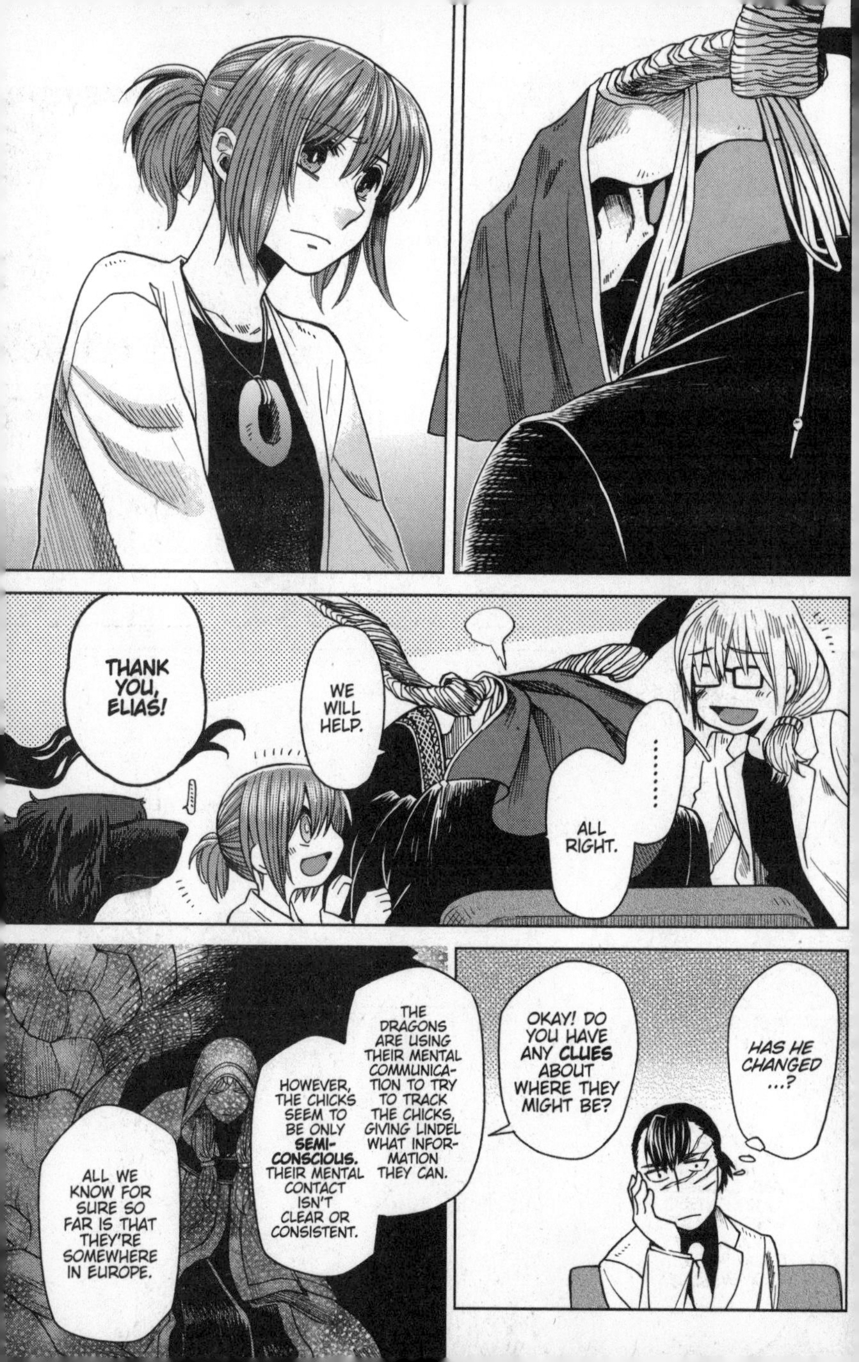
......
ALL RIGHT.
WE WILL HELP.
THANK YOU, ELIAS!
HAS HE CHANGED ...?
OKAY! DO YOU HAVE ANY CLUES ABOUT WHERE THEY MIGHT BE?
THE DRAGONS ARE USING THEIR MENTAL COMMUNICATION TO TRY TO TRACK THE CHICKS, GIVING LINDEL WHAT INFORMATION THEY CAN.
HOWEVER, THE CHICKS SEEM TO BE ONLY SEMI-CONSCIOUS. THEIR MENTAL CONTACT ISN'T CLEAR OR CONSISTENT.
ALL WE KNOW FOR SURE SO FAR IS THAT THEY'RE SOMEWHERE IN EUROPE.

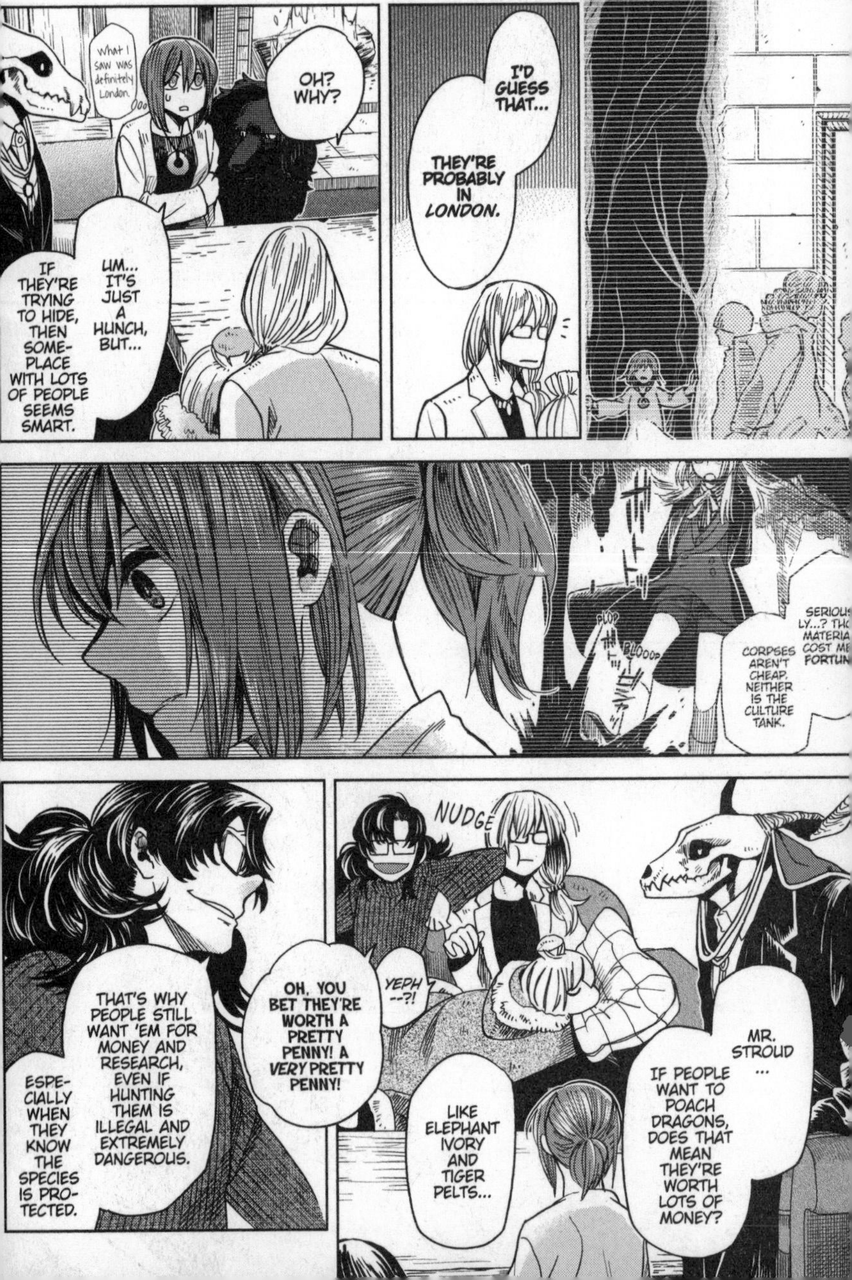
I'D GUESS THAT...
THEY'RE PROBABLY IN LONDON.
OH? WHY?
What I saw was definitely London.
UM... IT'S JUST A HUNCH, BUT...
IF THEY'RE TRYING TO HIDE, THEN SOMEPLACE WITH LOTS OF PEOPLE SEEMS SMART.
SERIOUSLY...? THO MATERIA COST ME FORTUN
CORPSES AREN'T CHEAP. NEITHER IS THE CULTURE TANK.
PLOP
BLOOOP
NUDGE
MR. STROUD ...
IF PEOPLE WANT TO POACH DRAGONS, DOES THAT MEAN THEY'RE WORTH LOTS OF MONEY?
LIKE ELEPHANT IVORY AND TIGER PELTS...
YEPH--?!
OH, YOU BET THEY'RE WORTH A PRETTY PENNY! A *VERY* PRETTY PENNY!
THAT'S WHY PEOPLE STILL WANT 'EM FOR MONEY AND RESEARCH, EVEN IF HUNTING THEM IS ILLEGAL AND EXTREMELY DANGEROUS.
ESPECIALLY WHEN THEY KNOW THE SPECIES IS PROTECTED.

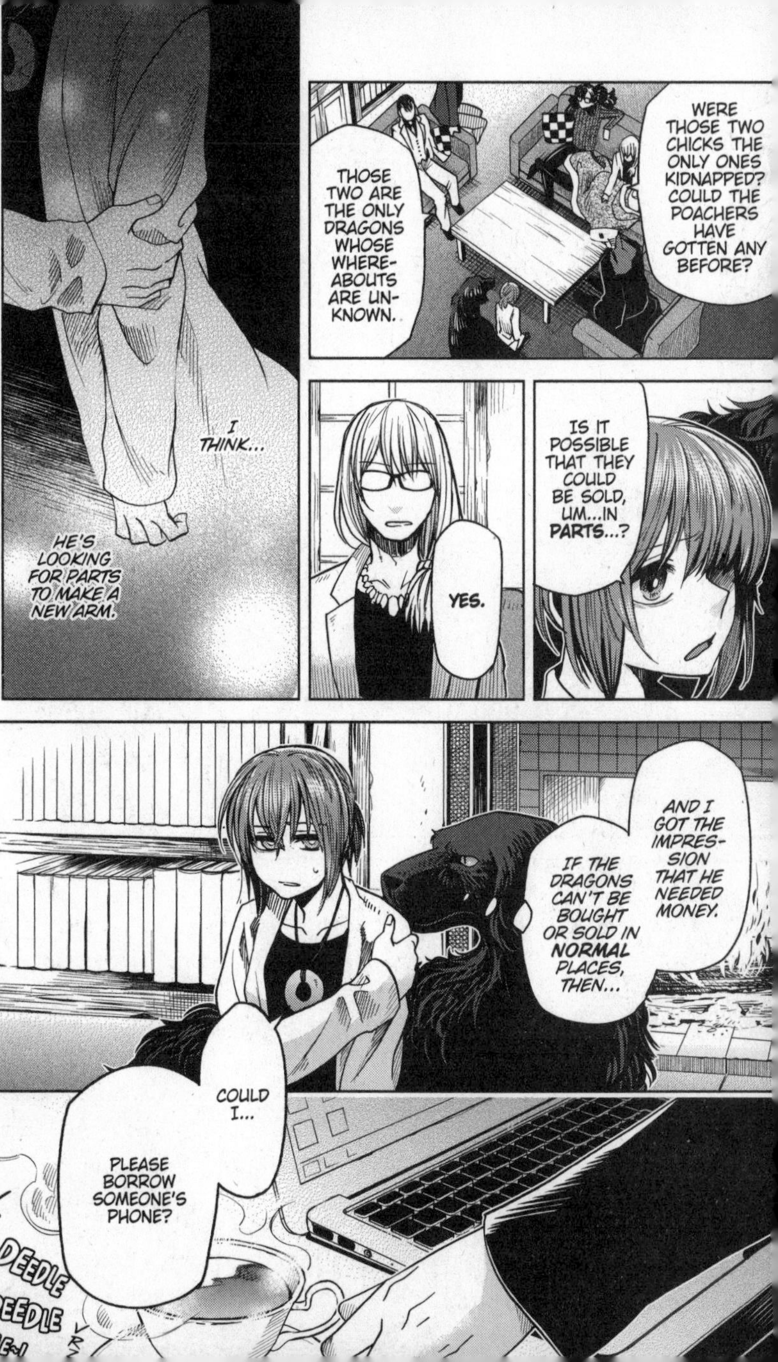
WERE THOSE TWO CHICKS THE ONLY ONES KIDNAPPED? COULD THE POACHERS HAVE GOTTEN ANY BEFORE?
THOSE TWO ARE THE ONLY DRAGONS WHOSE WHERE-ABOUTS ARE UN-KNOWN.
IS IT POSSIBLE THAT THEY COULD BE SOLD, UM...IN PARTS...?
YES.
I THINK...
HE'S LOOKING FOR PARTS TO MAKE A NEW ARM.
AND I GOT THE IMPRES-SION THAT HE NEEDED MONEY.
IF THE DRAGONS CAN'T BE BOUGHT OR SOLD IN NORMAL PLACES, THEN...
COULD I...
PLEASE BORROW SOMEONE'S PHONE?
VRRRZZZ
DEEDLE
DEEDLE
DEEDLE~!
VRZZ

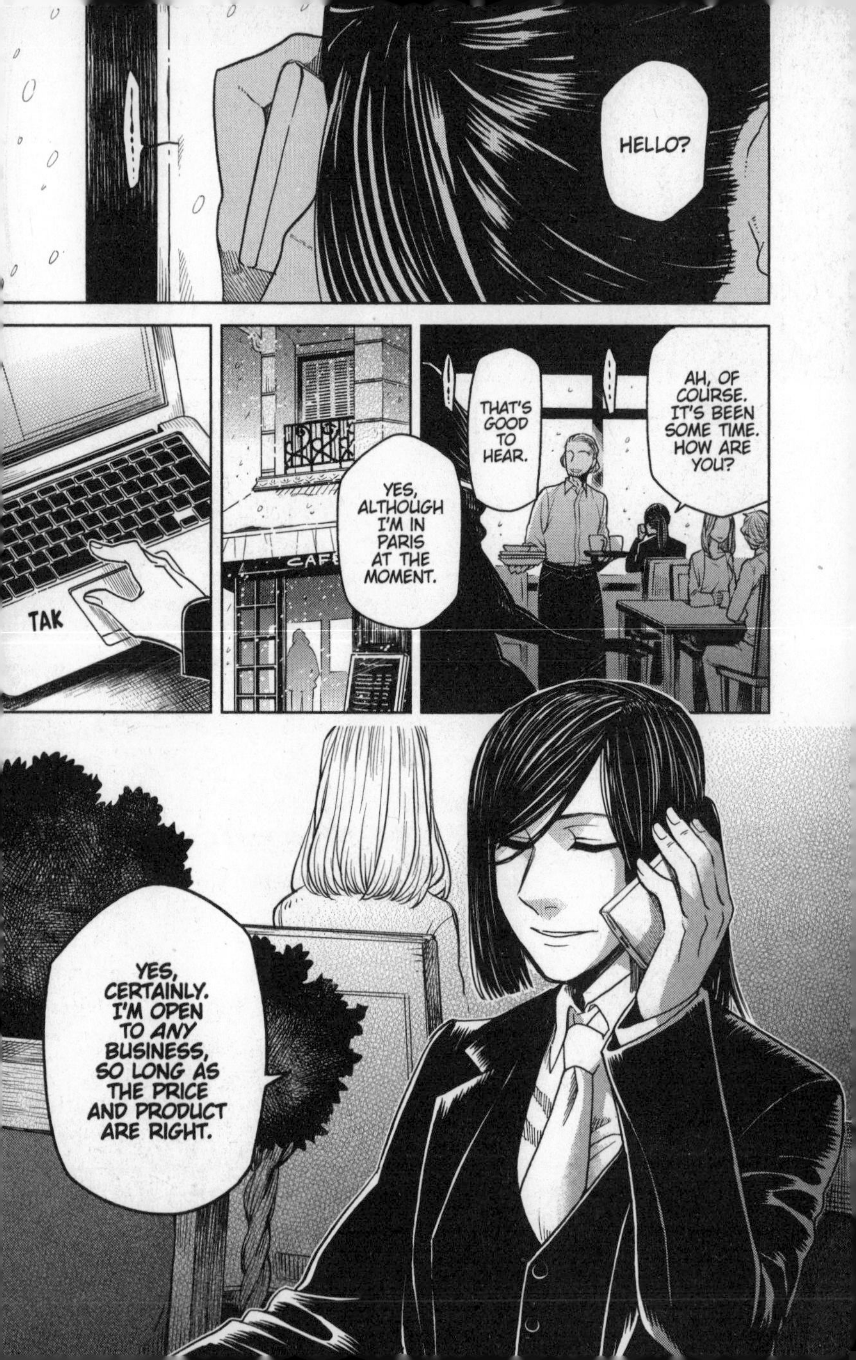
HELLO?
AH, OF COURSE. IT'S BEEN SOME TIME. HOW ARE YOU?
THAT'S GOOD TO HEAR.
YES, ALTHOUGH I'M IN PARIS AT THE MOMENT.
TAK
YES, CERTAINLY. I'M OPEN TO *ANY* BUSINESS, SO LONG AS THE PRICE AND PRODUCT ARE RIGHT.

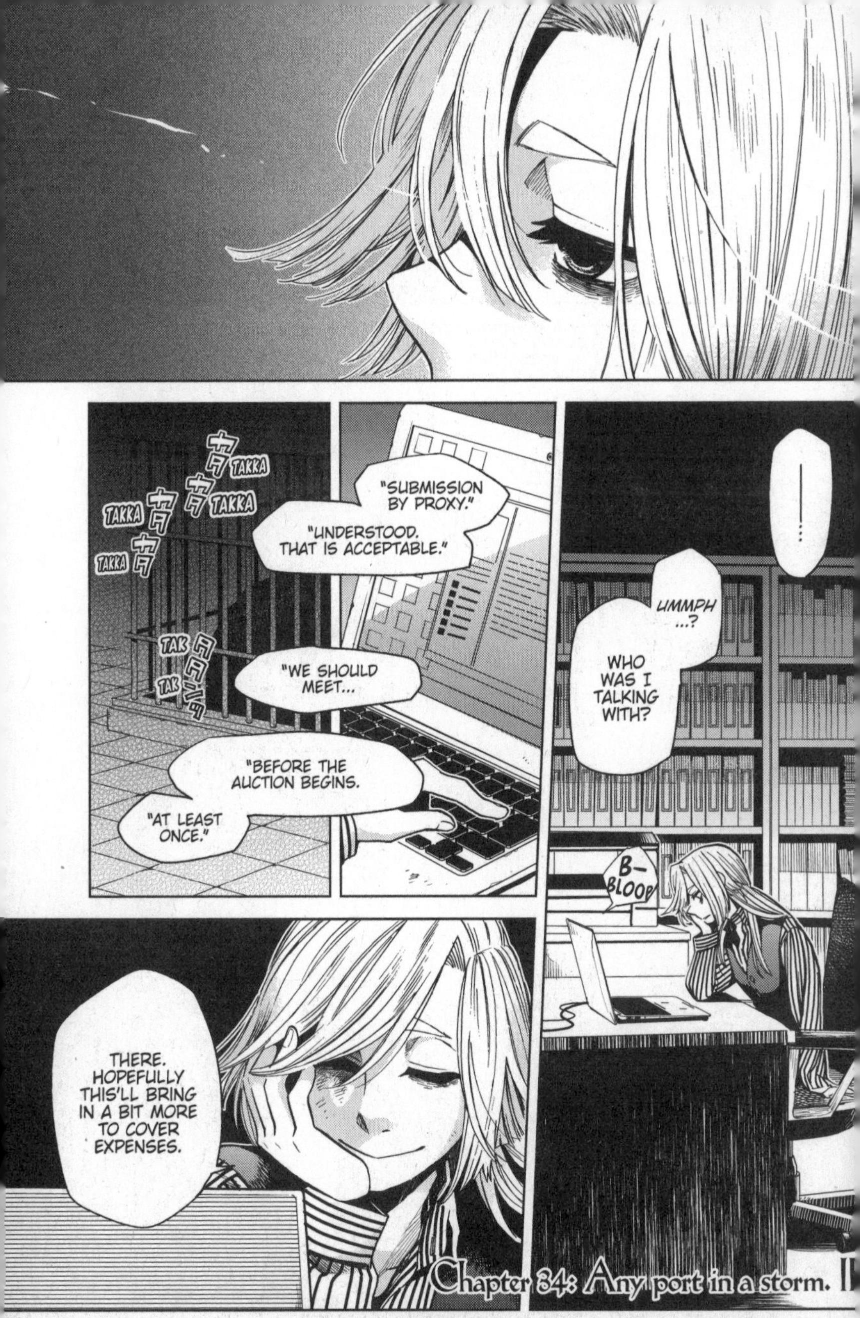
......
UMMPH ...?
WHO WAS I TALKING WITH?
B-BLOOP
"SUBMISSION BY PROXY."
"UNDERSTOOD. THAT IS ACCEPTABLE."
"WE SHOULD MEET...
"BEFORE THE AUCTION BEGINS.
"AT LEAST ONCE."
TAKKA TAKKA TAKKA TAKKA
TAK TAK
THERE. HOPEFULLY THIS'LL BRING IN A BIT MORE TO COVER EXPENSES.
Chapter 34: Any port in a storm. II

Chapter 34: Any port in a storm. II

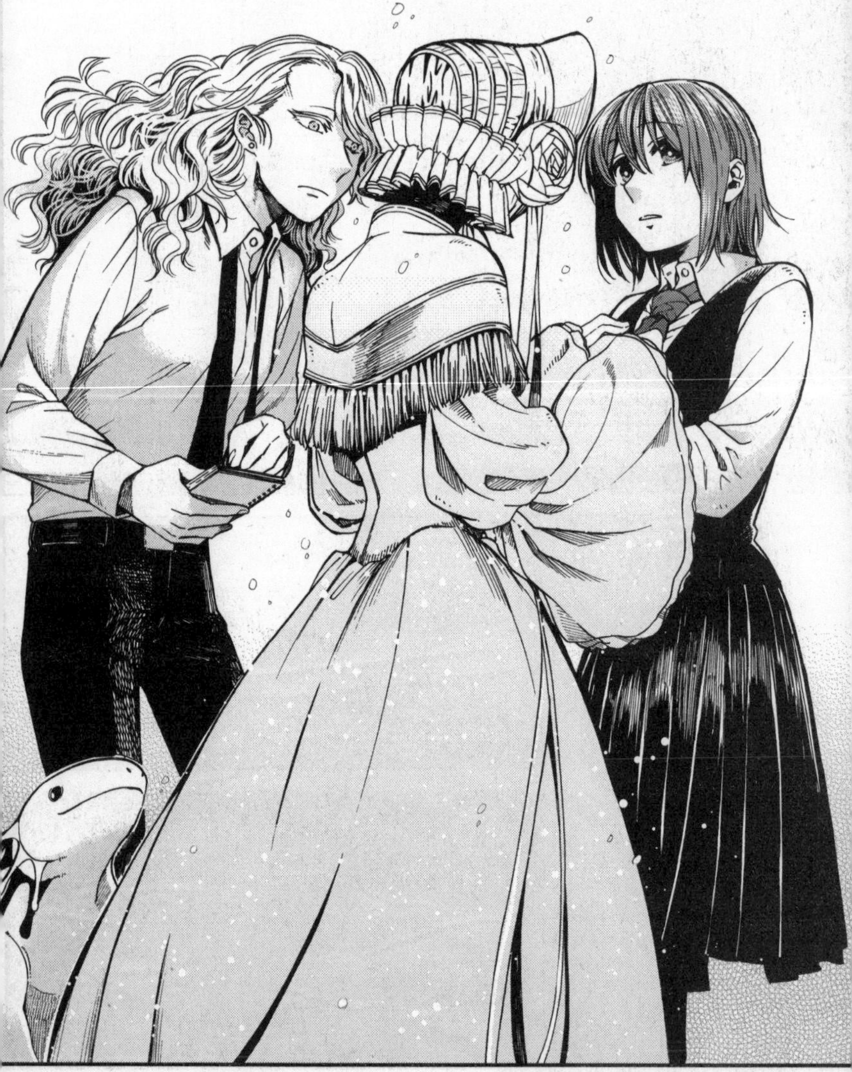

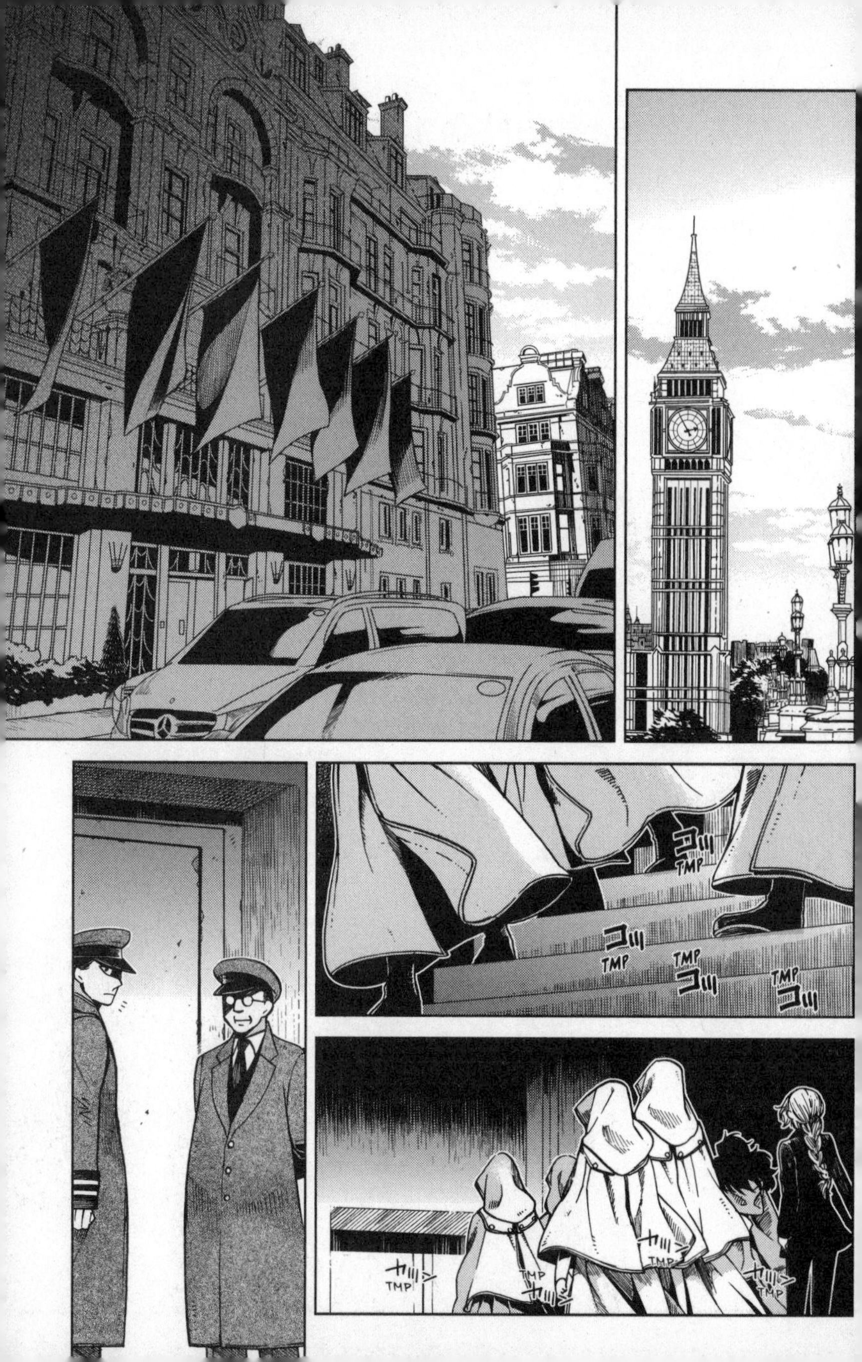
コッ
TMP
コッ
TMP
TMP
コッ
TMP
コッ
TMP
TMP
TMP
TMP

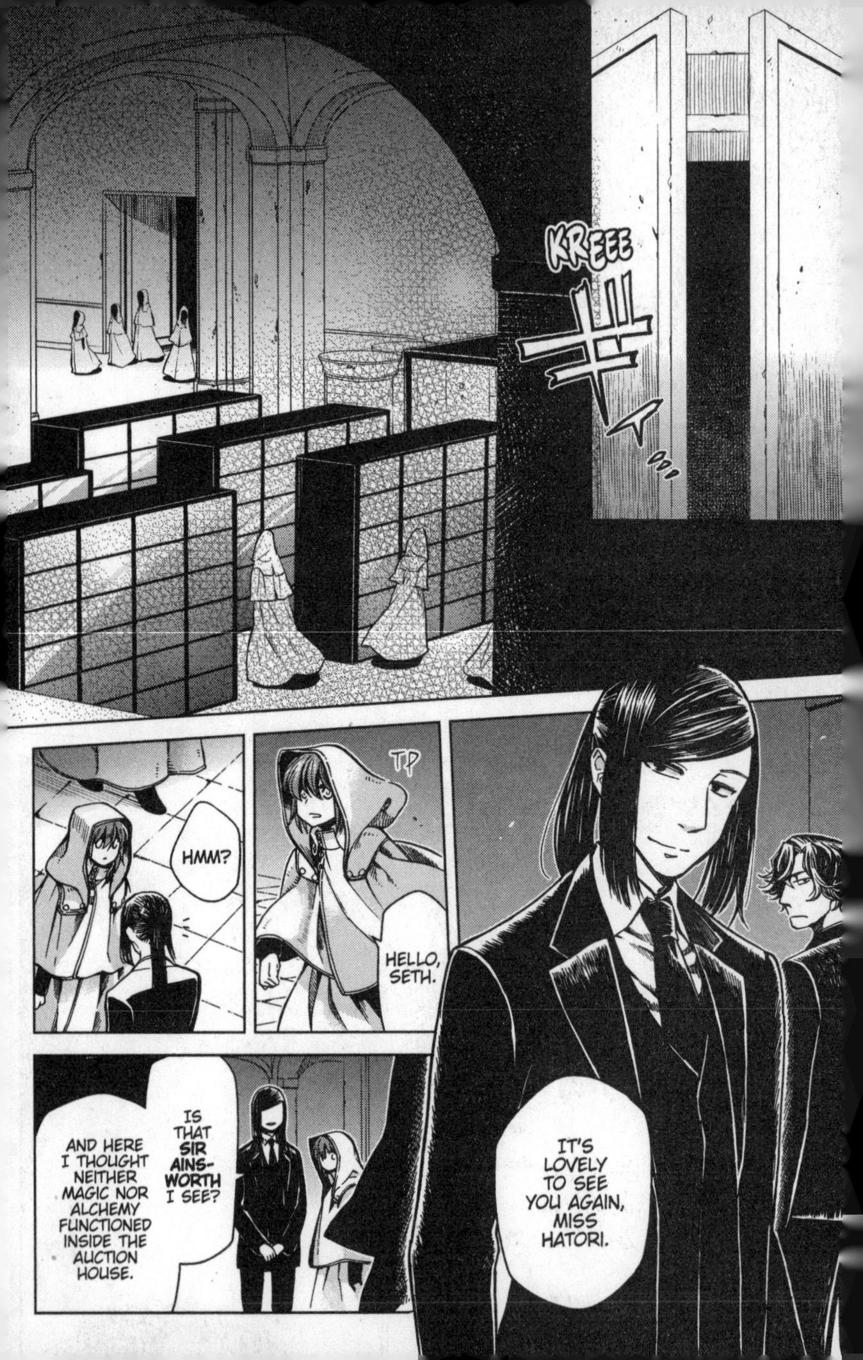
KREEE
ギィ…
IT'S LOVELY TO SEE YOU AGAIN, MISS HATORI.
TP
HELLO, SETH.
HMM?
IS THAT SIR AINSWORTH I SEE?
AND HERE I THOUGHT NEITHER MAGIC NOR ALCHEMY FUNCTIONED INSIDE THE AUCTION HOUSE.

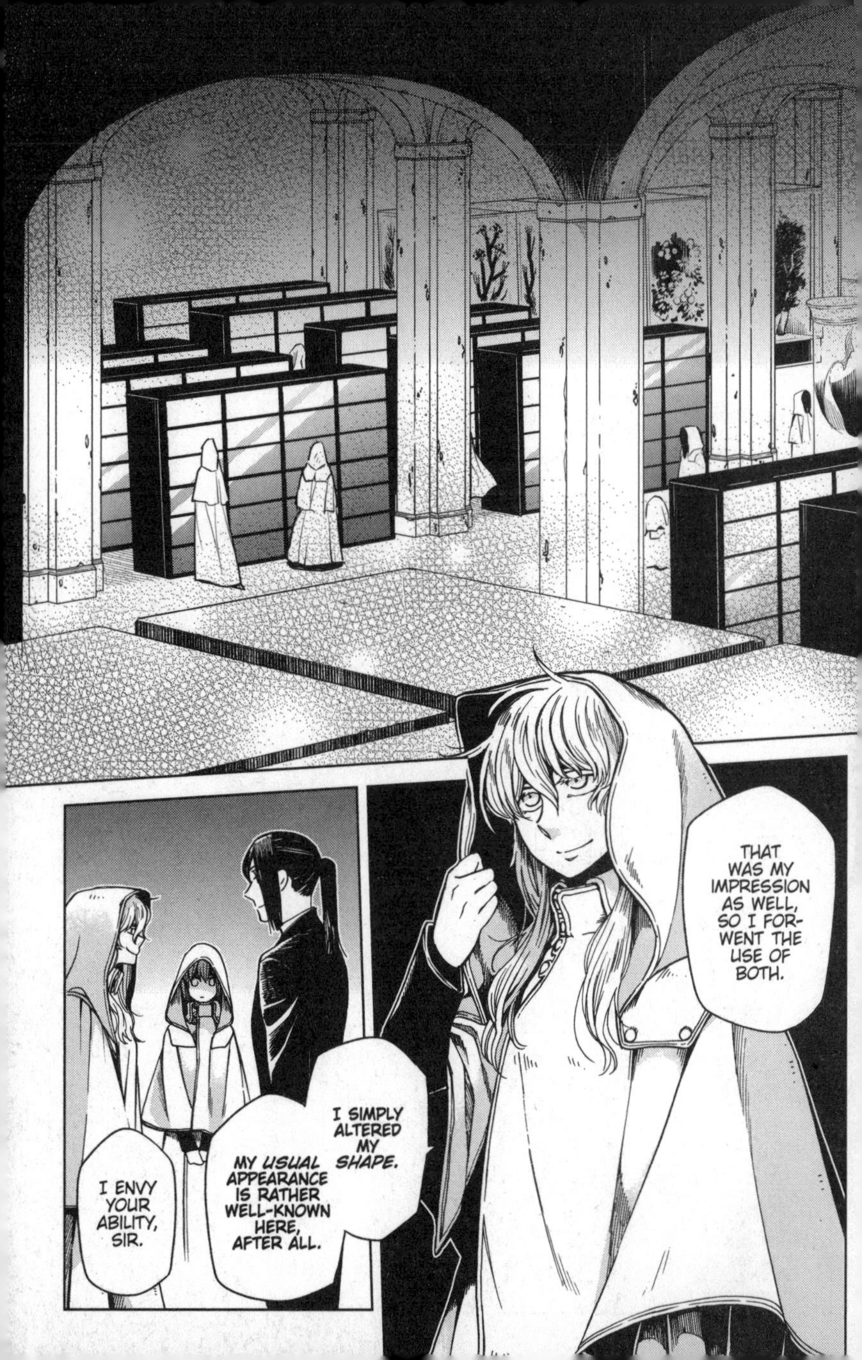
THAT WAS MY IMPRESSION AS WELL, SO I FOR-WENT THE USE OF BOTH.
I SIMPLY ALTERED MY *SHAPE*.
MY *USUAL* APPEARANCE IS RATHER WELL-KNOWN HERE, AFTER ALL.
I ENVY YOUR ABILITY, SIR.

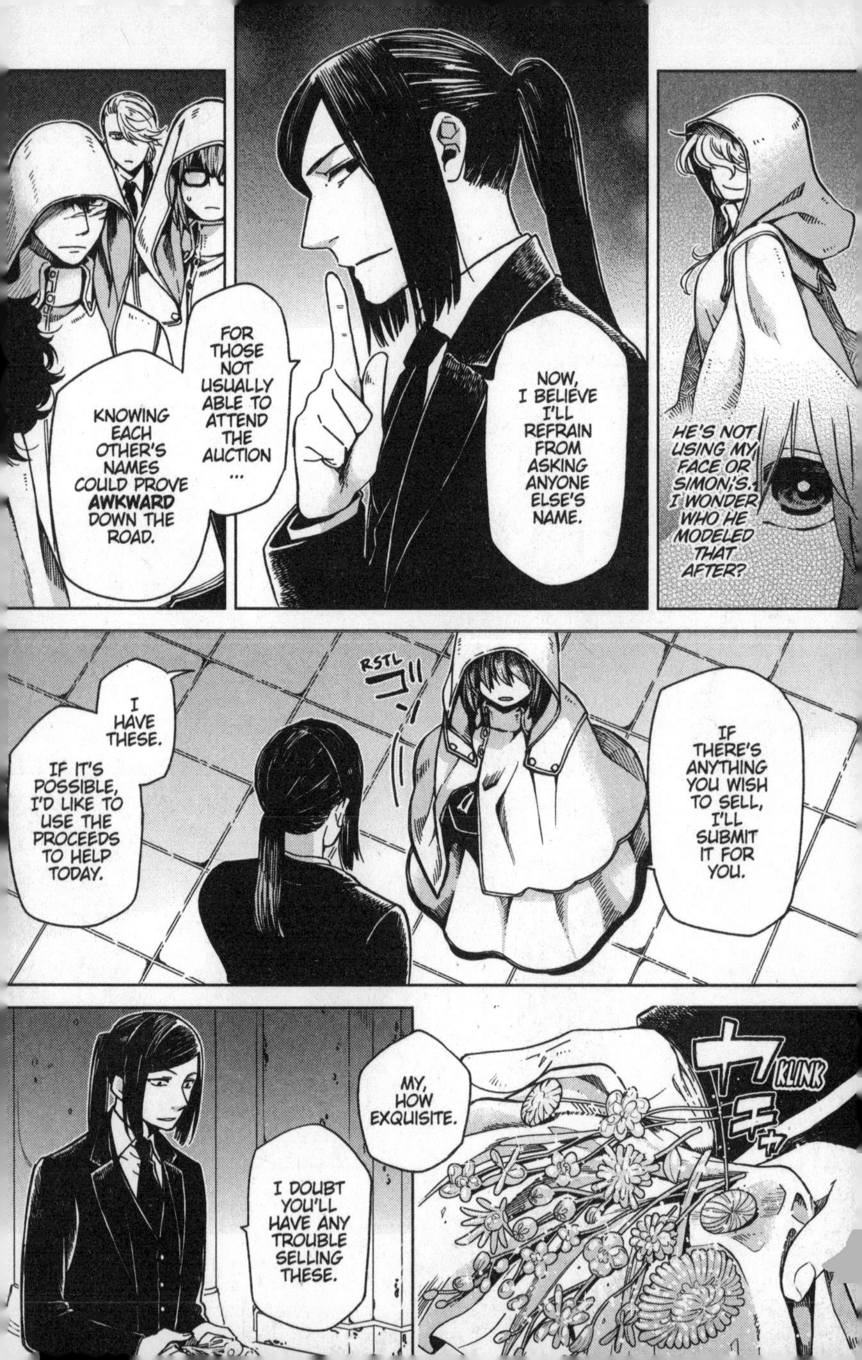
HE'S NOT USING MY FACE OR SIMON'S. I WONDER WHO HE MODELED THAT AFTER?
NOW, I BELIEVE I'LL REFRAIN FROM ASKING ANYONE ELSE'S NAME.
FOR THOSE NOT USUALLY ABLE TO ATTEND THE AUCTION ...
KNOWING EACH OTHER'S NAMES COULD PROVE AWKWARD DOWN THE ROAD.
IF THERE'S ANYTHING YOU WISH TO SELL, I'LL SUBMIT IT FOR YOU.
RSTL
I HAVE THESE.
IF IT'S POSSIBLE, I'D LIKE TO USE THE PROCEEDS TO HELP TODAY.
KLINK
MY, HOW EXQUISITE.
I DOUBT YOU'LL HAVE ANY TROUBLE SELLING THESE.

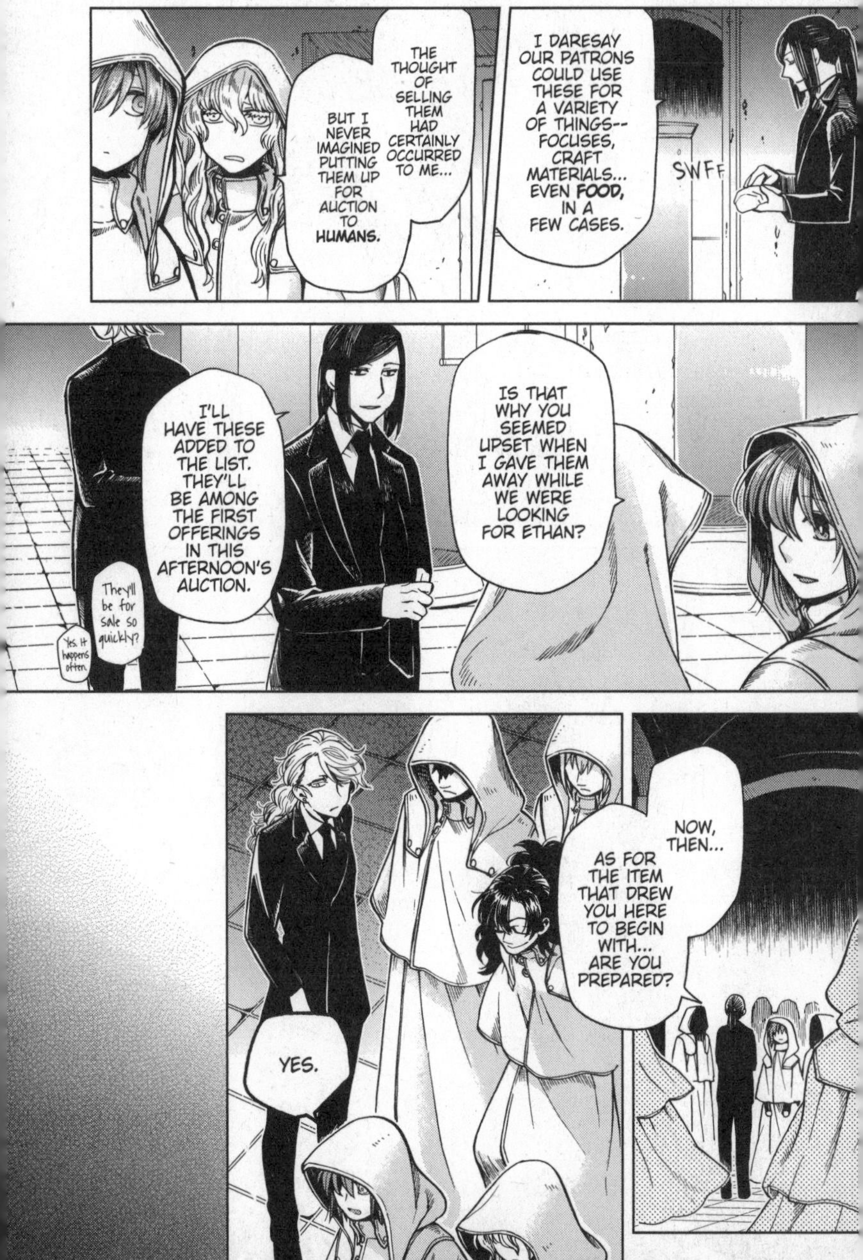
I DARESAY OUR PATRONS COULD USE THESE FOR A VARIETY OF THINGS-- FOCUSES, CRAFT MATERIALS... EVEN **FOOD,** IN A FEW CASES.
SWFF
THE THOUGHT OF SELLING THEM HAD CERTAINLY OCCURRED TO ME...
BUT I NEVER IMAGINED PUTTING THEM UP FOR AUCTION TO **HUMANS.**
IS THAT WHY YOU SEEMED UPSET WHEN I GAVE THEM AWAY WHILE WE WERE LOOKING FOR ETHAN?
I'LL HAVE THESE ADDED TO THE LIST. THEY'LL BE AMONG THE FIRST OFFERINGS IN THIS AFTERNOON'S AUCTION.
They'll be for sale so quickly?
Yes. It happens often.
NOW, THEN...
AS FOR THE ITEM THAT DREW YOU HERE TO BEGIN WITH... ARE YOU PREPARED?
YES.

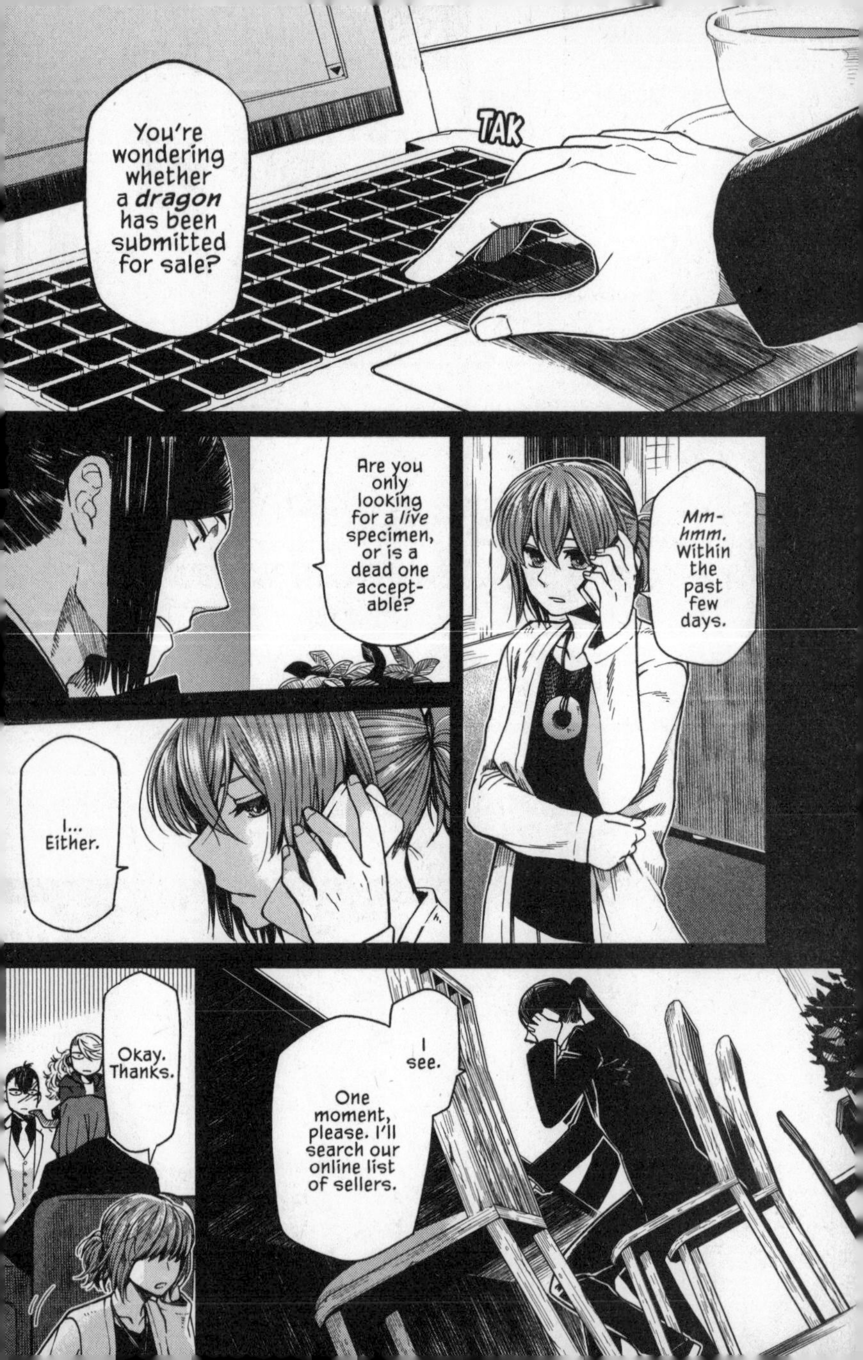
TAK
You're wondering whether a *dragon* has been submitted for sale?
Mm-hmm. Within the past few days.
Are you only looking for a *live* specimen, or is a dead one acceptable?
I... Either.
I see.
One moment, please. I'll search our online list of sellers.
Okay. Thanks.

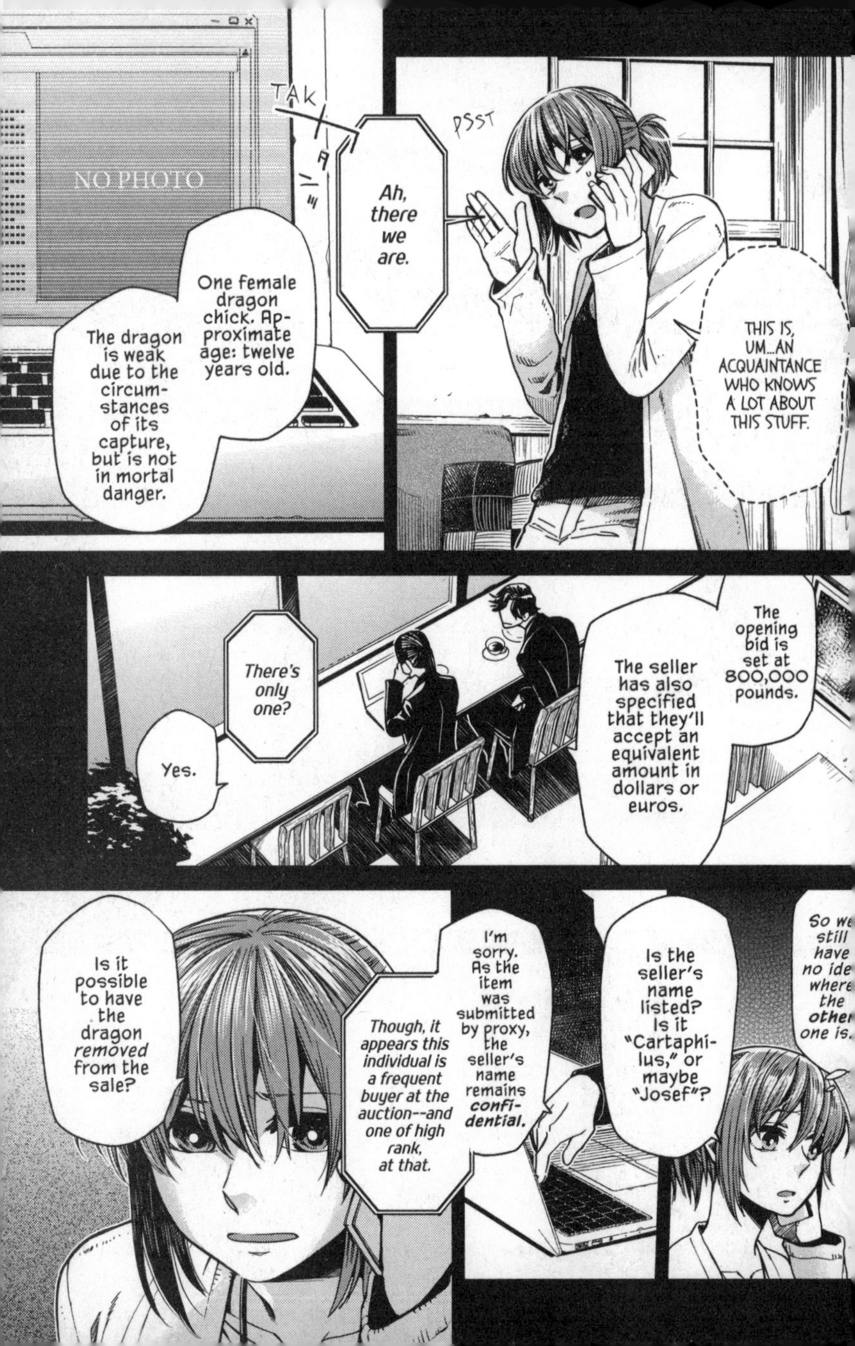
PSST
Ah, there we are.
THIS IS, UM...AN ACQUAINTANCE WHO KNOWS A LOT ABOUT THIS STUFF.
TAK
NO PHOTO
One female dragon chick. Approximate age: twelve years old.
The dragon is weak due to the circumstances of its capture, but is not in mortal danger.
The opening bid is set at 800,000 pounds.
The seller has also specified that they'll accept an equivalent amount in dollars or euros.
There's only one?
Yes.
So we still have no ide where the other one is.
Is the seller's name listed? Is it "Cartaphilus," or maybe "Josef"?
I'm sorry. As the item was submitted by proxy, the seller's name remains *confidential.*
Though, it appears this individual is a frequent buyer at the auction--and one of high rank, at that.
Is it possible to have the dragon *removed* from the sale?

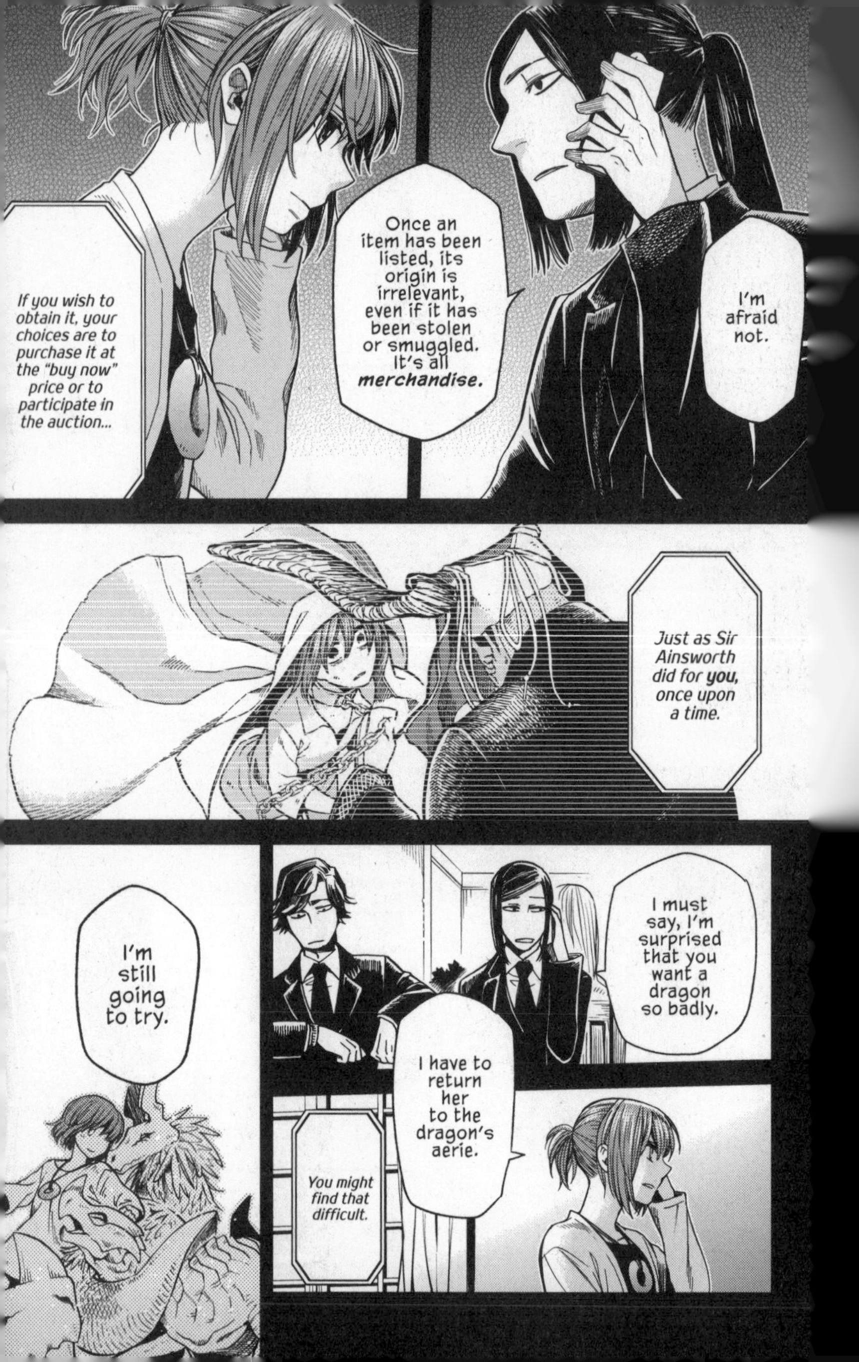
I'm afraid not.
Once an item has been listed, its origin is irrelevant, even if it has been stolen or smuggled. It's all **merchandise.**
If you wish to obtain it, your choices are to purchase it at the "buy now" price or to participate in the auction...
*Just as Sir Ainsworth did for **you**, once upon a time.*
I must say, I'm surprised that you want a dragon so badly.
I have to return her to the dragon's aerie.
You might find that difficult.
I'm still going to try.

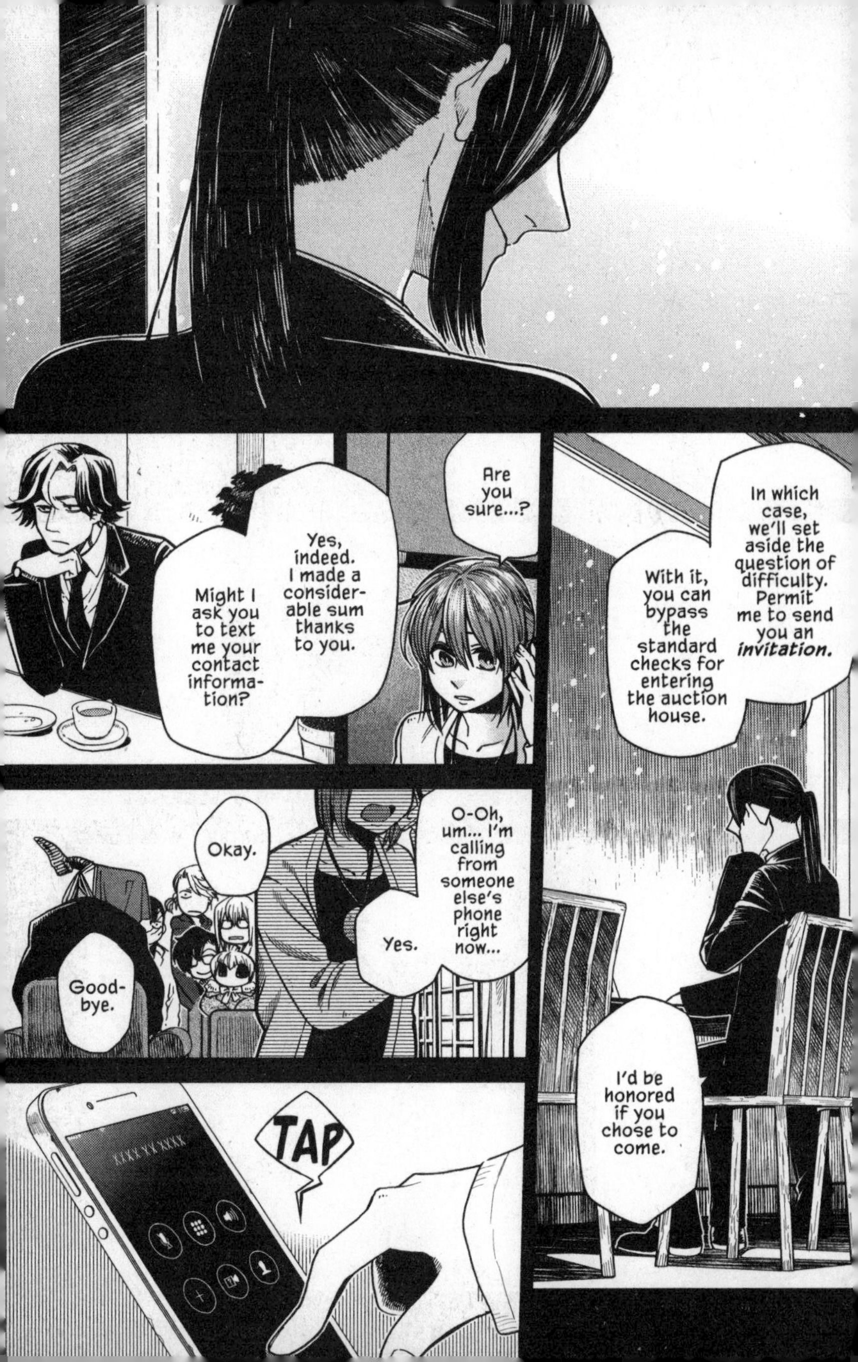

In which case, we'll set aside the question of difficulty. Permit me to send you an *invitation.*
With it, you can bypass the standard checks for entering the auction house.
I'd be honored if you chose to come.
Are you sure...?
Yes, indeed. I made a considerable sum thanks to you.
Might I ask you to text me your contact information?
O-Oh, um... I'm calling from someone else's phone right now...
Okay.
Yes.
Good-bye.
TAP

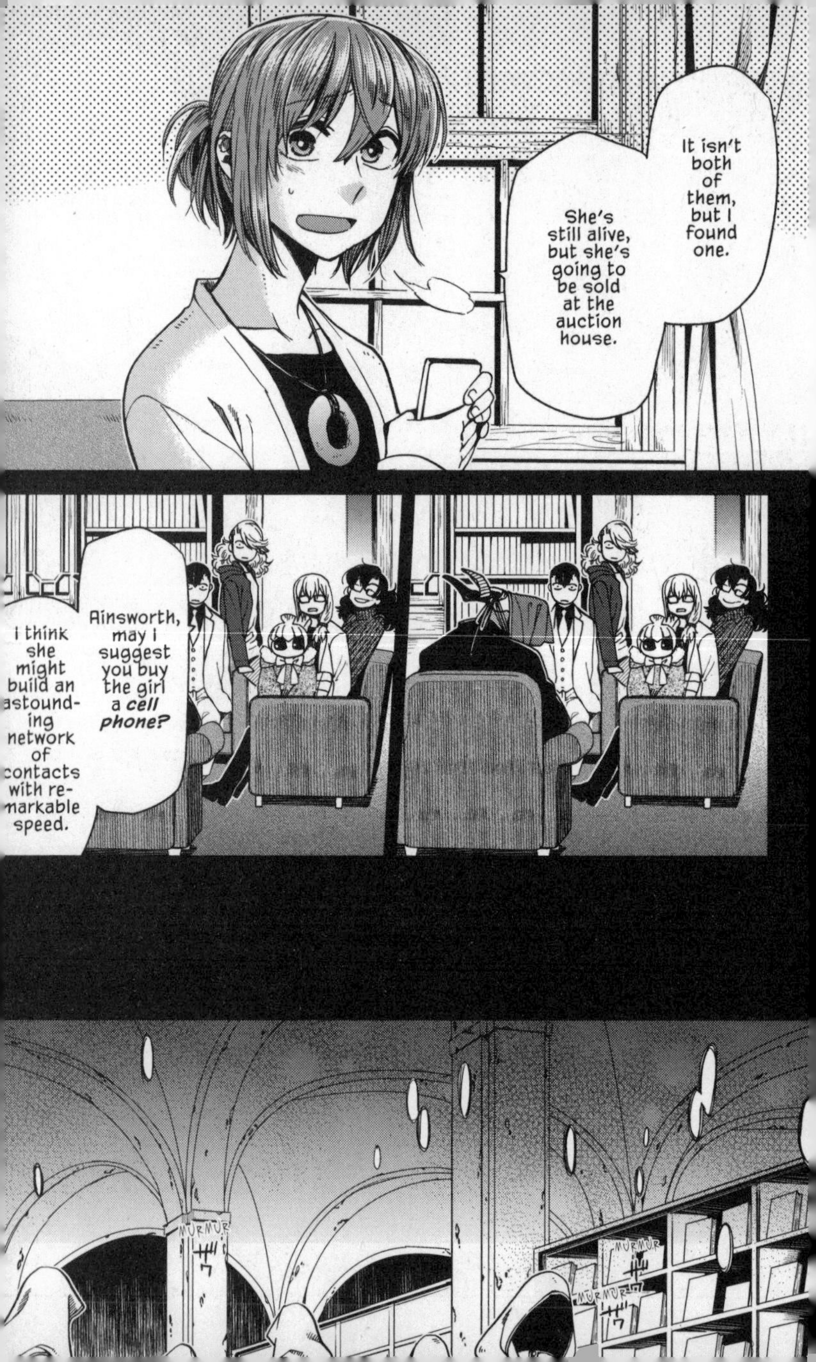
It isn't both of them, but I found one.
She's still alive, but she's going to be sold at the auction house.
Ainsworth, may I suggest you buy the girl a *cell phone?*
I think she might build an astounding network of contacts with remarkable speed.
MURMUR
MURMUR
MURMUR

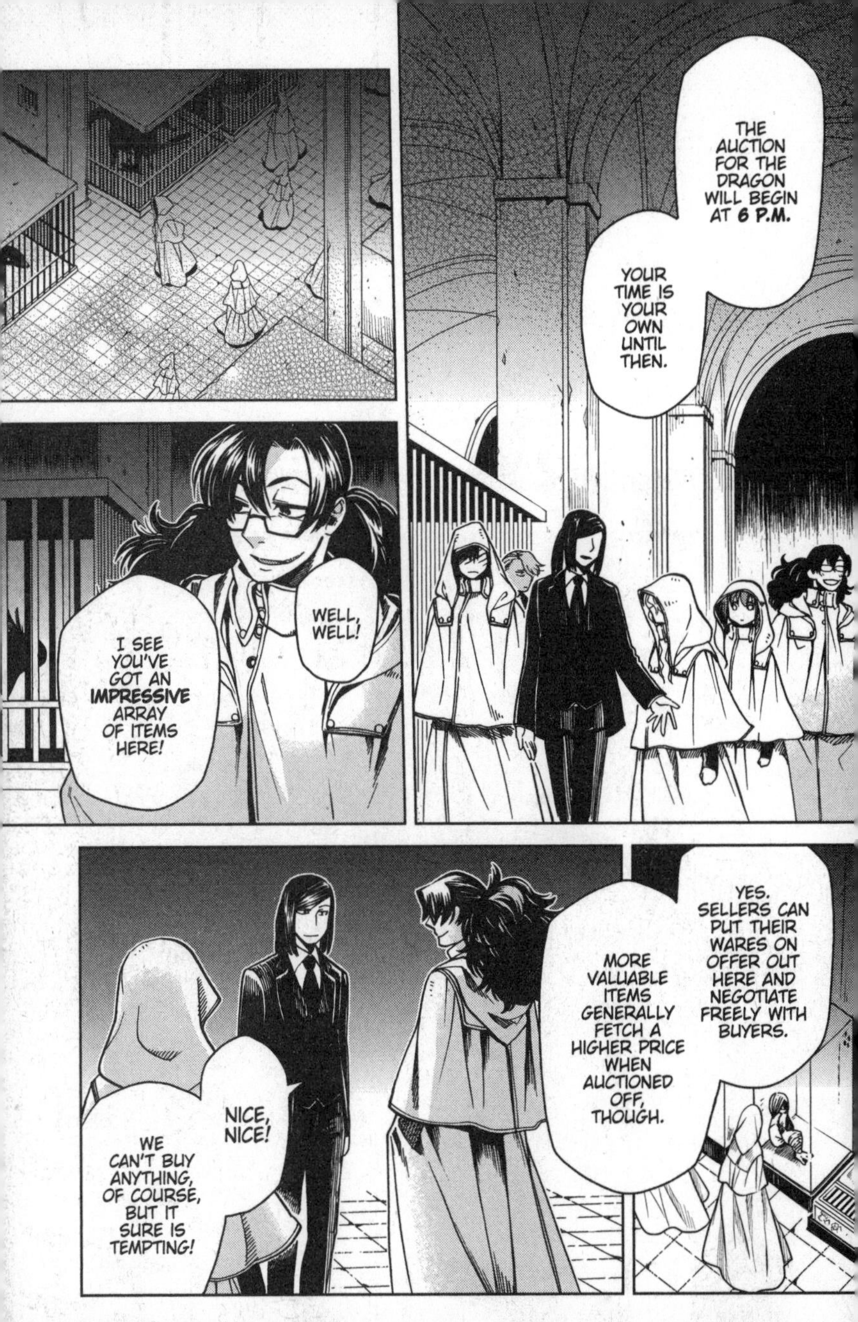
THE AUCTION FOR THE DRAGON WILL BEGIN AT 6 P.M.
YOUR TIME IS YOUR OWN UNTIL THEN.
WELL, WELL!
I SEE YOU'VE GOT AN IMPRESSIVE ARRAY OF ITEMS HERE!
YES. SELLERS CAN PUT THEIR WARES ON OFFER OUT HERE AND NEGOTIATE FREELY WITH BUYERS.
MORE VALUABLE ITEMS GENERALLY FETCH A HIGHER PRICE WHEN AUCTIONED OFF, THOUGH.
NICE, NICE!
WE CAN'T BUY ANYTHING, OF COURSE, BUT IT SURE IS TEMPTING!

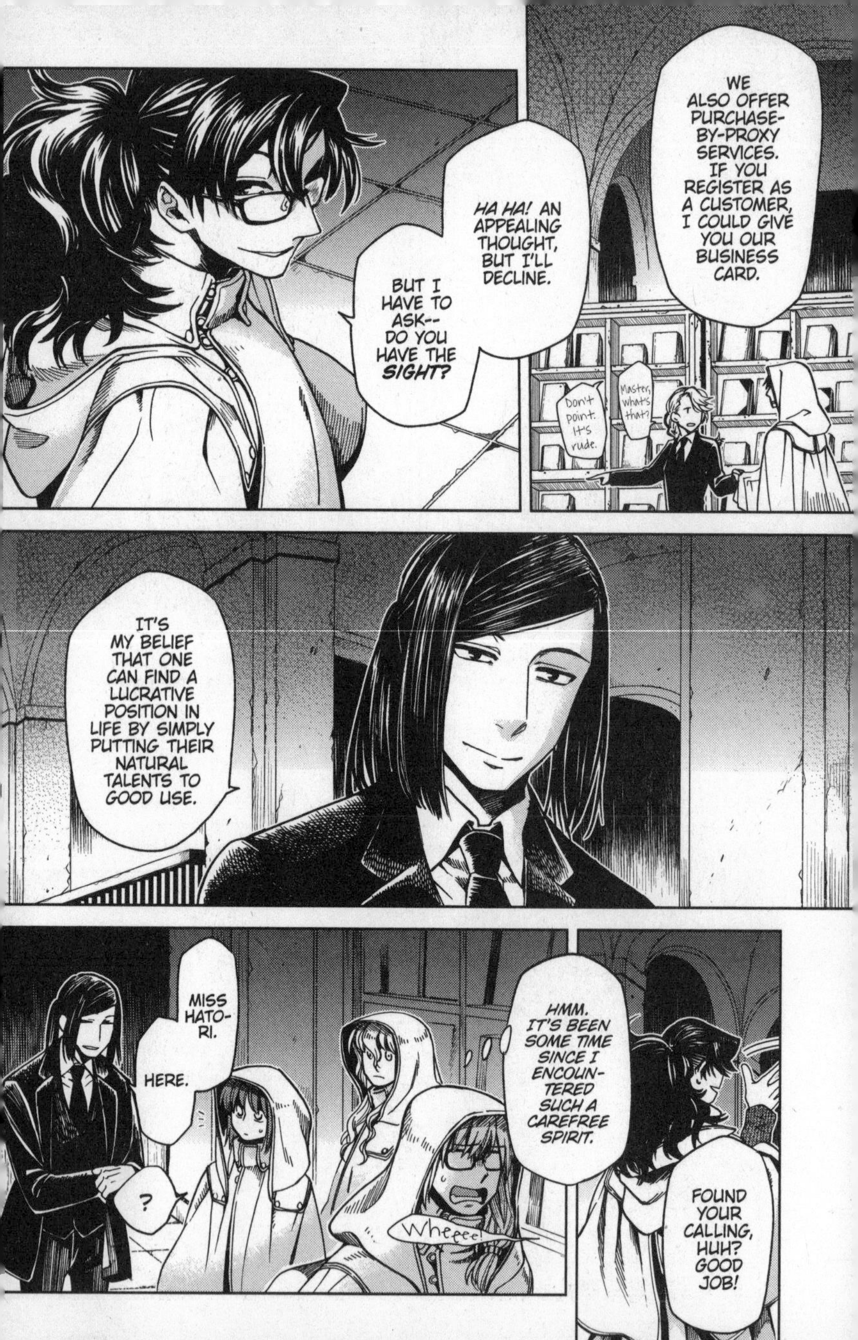
WE ALSO OFFER PURCHASE-BY-PROXY SERVICES. IF YOU REGISTER AS A CUSTOMER, I COULD GIVE YOU OUR BUSINESS CARD.
Master, what's that?
Don't point. It's rude.
HA HA! AN APPEALING THOUGHT, BUT I'LL DECLINE.
BUT I HAVE TO ASK-- DO YOU HAVE THE SIGHT?
IT'S MY BELIEF THAT ONE CAN FIND A LUCRATIVE POSITION IN LIFE BY SIMPLY PUTTING THEIR NATURAL TALENTS TO GOOD USE.
HMM. IT'S BEEN SOME TIME SINCE I ENCOUNTERED SUCH A CAREFREE SPIRIT.
FOUND YOUR CALLING, HUH? GOOD JOB!
MISS HATORI.
HERE.
?
Wheeee!

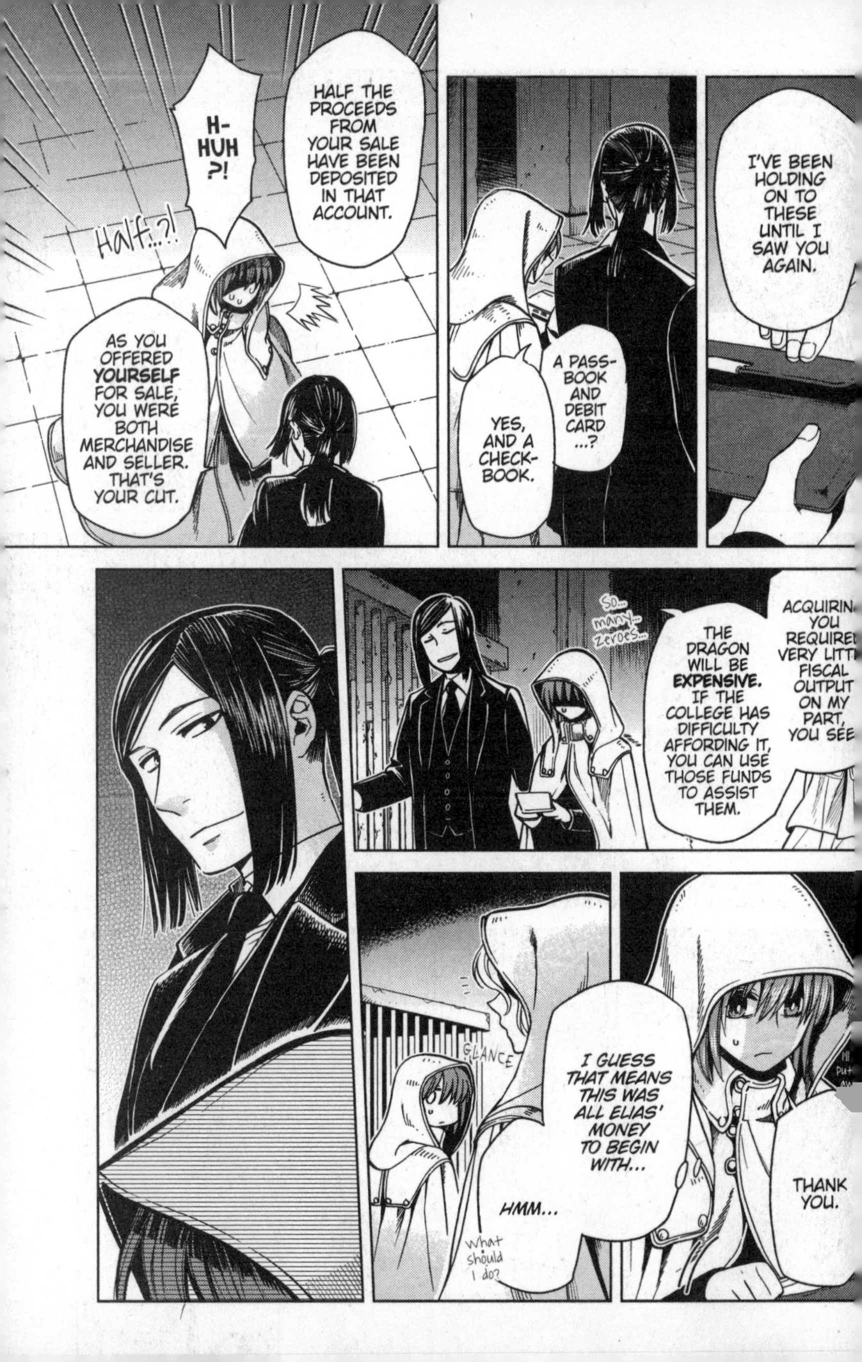
I'VE BEEN HOLDING ON TO THESE UNTIL I SAW YOU AGAIN.
A PASS-BOOK AND DEBIT CARD ...?
YES, AND A CHECK-BOOK.
HALF THE PROCEEDS FROM YOUR SALE HAVE BEEN DEPOSITED IN THAT ACCOUNT.
H-HUH ?!
Half...?!
AS YOU OFFERED **YOURSELF** FOR SALE, YOU WERE BOTH MERCHANDISE AND SELLER. THAT'S YOUR CUT.
ACQUIRIN YOU REQUIREI VERY LITTL FISCAL OUTPUT ON MY PART, YOU SEE
THE DRAGON WILL BE **EXPENSIVE.** IF THE COLLEGE HAS DIFFICULTY AFFORDING IT, YOU CAN USE THOSE FUNDS TO ASSIST THEM.
So... many... zeroes...
THANK YOU.
I GUESS THAT MEANS THIS WAS ALL ELIAS' MONEY TO BEGIN WITH...
GLANCE
HMM...
What should I do?

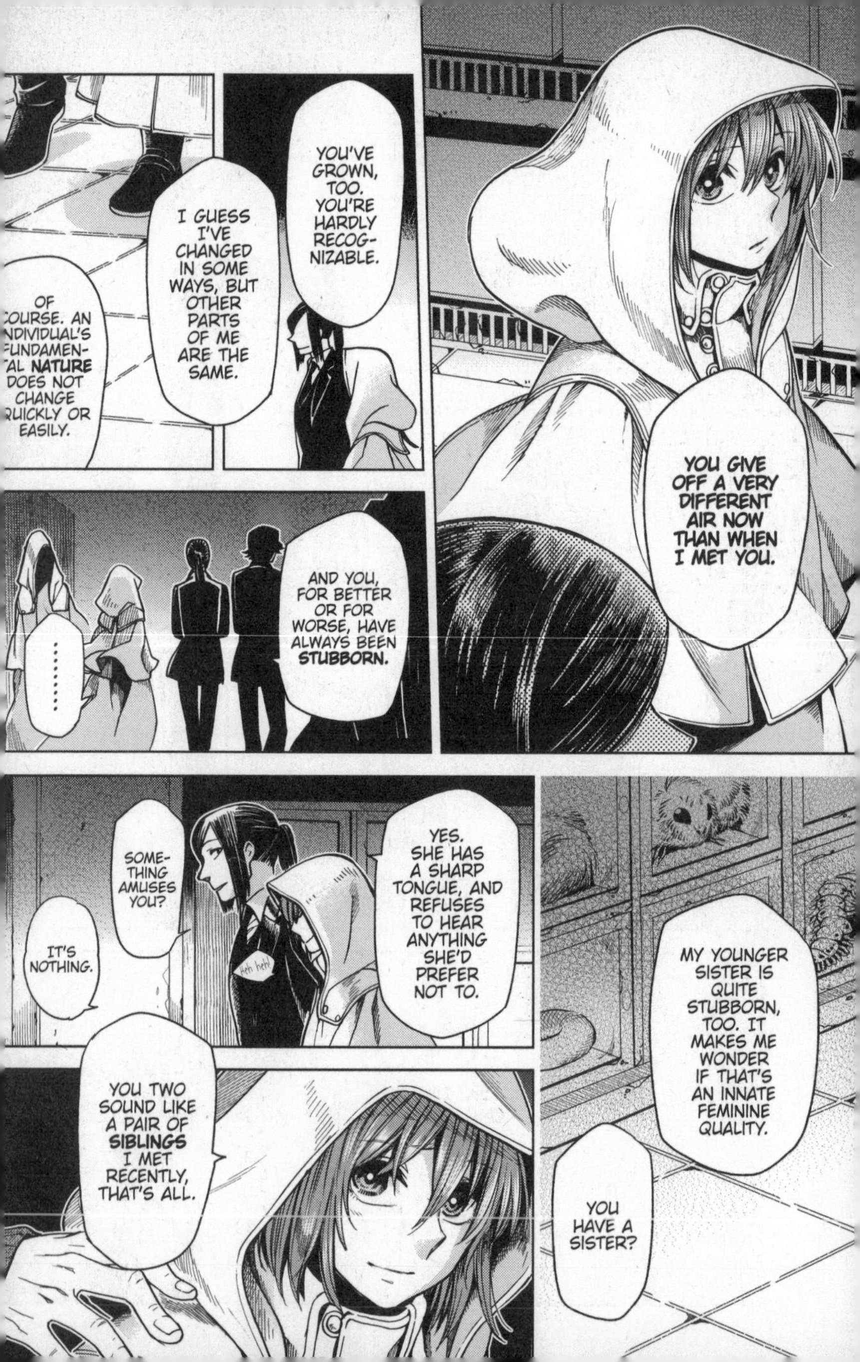
YOU GIVE OFF A VERY DIFFERENT AIR NOW THAN WHEN I MET YOU.
YOU'VE GROWN, TOO. YOU'RE HARDLY RECOG-NIZABLE.
I GUESS I'VE CHANGED IN SOME WAYS, BUT OTHER PARTS OF ME ARE THE SAME.
OF COURSE. AN INDIVIDUAL'S FUNDAMEN-TAL NATURE DOES NOT CHANGE QUICKLY OR EASILY.
AND YOU, FOR BETTER OR FOR WORSE, HAVE ALWAYS BEEN STUBBORN.
......
MY YOUNGER SISTER IS QUITE STUBBORN, TOO. IT MAKES ME WONDER IF THAT'S AN INNATE FEMININE QUALITY.
YOU HAVE A SISTER?
YES. SHE HAS A SHARP TONGUE, AND REFUSES TO HEAR ANYTHING SHE'D PREFER NOT TO.
heh heh
SOME-THING AMUSES YOU?
IT'S NOTHING.
YOU TWO SOUND LIKE A PAIR OF SIBLINGS I MET RECENTLY, THAT'S ALL.

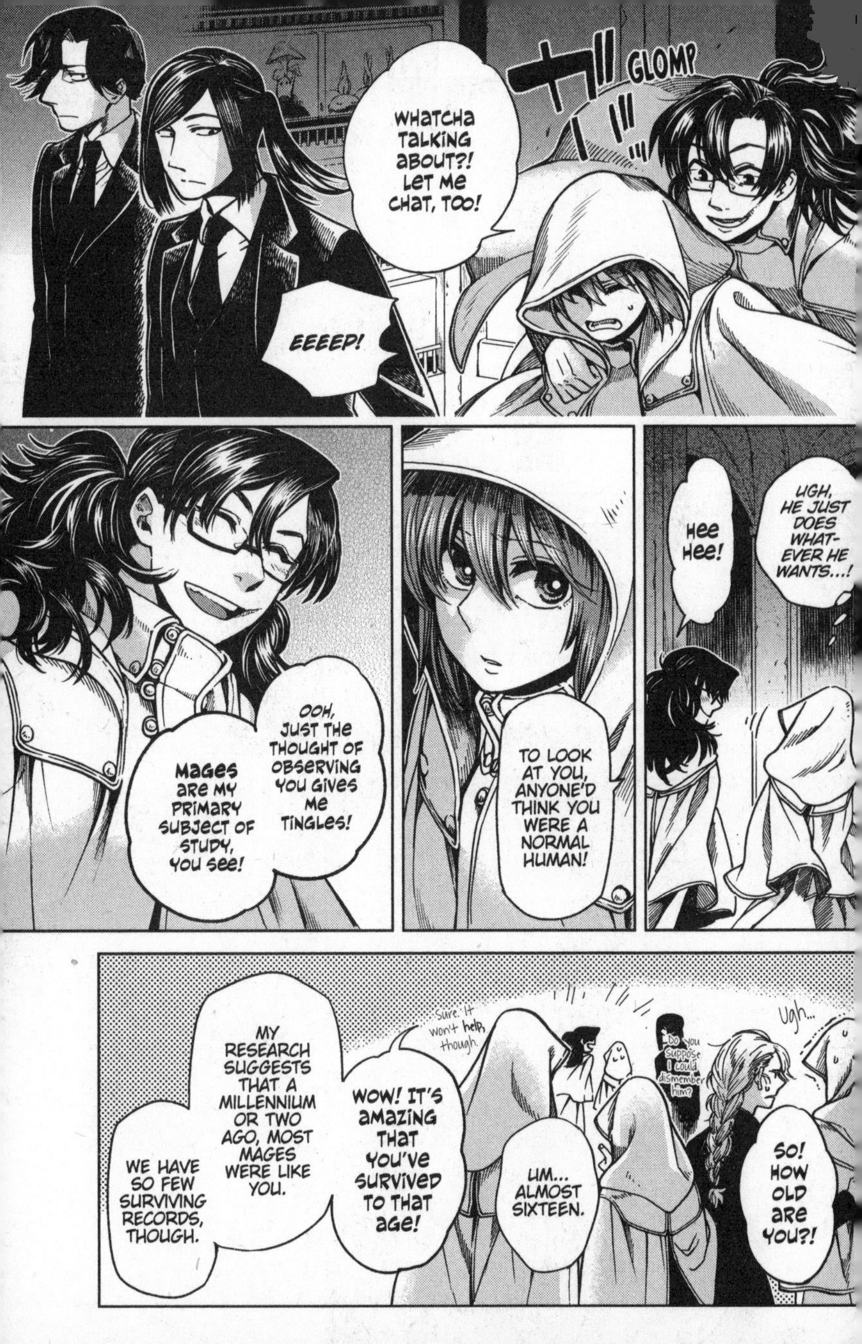
GLOMP
WHATCHA TALKING ABOUT?! LET ME CHAT, TOO!
EEEEP!
UGH, HE JUST DOES WHAT-EVER HE WANTS...!
Hee Hee!
TO LOOK AT YOU, ANYONE'D THINK YOU WERE A NORMAL HUMAN!
OOH, JUST THE THOUGHT OF OBSERVING YOU GIVES ME TINGLES!
Mages are my primary subject of study, you see!
Ugh...
SO! HOW OLD ARE YOU?!
Do you suppose I could dismember him?
Sure. It won't help, though.
UM... ALMOST SIXTEEN.
WOW! IT'S amazing THAT YOU'VE SURVIVED TO THAT age!
MY RESEARCH SUGGESTS THAT A MILLENNIUM OR TWO AGO, MOST MAGES WERE LIKE YOU.
WE HAVE SO FEW SURVIVING RECORDS, THOUGH.

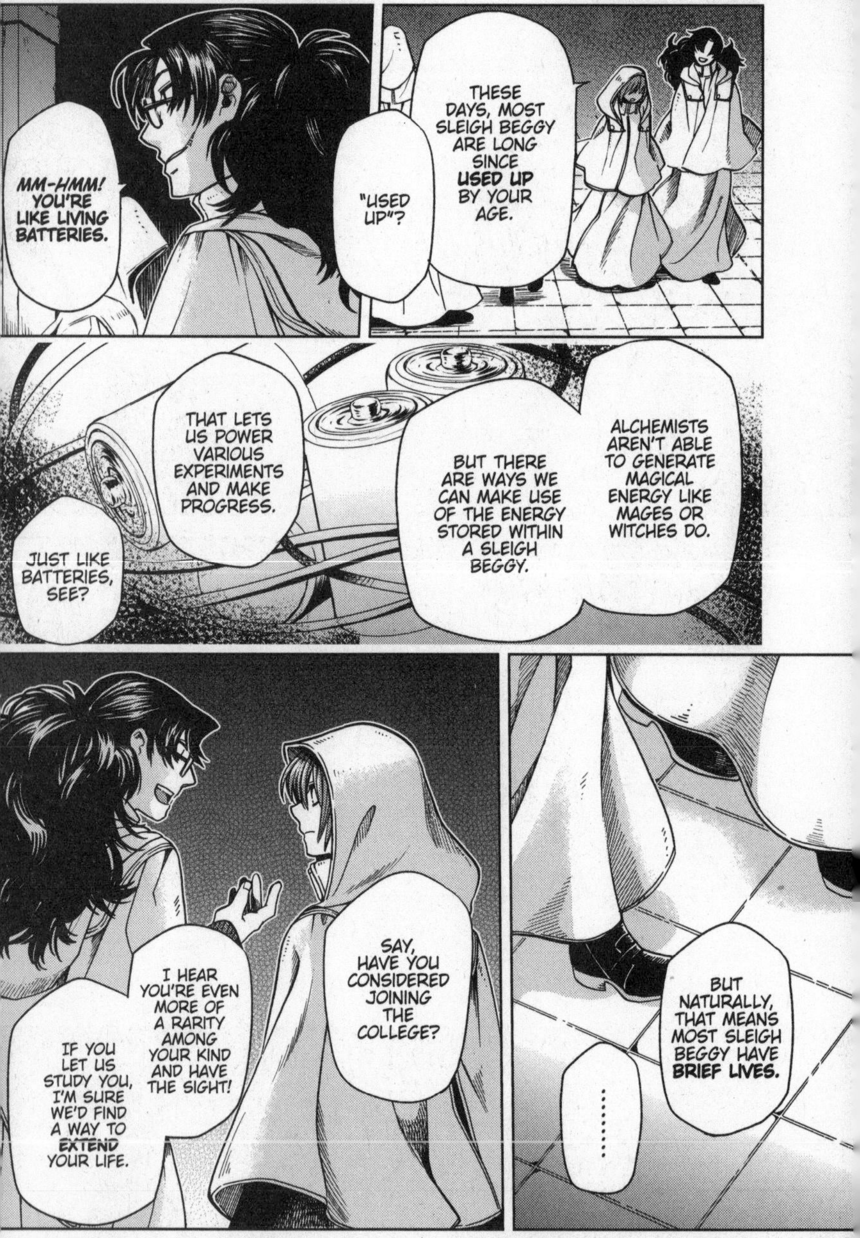
THESE DAYS, MOST SLEIGH BEGGY ARE LONG SINCE **USED UP** BY YOUR AGE.
"USED UP"?
MM-HMM! YOU'RE LIKE LIVING BATTERIES.
ALCHEMISTS AREN'T ABLE TO GENERATE MAGICAL ENERGY LIKE MAGES OR WITCHES DO.
BUT THERE ARE WAYS WE CAN MAKE USE OF THE ENERGY STORED WITHIN A SLEIGH BEGGY.
THAT LETS US POWER VARIOUS EXPERIMENTS AND MAKE PROGRESS.
JUST LIKE BATTERIES, SEE?
BUT NATURALLY, THAT MEANS MOST SLEIGH BEGGY HAVE **BRIEF LIVES.**
......
SAY, HAVE YOU CONSIDERED JOINING THE COLLEGE?
I HEAR YOU'RE EVEN MORE OF A RARITY AMONG YOUR KIND AND HAVE THE SIGHT!
IF YOU LET US STUDY YOU, I'M SURE WE'D FIND A WAY TO **EXTEND** YOUR LIFE.

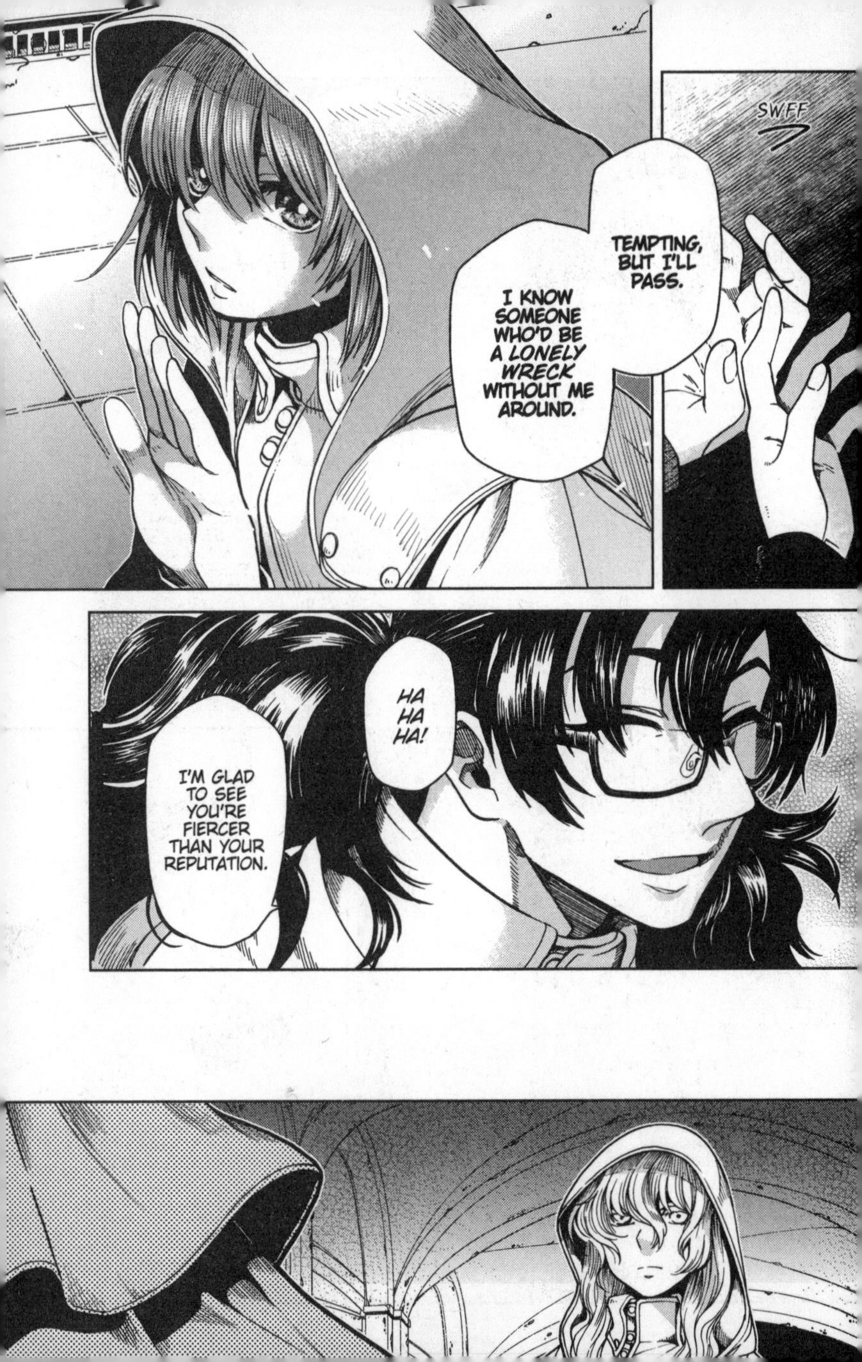
SWFF
TEMPTING, BUT I'LL PASS.
I KNOW SOMEONE WHO'D BE A *LONELY WRECK* WITHOUT ME AROUND.
HA HA HA!
I'M GLAD TO SEE YOU'RE FIERCER THAN YOUR REPUTATION.

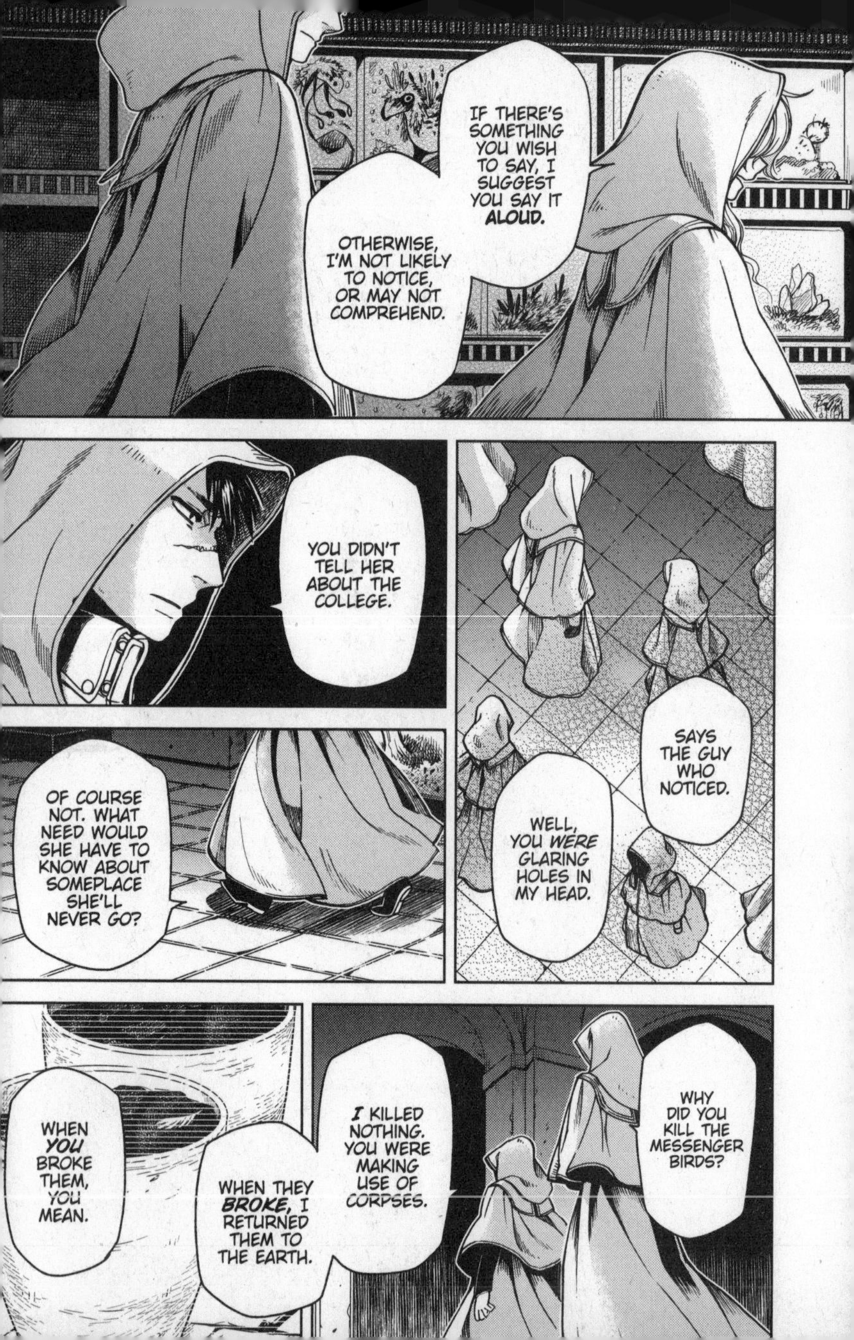
IF THERE'S SOMETHING YOU WISH TO SAY, I SUGGEST YOU SAY IT **ALOUD.**
OTHERWISE, I'M NOT LIKELY TO NOTICE, OR MAY NOT COMPREHEND.
SAYS THE GUY WHO NOTICED.
WELL, YOU *WERE* GLARING HOLES IN MY HEAD.
YOU DIDN'T TELL HER ABOUT THE COLLEGE.
OF COURSE NOT. WHAT NEED WOULD SHE HAVE TO KNOW ABOUT SOMEPLACE SHE'LL NEVER GO?
WHY DID YOU KILL THE MESSENGER BIRDS?
I KILLED NOTHING. YOU WERE MAKING USE OF CORPSES.
WHEN THEY ***BROKE,*** I RETURNED THEM TO THE EARTH.
WHEN ***YOU*** BROKE THEM, YOU MEAN.

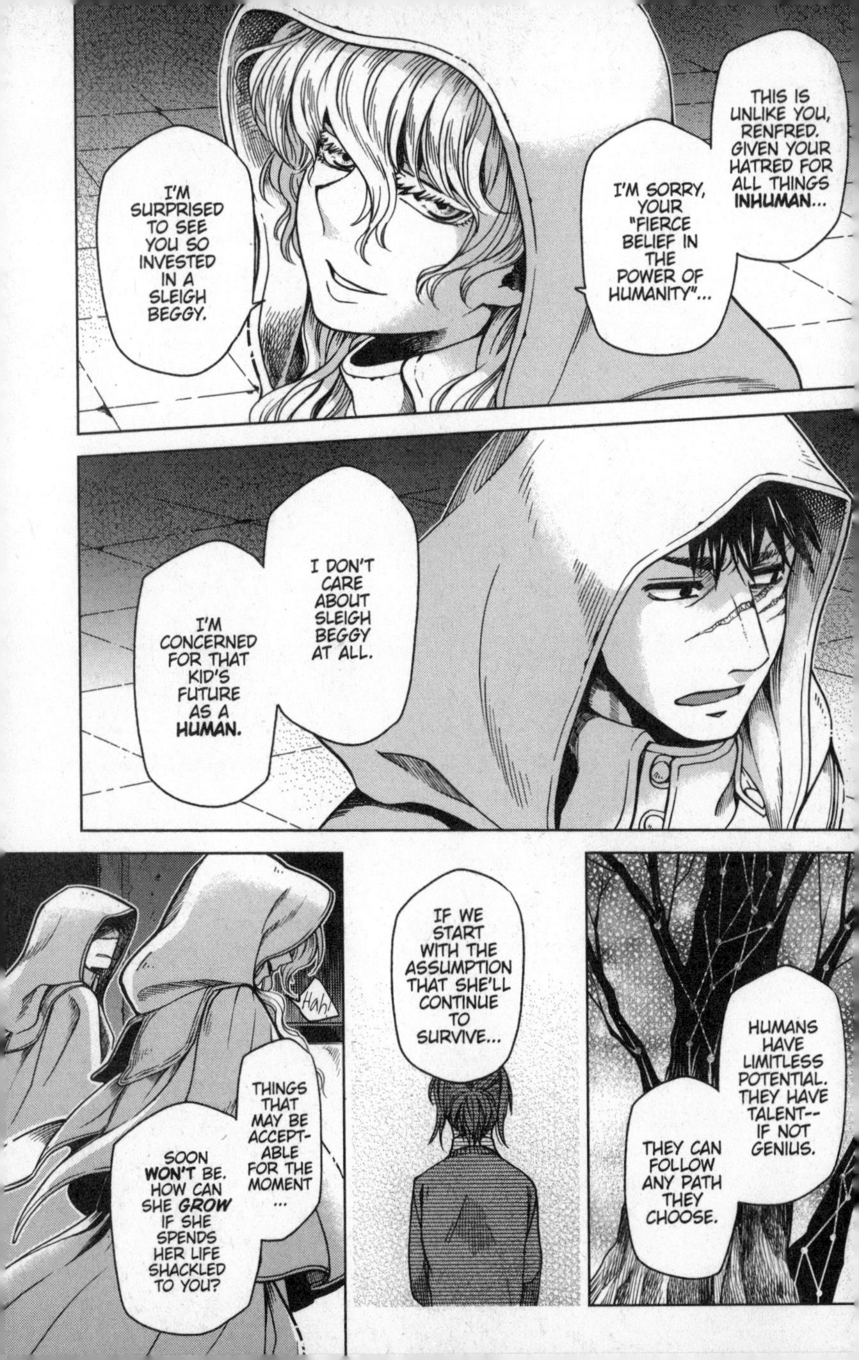
THIS IS UNLIKE YOU, RENFRED. GIVEN YOUR HATRED FOR ALL THINGS **INHUMAN**...
I'M SORRY, YOUR "FIERCE BELIEF IN THE POWER OF HUMANITY"...
I'M SURPRISED TO SEE YOU SO INVESTED IN A SLEIGH BEGGY.
I DON'T CARE ABOUT SLEIGH BEGGY AT ALL.
I'M CONCERNED FOR THAT KID'S FUTURE AS A **HUMAN.**
HUMANS HAVE LIMITLESS POTENTIAL. THEY HAVE TALENT-- IF NOT GENIUS.
THEY CAN FOLLOW ANY PATH THEY CHOOSE.
IF WE START WITH THE ASSUMPTION THAT SHE'LL CONTINUE TO SURVIVE...
Hah!
THINGS THAT MAY BE ACCEPT-ABLE FOR THE MOMENT...
SOON **WON'T** BE. HOW CAN SHE ***GROW*** IF SHE SPENDS HER LIFE SHACKLED TO YOU?

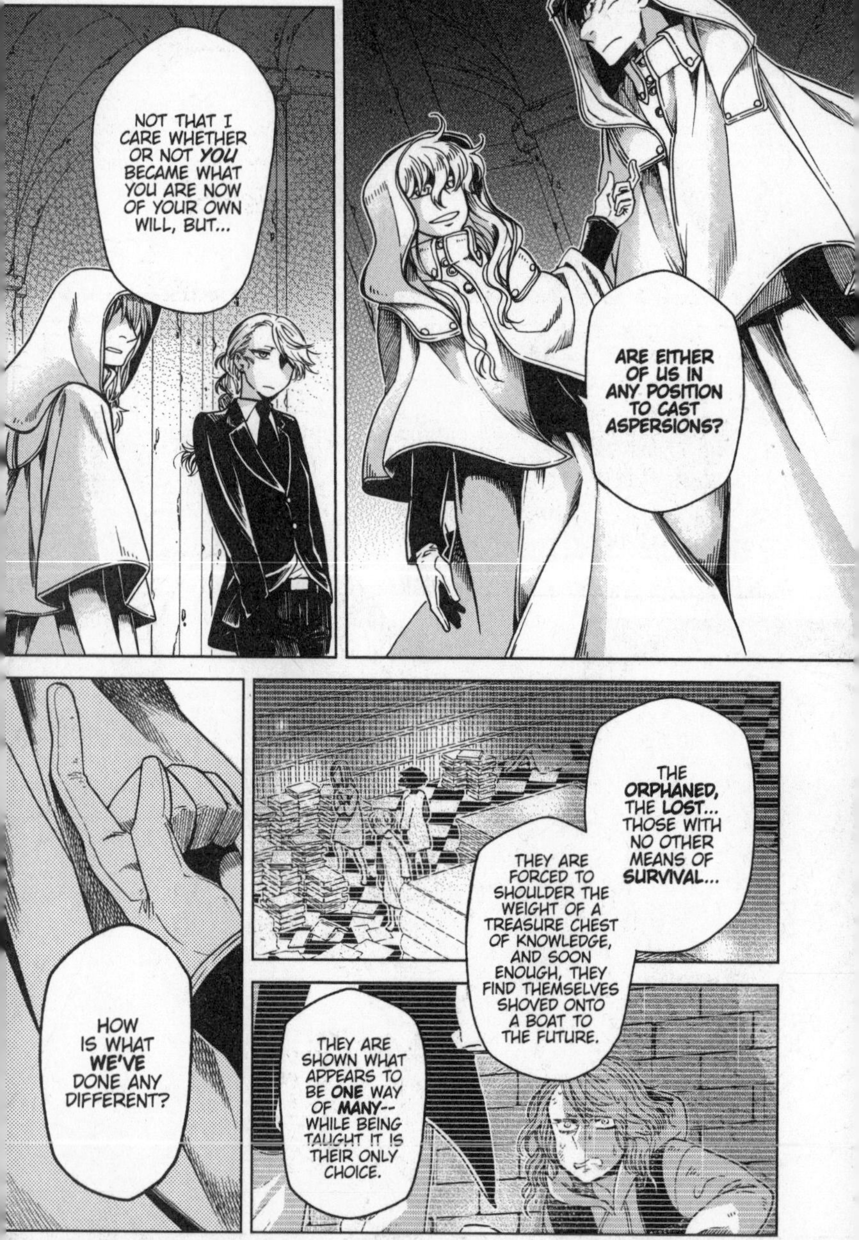
ARE EITHER OF US IN ANY POSITION TO CAST ASPERSIONS?
NOT THAT I CARE WHETHER OR NOT ***YOU*** BECAME WHAT YOU ARE NOW OF YOUR OWN WILL, BUT...
THE **ORPHANED**, THE **LOST**... THOSE WITH NO OTHER MEANS OF **SURVIVAL**...
THEY ARE FORCED TO SHOULDER THE WEIGHT OF A TREASURE CHEST OF KNOWLEDGE, AND SOON ENOUGH, THEY FIND THEMSELVES SHOVED ONTO A BOAT TO THE FUTURE.
THEY ARE SHOWN WHAT APPEARS TO BE **ONE** WAY OF **MANY**-- WHILE BEING TAUGHT IT IS THEIR ONLY CHOICE.
HOW IS WHAT **WE'VE** DONE ANY DIFFERENT?

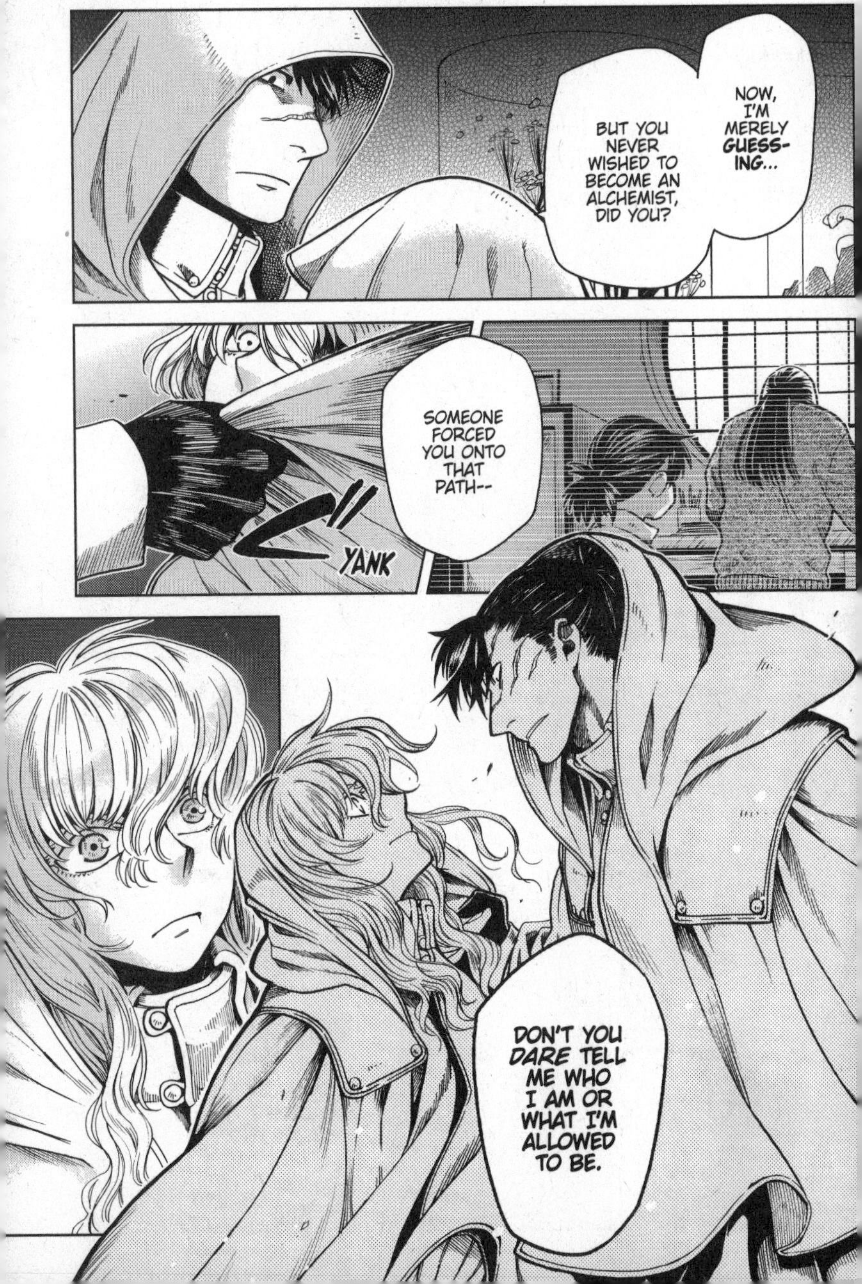
NOW, I'M MERELY GUESSING...
BUT YOU NEVER WISHED TO BECOME AN ALCHEMIST, DID YOU?
SOMEONE FORCED YOU ONTO THAT PATH--
YANK
DON'T YOU DARE TELL ME WHO I AM OR WHAT I'M ALLOWED TO BE.

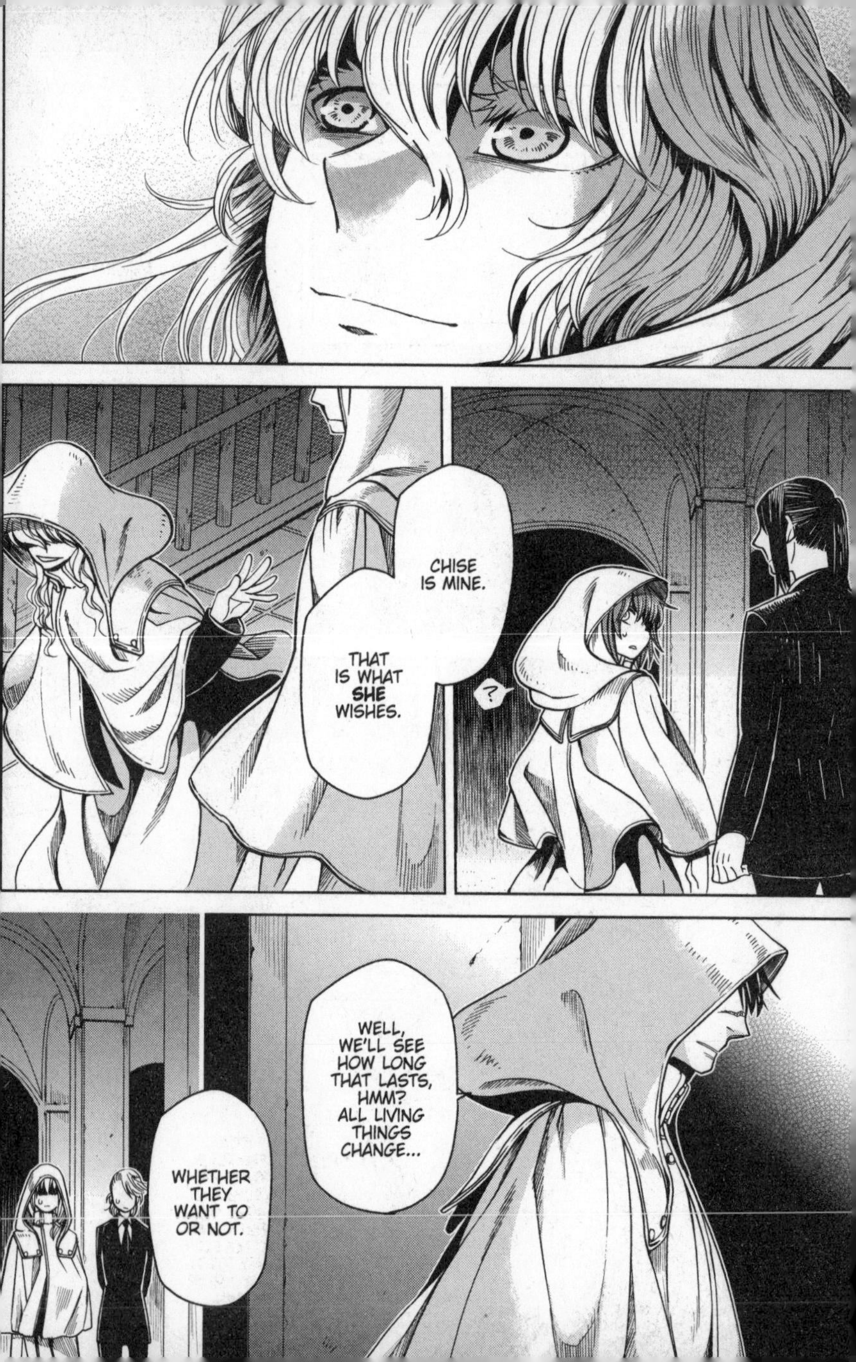
?
CHISE IS MINE.
THAT IS WHAT SHE WISHES.
WELL, WE'LL SEE HOW LONG THAT LASTS, HMM? ALL LIVING THINGS CHANGE...
WHETHER THEY WANT TO OR NOT.

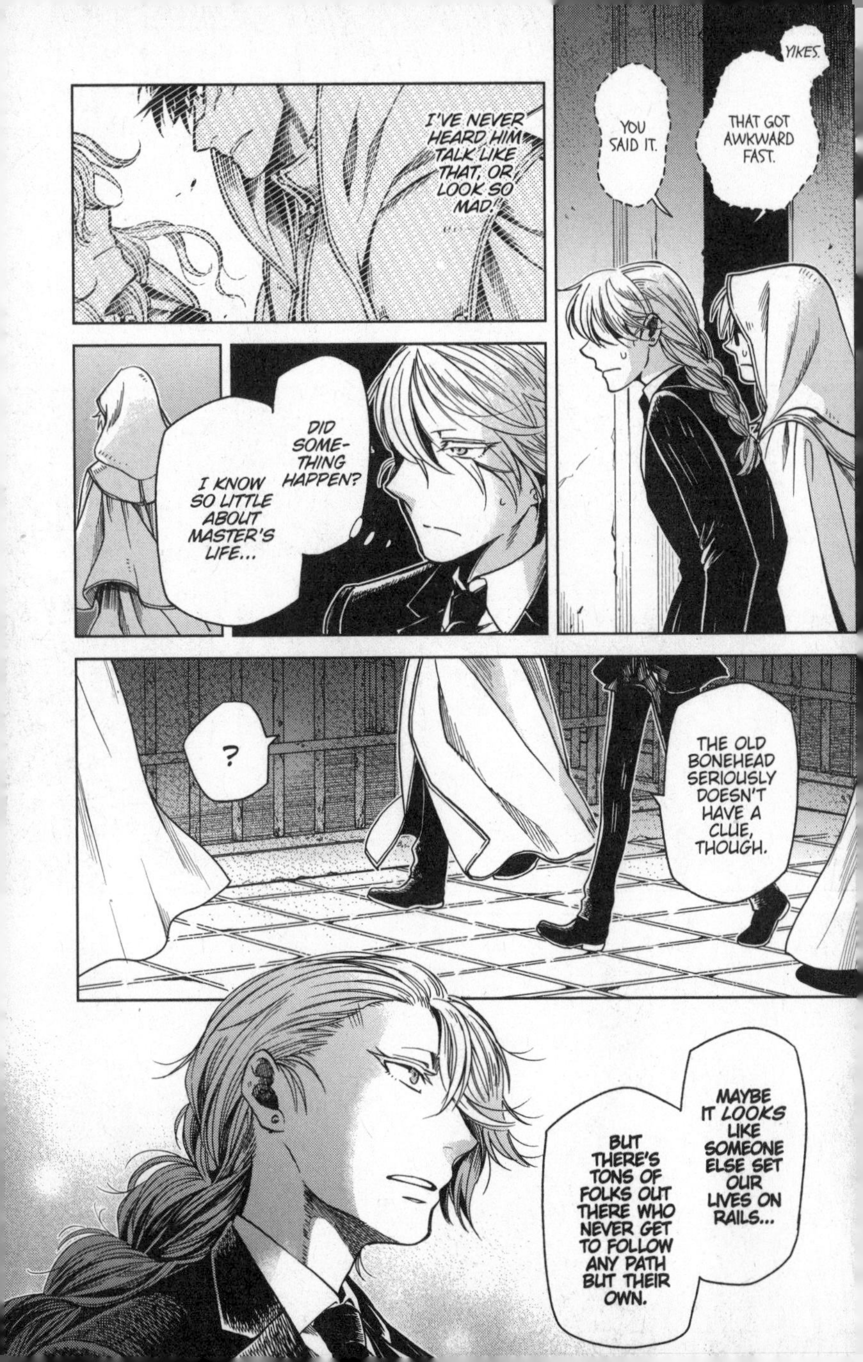
YIKES.
THAT GOT AWKWARD FAST.
YOU SAID IT.
I'VE NEVER HEARD HIM TALK LIKE THAT, OR LOOK SO MAD!
DID SOMETHING HAPPEN?
I KNOW SO LITTLE ABOUT MASTER'S LIFE...
THE OLD BONEHEAD SERIOUSLY DOESN'T HAVE A CLUE, THOUGH.
?
MAYBE IT *LOOKS* LIKE SOMEONE ELSE SET OUR LIVES ON RAILS...
BUT THERE'S TONS OF FOLKS OUT THERE WHO NEVER GET TO FOLLOW ANY PATH BUT THEIR OWN.

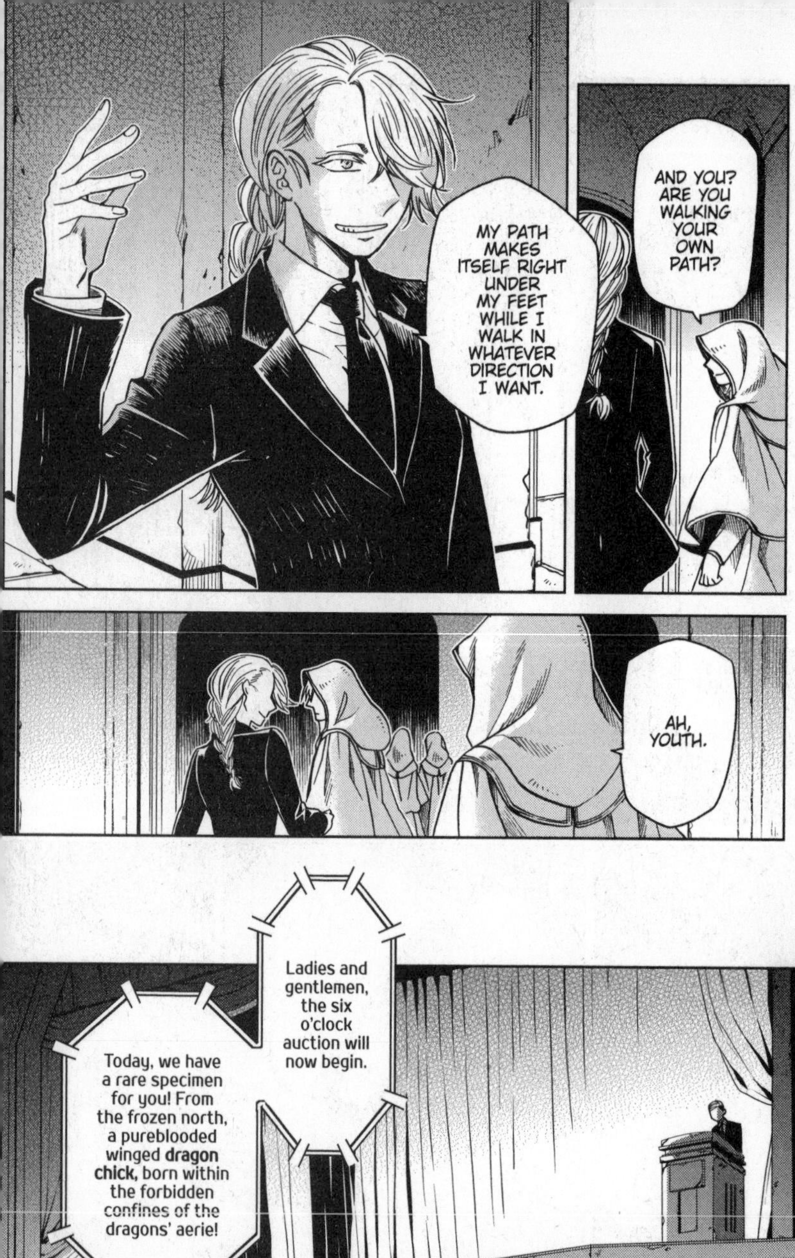
AND YOU? ARE YOU WALKING YOUR OWN PATH?
MY PATH MAKES ITSELF RIGHT UNDER MY FEET WHILE I WALK IN WHATEVER DIRECTION I WANT.
AH, YOUTH.
Ladies and gentlemen, the six o'clock auction will now begin.
Today, we have a rare specimen for you! From the frozen north, a pureblooded winged **dragon chick**, born within the forbidden confines of the dragons' aerie!

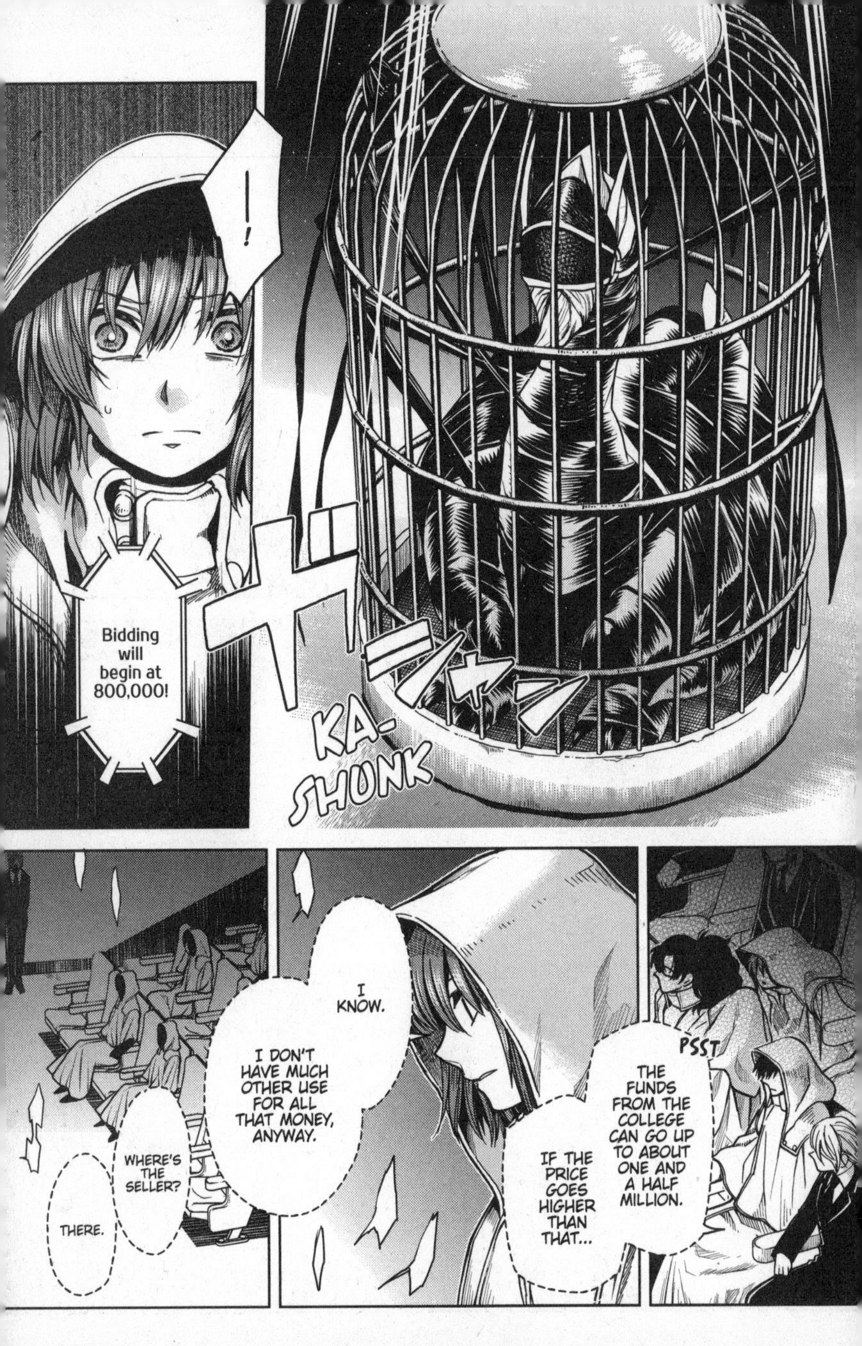
KA-SHUNK
!
Bidding will begin at 800,000!
PSST
THE FUNDS FROM THE COLLEGE CAN GO UP TO ABOUT ONE AND A HALF MILLION.
IF THE PRICE GOES HIGHER THAN THAT...
I KNOW.
I DON'T HAVE MUCH OTHER USE FOR ALL THAT MONEY, ANYWAY.
WHERE'S THE SELLER?
THERE.

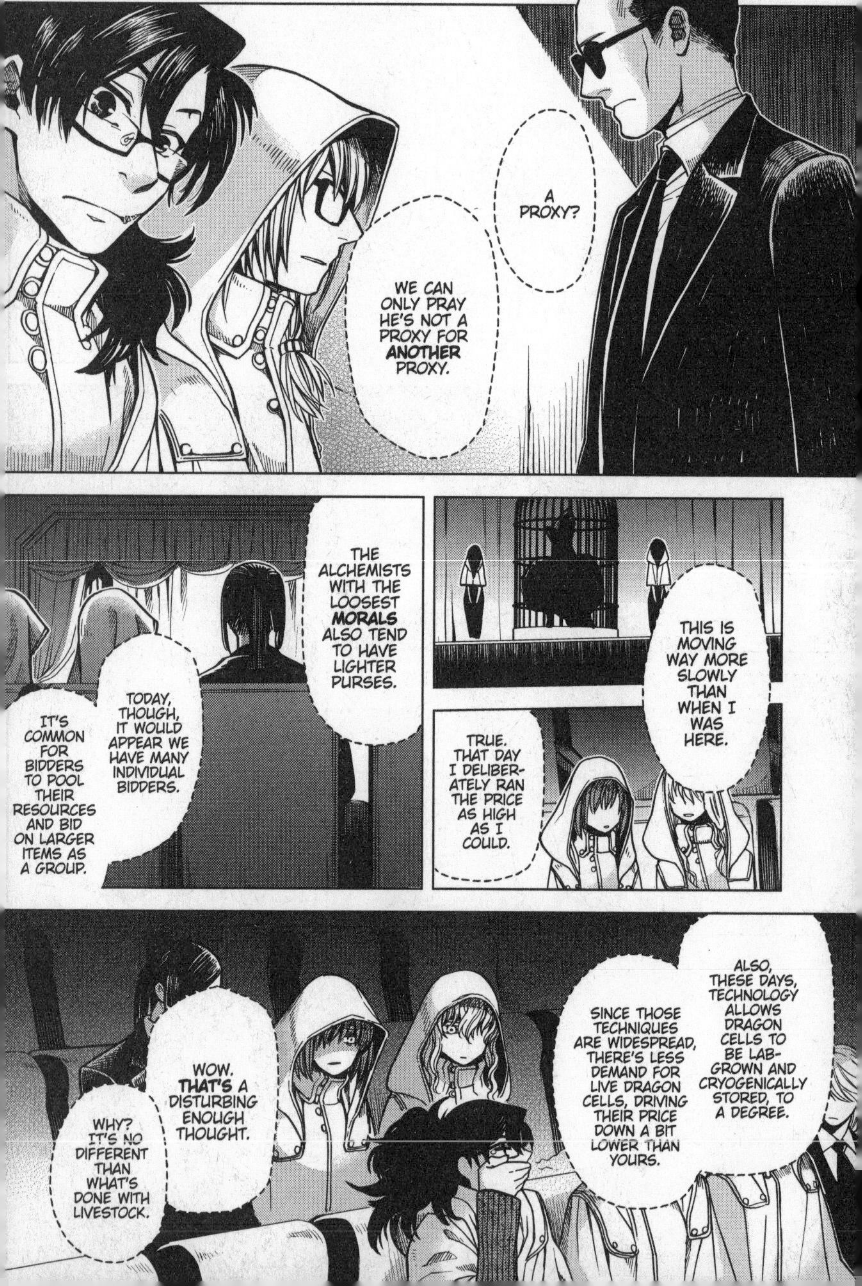
A PROXY?
WE CAN ONLY PRAY HE'S NOT A PROXY FOR **ANOTHER** PROXY.
THIS IS MOVING WAY MORE SLOWLY THAN WHEN I WAS HERE.
TRUE. THAT DAY I DELIBER-ATELY RAN THE PRICE AS HIGH AS I COULD.
THE ALCHEMISTS WITH THE LOOSEST **MORALS** ALSO TEND TO HAVE LIGHTER PURSES.
TODAY, THOUGH, IT WOULD APPEAR WE HAVE MANY INDIVIDUAL BIDDERS.
IT'S COMMON FOR BIDDERS TO POOL THEIR RESOURCES AND BID ON LARGER ITEMS AS A GROUP.
ALSO, THESE DAYS, TECHNOLOGY ALLOWS DRAGON CELLS TO BE LAB-GROWN AND CRYOGENICALLY STORED, TO A DEGREE.
SINCE THOSE TECHNIQUES ARE WIDESPREAD, THERE'S LESS DEMAND FOR LIVE DRAGON CELLS, DRIVING THEIR PRICE DOWN A BIT LOWER THAN YOURS.
WOW. **THAT'S** A DISTURBING ENOUGH THOUGHT.
WHY? IT'S NO DIFFERENT THAN WHAT'S DONE WITH LIVESTOCK.

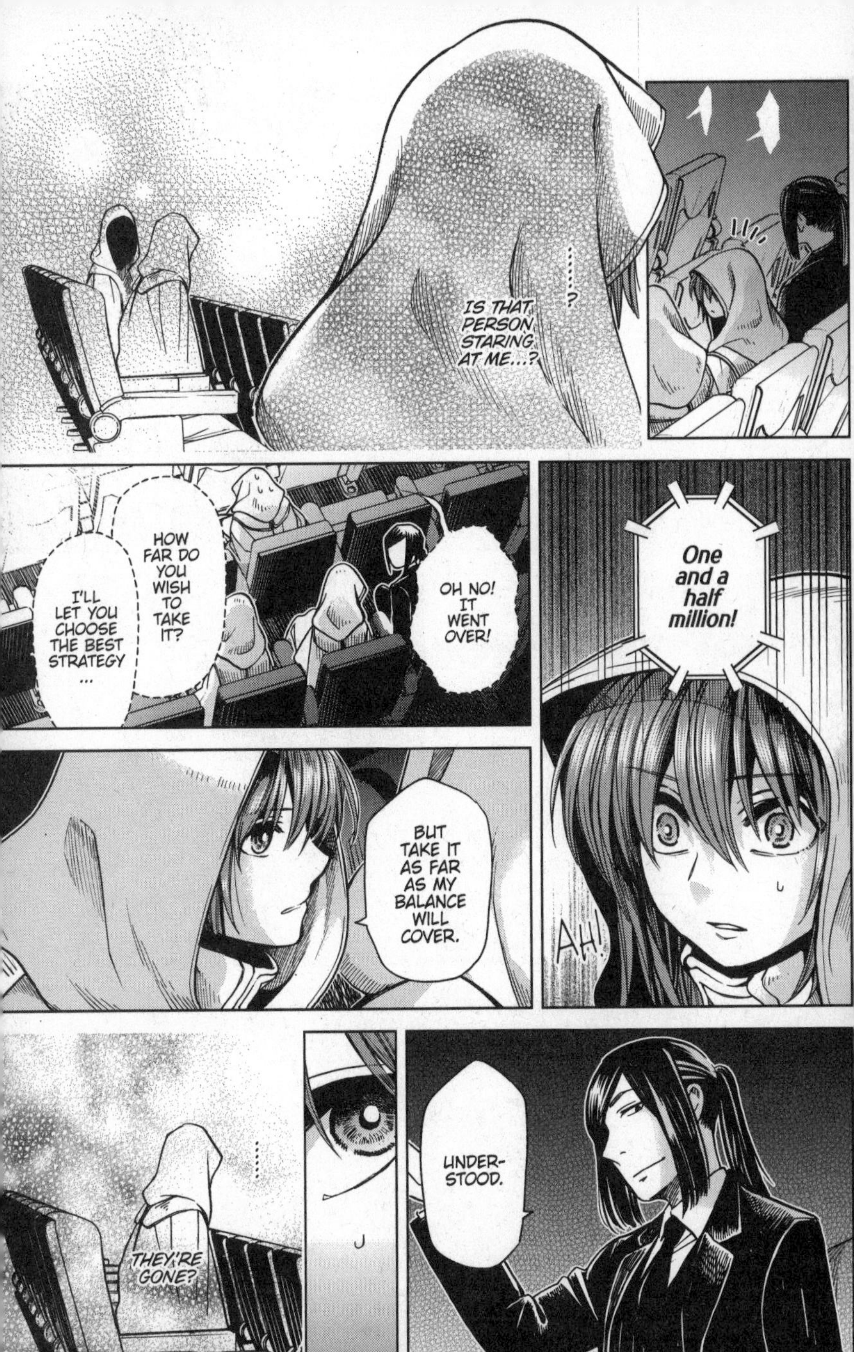
......?
IS THAT PERSON STARING AT ME...?
One and a half million!
AH!
OH NO! IT WENT OVER!
HOW FAR DO YOU WISH TO TAKE IT?
I'LL LET YOU CHOOSE THE BEST STRATEGY ...
BUT TAKE IT AS FAR AS MY BALANCE WILL COVER.
UNDER-STOOD.
......
THEY'RE GONE?

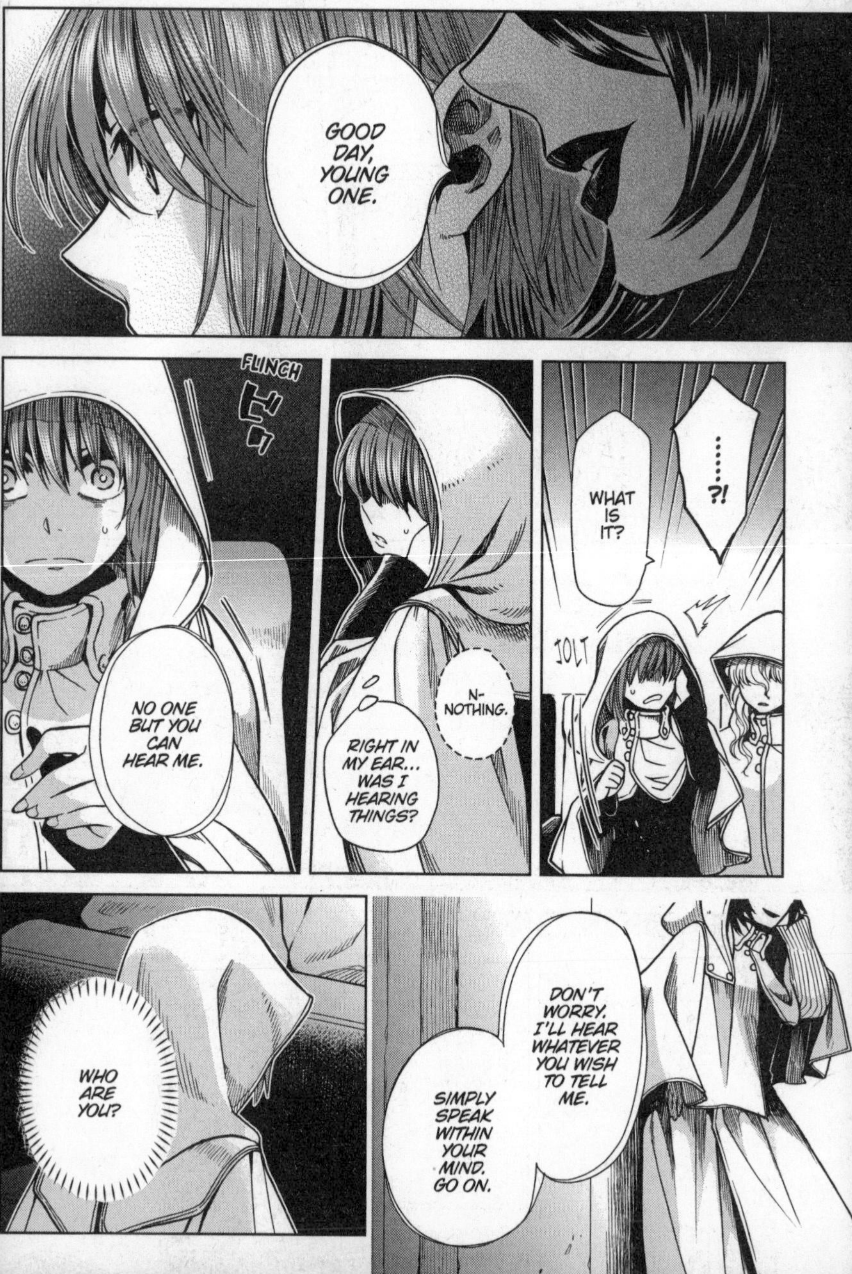
GOOD DAY, YOUNG ONE.
......?!
WHAT IS IT?
JOLT
N-NOTHING.
RIGHT IN MY EAR... WAS I HEARING THINGS?
FLINCH
NO ONE BUT YOU CAN HEAR ME.
DON'T WORRY. I'LL HEAR WHATEVER YOU WISH TO TELL ME.
SIMPLY SPEAK WITHIN YOUR MIND. GO ON.
WHO ARE YOU?

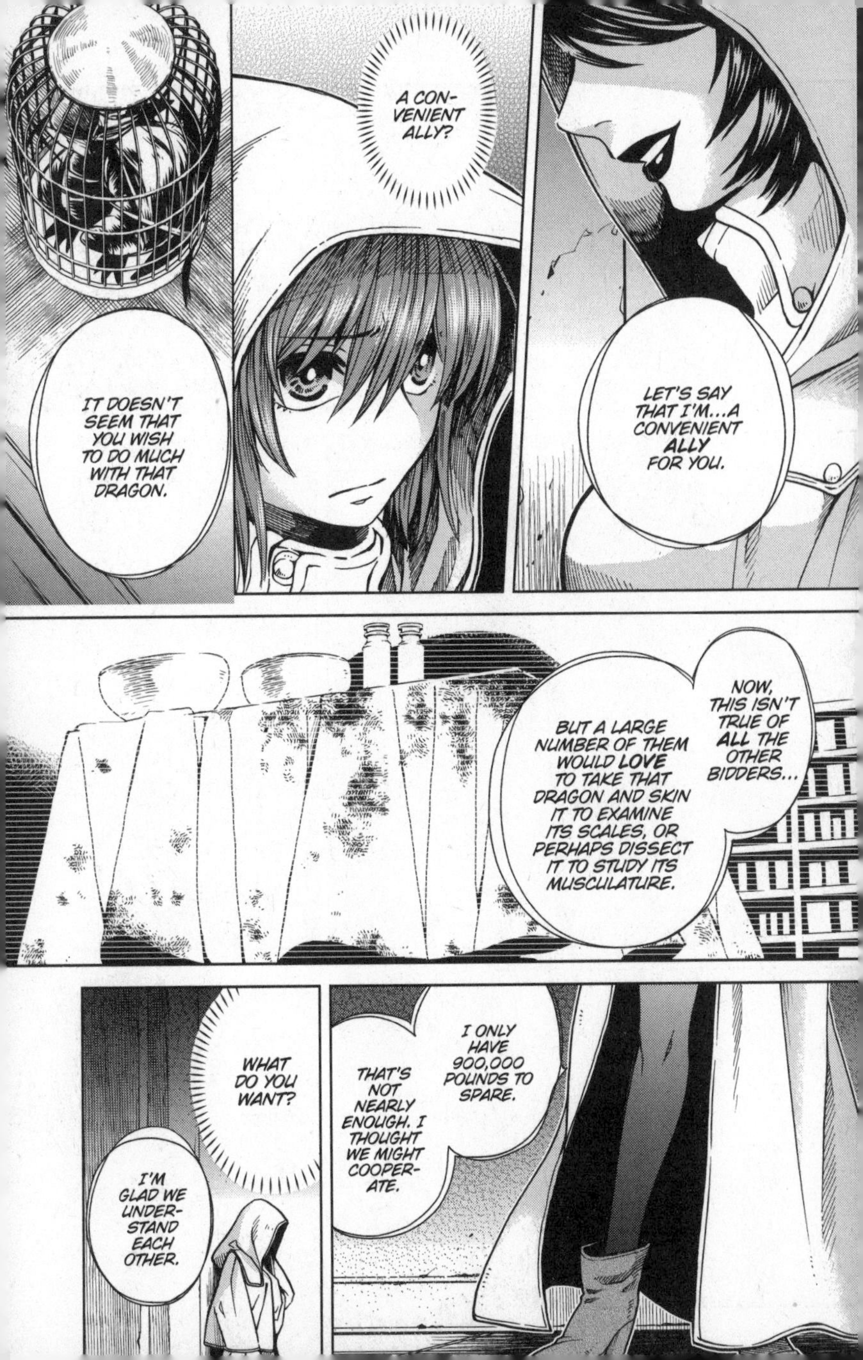
LET'S SAY THAT I'M...A CONVENIENT ALLY FOR YOU.
A CON-VENIENT ALLY?
IT DOESN'T SEEM THAT YOU WISH TO DO MUCH WITH THAT DRAGON.
NOW, THIS ISN'T TRUE OF ALL THE OTHER BIDDERS...
BUT A LARGE NUMBER OF THEM WOULD LOVE TO TAKE THAT DRAGON AND SKIN IT TO EXAMINE ITS SCALES, OR PERHAPS DISSECT IT TO STUDY ITS MUSCULATURE.
I ONLY HAVE 900,000 POUNDS TO SPARE.
THAT'S NOT NEARLY ENOUGH. I THOUGHT WE MIGHT COOPER-ATE.
WHAT DO YOU WANT?
I'M GLAD WE UNDER-STAND EACH OTHER.

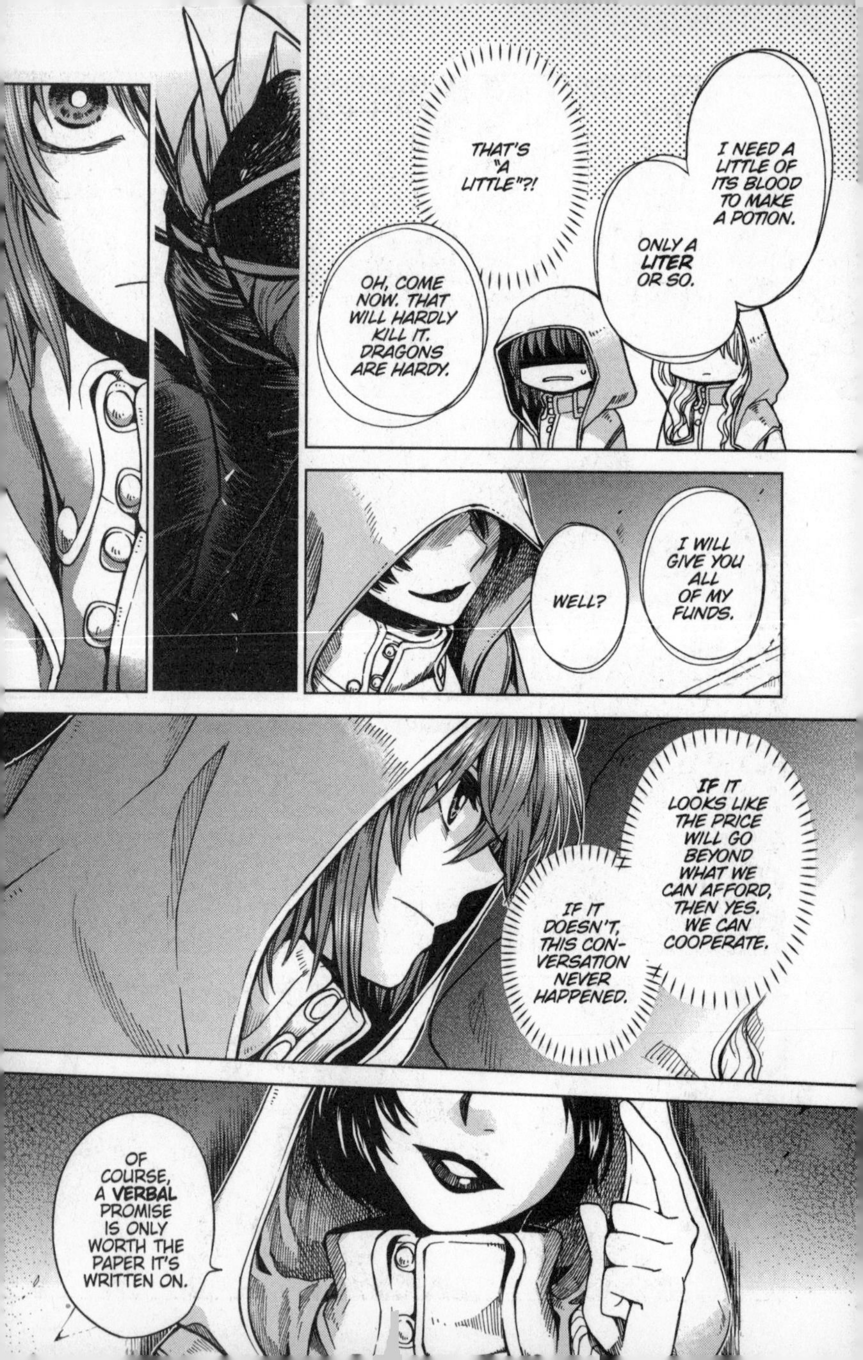
I NEED A LITTLE OF ITS BLOOD TO MAKE A POTION.
ONLY A **LITER** OR SO.
THAT'S "A LITTLE"?!
OH, COME NOW. THAT WILL HARDLY KILL IT. DRAGONS ARE HARDY.
I WILL GIVE YOU ALL OF MY FUNDS.
WELL?
IF IT LOOKS LIKE THE PRICE WILL GO BEYOND WHAT WE CAN AFFORD, THEN YES. WE CAN COOPERATE.
IF IT DOESN'T, THIS CONVERSATION NEVER HAPPENED.
OF COURSE, A **VERBAL** PROMISE IS ONLY WORTH THE PAPER IT'S WRITTEN ON.

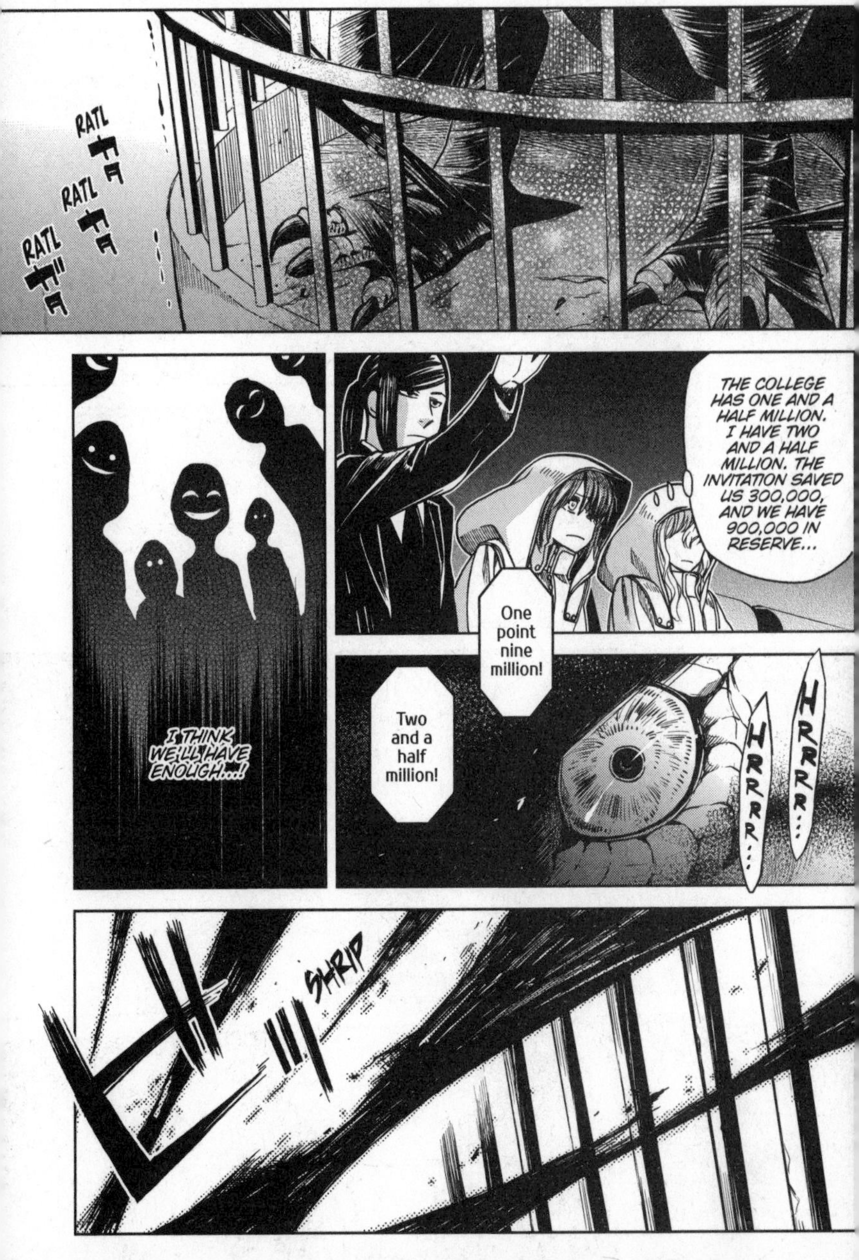
RATL
RATL
RATL
THE COLLEGE HAS ONE AND A HALF MILLION. I HAVE TWO AND A HALF MILLION. THE INVITATION SAVED US 300,000, AND WE HAVE 900,000 IN RESERVE...
One point nine million!
HRRRR...
HRRRR...
Two and a half million!
I THINK WE'LL HAVE ENOUGH...!
SHRIP

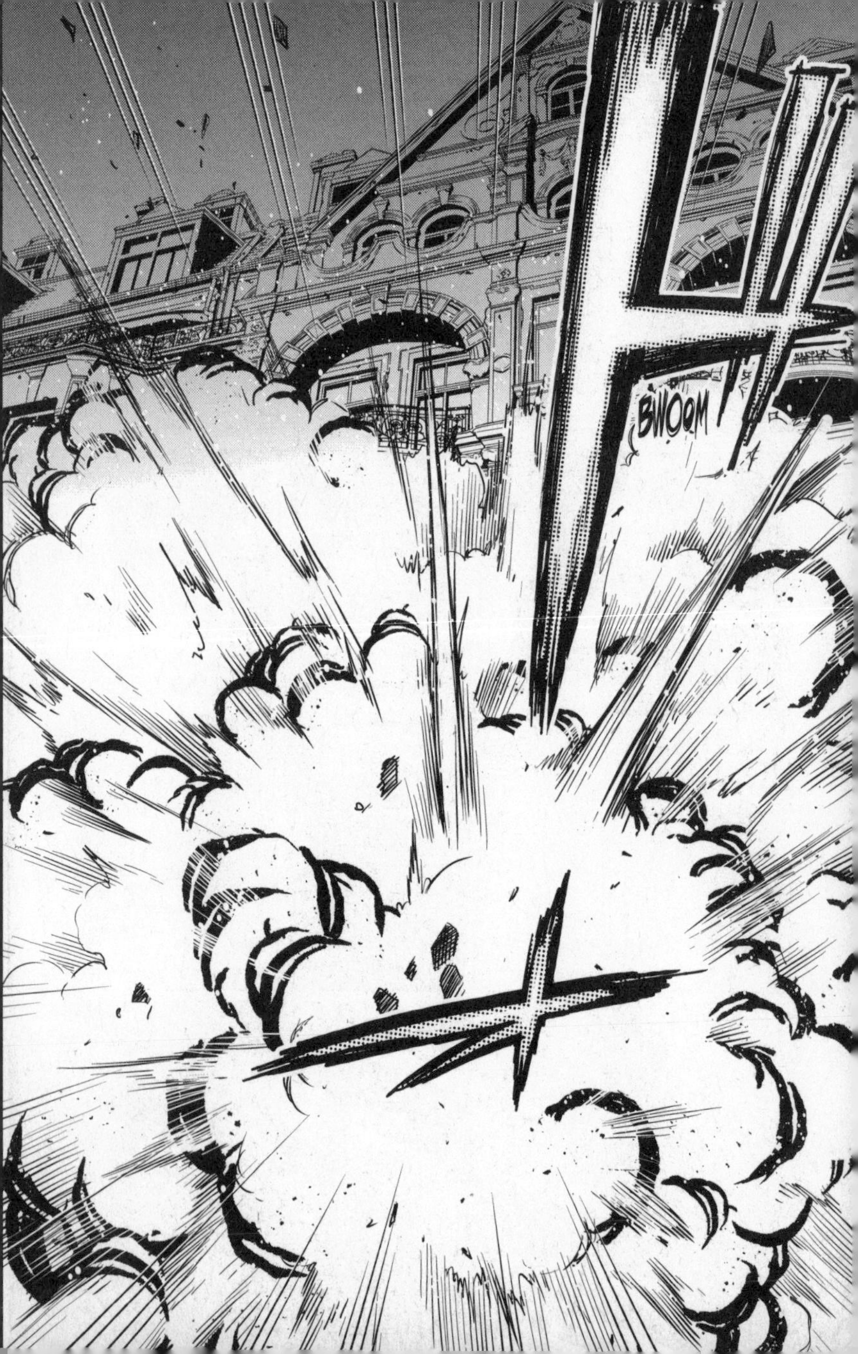
BWOOM

Chapter 35: Any port in a storm. III

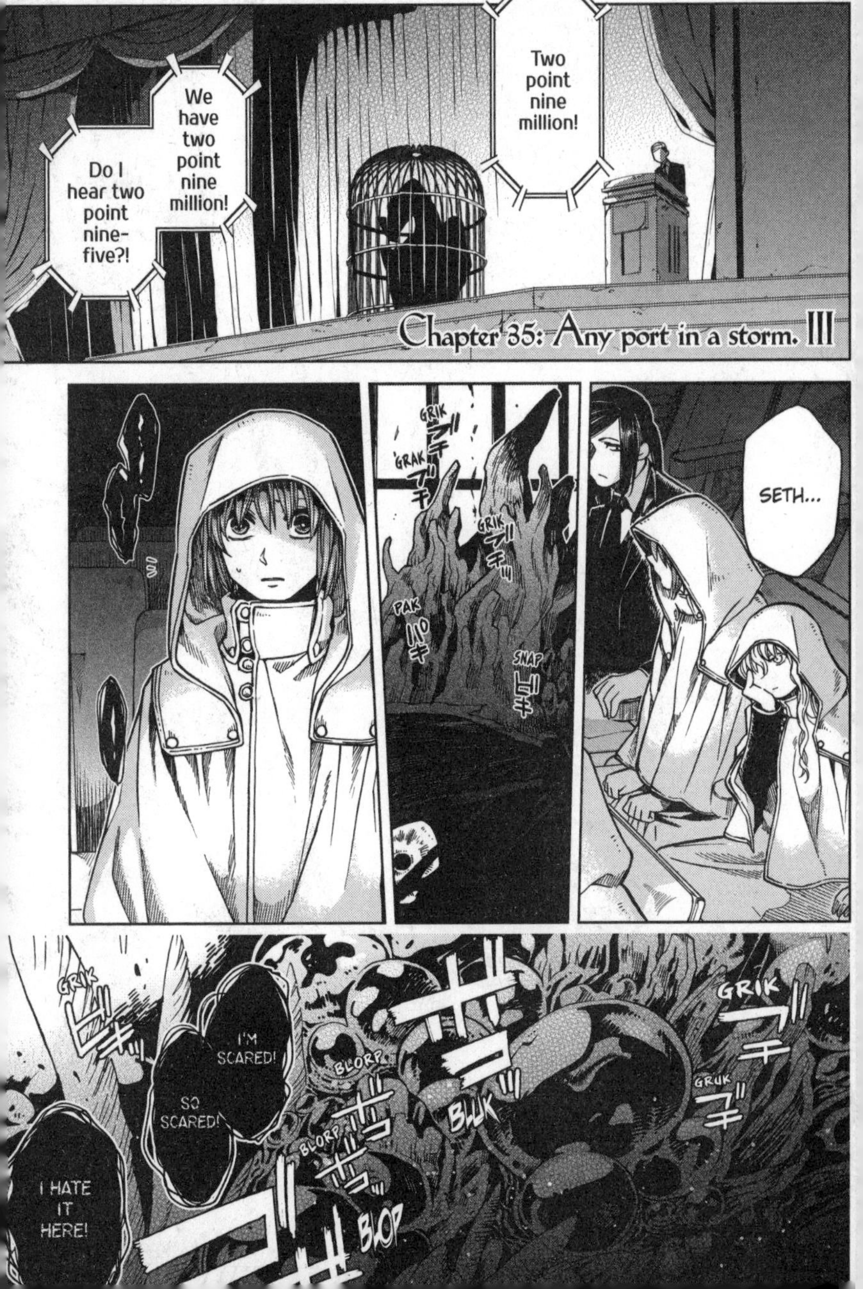

Two point nine million!
We have two point nine million!
Do I hear two point nine-five?!
Chapter 35: Any port in a storm. III
SETH...
GRIK
GRAK
GRIK
PAK
SNAP
GRIK
GRUK
BLUK
BLORP
I'M SCARED!
SO SCARED!
BLORP
GRIK
BLOP
I HATE IT HERE!

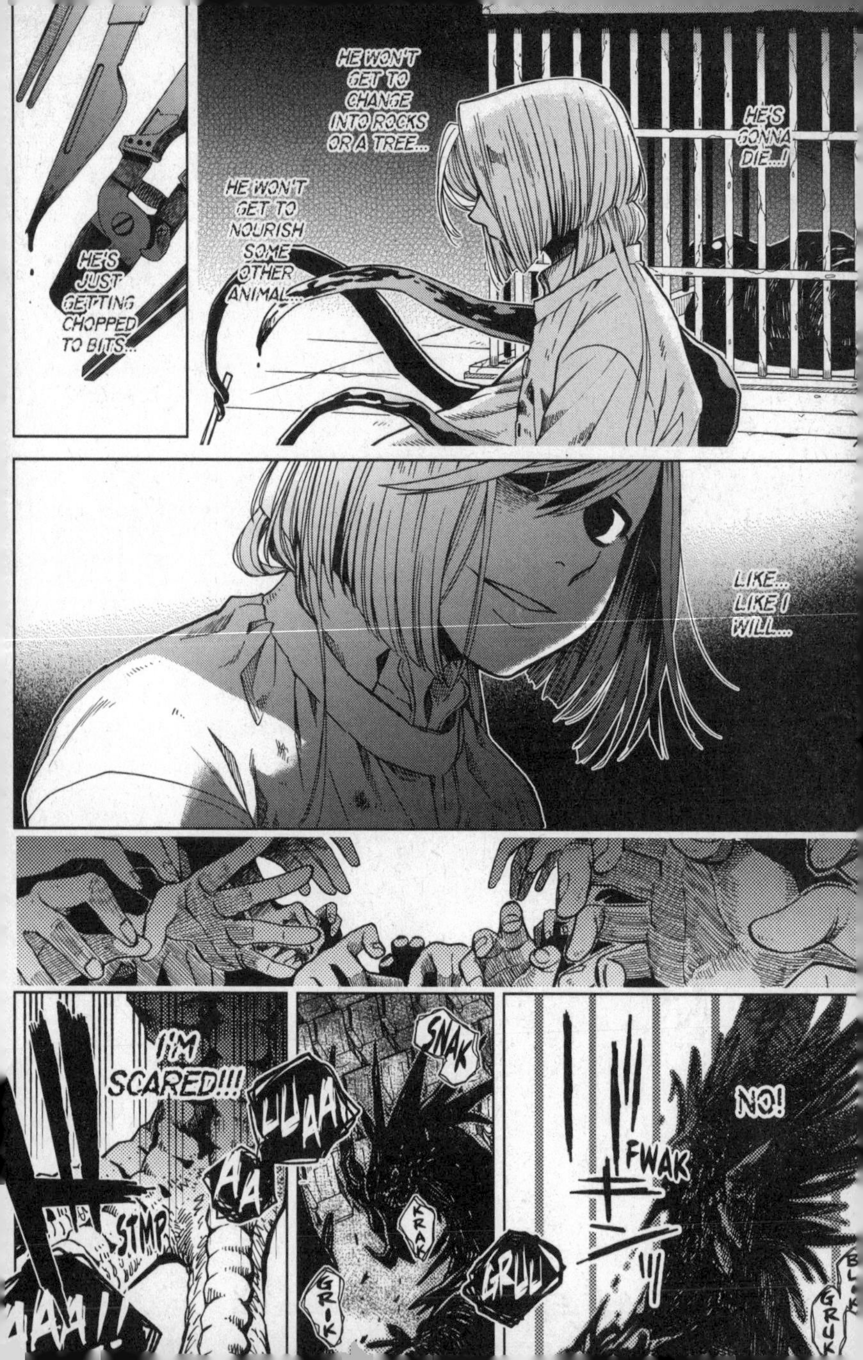
HE'S GONNA DIE...!
HE WON'T GET TO CHANGE INTO ROCKS OR A TREE...
HE WON'T GET TO NOURISH SOME OTHER ANIMAL...
HE'S JUST GETTING CHOPPED TO BITS...
LIKE... LIKE I WILL...
NO!
FWAK
GRUK
GRULL
SNAK
UUAA
AA
KRAK
GRIK
I'M SCARED!!!
STMP

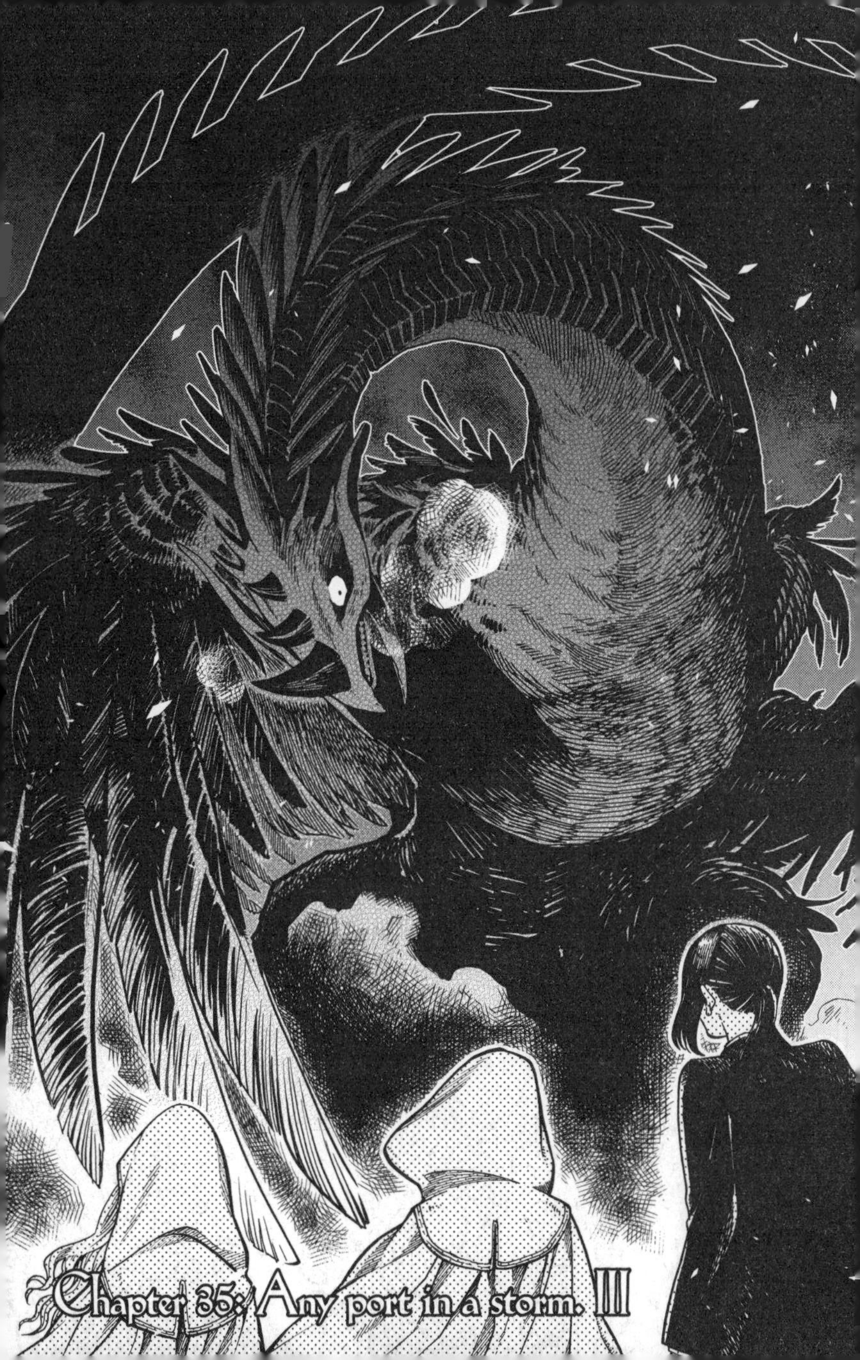

Chapter 35: Any port in a storm. III

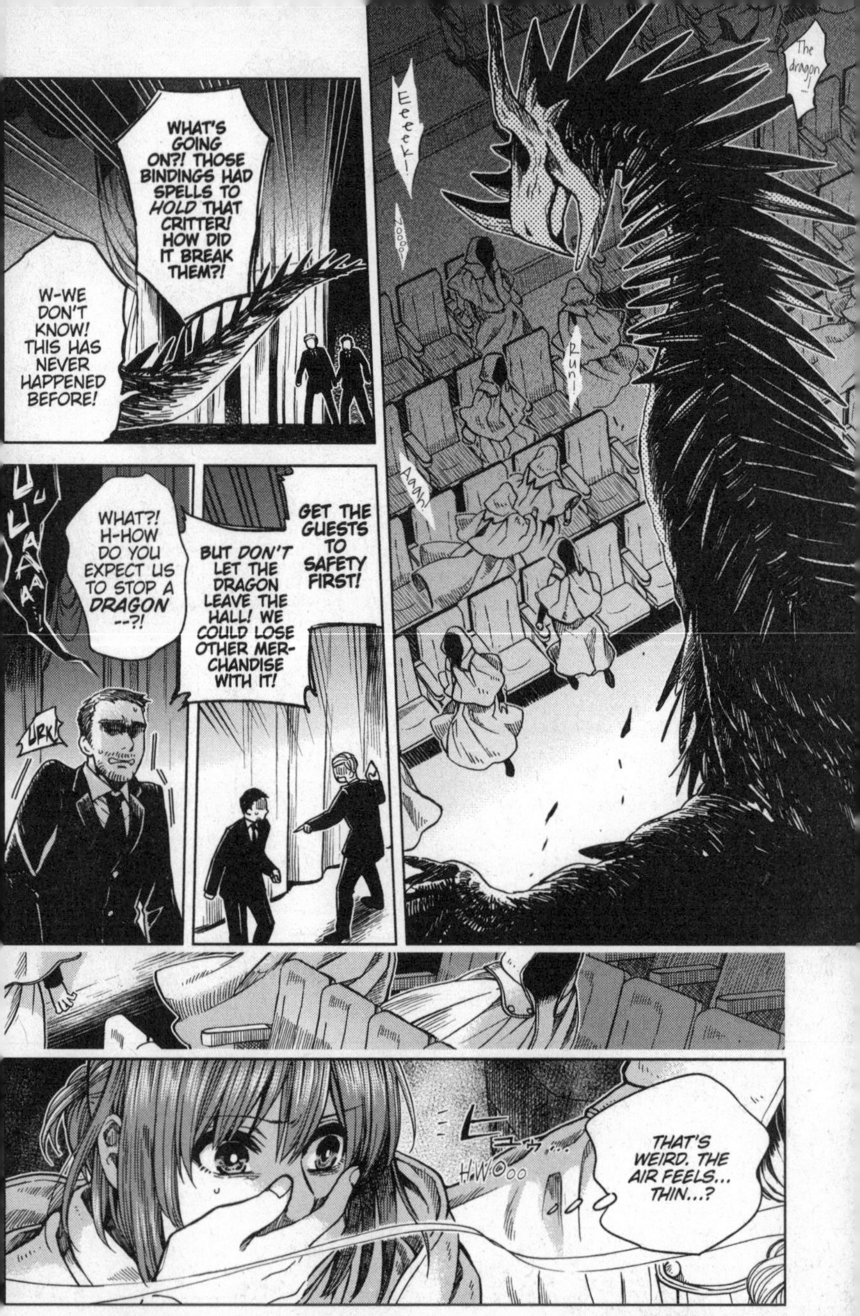
The dragon...!
Eeeek!
Noooo!
Run!
Aaah!
WHAT'S GOING ON?! THOSE BINDINGS HAD SPELLS TO HOLD THAT CRITTER! HOW DID IT BREAK THEM?!
W-WE DON'T KNOW! THIS HAS NEVER HAPPENED BEFORE!
GET THE GUESTS TO SAFETY FIRST!
BUT DON'T LET THE DRAGON LEAVE THE HALL! WE COULD LOSE OTHER MERCHANDISE WITH IT!
UUUAAAA...!
WHAT?! H-HOW DO YOU EXPECT US TO STOP A DRAGON--?!
URK!
ヒュゥ…
HWOOO
THAT'S WEIRD. THE AIR FEELS... THIN...?

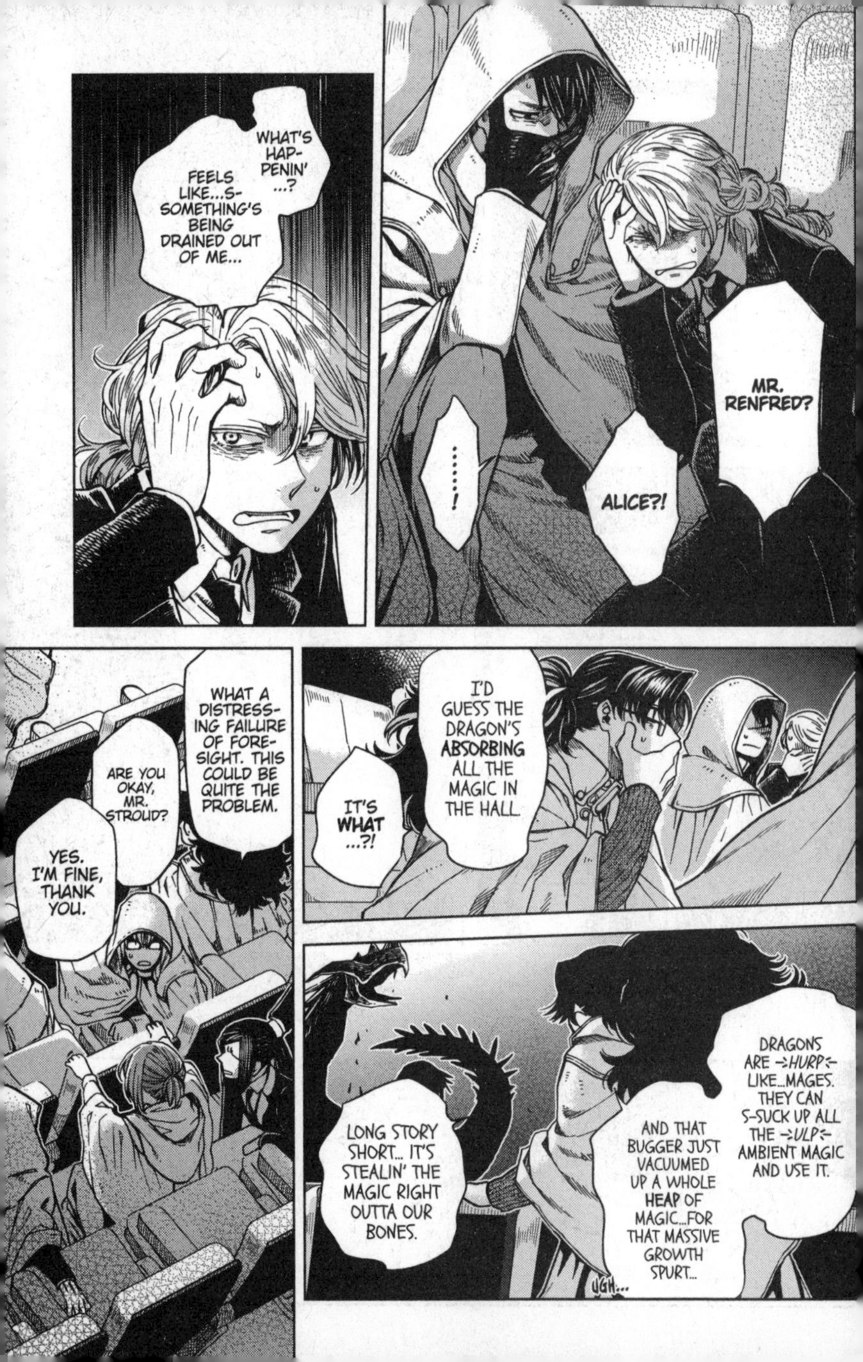
MR. RENFRED?
ALICE?!
......!
WHAT'S HAPPENIN' ...?
FEELS LIKE...S-SOMETHING'S BEING DRAINED OUT OF ME...
I'D GUESS THE DRAGON'S **ABSORBING** ALL THE MAGIC IN THE HALL.
IT'S **WHAT** ...?!
DRAGONS ARE ⇾HURP⇽ LIKE...MAGES. THEY CAN S-SUCK UP ALL THE ⇾ULP⇽ AMBIENT MAGIC AND USE IT.
AND THAT BUGGER JUST VACUUMED UP A WHOLE **HEAP** OF MAGIC...FOR THAT MASSIVE GROWTH SPURT...
LONG STORY SHORT... IT'S STEALIN' THE MAGIC RIGHT OUTTA OUR BONES.
UGH...
WHAT A DISTRESSING FAILURE OF FORESIGHT. THIS COULD BE QUITE THE PROBLEM.
ARE YOU OKAY, MR. STROUD?
YES. I'M FINE, THANK YOU.

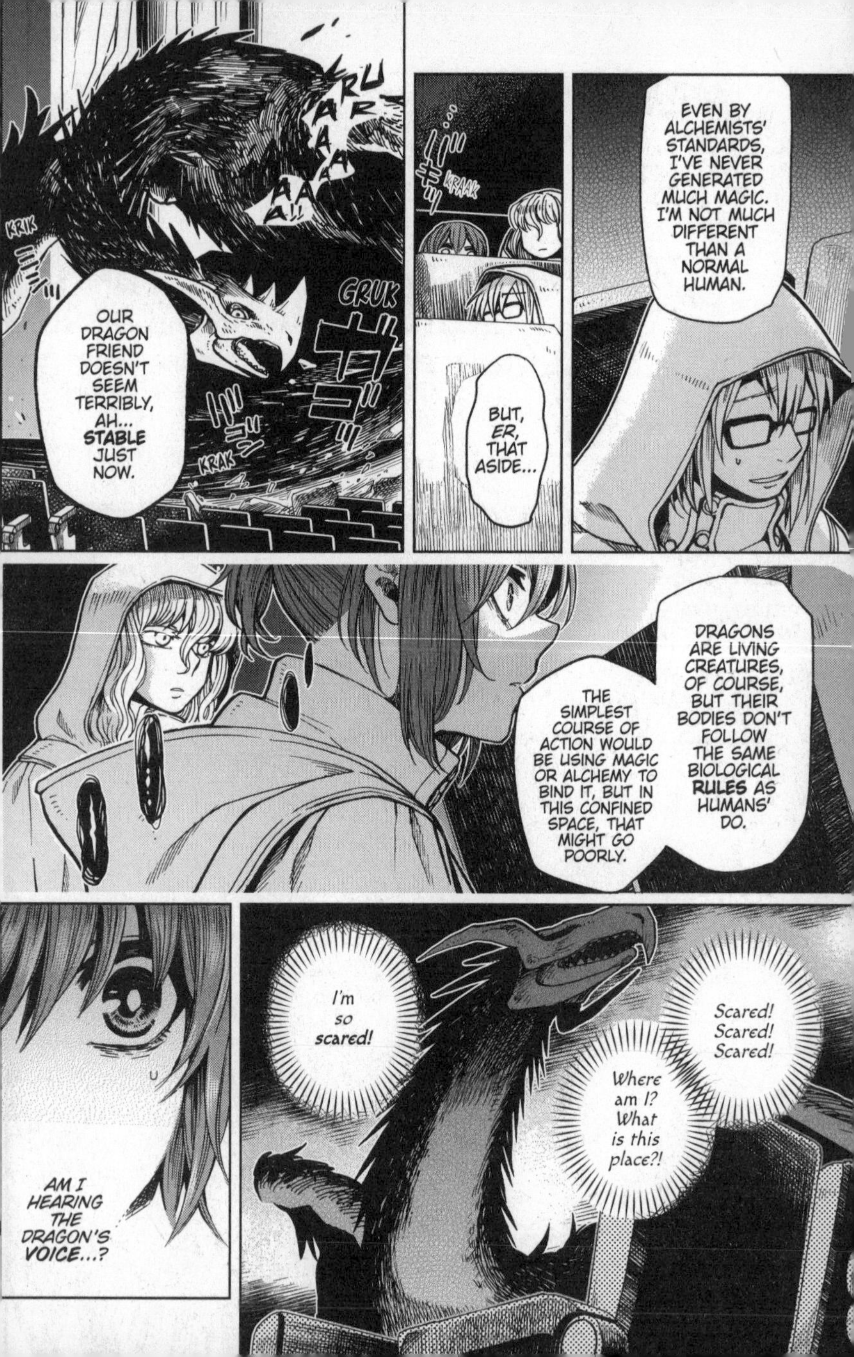
EVEN BY ALCHEMISTS' STANDARDS, I'VE NEVER GENERATED MUCH MAGIC. I'M NOT MUCH DIFFERENT THAN A NORMAL HUMAN.
KRAAK
BUT, *ER*, THAT ASIDE...
RU ARAAAAAAA!!
KRIK
GRUK
KRAK
OUR DRAGON FRIEND DOESN'T SEEM TERRIBLY, AH... **STABLE** JUST NOW.
DRAGONS ARE LIVING CREATURES, OF COURSE, BUT THEIR BODIES DON'T FOLLOW THE SAME BIOLOGICAL **RULES** AS HUMANS' DO.
THE SIMPLEST COURSE OF ACTION WOULD BE USING MAGIC OR ALCHEMY TO BIND IT, BUT IN THIS CONFINED SPACE, THAT MIGHT GO POORLY.
Scared! Scared! Scared!
I'm so scared!
Where am I? What is this place?!
AM I HEARING THE DRAGON'S **VOICE**...?

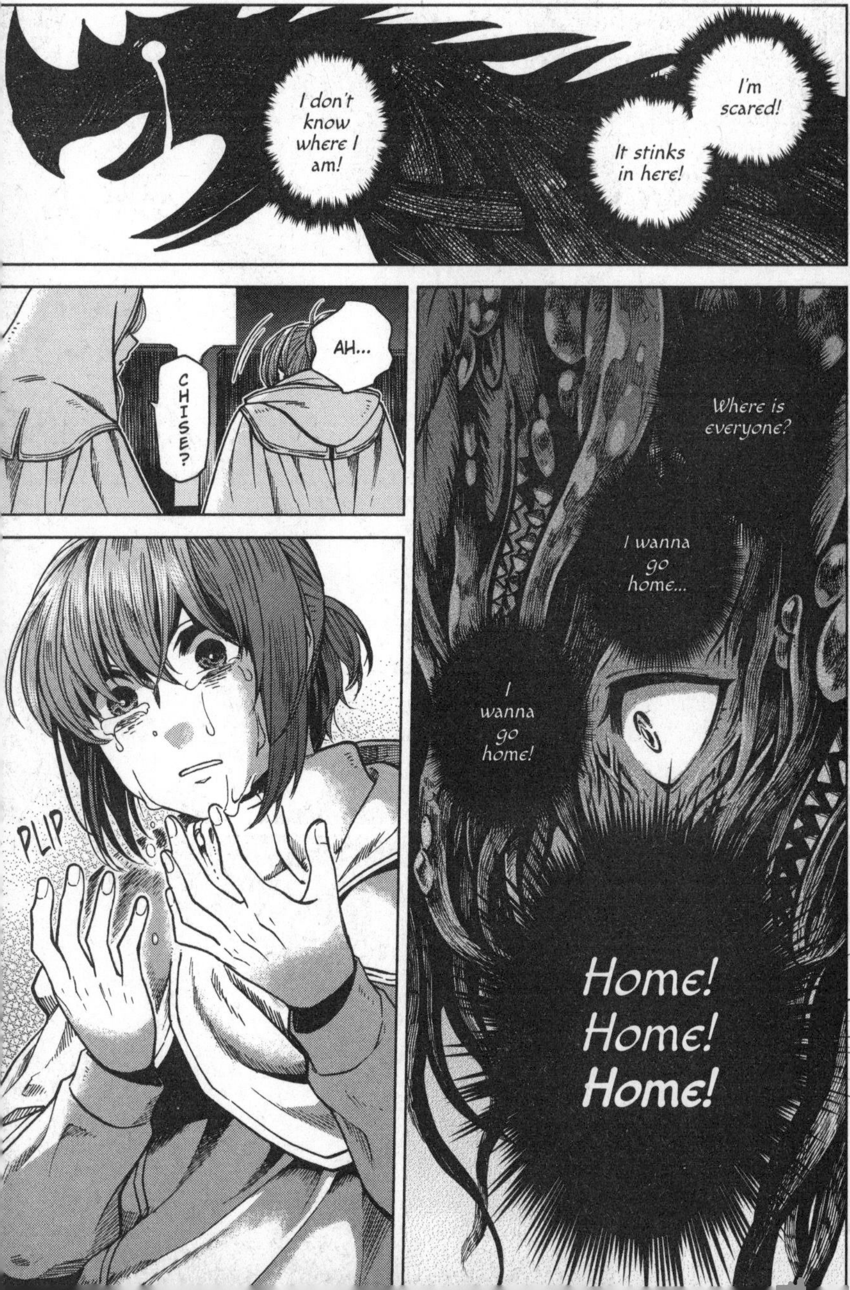
I'm scared!
It stinks in here!
I don't know where I am!
Where is everyone?
I wanna go home...
I wanna go home!
Home! Home! Home!
AH...
CHISE?
PLIP

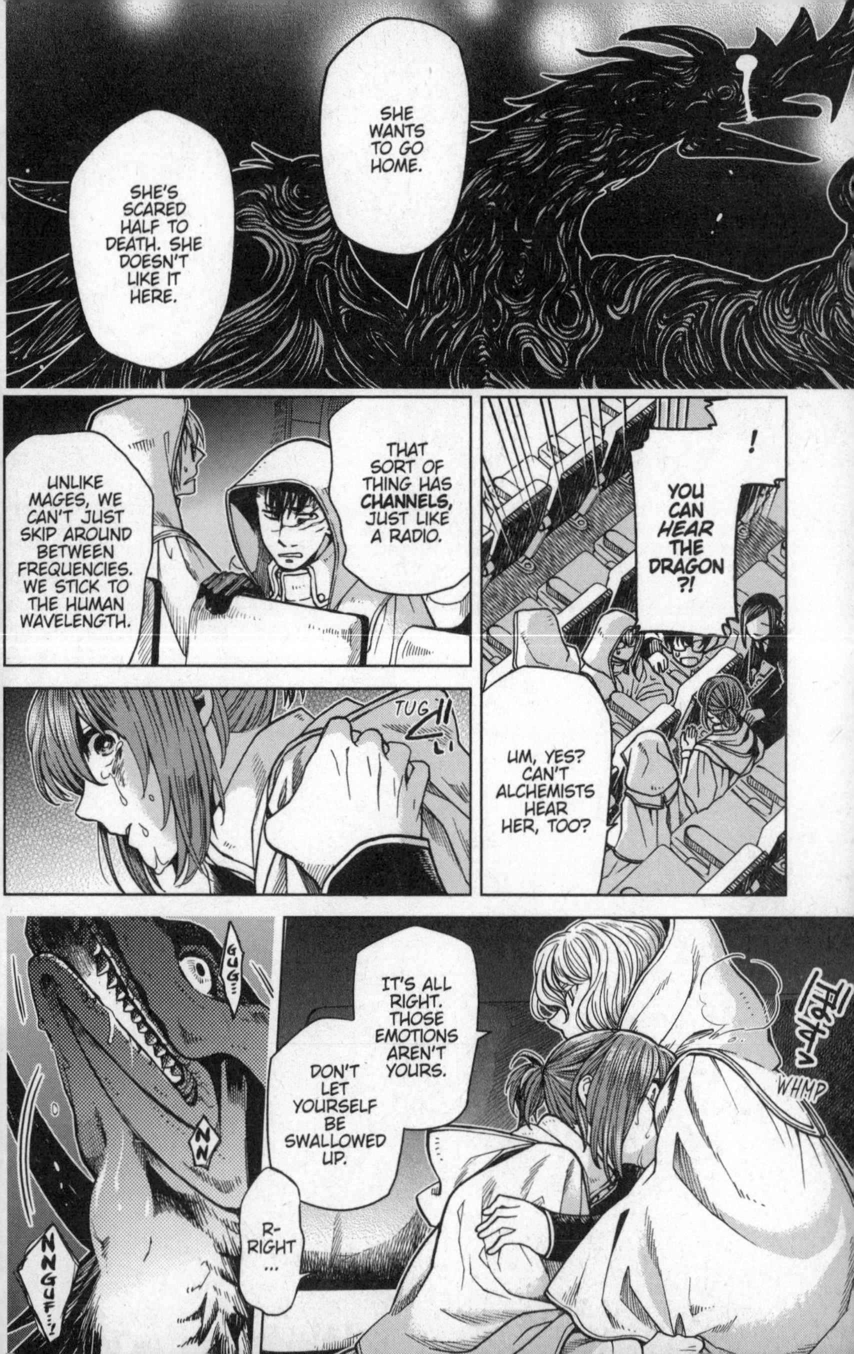
SHE WANTS TO GO HOME.
SHE'S SCARED HALF TO DEATH. SHE DOESN'T LIKE IT HERE.
!
YOU CAN HEAR THE DRAGON?!
UM, YES? CAN'T ALCHEMISTS HEAR HER, TOO?
THAT SORT OF THING HAS CHANNELS, JUST LIKE A RADIO.
UNLIKE MAGES, WE CAN'T JUST SKIP AROUND BETWEEN FREQUENCIES. WE STICK TO THE HUMAN WAVELENGTH.
TUG
WHMP
IT'S ALL RIGHT. THOSE EMOTIONS AREN'T YOURS.
DON'T LET YOURSELF BE SWALLOWED UP.
R-RIGHT...
GUG
NN
NNGUF...!

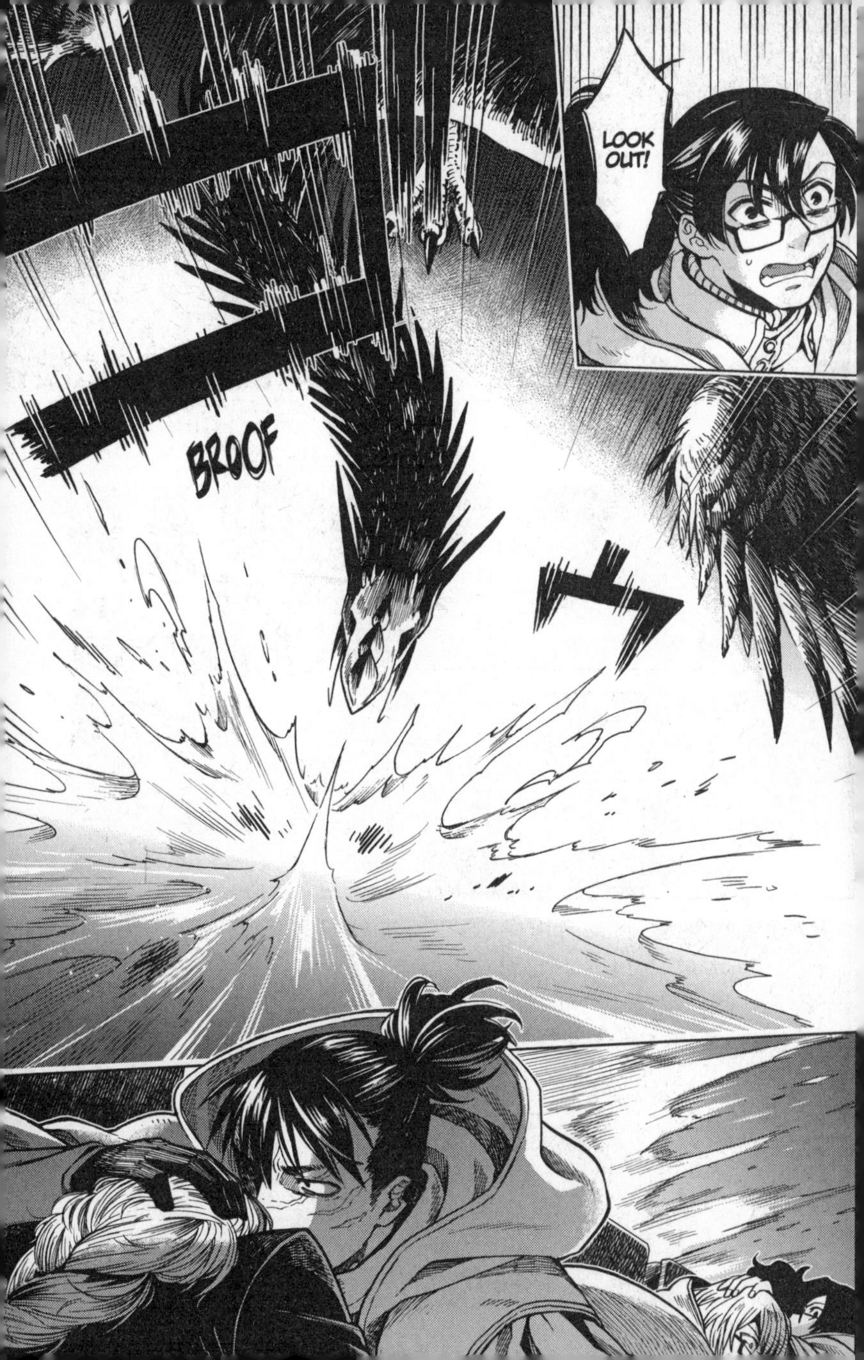
LOOK OUT!
BROOF

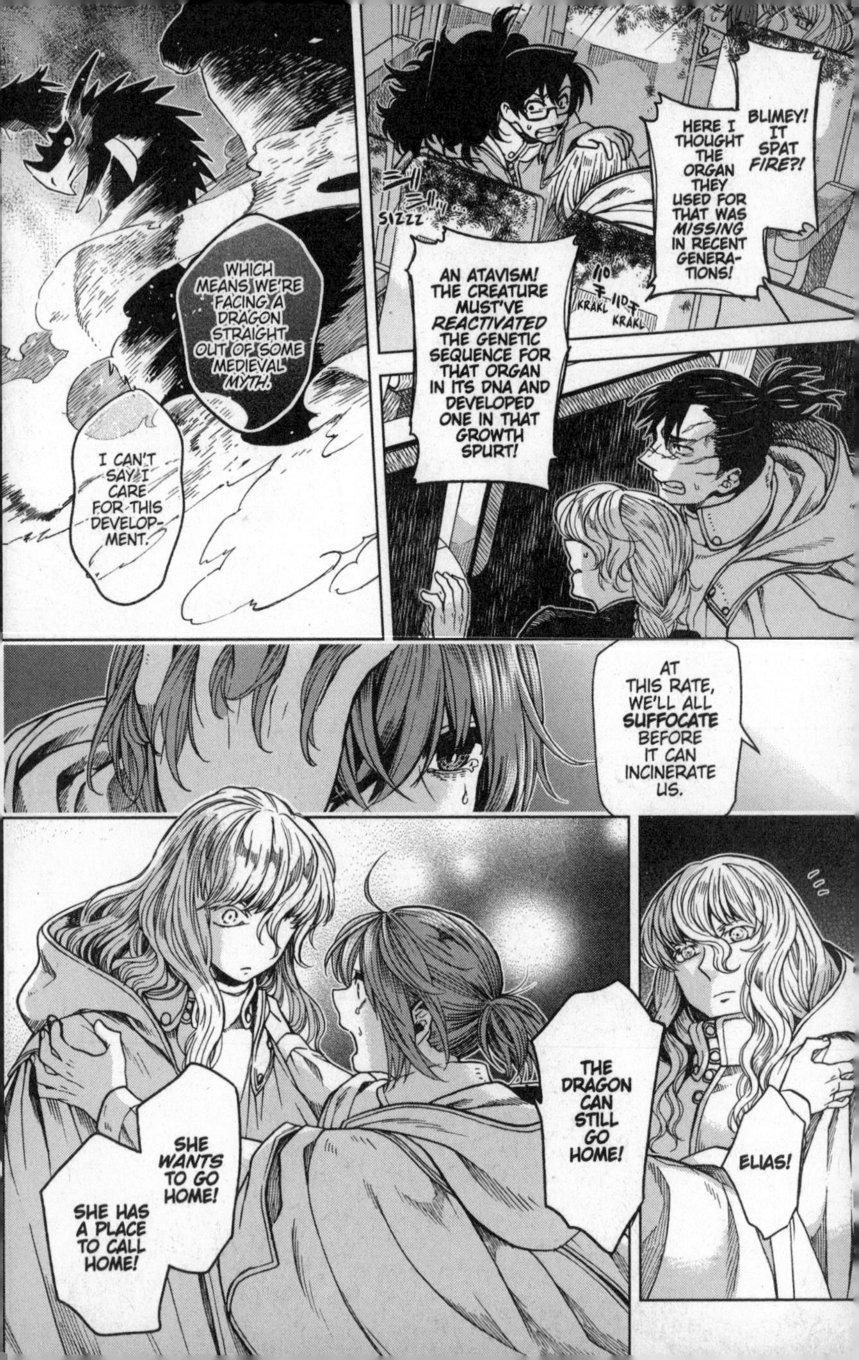
BLIMEY! IT SPAT FIRE?!
HERE I THOUGHT THE ORGAN THEY USED FOR THAT WAS MISSING IN RECENT GENERATIONS!
SIZZZ
KRAKL
KRAKL
AN ATAVISM! THE CREATURE MUST'VE REACTIVATED THE GENETIC SEQUENCE FOR THAT ORGAN IN ITS DNA AND DEVELOPED ONE IN THAT GROWTH SPURT!
WHICH MEANS WE'RE FACING A DRAGON STRAIGHT OUT OF SOME MEDIEVAL MYTH.
I CAN'T SAY I CARE FOR THIS DEVELOPMENT.
AT THIS RATE, WE'LL ALL SUFFOCATE BEFORE IT CAN INCINERATE US.
ELIAS!
THE DRAGON CAN STILL GO HOME!
SHE WANTS TO GO HOME!
SHE HAS A PLACE TO CALL HOME!

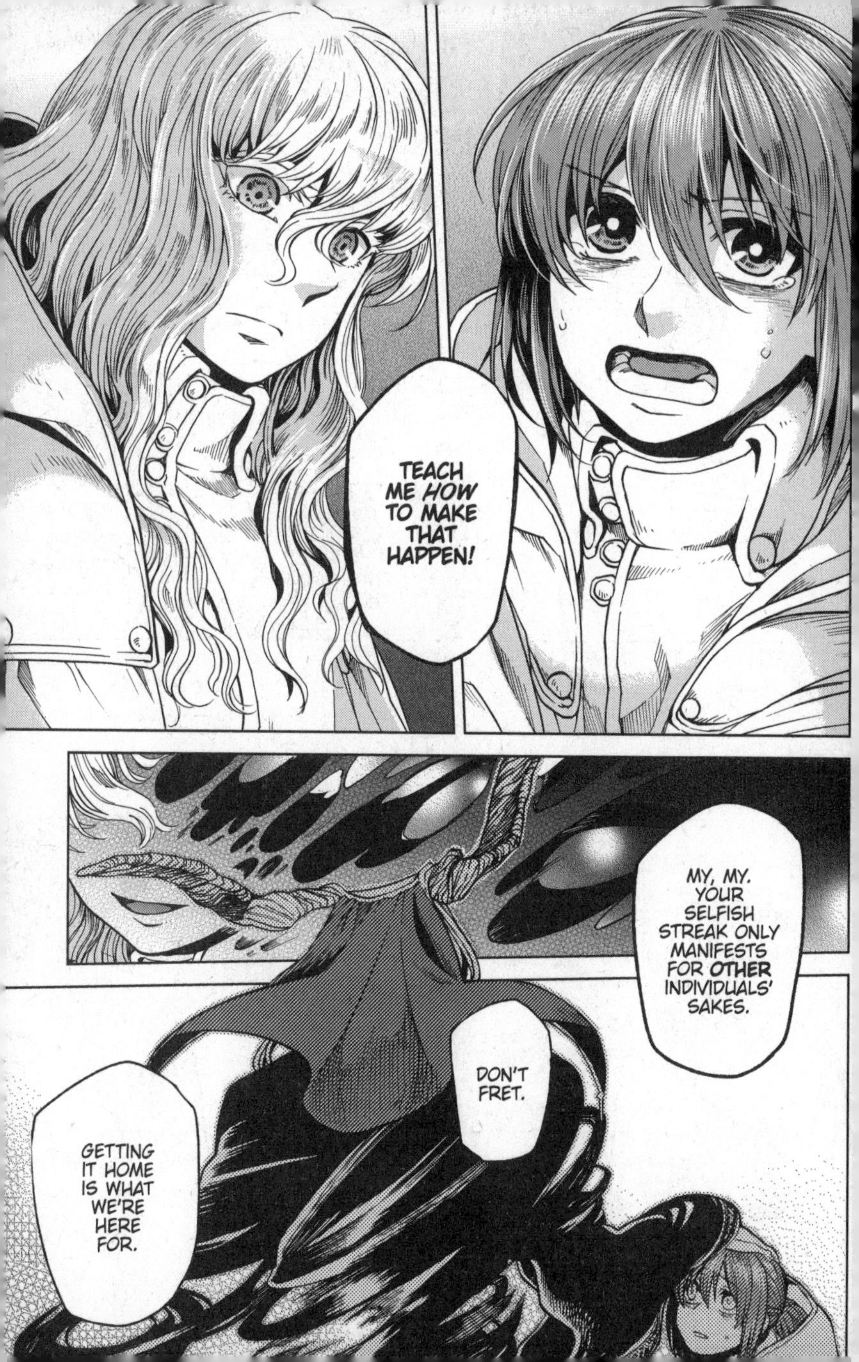
TEACH ME *HOW* TO MAKE THAT HAPPEN!
MY, MY. YOUR SELFISH STREAK ONLY MANIFESTS FOR **OTHER** INDIVIDUALS' SAKES.
DON'T FRET.
GETTING IT HOME IS WHAT WE'RE HERE FOR.

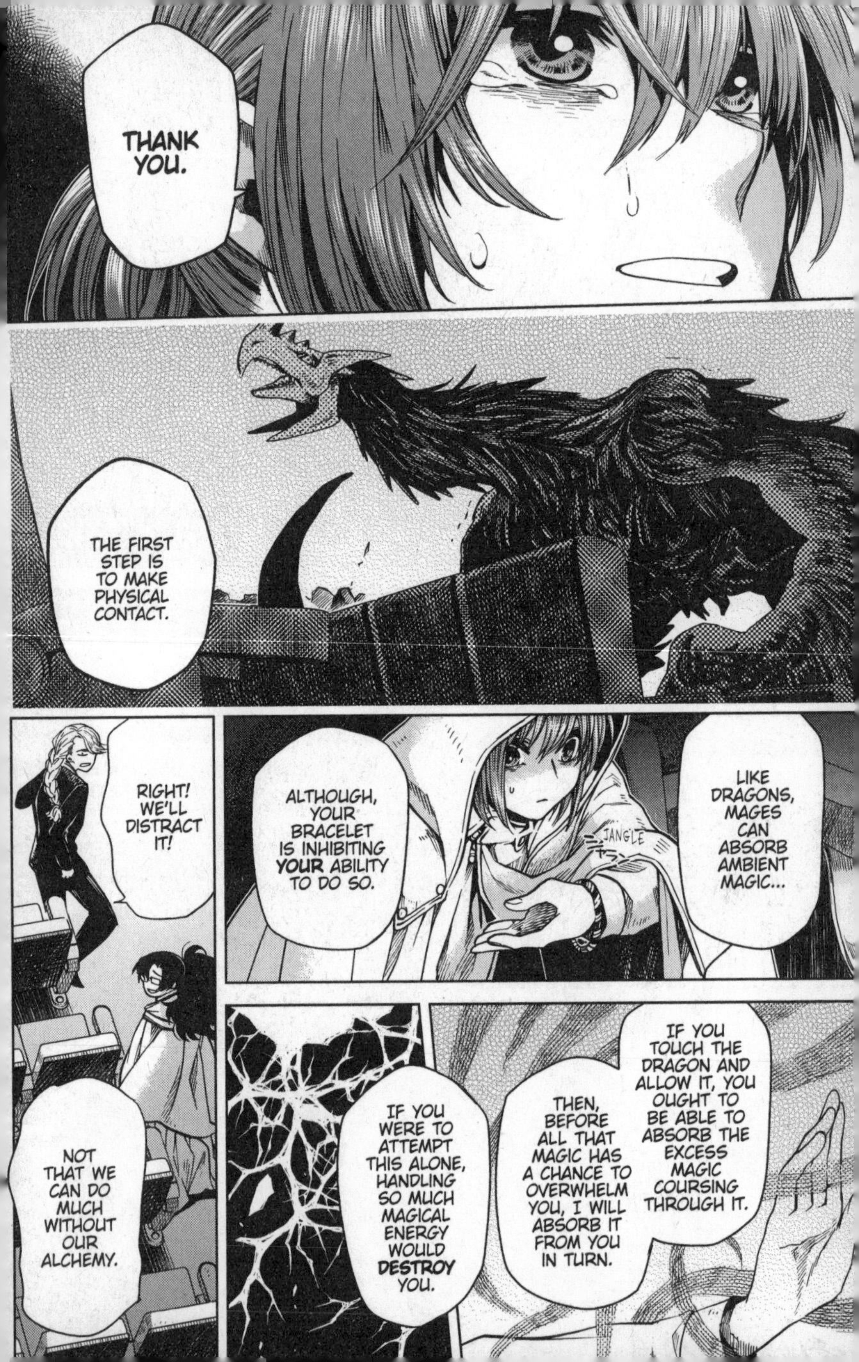
THANK YOU.
THE FIRST STEP IS TO MAKE PHYSICAL CONTACT.
LIKE DRAGONS, MAGES CAN ABSORB AMBIENT MAGIC...
JANGLE
ALTHOUGH, YOUR BRACELET IS INHIBITING **YOUR** ABILITY TO DO SO.
IF YOU TOUCH THE DRAGON AND ALLOW IT, YOU OUGHT TO BE ABLE TO ABSORB THE EXCESS MAGIC COURSING THROUGH IT.
THEN, BEFORE ALL THAT MAGIC HAS A CHANCE TO OVERWHELM YOU, I WILL ABSORB IT FROM YOU IN TURN.
IF YOU WERE TO ATTEMPT THIS ALONE, HANDLING SO MUCH MAGICAL ENERGY WOULD **DESTROY** YOU.
RIGHT! WE'LL DISTRACT IT!
NOT THAT WE CAN DO MUCH WITHOUT OUR ALCHEMY.

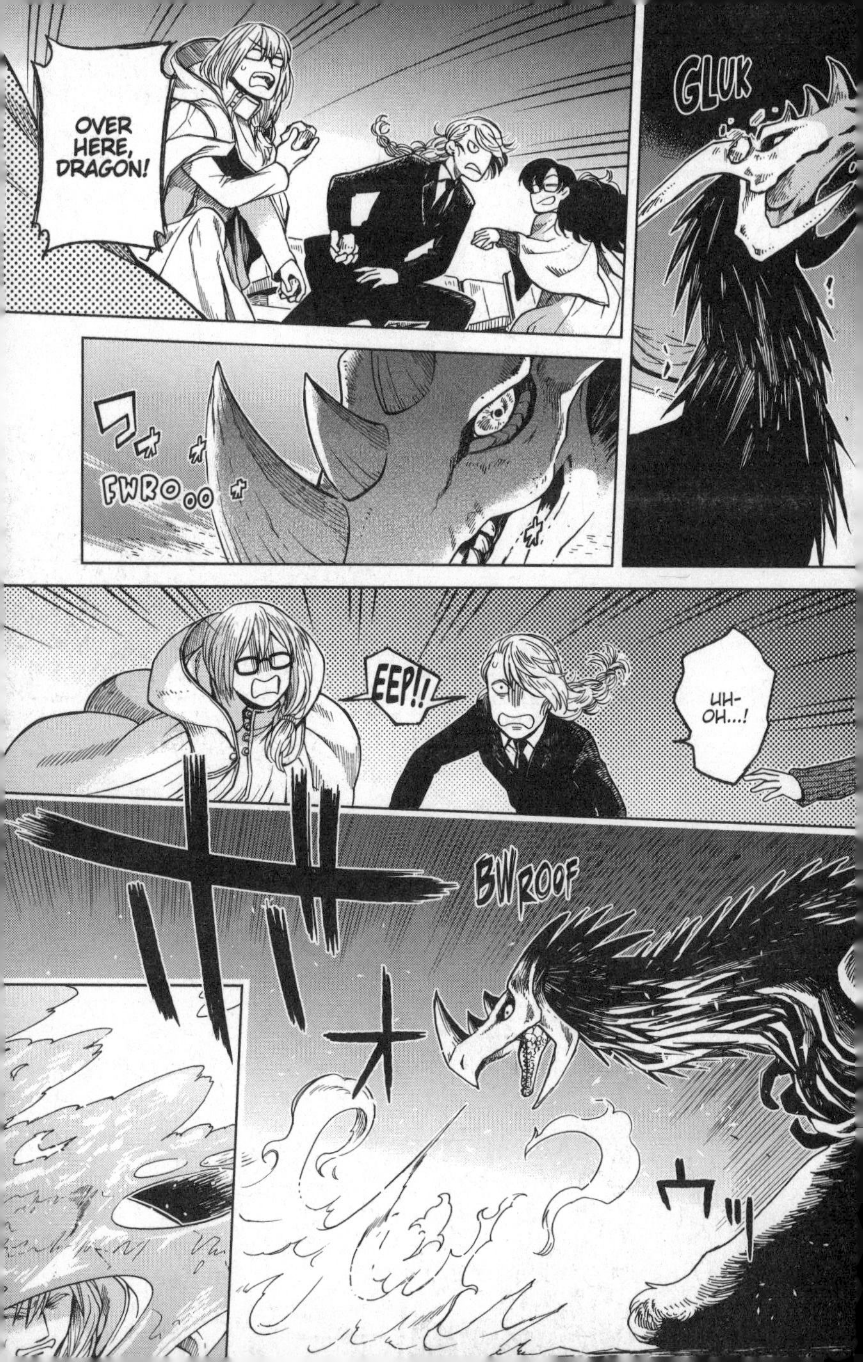
GLUK
OVER HERE, DRAGON!
FWROOOO
UH-OH...!
EEP!!
BWROOF

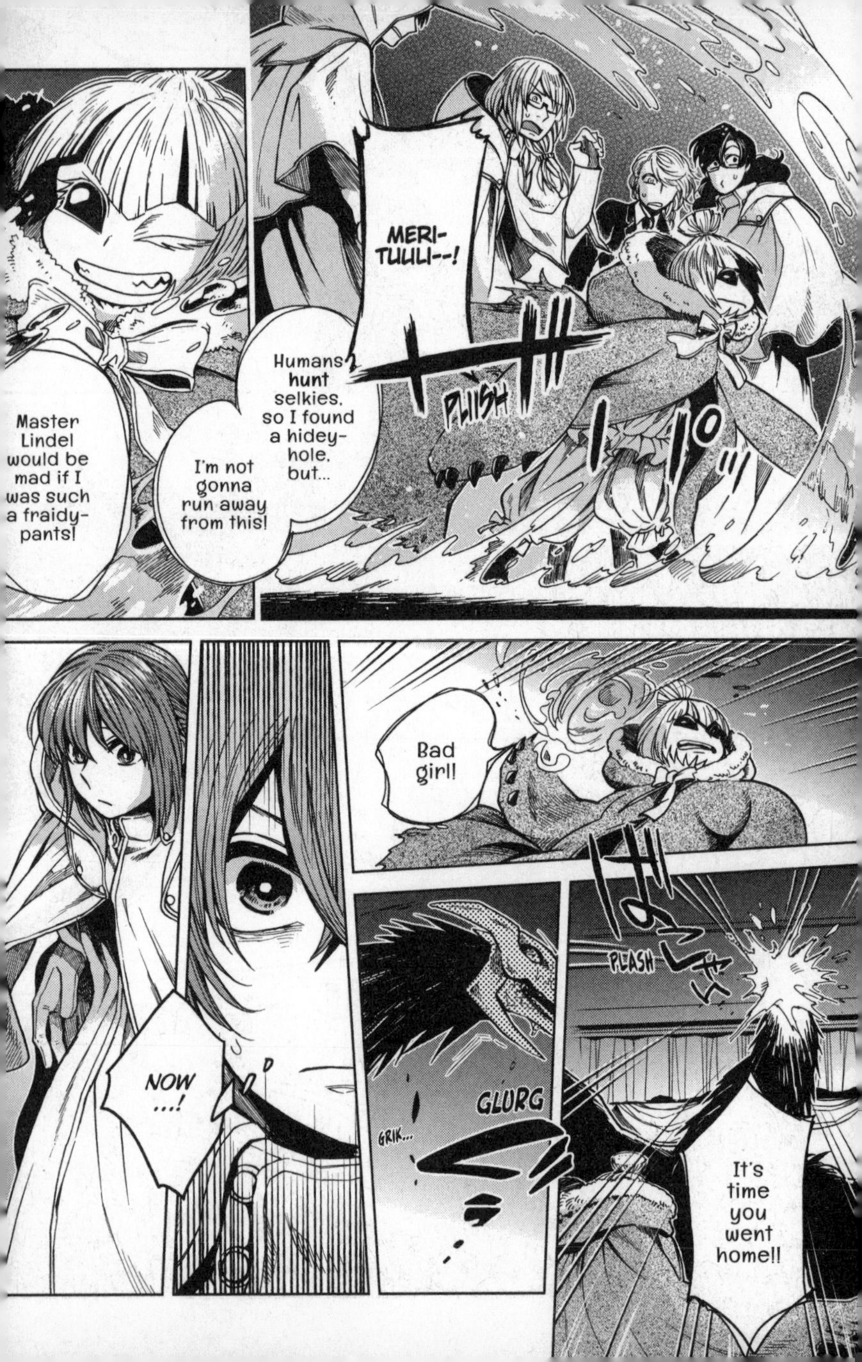
MERI-TUULI--!
Humans hunt selkies, so I found a hidey-hole, but...
I'm not gonna run away from this!
PLiiSH
Master Lindel would be mad if I was such a fraidy-pants!
Bad girl!
PLASH
It's time you went home!!
GLURG
GRIK...
NOW ...!

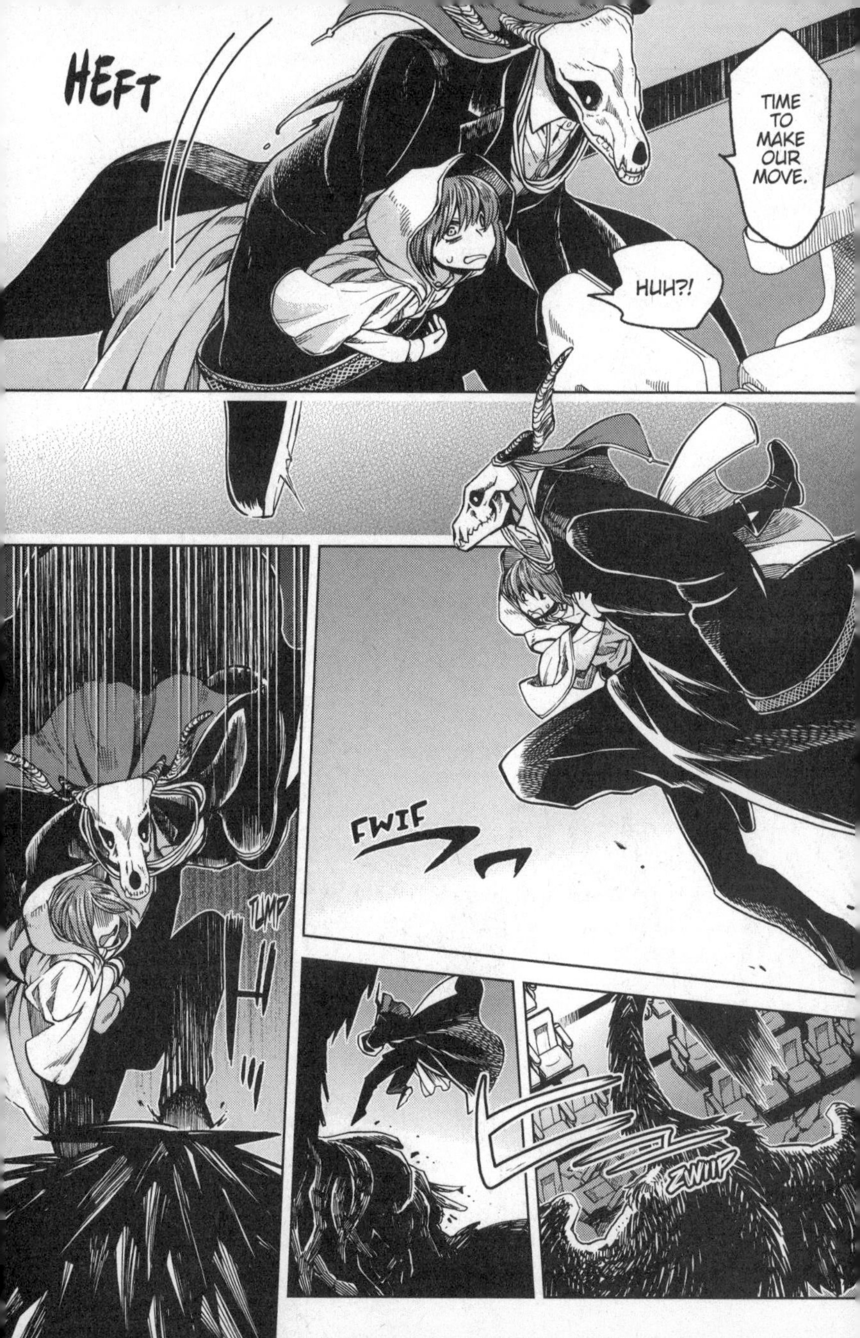
TIME TO MAKE OUR MOVE.
HUH?!
HEFT
FWIF
ZWIIP
TUMP

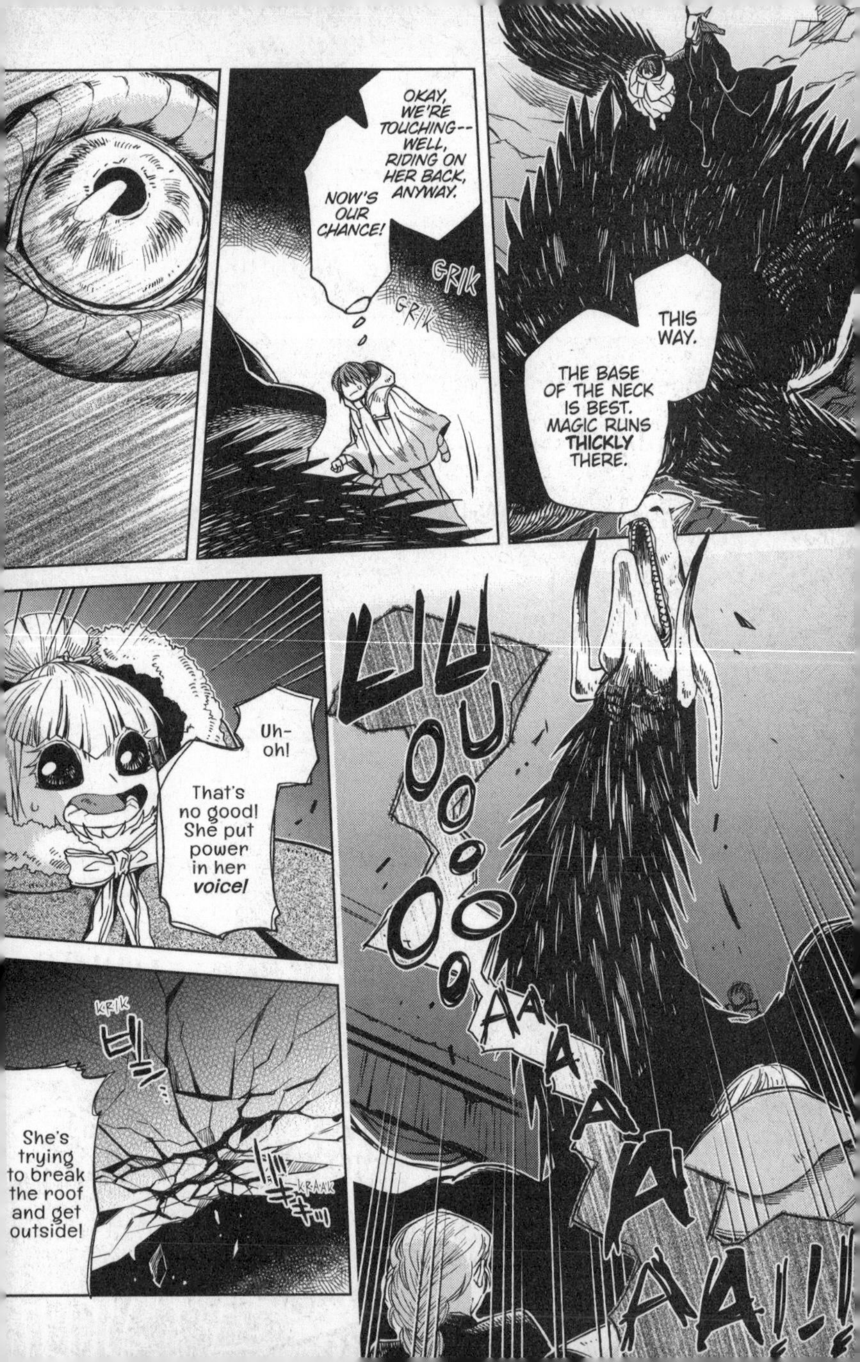

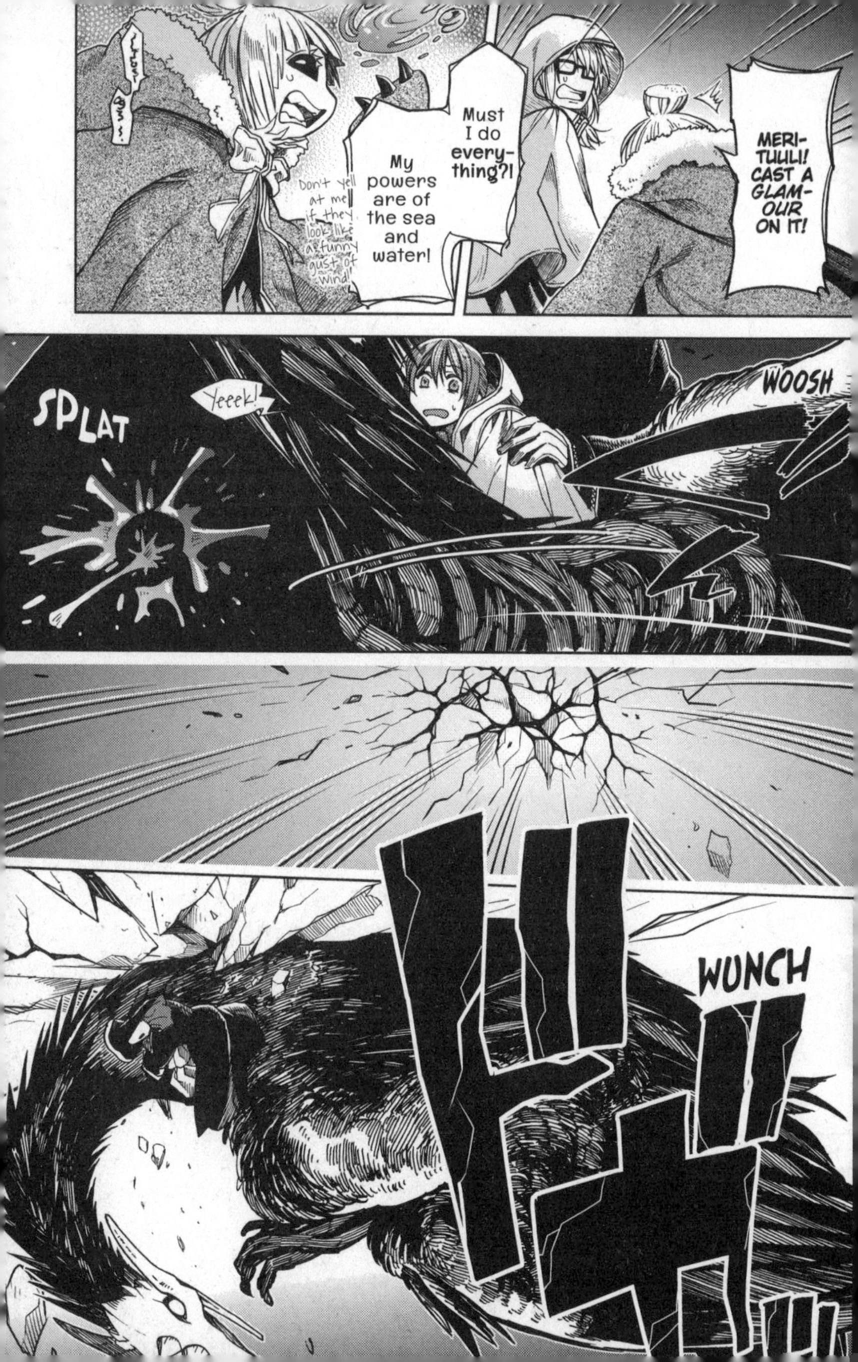
MERI-TUULI! CAST A GLAMOUR ON IT!
Must I do everything?!
My powers are of the sea and water!
Don't yell at me if they looks like a funny gust of wind!
WOOSH
Yeeek!
SPLAT
WUNCH

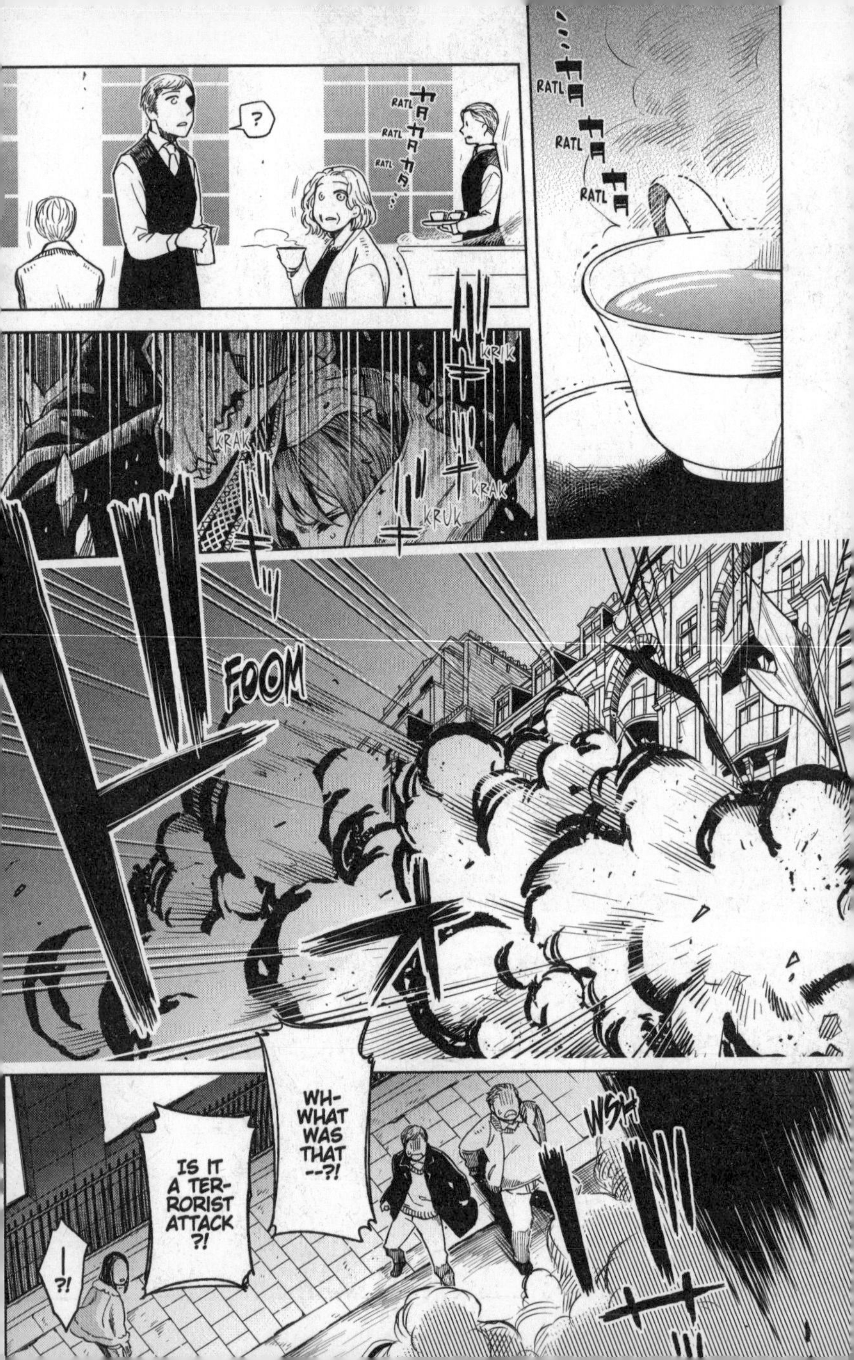
RATL
RATL
RATL
?
RATL
RATL
RATL
KRIK
KRAK
KRUK
KRAK
FOOM
WSH
WH-WHAT WAS THAT--?!
IS IT A TERRORIST ATTACK?!
—?!

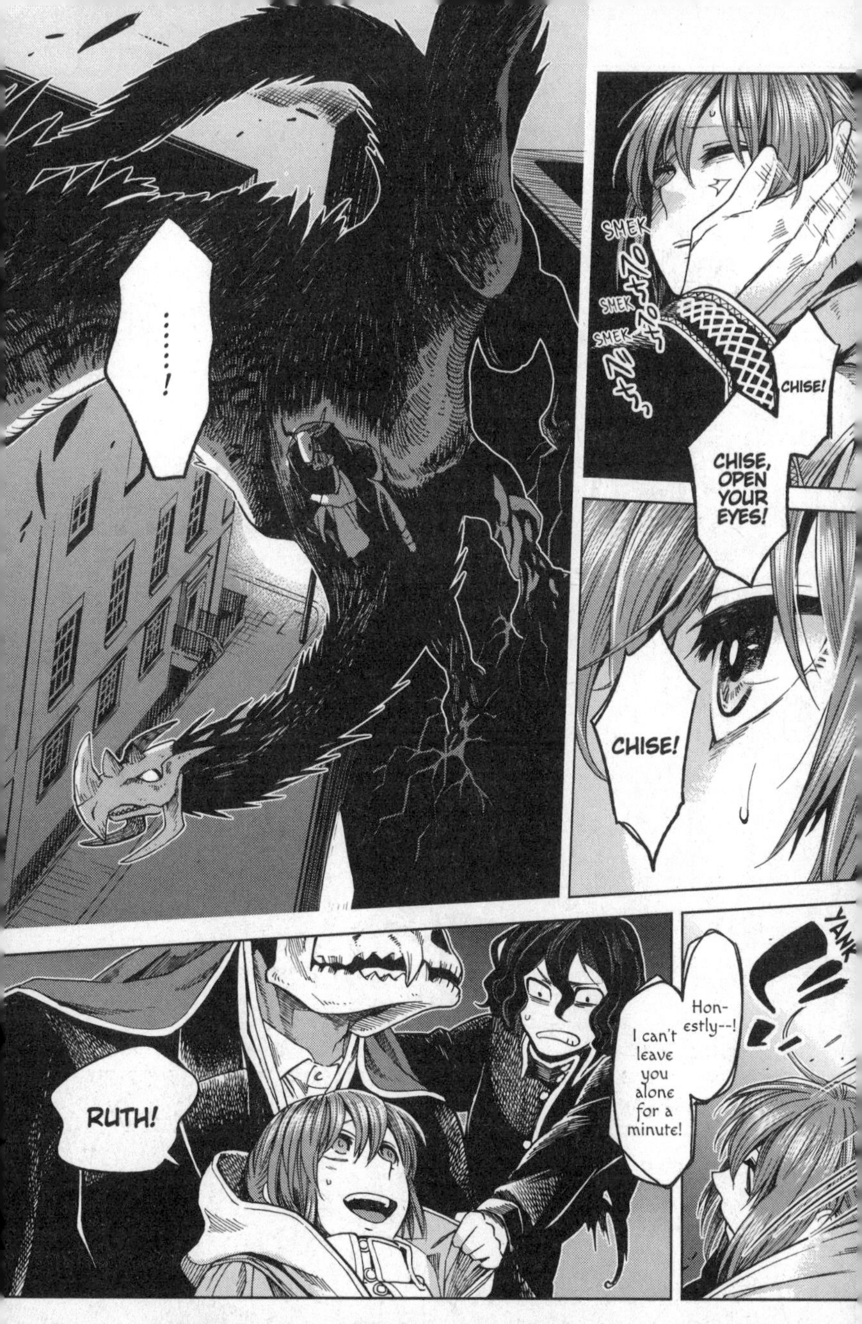
SMEK
SMEK
SMEK
CHISE!
CHISE, OPEN YOUR EYES!
CHISE!
......!
YANK
Hon-estly--!
I can't leave you alone for a minute!
RUTH!

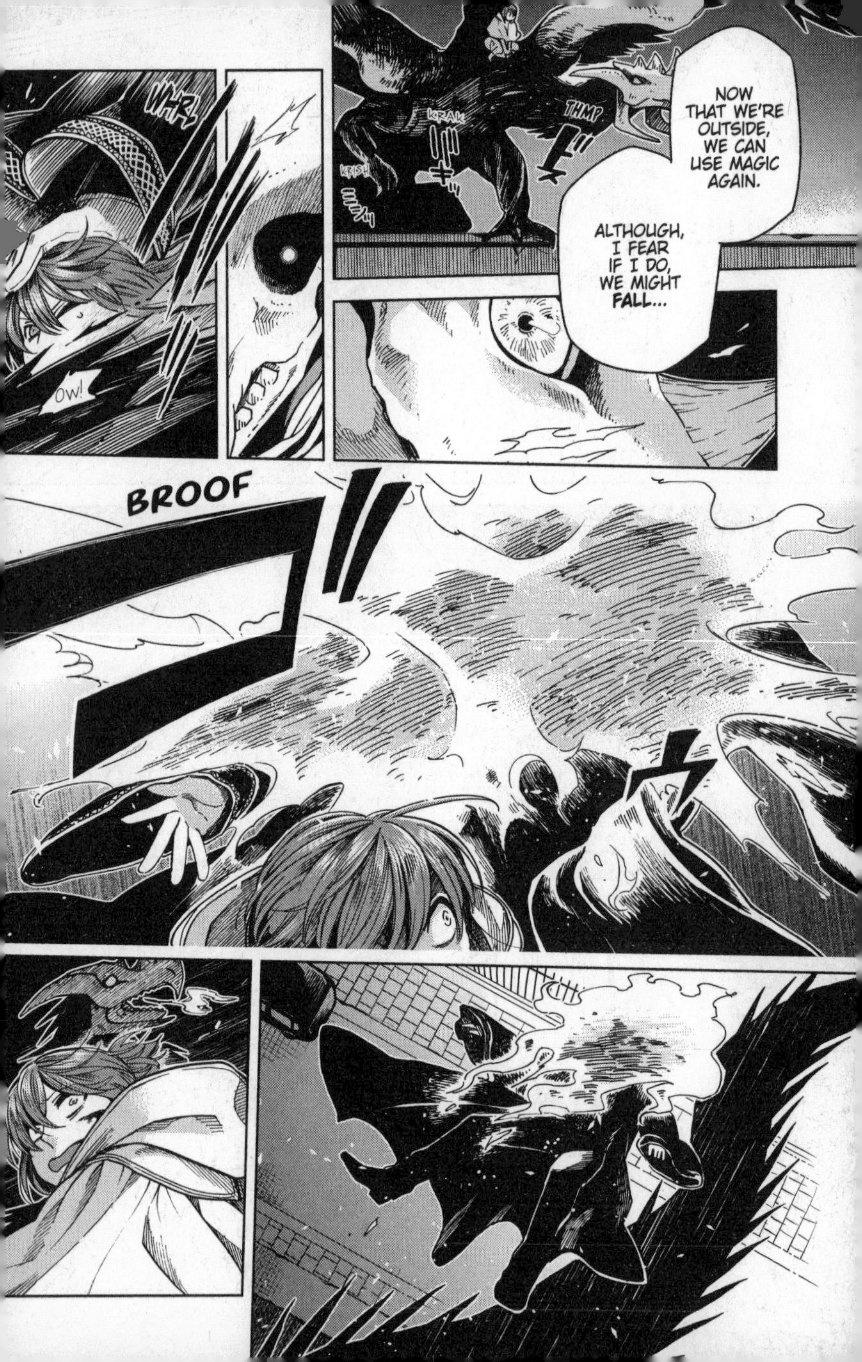
NOW THAT WE'RE OUTSIDE, WE CAN USE MAGIC AGAIN.
THMP
KRAK
KRISH
ALTHOUGH, I FEAR IF I DO, WE MIGHT **FALL**...
WHRL
Ow!
BROOF

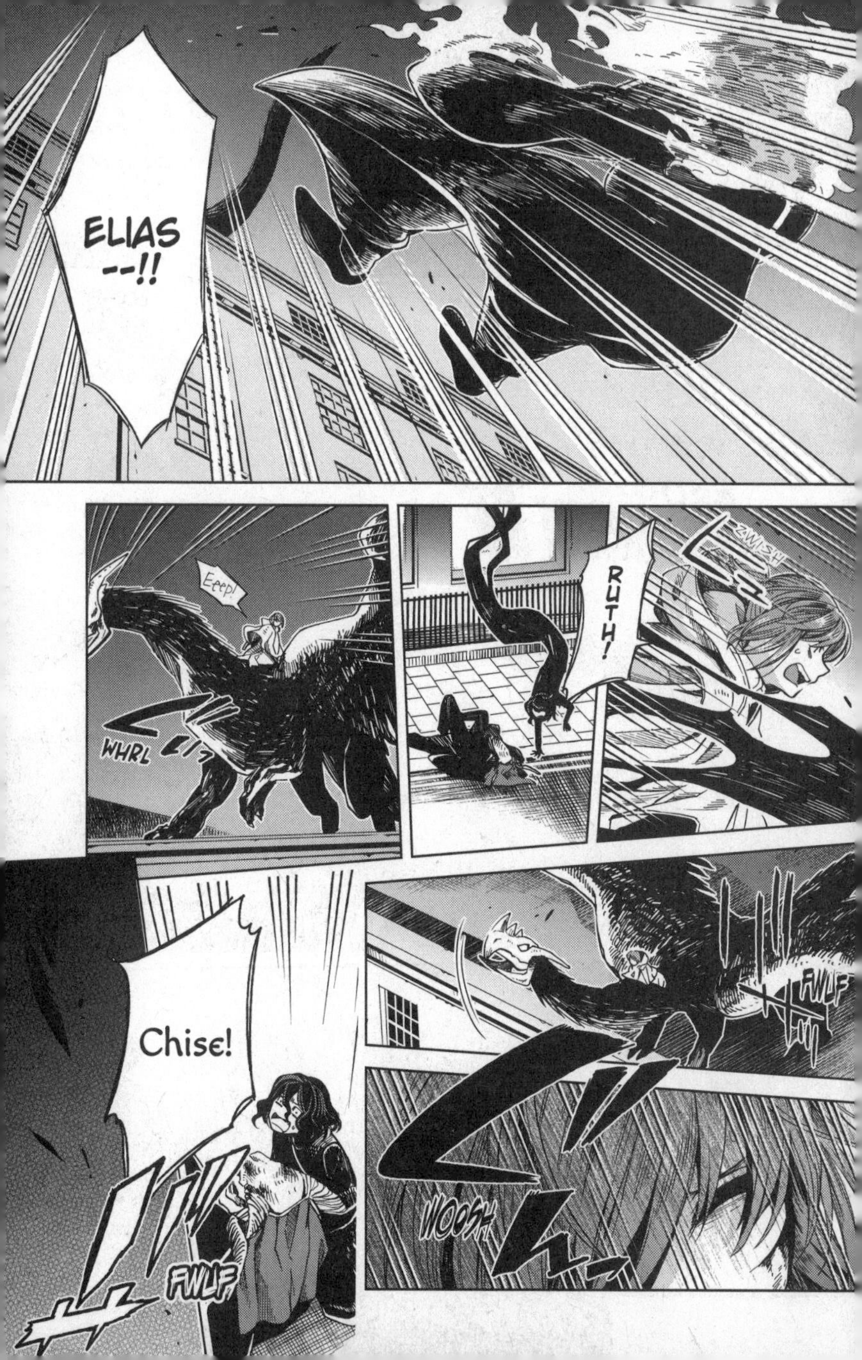
ELIAS --!!
ZWISH
RUTH!
Eeep!
WHRL
FWUF
WOOSH
Chise!
FWUF

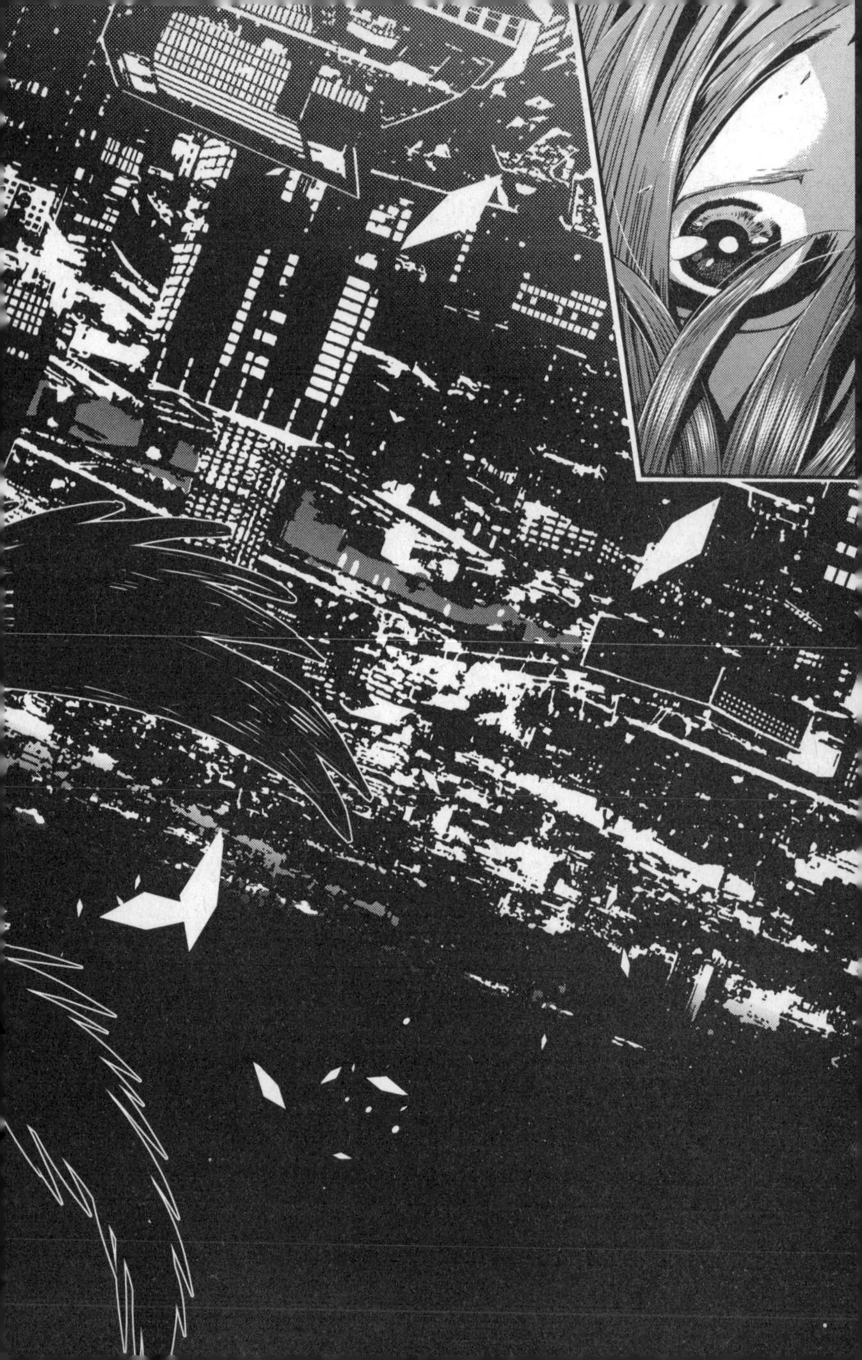

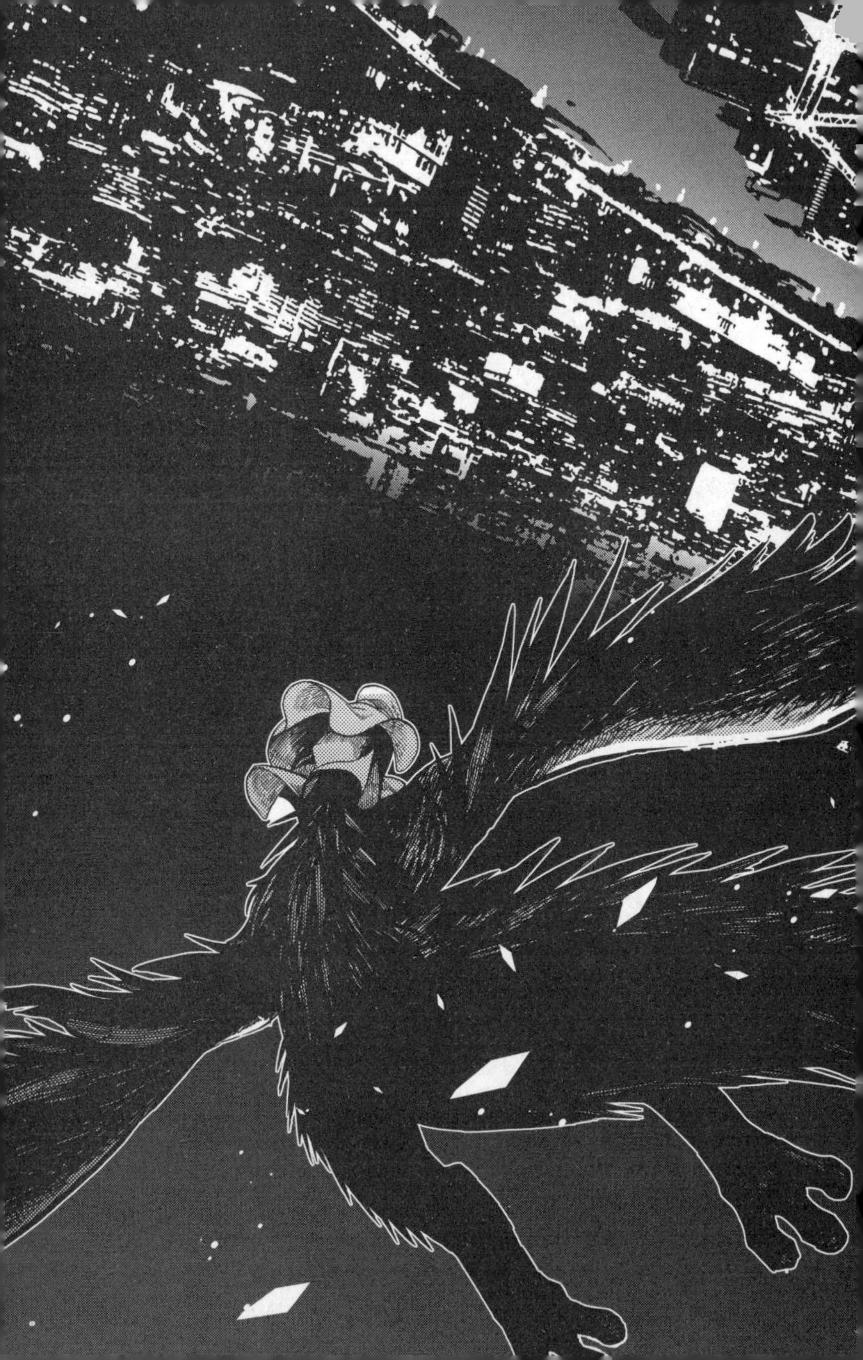

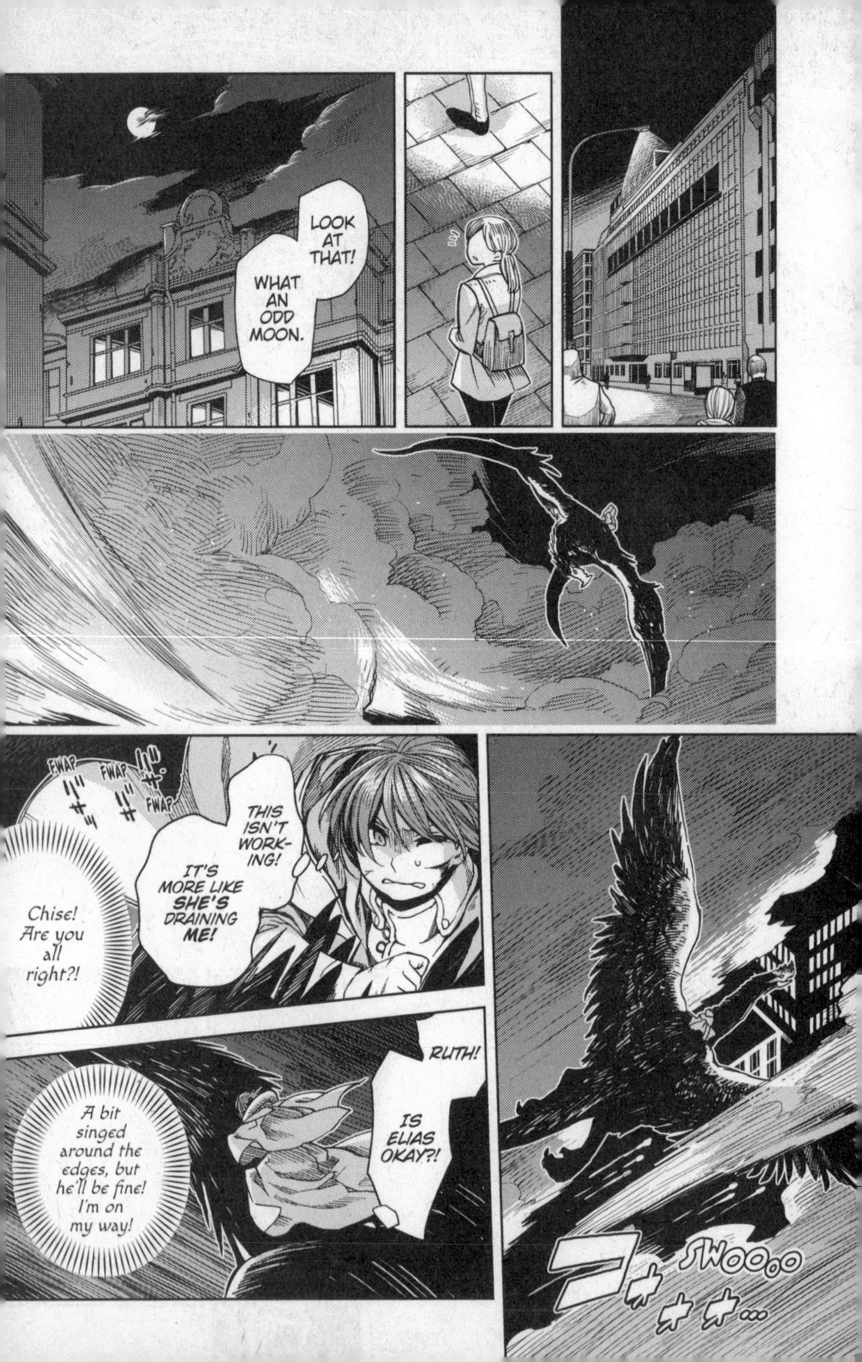

LOOK AT THAT!
WHAT AN ODD MOON.
SWOOOO
FWAP
FWAP
FWAP
THIS ISN'T WORKING!
IT'S MORE LIKE SHE'S DRAINING ME!
Chise! Are you all right?!
RUTH!
IS ELIAS OKAY?!
A bit singed around the edges, but he'll be fine! I'm on my way!

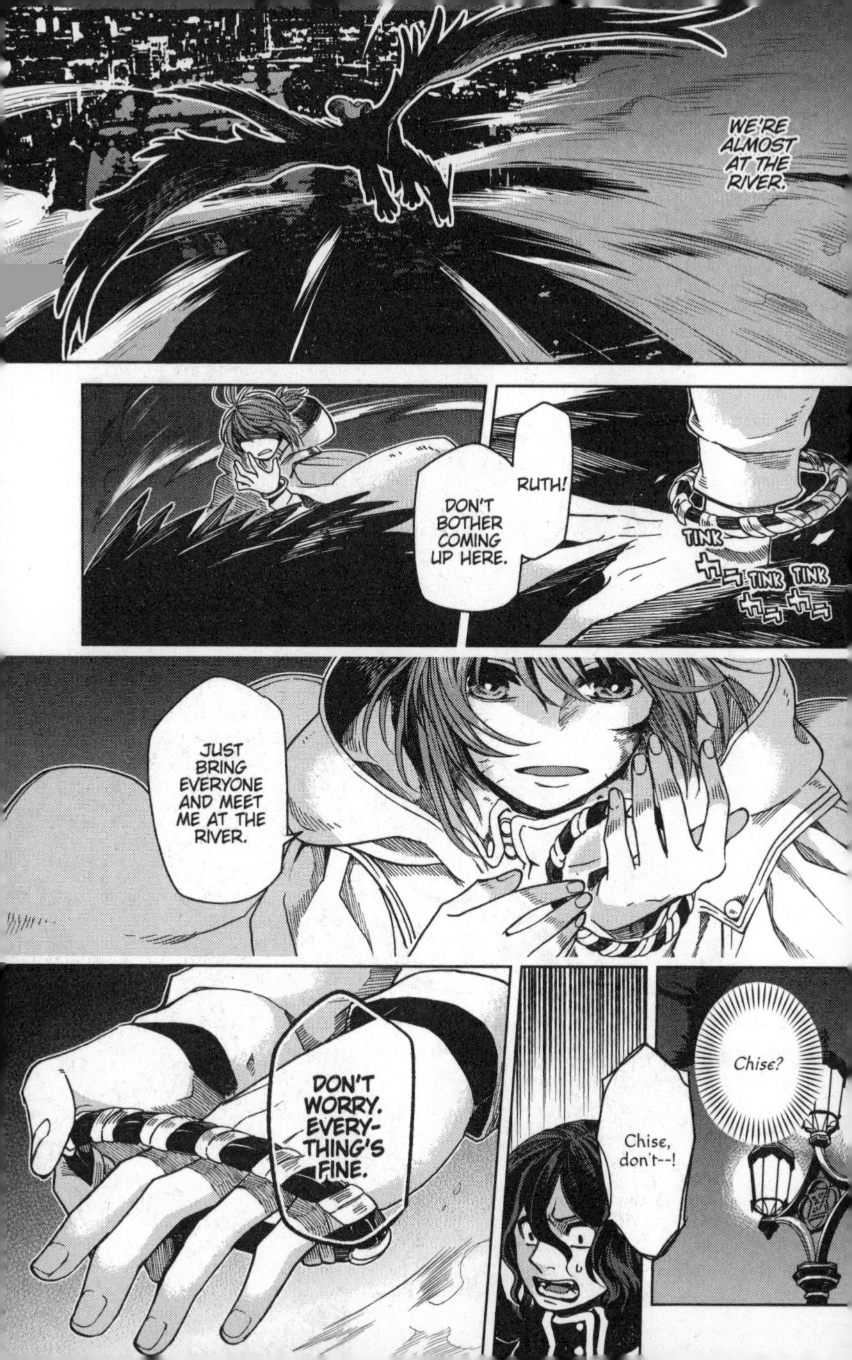
WE'RE ALMOST AT THE RIVER.
TINK
カラ
TINK
カラ
TINK
カラ
RUTH!
DON'T BOTHER COMING UP HERE.
JUST BRING EVERYONE AND MEET ME AT THE RIVER.
Chise?
Chise, don't--!
DON'T WORRY. EVERY-THING'S FINE.

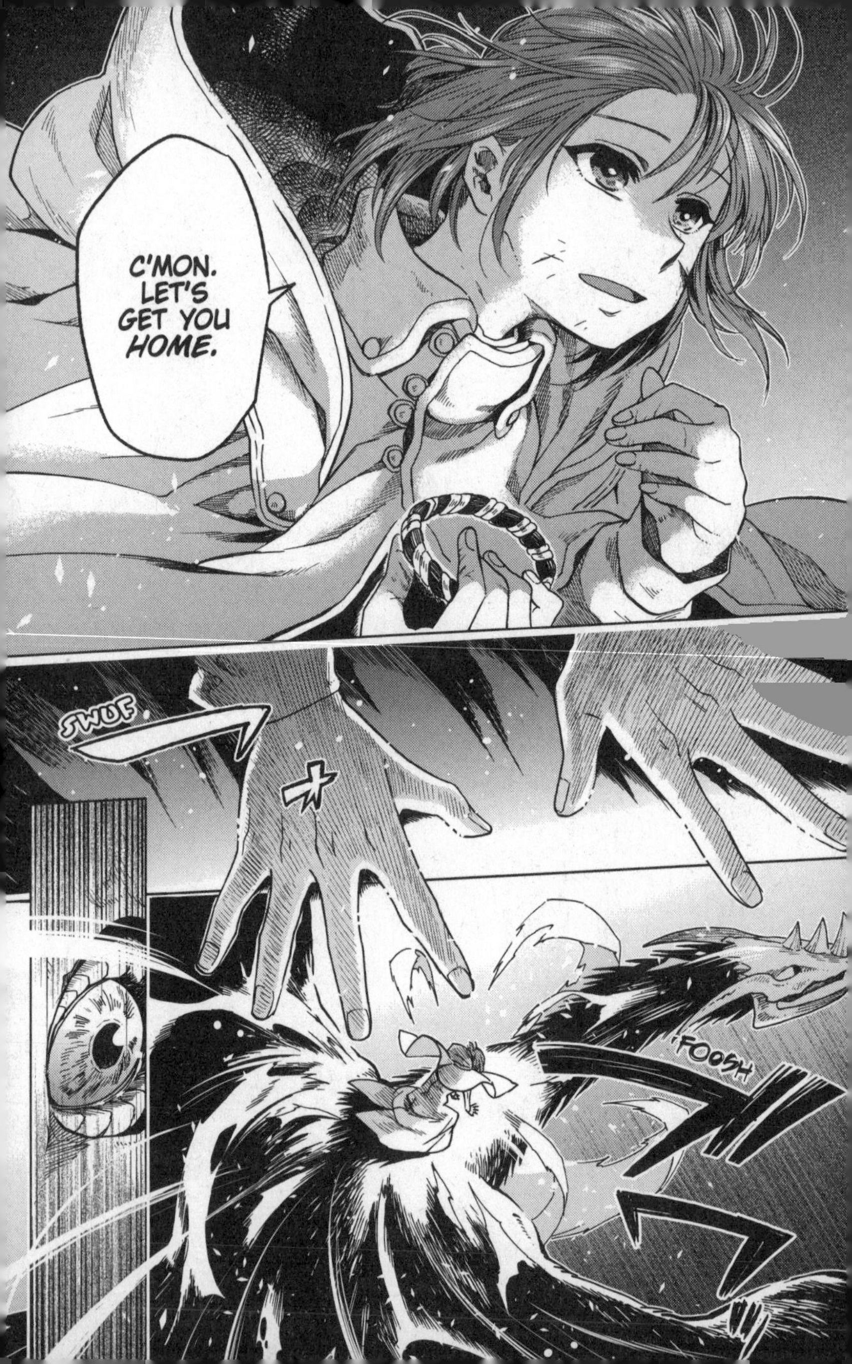
C'MON. LET'S GET YOU HOME.
SWUF
FOOSH

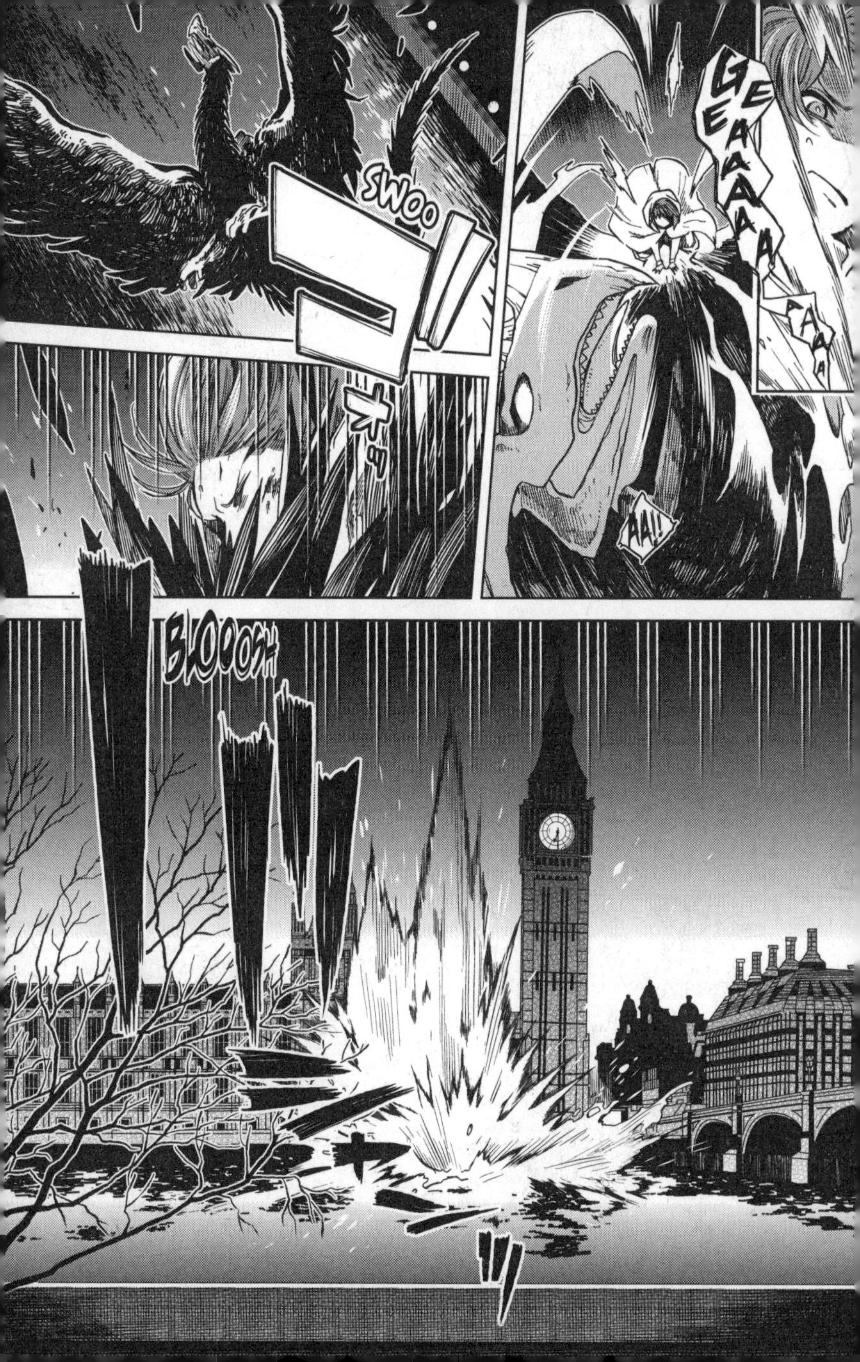
GEEAAAAA
AAAA
SWOO
AA!!
BLOOOSH

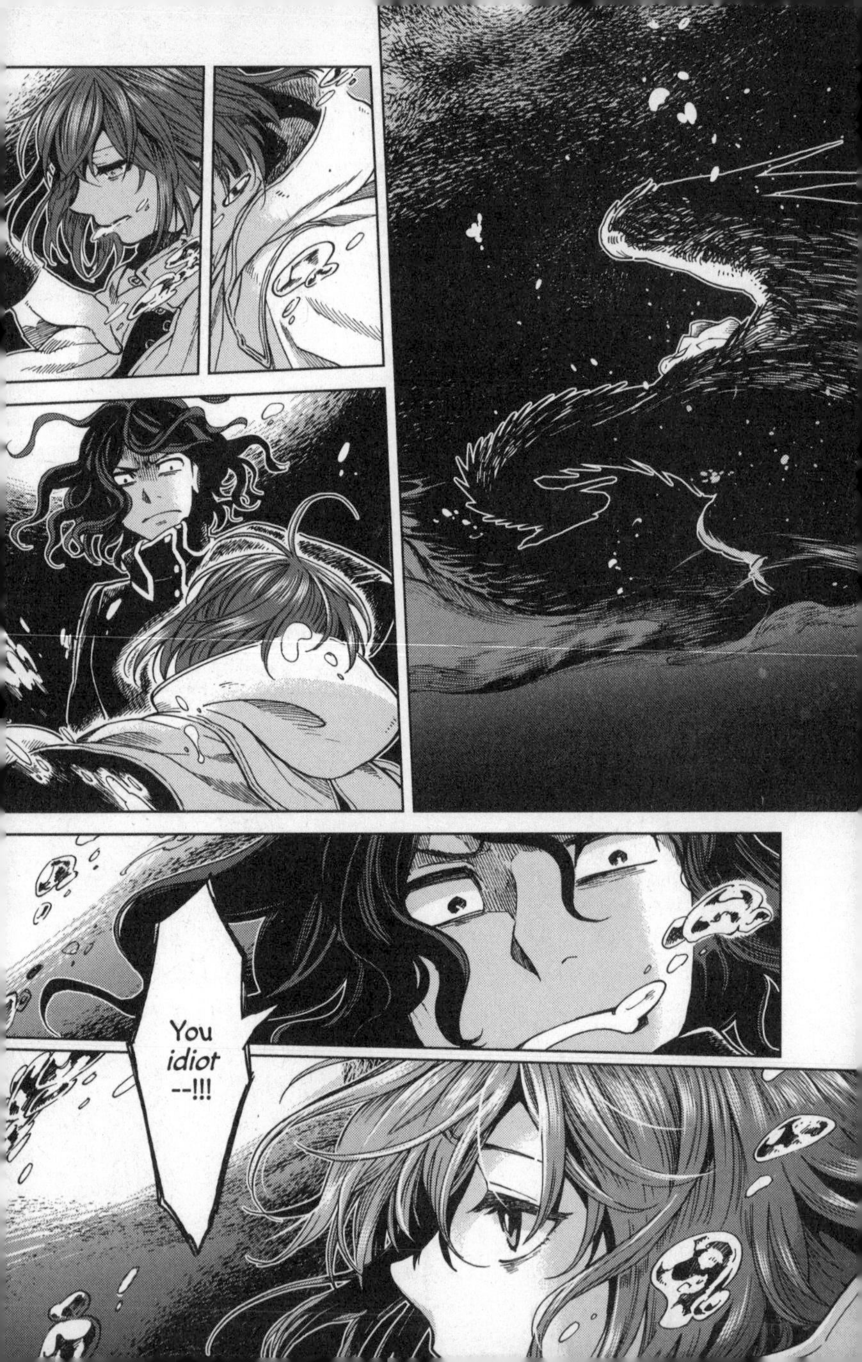
You idiot --!!!

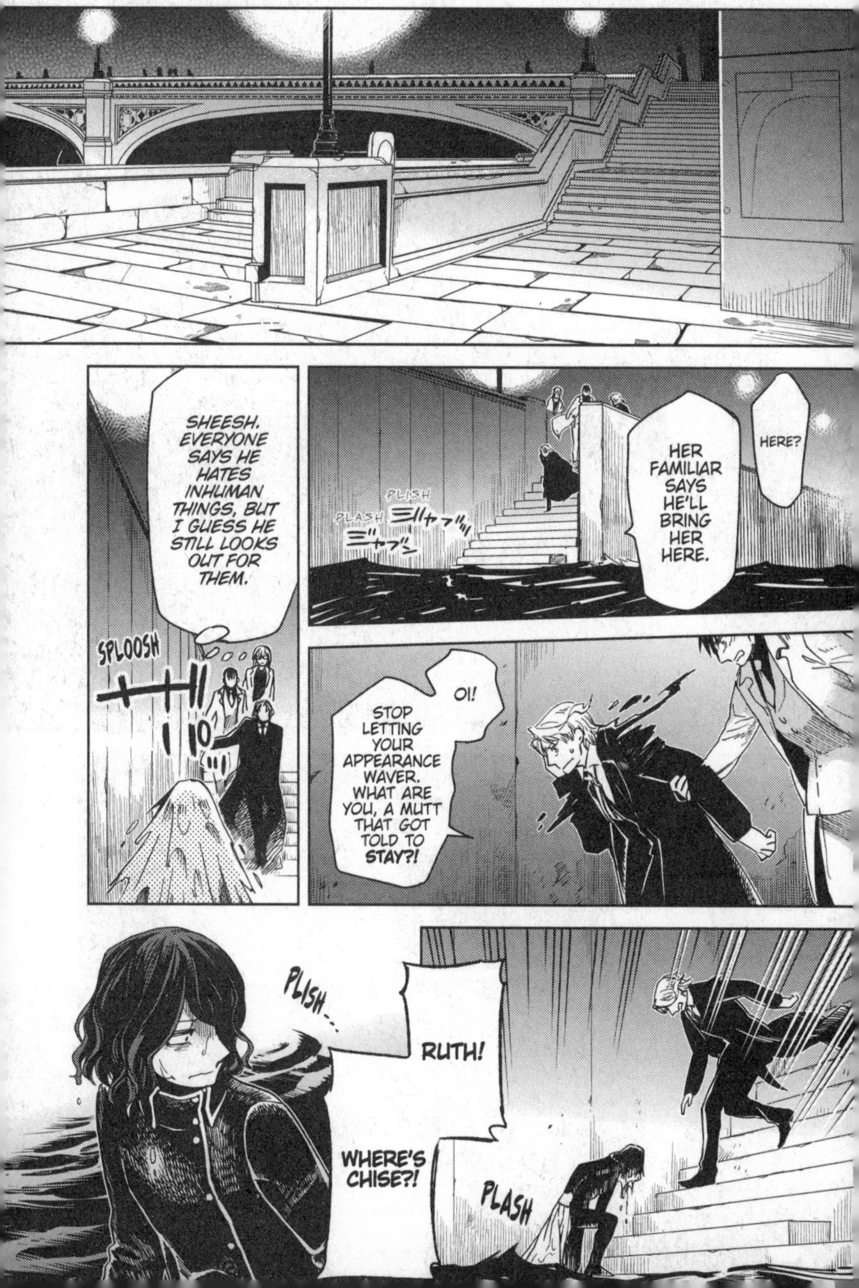
HERE?
HER FAMILIAR SAYS HE'LL BRING HER HERE.
PLISH
PLASH
OI!
STOP LETTING YOUR APPEARANCE WAVER. WHAT ARE YOU, A MUTT THAT GOT TOLD TO STAY?!
SHEESH. EVERYONE SAYS HE HATES INHUMAN THINGS, BUT I GUESS HE STILL LOOKS OUT FOR THEM.
SPLOOSH
PLISH...
RUTH!
WHERE'S CHISE?!
PLASH

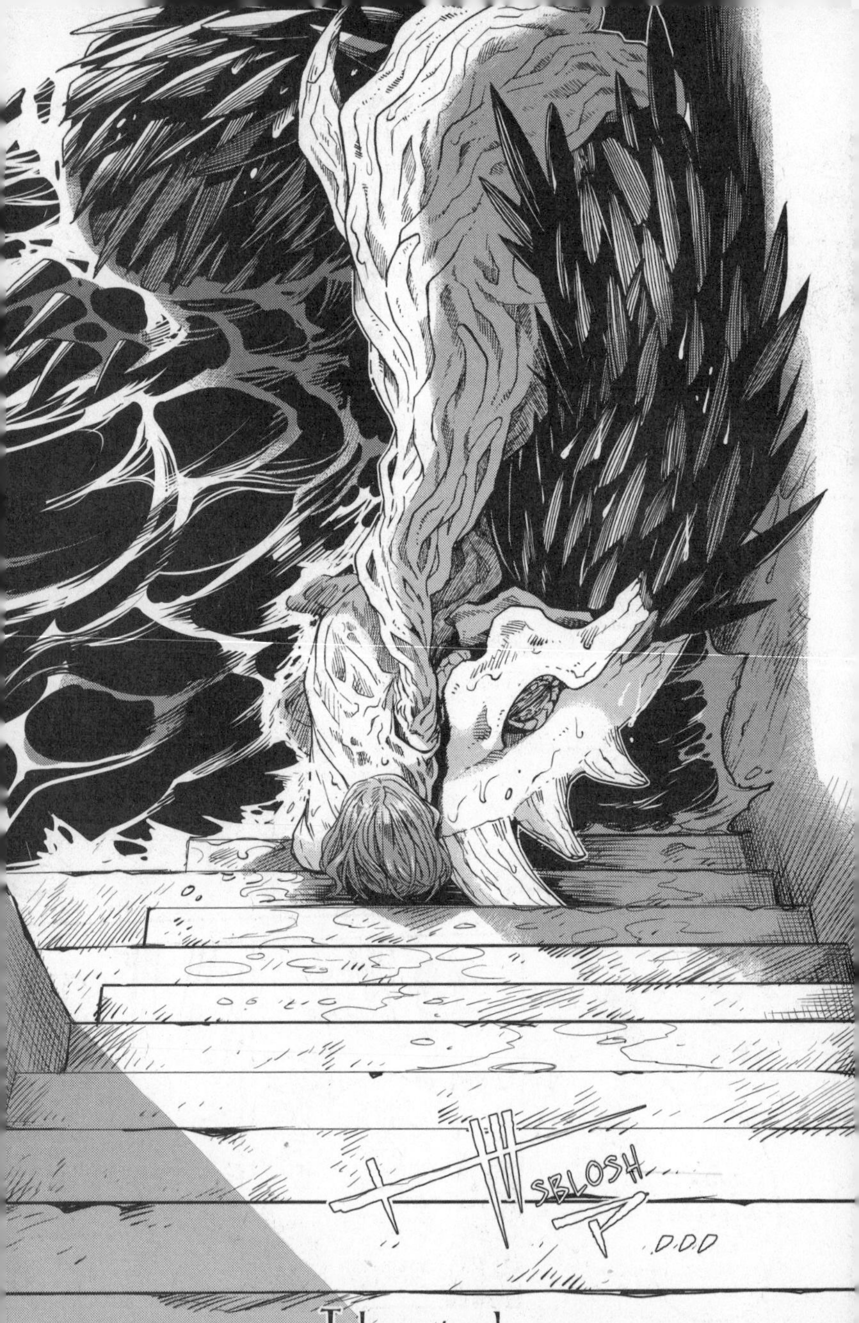
SBLOSH

To be continued...

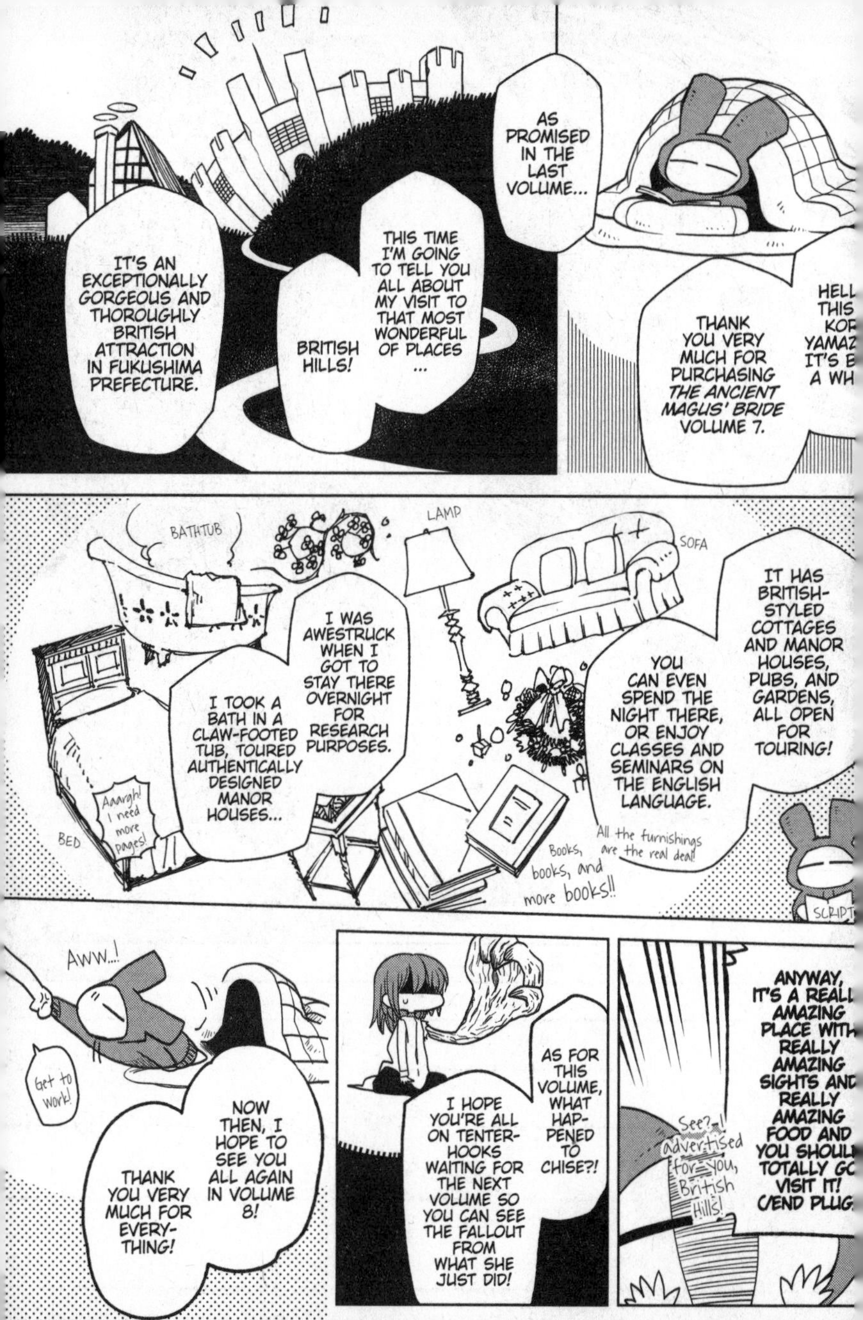

HELL THIS KOR YAMAZ IT'S B A WH
THANK YOU VERY MUCH FOR PURCHASING *THE ANCIENT MAGUS' BRIDE* VOLUME 7.
AS PROMISED IN THE LAST VOLUME...
THIS TIME I'M GOING TO TELL YOU ALL ABOUT MY VISIT TO THAT MOST WONDERFUL OF PLACES ...
BRITISH HILLS!
IT'S AN EXCEPTIONALLY GORGEOUS AND THOROUGHLY BRITISH ATTRACTION IN FUKUSHIMA PREFECTURE.
SCRIPT
IT HAS BRITISH-STYLED COTTAGES AND MANOR HOUSES, PUBS, AND GARDENS, ALL OPEN FOR TOURING!
SOFA
YOU CAN EVEN SPEND THE NIGHT THERE, OR ENJOY CLASSES AND SEMINARS ON THE ENGLISH LANGUAGE.
All the furnishings are the real deal!
Books, books, and more books!!
LAMP
I WAS AWESTRUCK WHEN I GOT TO STAY THERE OVERNIGHT FOR RESEARCH PURPOSES.
BATHTUB
I TOOK A BATH IN A CLAW-FOOTED TUB, TOURED AUTHENTICALLY DESIGNED MANOR HOUSES...
Aaargh! I need more pages!
BED
ANYWAY, IT'S A REALL AMAZING PLACE WITH REALLY AMAZING SIGHTS AND REALLY AMAZING FOOD AND YOU SHOUL TOTALLY GO VISIT IT! (END PLUG
See?! I advertised for you, British Hills!
AS FOR THIS VOLUME, WHAT HAP-PENED TO CHISE?!
I HOPE YOU'RE ALL ON TENTER-HOOKS WAITING FOR THE NEXT VOLUME SO YOU CAN SEE THE FALLOUT FROM WHAT SHE JUST DID!
Aww..!
Get to work!
NOW THEN, I HOPE TO SEE YOU ALL AGAIN IN VOLUME 8!
THANK YOU VERY MUCH FOR EVERY-THING!

Volume 8 Coming Soon!

I shall face myself.

After Cartaphilus, the Wandering Alchemist, kidnaps a dragon chick, Lindel appeals to both the college and Elias to help bring it home safely. Thanks to Chise's quick thinking and unexpected contacts, the rescuer team successfully manages to infiltrate the auction where the dragon chick is scheduled to be sold. But the scared, panicky dragon goes berserk--and Chise pays a hefty price to calm it, mutating her own left arm.

The curse her mother laid upon her... The curse of her birth... The curse of dragons.

When Chise decides to face those things she has hidden from for so long, the story will begin to undergo a drastic change...

A fairytale of adventure and otherworldly romance, with over 4 million copies in print!

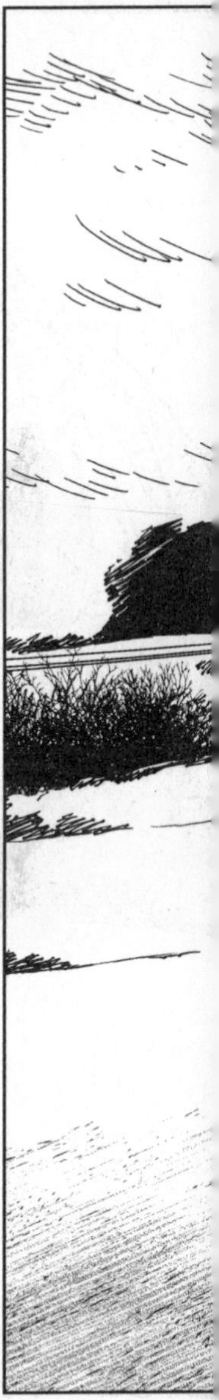

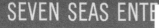

SEVEN SEAS ENTERTAINMENT PRESENTS

The Ancient Magus' Bride

story and art by **KORE YAMAZAKI**

TRANSLATION
Adrienne Beck

ADAPTATION
Ysabet Reinhardt MacFarlane

LETTERING AND RETOUCH
Lys Blakeslee

COVER DESIGN
Nicky Lim

PROOFREADER
Shanti Whitesides

ASSISTANT EDITOR
Jenn Grunigen

PRODUCTION ASSISTANT
CK Russell

PRODUCTION MANAGER
Lissa Pattillo

EDITOR-IN-CHIEF
Adam Arnold

PUBLISHER
Jason DeAngelis

Seven Seas books may be purchased in bulk for promotional, educational, or
business use. Please contact your local bookseller or the Macmillan Corporate
and Premium Sales Department at 1-800-221-7945, extension 5442, or by
e-mail at MacmillanSpecialMarkets@macmillan.com.

Seven Seas and the Seven Seas logo are trademarks of
Seven Seas Entertainment, LLC. All rights reserved.

ISBN: 978-1-626924-99-4

Printed in Canada

First Printing: July 2017

10 9 8 7 6 5 4 3 2 1

FOLLOW US ONLINE: *www.gomanga.com*

READING DIRECTIONS

This book reads from *right to left*, Japanese style.
If this is your first time reading manga, you start
reading from the top right panel on each page and
take it from there. If you get lost, just follow the
numbered diagram here. It may seem backwards at
first, but you'll get the hang of it! Have fun!!

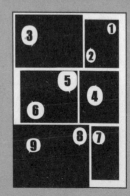